HEALTH PROMOTION AND HEALTH EDUCATION IN PRACTICE

MODULE 2

THE ORGANISATIONAL MODEL

Foreword by
Dr Ilona Kickbusch
WHO EURO

Barns Publications

ISBN 0-95-16973-1-5

Published by Barns Publications, 14, High Elm Road.
Hale Barns,
Altrincham, Cheshire, WA15 OHS, England.
FAX: 061-980-7446

CONTENTS

PART 3: CASE STUDIES

APPENDICES

FOREWORD

Ilona Kickbusch PhD, Director Lifestyles and Health, World Health Organisation, Regional Office for Europe, Copenhagen. [1]

This is the second book in a trilogy of handbooks intended for teaching and practising health promotion and health education (HP/HE). The first handbook (Baric, 1990) was concerned with the definition of problems and the choice of solutions. It differentiated between medical, health promotional and health educational definitions and choices. Its aims were to provide the reader with an insight into the latest theories and skills necessary for the planning, management and execution of HP/HE programmes. The third handbook will be concerned with the theories and skills, necessary for the planning, management and execution of monitoring, evaluation including quality assessment and auditing of HP/HE programmes and projects.

This, the second handbook, is concerned with the practical application of HP/HE. It includes a description of new developments in HP/HE theory and practice and presents examples of the practical application of HP/HE in different settings.

In recent years, health promotion has undergone a number of radical changes related to philosophical background and practical applications. The leading role of the World Health Organisation, Regional Office for Europe, has been enhanced by the creation of the Directorate for Lifestyles and Health. The changes have been described in detail elsewhere (Kickbusch, 1990a) and here it is only necessary to mention some major points to give the reader a general insight into the new movement.

The first component of the new Strategy for Health Promotion is concerned with "building and legitimating a framework for health promotion". This has included the development of the concept of health promotion and making health promotion visible and accepted. This ongoing process has been highlighted at a number of international conferences, which represent stepping stones in this endeavour.

---

[1] Dr Kickbusch has recently (1994) been appointed Director, Division of Health Promotion and Education, WHO, Headquarters, Geneva.

An important milestone was the Ottawa Conference (WHO, 1986) which resulted in the acceptance of "The Ottawa Charter". The Ottawa Charter was the result of the preceding work done by WHO EURO, including a survey of health promotion practices in a number of European countries and the development of the concept and principles of health promotion. The Ottawa Charter has widely dispersed intellectual roots in many disciplines, social movements and practical experience. It set a new direction for health promotion action.

The Ottawa Charter affirms the importance of fundamental living conditions and resources as prerequisites for health. Peace, shelter, education, food and income are defined as being essential for health. It was also the first WHO document to identify a stable ecosystem as a prerequisite for human health. The Ottawa Charter defines health promotion as the process of enabling people to increase control over and improve their health. Recognising that power and control are the essential issues in health promotion is a distinct shift away from the manipulative overtones of the social marketing and behavioural change of many government programmes, and points towards community empowerment. It describes health promotion in terms of advocacy, enabling and mediating, which implies a new type of institutional mandate beyond traditional health services, broader terms of reference beyond illness and disease, a different relationship with the community, new skills and different training. It outlines the five overlapping and interactive means of action, which constitute a comprehensive strategy for health promotion: building healthy public policy, creating supportive environments, strengthening community action, developing personal skills and reorienting health services.

The next important step in the development of a new health promotion movement has been the Second International Conference in Adelaide (WHO,1988), which aimed at exploring the effects of government decision-making on health, particularly in sectors not usually within the mandate of health planners. The theme of the Conference has embodied the political process which should lead to stronger foundations for health.

The Adelaide Conference adopted a consensus statement called the Adelaide Recommendations, which describe healthy public policy as being "characterised by an explicit concern for health and equity in all areas of policy and by an accountability for health impact". The Adelaide Recommendations identify four priority areas for immediate action for healthy public policy: supporting the health of women, improving food and nutrition, controlling the use of tobacco and alcohol, and creating supportive environments for health. The Conference advocated that the public health and ecological movements join together in pursuit of socioeconomic development that conserves our planet's resources. One year later, the World Health Assembly adopted a resolution (WHA42.26) on WHO's contribution towards the international efforts towards sustainable development.

A logical sequence to this development was the concentration on creating supportive environments for health, which was the topic of The Third International Conference on Health Promotion, held in Sundsvall (WHO,1991). One of the aims was to define the shared agenda between people who focus on public health and people who concentrate on environmental and ecological issues. The health of future generations is intimately linked to conserving the global environment, as outlined by the report of the World Commission on Environment and Development. Health beyond the year 2000 depends on sustainable development: development that meets the needs of the present generation without compromising the ability of future generations to meet their needs.

The three international conferences on health promotion convened over the five years provide a comprehensive framework for organised action, articulating a new role for government decision-making in promoting health and linking health and environment concerns.

In addition to the developments of a strategy for health promotion, important contributions have been made by WHO EURO in the practice of health promotion (Kickbusch, 1990b).

A key question in planning for health promotion is: where is health created? The approach implied by this question moves the focus of the discussion on health promotion far beyond existing organisational structures, means of financing and programme approaches. Health is created through a political and social process. The support of this process has been called a "new public health". An advocacy strategy and an implementation strategy are two key parts of such support.

The links between health, social action and social reform are the basis for the development of an advocacy strategy for public health with three elements: an informed citizenry, a mobilised advocacy lobby and contact points within the system.

An implementation strategy for health promotion should take action in 10 steps:

1. establishing credibility for the new health agenda;
2. developing foci for agenda setting in health policy;
3. demonstrating clear financial commitment and developing new funding mechanisms for health promotion;
4. creating and strengthening health promotion infrastructures;
5. facilitating intersectoral action;
6. creating accountability;
7. creating high-profile centres of excellence and models of good practice;
8. supporting innovations in health promotion development;
9. facilitating community empowerment;
10 creating visibility for health promotion.

This range of action steps shows clearly the range of strategic approaches necessary to implement health promotion successfully. Time and effort must go into not only implementing projects as such, but also into generating political support and commitment to health promotion action in all sectors of society. Health promotion is not just a "government exercise" - it is a responsibility of all major social actors in a developed industrial - or for that matter, post-industrial - society: it depends on partnership. This implies establishing a societal consensus that health is a priority goal.

The WHO strategy for health promotion is now five years old, which is a very short time in the history of ideas, and in terms of applying ideas in practice it is hardly any time at all. Current events suggest that new ideas are being translated into action.

However, the most important change initiated and developed by WHO EURO, which has occurred recently in the practice of health promotion and health education, is the shift from a problem-based to a settings-based approach. We are used to accepting aetiological and epidemiological studies as a basis for HP/HE interventions. This has meant that we spent our time and resources on studying different health problems and their causation, followed by population studies with the aim of establishing the prevalence and incidence of such diseases in defined populations. In other words, we studied the health problem and then tried to find out who suffered from that problem in a population. This has resulted in research and intervention programmes concerning specific diseases such as cancer, coronary heart disease, AIDS, etc. The logical consequence of the new ecological approach has been the shift of emphasis from problems to populations and their problems. People experience a number of different problems during their life, which are all a part of their lifestyle and affect their wellbeing. The new HP/HE approach targets people in their natural environment which is composed of different settings where they live, work, learn and play. These settings are the family, the community, the school, the workplace, the hospital, the health care system, etc. In each of these settings HP/HE aims at enabling people to become aware of and solve their own problems, by providing the necessary knowledge and skills. HP/HE also has the role of mediating between people in these various settings with the aim of enhancing their contribution to the improvement of health. There are also some cases where HP/HE has to take on the advocacy role in promoting the interest of individuals and communities.

It is important to recognise that we are dealing with a shift in emphasis and not a change of direction. Health promotion and health education are still concerned with alleviating, managing and preventing health problems. In so doing HP/HE is concerned with the most effective approach which seems to be directed towards the social and physical environment. It is for this reason that the most recent developments in HP/HE are concerned with bringing together the problem and the settings approach into a comprehensive ecological system of HP/HE interventions.

One area of application has been through the WHO "Healthy Cities" project, which began in 1986 and has achieved unprecedented popularity, with 300 cities actively participating in 13 national or linguistic Healthy Cities networks in Europe.

The Healthy Cities project has become the forerunner of an innovation in health promotion practice, characterised by the shift from a problem to a settings approach. This is best illustrated by the extension of the "Healthy Cities" concept to the new developments such as the "Health Promoting School", "Health Promoting Hospital" and a number of other settings.

This book reflects these new developments and aims to illustrate this new approach by means of a number of examples. It therefore represents a contribution to the raising of a practitioner's competence to engage in health promotion and health education.

INTRODUCTION

The general aim of this book is to give the readers an insight into the most recent advances in health promotion and health education, to provide them with a theoretical justification for the choice of available methods for a health promotion and health education intervention and to provide them with an opportunity of learning about the experience derived from applying this approach to various initial settings. To achieve this general aim, this book is divided into three parts.

Part 1: Historical Overview

The first part is concerned with an overview of the developments throughout the long history of health education and, later, health promotion. It does not claim to be an exhaustive history of the discipline and should be treated as the personal view of the author based on long involvement in health promotion and health education on an international, national and local level in the capacity of practitioner, academic lecturer and researcher. To achieve its aim this part includes the following topics:

- developments in health education in the pre Alma Ata period;
- health promotion and health education in the post Alma Ata period;
- developments in the UK.

The contents trace the historical development of health promotion and health education in practice. The developments in Europe are divided into the pre- and post-Alma Ata periods, with the Alma Ata Declaration being the point at which health education in Europe became integrated into health promotion. In the United States of America there has been continued development of health education, including the personal as well as social aspects, but a disregard for health promotion as a specific approach. The developments are traced through a number of models and approaches, evolving in both Europe and the USA.

Part 1 concludes with a description of the developments in the United Kingdom, with special reference to a number of documents published by the Department of Health, which have put health promotion and health education at the forefront of the reform of the NHS health care system in the United Kingdom.

Part 2: The Organisational Model

The second part of the book presents the reader with the latest developments in health promotion and health education. It provides a theoretical justification for the change in emphasis from problems to settings, which have led to the new organisational model, now being taken to its logical conclusion, with all its consequences. To achieve this aim this part includes the following topics:

- new approaches and developments arising from the paradigm shift, demographic changes, new developments in genetics and the subsequent new WHO approach;
- description of the organisational model with special reference to health promoting settings;
- quality management as a specific aspect of the organisational model;
- evaluation, quality assessment and audit as applied to the organisational model.

The above topics cover the shift from problems to settings and the consequent treatment of settings as organisations. The outcome for health promotion and health education has been the need to develop new theories and learn to interact with new partners. This is especially evident in the evaluation of health promotion and health education interventions, which requires the inclusion of quality assessment as a means of evaluating the processes and the outcomes.

Part 3: Case Studies

The third part presents a set of examples in the form of case studies. They are based on the experience collected by the author as a result of being involved as an external consultant in all these cases. They are used as an illustration of practical application of the organisational model to different settings. The specific aim of this part is to provide readers with an insight into the practical application of the new concepts and approaches by means of specific examples. The organisational model in fact operates on three levels. They include the ground work level, the implementation on the organisational level and the implementation on the client level. The whole movement is relatively new and many of the case studies show the developments on the first two levels, with only few attempting to reach the third or the client level. Ann early progress report should, however, be of interest to readers and enable them to follow the literature in this field. To achieve this aim this part includes the following examples:

- health promoting health care system;
- health promoting general practice;
- health promoting hospital;
- health promoting general dental practice;
- health promoting school;
- health promoting community services;
- health promoting charitablc organisations;
- health promoting enterprise;
- health promoting community.

Appendices

The recent literature which is relevant for these new developments in HP/HE is spread through many publications, some of which are not easily accessible. The Appendix, therefore, includes extracts from some of the documents that have been most important for the development of the new approach

Summary

The intention of the book can be summarised as an attempt to remedy the shortcomings of past developments in Europe. These have arisen because of the heavy emphasis given to health promotion and the failure to pay adequate attention to health education. The book aims to give a balanced view, including both health promotion and health education as equally important aspects of the organisational model. This is the logical consequence of the shift from problems to settings and the introduction of the organisational model. Since most of the settings in which health promotion and health education take place form part of the service industry sector, they are, by definition, concerned with the needs of their clients. Both approaches are relevant in that health promotion deals with the organisational aspects and health education with the client needs.

Implementation of the organisational model has brought HP/HE into contact with a new set of partners, who have different values and speak a different language. The summary description of the theories related to organisations and management and the ways they assess their achievements by means of quality control should help the health promotion and health education practitioners to become acquainted with this new area so that they could pursue it in greater detail if and when they become involved in the practical application of the organisational model. The case studies should illustrate how easy it is to sell the idea in various settings, especially in view of the attractiveness of international recognition and how easy it is to implement it on the first two levels (ground work and organisational level), but how difficult it is to get those involved in the various settings to implement it on the client level. Such problems will require further attention and study.

PART I

HISTORICAL OVERVIEW

INTRODUCTION

HEALTH EDUCATION
The Pre Alma Ata Period

THE ALMA ATA DECLARATION

HEALTH PROMOTION AND HEALTH EDUCATION
The Post Alma Ata Period

UK DEVELOPMENTS

SUMMARY

INTRODUCTION

Throughout their history, health education and more recently health promotion, have been undergoing changes concerning their place within other recognised branches of science, in the conceptual framework and in their approaches used in planned interventions. To understand these changes, it is necessary to explore the developments within a historical framework which is presented in three parts: the pre-Alma Ata period dealing with health education, the Alma Ata Declaration and the introduction of the concept of health promotion, and the post-Alma Ata developments concerning both health promotion and health education.

Before going into the description of the various developments, it will be necessary to explore the changes in the status of the activity from a skill to a scientific discipline. This has been achieved through developing a theoretical basis for the activity, which provided a basis for understanding what is happening as well as why it is happening. These changes have been closely related to the recognition of importance of research as a basis for providing a theoretical framework for the understanding of this activity.

The need for interaction between the behavioural sciences and medicine (Baric,1972) has arisen because of historical developments in both fields resulting in the changes of emphasis in medicine as well as in new insight into the etiology and epidemiology of a great many diseases.

With the Alma Ata Declaration a differentiation was made between health education (individual approach) and health promotion (societal approach), with the main emphasis in Europe given to health promotion.

The reform of the NHS and its expression in the document "The Health of the Nation" (DoH, 1992) gave health promotion and health education a central position in the care of people's health. Whereas the health promotion aspects have at this point in time been well developed, the health education aspects have been in Europe sadly neglected. The consequennces of this neglect are best illustrated in the example of the health promotion activities carried out by General Practitioners, who were contracted to carry it out and specially paid to do so. The lack of any visible success was due to their limited knowledge of health promotion and health education methods.

For example, an article by Peter Pallot in the Daily Telegraph of 19th July 1993 under the title "GP's £200m health drive 'is a flop' ", has or should have sent ripples throughout the health promotion community. There we were, smugly congratulating ourselves on the brilliant new approaches initiated by WHO, which seemed a logical answer to all our prayers. Shift from the medical problems to the people if you want to help them improve their health. That is exactly what we did, by focusing on the various settings, including that of general practice, and treating the practice population as a target, finding out about their needs and tailoring the programmes to meet them. The new contract signed by GPs gave them a paid opportunity to offer their patients services, which were meant to change their behaviour and life style, prevent disease and improve health. The patients made use of this offer and a variety of different health promotion clinics were organized and paid for.

So far this seemed to have been a story of success for health promotion. What has, however, been lost in the euphoria of the moment, expressed in all the expert committees, conferences, declarations and charters, was the fact that this new enthusiasm is resting on an inadequate development of the health education methods which were expected to bring about the desired changes and improvements in the target populations, such as, for example, the general practice patients. Before the Alma Ata Declaration and the introduction of health promotion, health education was slowly and gradually developing its methodology through introducing monitoring and evaluation, and when possible mounting small-scale research projects. This has been reflected in the gradual progression through a selection of "models", which has had a cumulative effect on the improvement of methodology. Just at the time when we reached the "ecological" model of health education, which combines the environmental and personal factors, the introduction of health promotion occurred. Consequently all the enthusiasm as well as resources went into developing an organisational framework for health promotion and the methodology of health education was disregarded.

The reason for stating that the GP activities in health promotion were a "flop" stems from reports mentioned in the newspaper article concerning two studies paid by the Department of Health, one costing £1.5m and the other £1m, which found that the GP activities in the form of health promotion clinics, costing £200m and raising the GP income on average by £2,400 each, have not been successful in meeting the expectations concerning the improvements in the health of the patients. The predominant method has been individual counselling and advice given to the patients by the practice nurse. The article states that a "fundamental rethink" is necessary if the Department of Health White Paper "Health of the Nation" targets are to be achieved.

There should be a fundamental rethinking of the means of supporting research and intervention studies concerning the health education methods, their effectiveness, efficiency, and possible side effects. The first steps have already been taken in this direction by concentrating on the quality assessment of health promotion, which includes the health education methods and by looking at the new developments in health education in the United States of America, where health promotion has not been accepted and where the main developments concentrated on health education. Thus, it can be hoped that the balance between the developments in health promotion and those in health education could be redressed and that this will result in a combined successful approach to the improvement of people's health, within a new organisational model.

HEALTH EDUCATION
The Pre Alma Ata Period

INTRODUCTION

Health education has a longer tradition than health promotion. During its past history health education has undergone a number of changes, mainly characterised by the introduction of more complex models, starting from the simple transmission of knowledge about health threats and prevention and management of diseases to an ecological approach taking into consideration the external as well as personal factors affecting health. The main change occurred after the Alma Ata conference when the concept of health promotion was introduced. The outcome of this event has been the differentiation of the activities of health education and health promotion within an ecological model of factors affecting health. At present **health promotion** has come to represent a unifying concept for those who recognise the need for change in the ways and conditions of living, in order to promote health. **Health education,** on the other hand, is concerned with the raising of individual competence and knowledge about health and illness; about the body and its functions, about prevention and coping; with raising competence and knowledge to use the health care system and to understand its function; and with raising awareness about social, political and environmental factors that influence health. The main difference, therefore, is not so much in the aims, but in the levels on which these are carried out.

Within this general framework of differentiation there are a number of issues which need further clarification and research for the development of appropriate theoretical support. There are a number of instances where health promotion is identified with health education and represents only a change in the label and where the activity is based on cognitive models depending solely on transmission of information for the desired actions to take place. This becomes more obvious with the advent of new health threats, such as the HIV epidemic, where the prevention is clearly defined and the outcomes can easily be assessed.

There are also political interests which influence the approaches used. If one simplifies the distinction between health promotion as being mainly concerned with cxternal factors and health education as mainly dealing with personal factors, it is evident that some people may prefer to concentrate on health promotion and others limit themselves to health education.

On the other hand, when the situation is examined according to the role of the agents, it is evident that certain agents will be restricted to a certain approach according to their professional role definition (Baric, 1992a).

The differentiation between health education and health promotion is the result of the Alma Ata Conference. Because of this the historical review of the pre-Alma Ata period will be concerned only with health education in terms of the existing approaches. These approaches have at the time been described as "models" and it is because of this that this summary uses the same terminology, although many of these so-called "models" would not meet the criteria associated with the concept of 'models'.

MODELS AND APPROACHES

There is no research without a conceptual framework, even if it is only implicit. Take, for example, research on whether the provision of anti-smoking clinics can be effective in reducing the incidence of lung cancer. A research project of this kind, even such a simple one, is based on several implicit models: one posits a direct relationship between smoking and lung cancer; another accepts the influence of an anti-smoking clinic on smoking, a third assumes that the provision of clinics is conversely related to their utilisation by smokers, etc. It seems logical for the researcher to be aware of the models used in order to be able to exploit them fully and avoid any omission of information about some aspect of the model.

Models, as tools of research, are abstract constructs, which define a system of interrelated parts such as objects, social positions, actions, etc. Theories, on the other hand, define the relationships between the parts of a model. We speak of more or less appropriate models, and specific relationships between the parts of the model, which can be supported or disproved by theories.

In the pre-Alma Ata period there were many different models in use in the field of health education. They range from the most simple ones (Knowledge-Attitude-Behaviour) to more complex ones such as the Health Belief Model (Behaviour-Perception of severity, of susceptibility, and of a way out). The problem, however, is that the simple models do not produce the desired results and the more complex ones are rarely used in everyday practice. Health behaviour, with its different aspects (acquisition, maintenance and change), seems to be the result of highly complex psycho-social processes. So far most studies have only partly covered the complexity of this process focussing on the specific interests of the researchers. In that period there have been many studies concerned with psychological aspects of a health behaviour, and only a few concerned with the socio-psychological aspects, with practically none using a sociological or an ecological model. The reason for this is that there have been many more psychologists than sociologists active in the field of health education, and even the few sociologists tended to be influenced by the psychological aspects of the problem under study.

For example, there are studies of doctor-patient communication carried out without exploring the professional and social background of the actors; there are studies of utilisation of preventive and screening services, without taking into account social expectations or norms; there are many studies which use social class as one of the variables, without defining what is meant for example by social class V in terms of a lifestyle of the population; there are studies of various personality characteristics associated with some form of behaviour, which do not examine whether these may possibly be disregarded if the social environment is changed, etc.

The examination of so-called models or approaches needs to start with the critical analysis of the term "model" in describing health education interventions. Some of the factors which need to be taken into account can be described by following statements:

- health education as a planned activity reflects the value orientation and scientific preferences of the agents of change;

- models are approximations of real life situations or concepts and represent a system composed of parts; the relationship between the parts is expressed in theories; models can be assessed as more or less appropriate representations of the reality, whereas the theories can be tested and falsified;

- all health education activities or interventions are based on certain model/s which can be implicit or explicit; they represent the conceptualisation of the problem and its relationship with the solution proposed;

- most of the models in health education use a reductionist approach which postulates that the effective solution can be derived from an insight into the problem; that is why most of the models use elaborate presentations of the problem, whereas the recommended solutions are based on a common-sensical approach;

- at the present state of development of health education as a discipline, it operates with models of a descriptive nature, without any original theories to explain the relationship between the parts based on empirical testing.

The main shortcoming of health education is that it lacks models and theories about solutions, as well as about the link between the problems and solutions.

Even the existing models about health educational problems can be criticised on a number of points:

- they do not give any rational explanation about the inclusion and exclusion of certain parts;
- they do not provide theories about the relationship between the parts;
- they operate mainly with theoretical constructs and do not provide a standardised way of measuring them;
- lack of an agreed upon way of defining and measuring the parts of a model prevent any comparison between the findings of different studies using the "same" model;
- without any theories, the relationship between the parts can go either way, and the model can still be wrongly accepted as valid;
- one can summarise that at present health education does not have any models in the true sense of the word, but uses only descriptive assumptions based on people's experiences, their professional orientation and common sense.

CLASSIFICATION SYSTEMS

The understanding of the development of health education will depend on the classificatory systems used in analysing the activities. There are a number of dimensions along which a classificatory system could be developed, two of which are set out below:

Value orientation

A very good review of changes in health education is given by Tones (1990) using the dimension of value orientation. It differentiates between the following models:

The preventive models

They are closely associated with the "medical model" and are criticised because of the tendency for "medicalisation" of certain behavioural problems related to the prevention of disease. They try to persuade individuals to undertake responsible decisions about health promoting kinds of behaviour. They differentiate the three levels of prevention (primary, secondary, tertiary). The criticism has been mainly about the "symptom" approach without regard to influencing causative factors, about the "blame the victim" orientation, and about creating a "healthist" movement which is individualistic in character and leaves out the political aspects of ill health.

Radical-political models

Those who reject the individualistic "blame the victim" approach may be described as subscribing to the radical-political model of health education. They are concerned with creating socio-political changes which in their opinion are the main cause of ill-health in our society. It is a political movement of social change with an improvement of health as one of its by-products. Some of its main representatives are the women's health movement, the environmentalist movement etc.

Self-empowerment models

These models are closely linked with the code of ethics developed by the Society for Public Health Education in USA which promotes "informed choice". They assume that people can make choices depending on the knowledge they have about a problem and the advantages of a certain solution. In their more sophisticated form the models supplement the simple cognitive approach with a value-clarification opportunity so that the people would not only know what is good for them, but also understand the value system on which such a decision is based. These models include the life-skills training which should empower an individual to make and apply the appropriate decisions concerning his/her health. In that sense one could say that the self-empowerment models not only facilitate educated choices but that they also promote positive health.

Theoretical orientation

Another dimension along which one can classify the various health education approaches during the pre-Alma Ata period is based on the theoretical assumptions used by health education agents in planning their interventions (Baric, 1990). It should be noted that the examination of health education interventions using a theoretical framework was relatively new. It started after the Second World War when the behavioural scientists in US Public Health Service, engaged during the war in contributing to the understanding and prevention of behavioural problems among the fighting forces, found themselves after the war involved in health education as a part of their new job. To be able to analyse the past health education activities, they developed conceptual frameworks to be able to define them. Looking at existing practices they were able to define them as using the "KAP" model (Knowledge-Attitudes-Practice). From this basic cognitive approach other approaches were developed, which are listed and supported by some examples:

Cognitive models

The upsurge of health education came with the discovery of germ theories when the health problem was understood and the solution was available. The solution required the participation of people at risk who needed information about the available way out. Until then most of solutions lay in the field of public health and depended on the provision of solutions by the society.

This tradition of basing health education on the need for knowledge persisted for a long time and was only questioned when even when they knew what to do, some people did not act in the expected way. The researchers tried to remedy this by including attitudes to a problem and its solution in addition to knowledge, as a required precondition for an action to take place.

In this way the concept of a link between *knowledge, attitudes and practice (KAP)* was accepted as the basis of health education activities. The ensuing **KAP model** *postulates a linear, causal and unidirectional* relationship between the parts.

The main area of application of the KAP model has been in the health education activities in the field of family planning (Berelson, 1965; Hamilton et al., 1980).

The main criticisms of the KAP model are:

- it lacks theoretical support for the main postulates and operates in a cultural and social vacuum;

- it is unidirectional and does not allow for feedback or a flow in the opposite direction;

- although it includes attitudes, the main direction of health education applications has been concerned with the knowledge aspect;

- the concept of knowledge has been accepted as an absolute and there is no differentiation between the different contents or amounts (minimal/optimal) of knowledge conducive for an action to take place;

- the most damaging criticism comes from the fact that when applied it did not work, as has been shown by the failure of many family planning programmes.

Psychological models

The best example of a psychological model is **The Health Belief Model**. There are a number of coincidental factors which can be said to have contributed to the development of the Health Belief Model (HBM). Some of them stem from the structural setup in the US Public Health Service and some are the consequence of the disappointment with the KAP Model.

During World War II, the US Public Health Service set up a Behavioural Sciences Department which produced the well known studies reported in *The American Soldier* (Stouffer, 1949). The tradition continued after the war and the behavioural scientists in the US Public Health Service attempted to develop a new approach which would examine the factors which could influence people's acceptance of preventive as well as curative services (Hochbaum, 1958; Kegeles, 1963; Leventhal et al., 1960, Rosenstock, 1960,1966; Beckcr ct al., 1974; ctc.).

The new approach was based on the theories developed by Kurt Lewin, best known for his "field theory" (Lewin, 1935). This theory was of a phenomenological orientation, which implies that emphasis is given to the various forms of consciousness and the ways in which people can apprehend the world in which they live. Field theory postulated that it is the world of the perceiver that determines action rather than the physical environment, except insofar as the physical environment comes to be represented in the mind of the behaving individual.

Following Lewin's theories, the researchers were of the opinion that the present state of affairs that determines action, with history playing a role only as it is represented in the present dynamics. In this way the HBM got rid of the reductionist approach based on the history of previous experiences.

Still also working within the KAP tradition, and concentrating on motivation and the perceptual world of the behaving individual, the researchers expanded the notion of attitudes by subdividing them into their components: the cognitive, affective and the action aspects.

The HBM Model depended strongly on the concept of an "economic man" who can make rational decisions. If this rationality becomes distorted, for example through excessive fear, he may not be able to think objectively and act rationally (Atkinson, 1957).

The main postulates of the HBM Model gradually developed during the 1950s. In its final version it includes the following components:

- the individual's psychological readiness to take action relative to a particular health condition, determined both by person's perceived "*susceptibility*" or vulnerability to the particular condition, and by his/her perceptions of the "*severity*" of the consequences of contracting the condition;

- the individual's evaluation of the advocated health action's potential "*benefits*" in reducing actual (or perceived) susceptibility and/or severity, weighed against the perceptions of "psychological" and other "barriers" or "costs" of the proposed action;

- finally, a "*stimulus*" either "internal" or "external" must occur to trigger the appropriate health behaviour, i.e. "*the cue to action*".

There have been a number of criticisms of the HBM in the last three decades of its existence:

- the factors related to readiness for action assume that the decision is a single act, and not as some others (Parsons, 1951; Freidson, 1961; Zola, 1964) have postulated, a series of steps or phases, each of which has an independent probability of being positive or negative;

- there has been no single operational definition of the variables included and various researchers have used different questions to ascertain the same variable;

- the model showed the best results when applied to voluntary behaviour not accompanied by any symptoms;

- there has been no evidence about the optimal relationship between the variables for an action to take place; their relative contributions are still open to speculation, as a number of studies applying the model showed;

- the concept of a "cue to action" has not been fully explored and identified; it seems to be composed of the residue of unexplained factors influencing an action.

Psycho-social models

Following the HBM, the **Green Model** (Green, 1970) combined the two aspects of health behaviour, i.e. the social and personal, and included them into a two-dimensional model. On one axis he maps the elements of *psychological readiness* and on the other the elements of *social support*. By psychological readiness, Green understands the attitudinal dimension, which he thinks is important for health action to take place. He is, however, critical of treating the issue of attitudes in isolation and lists objections to a general approach to attitude change. To reduce this danger he proposes the inclusion of a social dimension represented by the *social support* of the lay referral system.

More recently, Green (1990) has updated his approach and described it in what he has called the *Precede* model, which includes also elements of marketing and health promotion.

Sociological models

Suchman (1963, 1965, 1966, 1969, 1970), as a researcher into health behaviour, began by being attracted to the HBM and applying it in his research in Puerto Rico (Sugar cane cutters). As a sociologist he became more interested in the societal aspects of the "cue to action" and consequently developed a model (the **Suchman Model**) which depended heavily on people's orientation towards medical care.

Suchman's major hypothesis was that those individuals who belong to relatively homogeneous and cohesive groups will be more likely to react to illness and medical care in terms of the social group's definition and interpretation of appropriate medical behaviour rather than the formal and non-personalised prescriptions of the medical care system.

The model postulates a divergence between the patient and the doctor in terms of concern, aims and reliance.

The postulated effects of this divergence have been tested in terms of *social group organisation* (including ethnic exclusivity, friendship solidarity and family tradition and solidarity) and *individual medical orientation* (including knowledge about disease, scepticism of medical care and dependency in illness).

The revised model consists of social, socio-medical and medical factors, which influence individual medical orientation and consequently health behaviour.

The model has been positively accepted by many researchers in the field, who have applied the general sociological approach initiated by Suchman in their own work. The main criticism, however, has been of the very general and broad categories used in the model, such as "health orientation", to predict a specific health behaviour.

In addition to developing this model, Suchman made a significant contribution to health education by drawing the attention to the structural aspects of health behaviour. He analysed "sick role" behaviour based on a concept developed by Parsons (1951), and listed the various stages involved.

Descriptive models

Tones (1990) developed a **"Health Action Model"** which he defines as a "mapping model". This seeks to provide a comprehensive framework within which the major variables influencing health choices and actions and their relationships are described and categorised. The Health Action Model, therefore, incorporates elements of a number of existing models such as the Health Belief Model, Reasoned Action Model, Lay Referral System Model and the important work on health locus of control (Rotter 1966). The Health Action Model recognises three categories of health action: routines, quasi-routines and discrete single time choices. It is mainly concerned with the latter. The elements of the model may be influenced by two kinds of input, which are interdependent processes of education and public policy making. The model attempts to bring together health education and health promotion activities.

Mckinley (1971) developed a **careers approach** to the study of patients' behaviour. He includes the general elements of disease distribution, the illness behaviour aspects and the relationship between doctor and patient in terms of roles and expectations.

Baric (1979) developed a **smoker's career model** which includes the phases of acquisition and maintenance of the behaviour and compares them with the relevant causes/effects, social statuses and behaviour.

Social Marketing Model

The idea of "selling" health as just another product prompted some health educators to try applying **marketing principles** to the practice of health education. It was very soon obvious that selling health is different from selling shoes or some similar product. The differences were quoted as:

- marketing a product meets a certain need felt by people, whereas marketing health requires people to abandon some of their deeply felt needs such as smoking, enjoying overeating etc.;
- marketing is satisfied with a small percentage increase in take up, which in terms of money can mean huge profits, whereas health education usually aims at changes in the range of 80% or more;
- advertising as a part of the marketing approach need not aim only at the increase in sales of products but can be successful through increasing awareness of the brand image or the habit as such, whereas health education needs behavioural results in terms of reducing risk and increasing positive aspects of health;
- and, finally, one of the most commonly quoted reasons for differences is the enormous disparity in resources spent on

marketing a product compared with resources devoted to health education.

Accepting most of these arguments, some health educators (Marsden and Peterfreund, 1984) subscribe to the idea that in spite of the differences, there are still certain advantages to be gained from applying certain marketing principles to health education activities. Solomon (1981), following the same line, identified a number of key marketing concepts relevant to health education, which should enable health educators to apply marketing expertise to their activities.

The still unanswered question is whether the attempts to turn marketing into a scientific subject will help health education, or is it merely another way marketing experts can sell their services to industry and commerce.

At risk role model

Based on Talcott Parsons' (1951) concept of the "sick role", designed to explain patients' behaviour, Baric (1969) developed the **"at-risk role"** concept, which explores this conceptualisation for the purpose of examining the behaviour of people at risk.

The model explores the existence of formally recognised at-risk status for a number of health risks and indicates the problems that health education has in changing people's behaviour in cases where such a formalised status does not exist.

This raises the question of conformity and deviance related to a formalised status supported by norms (Baric,1975) and postulates that health education should attempt to create a recognised status and formalised norms in cases where such a status does not exist, before engaging in adjusting people's behaviour.

Ecological approach

The **Social Intervention Model (SIM)** was the percursor of the now widely accepted "ecological" approach, which looks at people in their natural and social environment. This model, developed by

Baric (1979), deals with such concepts as the systems approach, the shift in emphasis from problems to people and the lifestyle approach. It explores the complexity of health problems by using as a case study the planning of health education as a part of an inner city development programme.

An urban setting, fraught with numerous problems due to unemployment, urban blight, resettlement and migration, represents a complex system of interacting factors and processes. The character of these problems can be economic, social, political and health-based. Because of their complexity any solutions will require a concerted and coordinated approach, requiring the participation of many agencies and services, of which the health education service is only one.

Three different types of health problems can be recognised originating in environmental factors, socio-economic factors and personal factors. The problems due to environmental factors are manifested in dilapidated and run down housing, lack of amenities, limited transport etc. The problems due to socio-economic factors are manifested in the threat of unemployment and migration, low educational achievement, overcrowding, delinquency, vandalism, etc. The problems due to personal factors are manifested in widespread ignorance, self-defeating personal habits, alienation, lack of future orientation, poverty, etc.

This whole complex system of health problems in an urban setting can be represented by a matrix of problems according to their origin and the institutions dealing with them. The purpose of representing a complex problem area in the form of a matrix is to help the planners of interventions to take into consideration more of the relevant interrelationships in deciding where the intervention should take place. For example, economic problems in a specific urban area may be due to environmental factors, such as lack of proper transportation and infrastructure; socio-economic, such as lack of employment because there are no industries leading to migration of young people into more prosperous parts of the country; or they may be personal due to a high proportion of immigrants who have not yet been able to adjust to local conditions. The matrix serves only as an example of a systems approach in planning intervention, since it represents the whole problem area in a very simplified way.

Nevertheless, it serves to illustrate that health problems are only one of the many problems that coexist. Developed in greater detail the matrix should also show that health problems in their own right are highly complex. This complexity has so far been disregarded because of a lack of coordination of the various concepts and empirical findings into a coherent system. For example, we have all accepted the WHO definition of health as a state of physical, mental and social wellbeing and not merely absence of disease. And yet, in all our programmes, usually only one dominant aspect of a health problem is taken into consideration. For instance, coronary heart disease is considered in the first place as a physical illness, while the mental and social aspects of a patient who recovers his/her physical health, are not generally taken into account and no specific services are provided to deal with them in the same extensive way as with physical aspects of the disease. If one takes the complete WHO definition of health into consideration then the complexity of the matrix will be increased by including the elements of health and risk.

Breaking up a problem into a number of categories on two axes (Health, Origin) should be considered only as an initial conceptual tool, to remind us of all the relevant aspects of the problem involved. The categories should not be treated as exclusive units because most health problems spread across the boundaries. As an illustration we can look at the problem of cigarette smoking. This represents a health problem affecting physical (lung cancer) and mental (addiction, dependence) wellbeing and its origins can be traced to socio-economic and personality sources. A useful conceptualisation of the problem of smoking is possible if we begin with the matrix as a general background and locate the problem of cigarette smoking in the appropriate cells. Some pieces of research may locate the main problem of smoking differently, and others may cover different areas of the matrix. This, however, does not reduce the value of the approach recommended nor its implications for a health education intervention. One of the main implications of using such a complex matrix is that health education will in the future have to change its simplified approach to a more complex one. Health education so far has informed people about the dangerous consequences of smoking, recommended stopping smoking and provided professional help for those who could not do it on their own. The first contribution of the SIM is, therefore, to make health education practitioners aware of the complexity of the problem with which they are dealing.

The second contribution of the SIM is to draw our attention to the need for changing the emphasis in the relationship between the problem and the population affected. At present, health education is problem-oriented and uses the medical model, which treats the health threat as the independent variable. For example, we treat the problem of smoking as given and try to find differences among smokers that would help us in finding a solution. The use of the SIM helps us to become people-oriented, to choose one population group and treat it as the independent variable and cxamine the variations in the problems treating them as independent variables. We can consider pregnant women as the independent variable and the threat to the unborn child from smoking during pregnancy as the dependent variable. We thus examine the different aspects of smoking (amount, inhaling, brand of cigarette, etc.) for a specified population.

Although this increases the complexity of the model and changes the emphasis from the problem to the population group, we are still using a medical framework that is limited to one health threat at a time. This has been the case so far in most health education interventions, which have been concerned with 'smoking', 'toothbrushing', etc. as specific problems, no matter whether the emphasis was on social or personal factors.

The third contribution of the SIM is considered to be an innovation of the greatest importance. Experience has taught us that in solving one problem we may create another, as in the case of a person who stops smoking and gains weight. This leads us to take to its logical conclusion the change of emphasis from an individual health threat to a population group. In applying a systems approach to the population as well as to the problem wc can observe that health behaviour (smoking) does not exist in a vacuum, but is a part of a complex behavioural system which can be called "the lifestyle" of an individual.

The extension of the model to include the lifestyle of a population group illustrates the highly complex interrelationship of a great number of variables to be taken into account by a health education intervention such as the following:

- definition of the population group, which can be achieved by examining the distribution of the problem in a population and finding certain common denominators shared by certain easily defined subgroups such as social class, age, and sex;

- definition of the effects of the problem on all three aspects of the concept 'health', as defined by WHO, which can be achieved by taking a specific population group (pregnant women) and seeing which aspect of health is most important, as perceived by the women, and as compared with the 'objective' assessment of this importance by the medical profession; if we refer again to the example of smoking and examine its effects on different aspects of 'health' for different population groups, we may find out that it affects pregnant women by creating anxiety (mental wellbeing), whereas it may have as well as health, social implications for babies (social wellbeing), in reducing their potential mental functions in later life;

- ranking of the problems affecting a population group according to perceived importance, prevalence, stigmatisation, etc; this will be achieved by consulting with the medical profession (importance), using epidemiological studies (prevalence), examining the social norms and sanctions (stigmatisation), etc; the process of ranking will include the 'objective' assessment made by the medical profession and the 'subjective' perception of importance by the population at risk;

- examination of the origins of a specific problem in a specific population: this will enable the health educator to decide whether the main reasons for the existence of the problem lie in the environment, in the socio-economic position or in the personality of the individual; we know, for example, that high rise flats are associated with loneliness and depression, lower social class and economic deprivation, involving the under utilisation of preventive services; we also suspect that ambition and competitiveness are associated with cardio-vascular disease.

At the time when it was put forward in 1978, the SIM was considered to be to radical and not in line with the thinking of the day. Its recommendations included the following ideas:

- the use of a systems approach based on the SIM revealed the complexity of the task facing health education in the maintenance of health and prevention of disease;
- it also drew our attention to the many cells in the matrix which must at present remain empty since there is no information or knowledge available;
- to fill these cells additional research would be required, which so far has not been carried out; one reason for this is that we have not developed appropriate methods and indicators which could be used to provide us with the necessary additional information; one could, therefore, conclude that the application of the SIM indicates the way future research in health education should go, i.e. to develop appropriate methods and reliable indicators before any relevant information can be collected.

The application of the SIM in health education shows the limitations of our present knowledge in a number of areas:

a) The team approach An insight into the complexity of problems facing health education makes it obvious that the task of solving such a set of complex problems forming a part of a population lifestyle cannot be solved by one person, or even by one profession. The complexity of the problems will require the concerted efforts of a whole range of agents and services of which health education is only one among many. Because the SIM helps to outline the various aspects of a set of problems it should also help in the more precise distribution of specific tasks among different agents. We all agree, for example, that teachers, doctors, nurses, etc. have an important role in health education. Nobody has so far defined what this role is and in practice it is usually limited to transmitting information to clients or patients. In the area of doctor-patient communication health education practitioners are concerned about the amount of information the doctor transmits and the amount the patient recalls, they use nurses and health visitors to give talks in schools, and encourage teachers to include health information in their regular lessons. The transmission of information may be considered by some as a very important part of a health education intervention, but it certainly cannot be considered to be the only one. We have moved on from the simple model of equating knowledge with recommended behaviour. The application of the SIM should help us not only to see the complexity of the processes and agents involved, but also to decide who should do what in each part of the model. Thus, the SIM will enable the health educator to fulfil his role as a coordinator of various agents and services by defining their contributions to the solution of the problems. It should also increase the probability of the participation of these agents and services. They will know not only what is expected from them, but also why, and with what outcome that can be monitored and evaluated.

b) Choice of methods The differentiation of the tasks of services will require the choice of an appropriate approach or method for each one. Health education has at present a range of methods and aids which are used in various programmes. Many of the methods and aids have been evaluated and in many instances we know what each of them can offer in terms of efficiency and effectiveness. In the same way as the use of the SIM enables us to place various agents and services into different cells and thus define their task and role, this system approach as outlined in relation to the SIM should enable us to do the same with the identification of different approaches corresponding with the different tasks of different agents, and covering specific areas of the complex problem. To do this, however, we need additional knowledge about the relationship of a specific approach not only to a specific form of health behaviour but to the whole complex of a person's lifestyle. This knowledge does not always exist and will have to be acquired by research and evaluation of a new kind as far as health education is concerned.

The research required will have to use pretested instruments and indicators which are not readily available. One such instrument, for example, has been applied in the measurement of social expectations or norms related to smoking (Baric and Fisher, 1978). At the time of the study it was established that there was no such standardised instrument available, nor was there a general agreement how one can measure norms. For this reason the greater part of the study was devoted to the development of a theoretical model and a specific method for the measurement of norms.

c) Making inferences In addition to the development of new instruments, future research needs to develop new ways of analyzing the findings and drawing inferences from them. At present we use simple models and are satisfied with simple analysis, by using two by two tables and Chi-square tests of association. We also use ready-made computer programs (SPSS) which limit the analysis to a standardised set of answers. The SIM helps us to see the totality of a process which cannot be fully understood by examining the various parts separately. A systems approach requires a complex method of analysis providing us with new insights into the problem as well as the consequences of the solution applied.

d) Evaluation This represents a very important area of development for the needs of health education. One should, however, draw the distinction between evaluation and the assessment of effectiveness, efficiency, effort, etc. The difference has so far been disregarded and we can find examples of simple assessments being defined as evaluation. Evaluation should be primarily interpreted as the process of judging the value of something. This interpretation is in accordance with the general notion that health education is based on and derives its justification from the value system of the social group within which it operates. We make such value judgements as "it is better to prevent than cure", or "saving a life is good", etc. which, although we take for granted, nevertheless reflect the value system of our society. Consequently, evaluation should primarily be concerned with assessing the correspondence between the values held and the results achieved by health education.

For example, in the UK in 1994 there was a threat of an epidemic of whooping cough. We know that whooping cough in a certain number of cases will be fatal; at the same time we have a possibility of vaccinating the children but this may (although rarely) produce brain damage in the children. The critical decision of health education in this area should initially include an 'evaluation' and only subsequently an 'assessment' of its effectiveness, efficiency, etc. The evaluation needs to answer a number of pertinent questions: do we compare the number of deaths with the number of brain damaged children, and if so, do we compare them on a 1:1 basis or do we introduce a weighting factors, such as 2 dead to one brain damaged child? How do we derive the weighting factor? By asking parents, would they prefer their child to die immediately, or to live as a mentally handicapped member of their family and the society? This evaluation is performed unconsciously, but its rationale has so far been neglected by health educators, although they have to make such decisions, as for example, whether they should promote vaccination against whooping cough or not and whether they should make certain that if they do there will be an adequate support service for cases where there is some undesirable side-effect? If such an evaluation is carried out, the answer might represent a compromise based on the notion of *'differential risk'*: since brain damage from vaccination occurs every year and the whooping cough epidemic has a four years cycle, and the danger is the greatest in the first year of a child's life, a changing vaccination pattern could be the answer, to accommodate all the different risk factors involved. Only after this kind of evaluation is carried out, should the assessment of the effectiveness and efficiency take place, including long and short-term effects, as well as possible side effects of a health education intervention.

This issue can be illustrated by a study of anti-smoking clinics. It was found that although the short-term effects were positive and clinics have been successful in helping people to stop smoking, there might be some negative effects in the long term. The result of such an assessment could be to draw our attention to the real problem, which is relapse. We may find that the possible negative effects of such clinics could be neutralised by providing follow-up services such as 'clubs for ex-smokers'.

Another illustration is the health education programme aimed at pregnant women, who should not smoke, at least during pregnancy. The use of mass media in promoting the idea of the risk to the unborn baby may be effective in creating social expectations (norms) which provide the necessary social pressure on pregnant women. An assessment of possible side effects could produce evidence of negative effects on those women who smoked while pregnant in the past and did have a handicapped baby. The result of such an assessment could be to limit health education against smoking in pregnancy to a person-to-person interaction between the medical profession and the pregnant woman and avoid stigmatisation of some mothers who cannot do anything about it.

The ideas originally presented in the SIM have been gradually incorporated in later approaches in line with the original ideas expressed in the SIM

There are, therefore, many models in health education. Although they were very important in their day, in that they provided a theoretical underpinning for professional action, they all have in common the general shortcomings described earlier in the critical analysis of models. Now that health promotion is becoming as important as health education the issue of models is rapidly becoming obsolete in that the idea of models has been replaced by the idea of approaches. This has been the result of the Alma Ata Declaration and is discussed in the following chapter.

THE DECLARATION OF ALMA ATA

The watershed Declaration of Alma Ata published in 1978 needs to be examined in detail. It is set out below:

"The International Conference on Primary Health Care, meeting in Alma-Ata this twelfth day of September in the year nineteen hundred and seventy-eight, expressing the need for urgent action by all governments, all health and development workers, and the world community to protect and promote the health of all the people of the world, hereby makes the following Declaration (WHO,1978):

I The Conference strongly reaffirms that health, which is a state of complete physical, mental and social wellbeing, and not merely the absence of disease or infirmity, is a fundamental human right and that the attainment of the highest possible level of health is a most important world-wide social goal whose realization requires the action of many other social and economic sectors in addition to the health sector.

II The existing gross inequality in the health status of the people particularly between developed and developing countries as well as within countries is politically, socially and economically unacceptable and is, therefore, of common concern to all countries.

III Economic and social development, based on a New International Economic Order, is of basic importance to the fullest attainment of health for all and to the reduction of the gap between the health status of the developing and developed countries. The promotion and protection of the health of the people is essential to sustained economic and social development and contributes to a better quality of life and to world peace.

IV The people have the right and duty to participate individually and collectively in the planning and implementation of their health care.

V Governments have a responsibility for the health of their people which can be fulfilled only by the provision of adequate health and social measures. A main social target of governments, international organisations and the whole world community in the coming decades should be the attainment by all people of the world by the year 2000 of a level of health that will permit them to lead a socially and economically productive life. Primary health care is the key to attaining this target as part of development in the spirit of social justice.

VI Primary health care is essential health care based on practical, scientifically sound and socially acceptable methods and technology made universally accessible to individuals and families in the community through their full participation and at a cost that the community and country can afford to maintain at every stage of their development in the spirit of self-reliance and self-determination. It forms an integral part both of the country's health system, of which it is the central function and main focus, and of the overall social and economic development of the community. It is the first level of contact of individuals, the family and community with the national health system bringing health care as close as possible to where people live and work, and constitutes the first element of a continuing health care process.

VII Primary health care:

1. *reflects and evolves from the economic conditions and sociocultural and political characteristics of the country and its communities and is based on the application of the relevant results of social, biomedical and health services research and public health experience;*

2. *addresses the main health problems in the community, providing promotive, preventive, curative and rehabilitative services accordingly;*

3. *includes at least: education concerning prevailing health problems and the methods of preventing and controlling them; promotion of food supply and proper nutrition; an adequate supply of safe water and basic sanitation: maternal and child health care, including family planning; immunization against the major infectious diseases; prevention and control of*

locally endemic diseases; appropriate treatment of common diseases and injuries; and provision of essential drugs;

4. *involves, in addition to the health sector, all related sectors and aspects of national and community development, in particular agriculture, animal husbandry, food, industry, education, housing, public works, communications and other sectors; and demands the coordinated efforts of all those sectors;*

5. *requires and promotes maximum community and individual self-reliance and participation in the planning, organization, operation and control of primary health care, making fullest use of local, national and other available resources; and to this end develops through appropriate education the ability of communities to participate;*

6. *should be sustained by integrated, functional and mutually-supportive referral systems, leading to the progressive improvement of comprehensive health care for all, and giving priority to those most in need;*

7. *relies, at local and referral levels, on health workers, including physicians, nurses, midwives, auxiliaries and community workers as applicable, as well as traditional practitioners as needed, suitably trained socially and technically to work as a health team and to respond to the expressed health needs of the community.*

VIII All governments should formulate national policies, strategies and plans of action to launch and sustain primary health care as part of a comprehensive national health system and in coordination with other sectors. To this end, it will be necessary to exercise political will, to mobilize the country's resources and to use available external resources rationally.

IX All countries should cooperate in a spirit of partnership and service to ensure primary health care for all people since the attainment of health by people in any one country directly concerns and benefits every other country. In this context the joint

WHO/UNICEF report on primary health care constitutes a solid basis for the further development and operation of primary health care throughout the world.

X An acceptable level of health for all the people of the world by the year 2000 can be attained through a fuller and better use of the world's resources, a considerable part of which is now spent on armaments and military conflicts. A genuine policy of independence, peace, detente and disarmament could and should release additional resources that could well be devoted to peaceful aims and in particular to the acceleration of social and economic development of which primary health care, as an essential part, should be allotted its proper share."

The International Conference on Primary Health Care calls for urgent and effective national and international action to develop and implement primary health care throughout the world and particularly in developing countries in a spirit of technical cooperation and in keeping with a New International Economic Order. It urges governments, WHO and UNICEF, and other international organisations, as well as multilateral and bilateral agencies, non-governmental organisations, funding agencies, all health workers and the whole world community to support national and international commitment to primary health care and to channel increased technical and financial support to it, particularly in developing countries. The Conference calls on all the aforementioned to collaborate in introducing, developing and maintaining primary health care in accordance with the spirit and content of this Declaration.

HEALTH PROMOTION AND HEALTH EDUCATION - THE POST ALMA ATA PERIOD

INTRODUCTION

This section deals with the new tasks and demands facing health promotion and health education in a changing world where the established values and accepted paradigms have not only been challenged but more often completely rejected and where new roles are being allocated and accepted by the existing agents who are expected to change and cope with the new expectations.

The understanding of the new expectations facing health promotion and health education forces us to examine the new situation which has been the result of a series of most rapid and radical changes that have been and still are occurring throughout the world and especially in Europe. Although one could analyse these changes in terms of political and economic parameters, the underlying element is social change expressed in terms of radically different value systems, including the value given to health.

It may be a platitude to say that most people never believed that they would witness such changes in their lifetime, and this is even more true of people who have been directly involved in bringing about these changes.

The radical character of these changes is due to the wide range of implications and the depth of new adjustments necessary for people to be able to accommodate, manage and cope with new roles, norms, and a completely new value system as a part of the new situations. Historically speaking, there have been well known changes in terms of scope and depth, which have changed the established conditions of life. The Second World War, changed the map of the world and the power structure between and within many nations, creating the world in which we have lived and grown up. These changes were not smooth and in many instances produced great upheavals and disruptions. One of the consequences was the division of the world into two main ideological camps with different socio-political and economic systems, ambitions and programmes.

After the War, depending on the decisions of the winners, the losers found themselves living and working under new conditions. The value systems were changed and people needed to adjust to new conditions. In a divided world, the immediate post-war period was characterised by great efforts to reeducate whole populations to adjust to the new values promoted in each camp and be able to meet the new expectations. In the Eastern bloc countries this was defined as 'political indoctrination', whereas in the Western World of which the conquered as well as newly liberated countries became a part this was called the process of 'democratisation'.

The collapse of Eastern bloc ideologies, which started a few years ago and is still continuing together with the introduction of a 'democratic' system based on a market economy in countries that have been living and working for nearly half a century under one set of values, represents as great an upheaval as the one facing the world after the Second World War, and may require an intensive programme of reeducation similar to the one that took place immediately after the War.

Within this broad framework of socio-political and economic changes, the changes that will be necessary in the field of health promotion and health education to match the changes that are taking place in the health care delivery system are of special interest. At present, it is difficult if not impossible to allocate the responsibilities for meeting these new demands to any specific institution or organisation, since they themselves are changing in their roles and activities. Prominent here are the CEC (in Europe) and the World Health Organisation. Although traditionally the WHO was seen as dealing with health problems, in the new situation in Europe, the CEC is showing an increased interest and willingness to play an important role in this field. At present there are many indications of involvement of either or both of these organisations in the field of health and of the considerations these organisations are giving to adjusting their existing programmes and approaches to accommodate the new situation with its specific demands.

It should be, however, recognised that the WHO has to some extent anticipated the coming changes by putting forward the Alma Ata Declaration, which recognises and deals with many of the new needs. One of the most radical innovations has been the shift of responsibility for health, from society to the individual, employing the concept of 'self-reliance'. This implies that people are responsible for their own health and that the society can only play a supporting role in providing 'equality' in opportunities and the necessary health care services. Furthermore, the support provided by the society will depend on people's 'participation' in the decision making processes involved in creating and maintaining the health care systems, which should be accessible to people and sensitive to their needs.

HEALTH PROMOTION AND HEALTH EDUCATION

HEALTH PROMOTION

Post Alma Ata Declaration, the WHO HQ as well as its Regional Offices were concerned with clarifying concepts mentioned in the Declaration.

Targets for Health for All (HFA)

In 1985, the WHO EURO published a list of targets in support of the European regional strategy for Health For All.

The reasons given for setting the targets were:

- to propose improvements in the health care delivery system;
- to indicate where these improvements should be made;
- to provide a tool for monitoring and evaluation of the improvements made.

The main themes covered by the 38 targets were:

- equity in health;
- emphasis on promotion of health;
- using full community participation;
- employing a multisectoral approach;
- full use of primary health care system;
- strengthening of international cooperation.

Changes in European health development were expected to ensure:

- that each baby will be born healthy and wanted;
- that a child's education will make health a valued aspect of life;
- that each child will be provided with basic requirements for health.

To achieve these aims, the following achievements of prerequisites for health were indicated as required:

- freedom from war;
- equal opportunities;
- satisfaction of basic needs
    - i) food
    - ii) education
    - iii) water and sanitation
    - iv) housing
    - v) secure work and useful role;
- political will and public support.

The WHO strategy was summarised in 38 targets (see Appendix 7) which should permit the achievement of the Health for All by the Year 2000.

Since some of the concepts have been in use for a great number of years, the interpretation given by the Declaration requires further description of the new meanings and implications given to some of these concepts.

The New Concept of Health Promotion

Health promotion stands for the collective effort to attain health. Governments, through public policy, have a special responsibility to ensure the basic conditions for a healthy life and for making the healthier choices the easier choices. At the same time, supporters of health promotion within governments need to be aware of the role of spontaneous action for health, i.e. the role of social movements, self-help and self-care, and the need for continuous cooperation with the public on all health promotion issues. This implies paying attention to the following points:

a) *The concept and meaning of "health promotion" should be clarified at every level of planning,* emphasising a social, economic and ecological, rather than a purely physical and mental perspective on health. Policy development in health promotion can then be related and integrated with policy in other sectors such as work, housing, social services and primary health care.

b) *Political commitment to health promotion* can be expressed through the establishment of focal points for health promotion at all levels - local, regional and national. These would be organisational mechanisms for intersectoral, coordinated planning in health promotion. They should provide leadership and accountability so that, when action is agreed, progress will be secured. Adequate funding and skilled personnel are essential to allow the development of systematic long-term programmes in health promotion.

c) In the development of health promotion policies, there should be *continuous consultation, dialogue and exchange of ideas* between individuals and groups, both lay and professional. Policy mechanisms need to be established to ensure opportunities for the expression and development of public interest in health.

d) *When selecting priority areas for policy development a review should be made of:*

- indicators of health and their distributions in the population;
- current knowledge, skills and health practices of the population;
- current policies in government and other sectors.

Further, an assessment should be made of:

- the expected impact on health of different policies and programmes;
- the economic constraints and benefits;
- the social and cultural acceptability;
- the political feasibility of different options.

e) *Research support is essential for policy development and evaluation,* in order to provide an understanding of influences on health and their development, as well as an assessment of the impact of different initiatives in health promotion. There is a need to develop methodologies for research and analysis and, in particular, to devise more appropriate approaches to evaluation. The results of research should be disseminated widely and comparisons made within and between nations.

Health-related public policy will always be confronted with basic political and moral dilemmas, since it aims to balance public and personal responsibility for health. Those involved in health promotion need to be aware of possible conflicts of interest both at the social and the individual level, such as:

a) *There is a possibility with health promotion that health will be viewed as the ultimate goal, incorporating all life.* This ideology, sometimes called healthism, could lead to others prescribing what individuals should do for themselves and how they should behave, which is contrary to the principles of health promotion.

b) Health promotion *programmes may be inappropriately directed at individuals at the expense of tackling economic and social problems.* Experience has shown that individuals are often considered by policy makers to be exclusively responsible for their own health. It is often implied that people have the power completely to shape their own lives and those of their families so as to be free from the avoidable burden of disease. Thus, when they are ill, they are blamed for this and discriminated against.

c) *Resources, including information, may not be accessible to people in ways that are sensitive to their expectations, beliefs, preferences or skills.* This may increase social inequalities. Information alone is inadequate; raising awareness without increasing control of prospects for change may only succeed in generating anxieties and feelings of powerlessness.

d) *There is a danger that health promotion will be appropriated by one professional group and made a field of specialisation to the exclusion of other professionals and lay people.* To increase control over their own health the public require a greater sharing of resources by professionals and government.

The New Concept of Lifestyles

The concept of lifestyle, is closely associated with the feeling of wellbeing, as the expression of health. The use of this concept avoids the overemphasis on specific risky behaviours which have been associated with certain diseases. Instead of concentrating on nutrition, smoking, hygiene, exercise, etc., one looks at different life-styles, some of which may include activities like smoking or exclude some, like exercise. By treating a life-style as a system one can apply a systems approach and treat parts of a system as forming an interrelated whole. It is not possible to change one part of the system without affecting the rest of the system; but one part of the system can be affected if one manipulates the whole system appropriately and allows for simultaneous changes.

Because so many agents are directly or indirectly influential in affecting lifestyles of a certain population group, one cannot depend solely on the health care system. On the other hand the life-style approach requires a very specific division of labour and role definition for each and every agent involved. It is not enough to say that everybody should do something; it is necessary to state clearly who should do what and, at the same time, ensure that a coordination of effort takes place. In the past, the political, economic and social environments were taken as given, and health care was supposed to enable people to lead as healthy a life as possible under the circumstances. The concept of "optimal health" was used to describe this situation. The aim was to adjust people to the system and optimise their utilisation of existing possibilities. The new approach looks at the system, including the environment as well as the people, and maintains the view that both the environment and the individuals need to undergo a change in order to create both desirable conditions and the possibility of deriving the best advantage from them.

The question of lifestyles was central to the Technical Discussion at the Thirty-third Session of the Regional Committee of the WHO EURO which published its views in "Life-styles and their Impact on Health" (1982). Sections of the Report are reproduced as being relevant to our discussion:

"In the 19th century great improvements in health were brought about by what might be called 'engineering methods' - the building of safe water supply and sewerage systems in the towns and the use of mechanised agriculture to provide cheap food for the urban population. Such methods of improving health are still important in

the poorer parts of the Region. The first sixty years or so of the 20th century could be termed the 'medical era', in which allopathic medicine emerged as the dominant approach to health care; this was based on mass vaccination and the extensive use of antibiotics and is still the main approach in some parts of the Region. Now, however, the industrialised parts of the Region have entered upon a 'post-medical' era, in which physical wellbeing is undermined by certain types of individual behaviour (e.g. smoking), failures of social organisation (e.g. loneliness), economic factors (e.g. poverty, over-eating) and factors in the physical environment (e.g. pollution), that are not amenable to improvement by medicine, which now has in many parts of the Region only a limited capacity to effect further improvements in health. Whereas in the 'medical' era health policy has been concerned mainly with how medical care is to be provided and paid for, in the new 'post-medical' era it will focus on the attainment of good health and wellbeing.

The debate on life-styles and their impact on health is an expression of the search for ways of meeting the new situation, in which chronic conditions, particularly cardiovascular disorders and cancer, make up the bulk of morbidity, and psychological disorders such as depression and the repercussions of stress are becoming increasingly important.

At first the key to preventing many of these conditions was considered to be a change in the health behaviour of the individual and it is, of course, true that excessive drinking and smoking, over-eating and faulty nutrition, lack of exercise and misuse of drugs and other medicines have a deleterious effect on wellbeing and health. Much more controversial is the question of why unhealthy life-styles have become so widespread and what practical conclusions should be drawn from the knowledge accumulated in the past decade about this situation, especially since industrialised countries are exporting unhealthy life-styles to the poorer parts of the world. Researchers are now acknowledging that the standard risk factors do not explain everything and are beginning to study the combined influence of life-styles, psychological factors and social conditions on human wellbeing as a basis for their concepts. With poverty still present and health contrasts due to socioeconomic inequalities even increasing in some parts of the Region, it is one of

WHO's responsibilities to ensure that the life- style concept is used not as a blanket explanation in which the victim is always blamed, but as a means of stressing how great an impact living conditions have on individual wellbeing and health behaviour.

The transition from emphasis on types of individual behaviour to emphasis on the social factors affecting health means a change in the pattern of thinking and such changes take time and require a fundamental reorientation of beliefs and attitudes. Different societies differ in their degree of readiness to accept the life-styles approach to health, so that the implications of a shift of perspective must be taken into account in any policies and strategies regarding research on life-style and action to change them.

While the term 'lifestyle' is currently used in ordinary speech it has not yet become firmly established in scientific parlance. It was, therefore, necessary for the Regional Office as a first step to clarify what is meant by 'life-styles', so that common patterns and major differences between the various countries can be distinguished and a basis laid for policies forming part of the regional strategy that will reflect the needs, cultures, traditions and economic and political features of Member States. To this end a series of meetings has been held over the last two years to seek information from all parts of the Region, as well as from sectors and disciplines not usually involved in WHO work. This paper should, therefore, be considered as a first summary of a continuous and long-lasting process. Fortunately, it has been possible to combine this process of clarification with the formulation of the life-style section of the regional target document, thus providing an opportunity for this Regional Committee to discuss both the analytical base and the policy implications of an approach to health concerned with life-styles.

There is almost no agreement either in theory or practice as to what constitutes a 'life-style'. Some use it to denote a number of health-relevant patterns of consumption and general living, but often in too broad and general a way to enable specific health consequences to be determined. Others use 'life-style' in a sense implying that the individual has chosen particular types of behaviour and particular habits of his own free will; here the term refers to individual types of behaviour that are hazardous to health and does not leave room for clear differentiation between a particular habit that is injurious to health and a specific life-style.

In the regional strategy and the target document, the term 'life-style' is taken to mean ***a general way of living based on the interplay between living conditions in the wide sense and individual patterns of behaviour as determined by socio- cultural factors and personal characteristics.*** *The range of behaviour patterns open may be limited or extended by environmental factors and also by the degree of individual self-reliance. The way in which an individual lives may produce behaviour patterns that are either beneficial or detrimental to health. If health is to be improved, action must be directed at both the individual and environmental factors affecting life-style.*

For example, there is extensive evidence of relationships between socio-economic status (including occupation) and morbidity, disability and mortality, and between level of education and health maintaining practices and health status.

Another potential source of confusion in attempts to detect associations between daily living habits and morbidity and mortality is a stressful life situation due to causes other than insufficient income or an unhealthy work environment. Stressful events or situations have often been found to have adverse effects on health and persons exposed to them may become more neglectful of health.

It has also been shown that social intercourse and support help to reduce the deleterious effects of stress, perhaps by influencing health behaviour.

Finally, what people believe about health affects their attitude to healthful behaviour, their utilisation of preventive health and screening services, their behaviour responses to illness and even the degree to which they report illness.

One working definition of life-styles that attempts to cover the multitude of background factors, reads as follows:

'Lifestyles are patterns of (behavioral) choices made from the alternatives that are available to people according to their socio-economic circumstances and to the ease with which they are able to choose certain ones over others.' (Milio 1981).

This definition links the consciousness, experiences and behaviour patterns of individuals and social groups to identifiable structural patterns within a given society, and thus provides a basis for health policy decisions, health promotion and health education."

Definition of lifestyles

WHO EURO in their document on "Lifestyles and their Impact on Health" (WHO 1982) defined and described the concept as follows:

"For the purpose of analysis, lifestyle has to be defined in relation to collective and individual experiences and to conditions of life. The range of options open to an individual is confined to the area in which the two groups of factors overlap.

The lifestyle of a social group comprises a range of socially determined patterns of behaviour and interpretations of social situations, developed and used jointly by the group to cope with life.

An individual's lifestyle is made up of the standard reactions and behaviour patterns that are developed through processes of socialisation. They are learnt through social interaction with parents, peer groups, friends and siblings or through the influence of schools, the mass media, etc. They are continually interpreted and tested out in social situations and are, therefore, not fixed once and for all but subject to change based on experience and reinterpretation. The lifestyle of an individual provides a framework for different sorts of behaviour: choice of a particular behaviour pattern will depend on this cognitive and emotional make-up and the constraints and contradictions of the surrounding social work. Thus research on the effects of lifestyles on health is bound to be an extremely complex matter.

Since no individual lives for himself or herself alone, and no social group exists without links to the near and far environment and without reference to its tradition and culture, there must be identifiable elements within the social system to transmit its broad values down to the level of daily behaviour. These elements are institutionalised in various forms (kinship, family, school, religion) and act as intermediaries between the lifestyle of a society and the lifestyle of the groups and individuals that make it up. The lifestyle of a society as whole will be affected by modernisation and social change and these will reach different groups at different points in time and space.

Individual behaviour occurs against a background of past experiences, stresses, social relationships and knowledge within the cultural, political and economic environment characteristics of the society concerned. Many factors they know to be detrimental to health cannot be affected by individuals. It must also be borne in mind that the attainment of health in a society in which some social groups (e.g. women, the elderly, the poor) are systematically at a disadvantage is problematical. A healthy community cannot be based on exploitative, i.e. unhealthy human relations."

Experience so far has not been encouraging. Measurement of life-styles lacks precision and its relationship to health is even more difficult to establish. One attempt at measuring life- styles has been made by Sobel (1981) in his study of the concept, definition and analysis of life-styles. Sobel found that there is no agreed definition of thc word amongst scientists, although there is an obvious shared understanding about its meaning among lay people. He felt obliged to define it for his own purposes as any distinctive and therefore recognisable, mode of living. Life-styles are composed of "expressive" behaviours that are directly observable and deducible from observations. Which "behaviours" to include in describing a life-style is debatable, and Sobel proposes those that are most salient within a given time and space. For Sobel's purpose the most obvious ones seemed to be consumption, leisure and work. In the end, Sobel limits himself to consumption, since he treats leisure as a part of consumption and work for him is not typically an expressive activity. The differences in life-styles depend on the different reference-sets that individuals maintain, which are in turn dependent on the status or position of individuals in a society. Thus, lifestyle differentiation stems from differentiations within the social structure.

Socio-economic characteristics are closely associated with lifestyles. In his study Sobel examined education, socio-economic status and consumption. Consumption was studied in terms of food eaten at home and outside the home, alcohol consumption, housing, household textiles, furniture, decoration, different kinds of clothing, personal care, vacations and gifts. Sobel found that the most powerful factors in differentiating life-styles were occupational status and income, whereas education was not significantly influential.

For analytical purposes it will be necessary to combine the great variety of individual life-styles into recognisable groupings. In his discussion of the definition of a life-style, Sobel concentrates on the term 'style' and its many meanings: the general formulation of the concept hinges on the descriptive word 'style' defined as 'any distinctive and therefore recognisable way in which an act is performed or an artifact made or ought to be performed and made' (Gombrich, 1968). Under a life-style Sobel understands a distinctive and recognisable mode of living, which is characterised by different factors which constitute a stylistic unity (e.g. a normal everyday expenditure factor, an entertainment factor, etc). These factors need not be activated all at the same time. One can, therefore, conclude that a certain life-style is composed of certain behavioral patterns but at the same time, these need not be activated consistently to form a life-style. Certain patterns may even change, whereas the life-style may remain the same.

This conceptualisation is very important if one wants to use the concept 'life-style' as an analytical tool for defining a health problem. The concept was introduced in WHO documents with the aim of changing the approach from emphasising individual actions or behaviour to a more general combination of activities or behaviours within a life-style. The intention was to promote a holistic approach to a person and his/her survival in a physical and social world. One has to accept that 'life-style' is a theoretical construct and needs to be clearly defined before one can use it for interventions aimed at improving health. The great expectations of health promotion as well as health education related to the achievement of 'Health for All by the Year 2000' are not at present justified because the definition of the concepts is very often vague.

For health education purposes the definition of the health problems should include the following:

- the description of the health problem;
- the causal and contributing factors;
- the behavioral and/or environmental factors related to causation, persistence or outcome;
- the indication of a minimal and optimal solution;
- the epidemiological data concerning the problem as well as the behavioral and social factors;
- the psychological and social characteristics of the population at risk and their social environment.

The information required for such a definition of a health problem should be based on medical, epidemiological, psychological and sociological theories and models. The concepts, criteria and indicators should be precise enough to allow for the operationalisation of the data in terms of an intervention.

Based on this kind of background data, health education should be in a position of carrying out a *differential diagnosis* of the problem, using a holistic or systems approach. A differential diagnosis implies the exploration of a range of factors out of which only those are selected which are relevant for the solution of the problem. The concept of a differential diagnosis for health education intervention assumes that in real life situations a choice will have to be made among the various factors present to satisfy the requirements of a minimal solution since the optimal solution is often not possible. This approach requires the listing of all causal and contributing factors, followed by an assessment of prevalence, which will allow for the selection of those factors which contribute to at least 75% of cases. In this way the differential diagnosis will ensure the minimal required intervention to achieve most results.

The holistic approach is achieved by concentrating on the concept of a 'life-style'. The implications of the meaning of a 'style' and 'stylistic unity' have been discussed. The term 'life' covers all the activities of a living human being, and for health education purposes it will be necessary to select those which are associated with causal and contributing factors for better health. In this way a precise definition of the problem will allow for the selection of relevant aspects of 'life' to be included as aims in planning a health education intervention.

The Concept of Primary Health Care

Primary health care is considered to be the basis for successful improvement in the health of a nation and forms a vital part of health promotion aiming at the adjustment of people's lifestyles for better health. **Primary health care is manifested in the first contact with a health threat or problem**. It is practised by individuals on their own or within families and includes the first awareness of a problem, its diagnosis and the decision about its management. The decision can be to do nothing about it, to use self-medication or to seek medical support.

The first contact with the health care system is only one of the many possible aspects of primary health care. Primary health care is of course also in operation before any problem occurs and includes prevention of illness and promotion of health. Primary health care includes knowledge about health matters, which is the background for the awareness and recognition of potential threats and the appropriate interpretation of experienced symptoms or signs indicating the possible presence of a disease. This includes knowledge about the human body and how it works, its needs, such as nutrition, stimulation and relaxation, as well as the potential threats. It also includes knowledge of the causes and processes of different diseases so that one can interpret their seriousness and predict the outcome. All this together will indicate the ability to carry out self-diagnosis as the first step in primary health care.

The second step in primary health care includes the competence to act upon the results of such a self-diagnosis by choosing the appropriate measures. It may happen that the diagnosis results in deciding that the situation is not serious enough to merit an action and no specific action will take place. If the situation is assessed as meriting an action, this may take the form of self-care which will include self-medication. If the problem is not resolved and further help is deemed necessary, outside help may be mobilised. This may take the form of joining a self-help group or a visit to the general practitioner as the first level of primary medical care. Once this help has been mobilised the person enters into a contractual relationship with the medical system by taking on a "sick role" with the accompanying rights and duties of a patient.

In their final report, the Working Group on Primary Health Care (WHO, 1981) produced an analysis of the content of the eight essential elements of Primary Health Care which are:

1. education concerning the prevailing health problems and methods of preventing and controlling them;
2. promotion of food supply and proper nutrition;
3. adequate supply of safe water and basic sanitation;
4. maternal and child health, including family planning;
5. immunization against the major infectious diseases;
6. prevention and control of locally endemic diseases (examples: malaria, hypertension);
7. appropriate treatment of common diseases and injuries(examples: diarrhoeal diseases, common accidents in the home);
8. provision of essential drugs.

The Working Group recognised that primary care operates on four levels which are:

i) *Home Level*: This refers to the basic unit in any community: the household. The family members are those primarily responsible for activities at this level, whether they are seen as individuals, mothers or fathers of children or heads of the household. People, from the neighbourhood, as well as home-visiting community workers of various kinds (including trained health workers), interact with the family and are directly involved in activities at this level.

ii) *Community Level*: Activities at this level concern the health of a whole community (village/town or group of villages) and require common facilities and/or the joint voluntary efforts of community members. Examples are cleaning campaigns, construction of facilities, information/education about immunization sessions.

The Community Development Committee, or its equivalent is the central coordinating mechanism for activities at this level, but it also provides support to activities at the other levels, in particular that of the home. The Community Development Committee interacts with, and is supported by, the individual community members, in addition to various community groups and those concerned with national sectoral programmes including health.

Community health workers as well as other community workers and volunteers, function also at this level both in promotion/ informational activities and in planning and/or implementation of communal health activities. Many communities have created an actual facility for the community health worker at this level.

iii) *First Health Facility Level*: This refers to the first level at which a trained health professional is available and where facilities are available for running clinic sessions. The kind of facility and the type of staff available will vary from country to country.

In addition to the standard clinical activities, the staff interact both on the home level (during home visits) and on the community level. Acting at this level also fills a major supportive role in training and supervision of all kinds of community health workers.

iv) *First Referral Level*: There are two types of referral systems in a Primary Health Care strategy. The first is a clinical referral system which includes the supervision of performances at lower levels. The second is an administrative referral system - usually the District Health Office. This is the level involved in planning, management and support of activities related to sanitation, health education/information, disease control campaigns, etc.

The Concept of Community Participation

The idea of actively involving a community in health promotion and health education activities is not new and has existed in practice for decades. A distinction has been drawn between the concepts of 'community organisation' and 'community development'. The former is concerned with activating the existing forces in a community whereas the latter is concerned with developing new potentials. In order to contribute to the promotion of primary health care, some aspects of health promotion and health education need reorientation, one of them being community participation. In their report, a WHO expert committee on "New Approaches to Health Education in Primary Health Care" (WHO, 1983) states:

"For one thing, it is necessary for the health care providers to develop a better understanding of what can be called the 'health culture' of a community and how this culture is influenced by social forces such as the dynamics of social and cultural change and the political and economic organisation of the community.

The cultural perception and the meaning of various health problems, the response of the community to these problems, and the various customs of the community constitute the three major interacting elements that give to the health culture of a community its particular characteristics.

A people-orientated health technology will require a fundamental change in the relationship between the community and the health care providers. In essence, it implies that people will no longer be fitted into a predetermined framework of health care. Instead, the approach adopted will enable community members to play an active role in the planning and setting up of health care programmes. This calls for a thorough understanding by the health care providers of the people's perception of their health needs and their acceptance and utilisation of different health care technologies - influenced as these are by socio-cultural and economic factors. There is an area where health care providers and the community share the same views on health problems, health needs and the appropriate solutions. As the exchange of ideas, information and technology between the health care providers and the community increases, so does this area of 'interface'. Health education plays a key role in increasing such common thinking.

While health care workers should not compel communities to accept the health technologies they propose, they should also not allow themselves to be forced into a situation where they have to abdicate their views on technical matters. The common ground between the two groups should serve as a basis for a fruitful dialogue, which may lead to change, provided health workers keep in mind that socio-cultural factors and beliefs are not necessarily obstacles to development; in fact they can be points of departure for development."

The Relationship Between HP and HE

Health behaviour is associated with lifestyles and both are affected by social and personal factors. Health promotion may affect lifestyles by influencing and changing social factors. Health education may influence lifestyles by manipulating personal factors which are closely related to health problems and through them it will influence lifestyles. The evaluation can use indicators to measure the changes in the enabling social factors and contributing personal factors, and associate them with the changes in a specific health behaviour. For example, one can mount an anti-smoking campaign, using health promotion to increase the price of cigarettes, and a health education programme to increase knowledge about the risk of smoking and support any attempts at changing relevant behaviour. The indicators for the health promotional aspect of the intervention will include the price of cigarettes before and after the intervention, whereas the indicators for the health educational aspect will include level of knowledge and degree of dependency. The evaluation of the campaign will associate the results of such measurements with the changes in the smoking habit and thus provide a positive or negative evaluation of the campaign.

If the aim of the intervention is a change in the lifestyle of the target population in such a way that the new lifestyle will not include smoking, the campaign may still follow the same pattern. The evaluation will, however, have to use different indicators: for the health promotional aspect it will not be enough to record the changes in the price of cigarettes, but also the effects of such changes on the local economy (reduced profits of tobacconists, reduction in sales of cigarettes, and the threat to the labour force in the tobacco industry and other industries associated with the production and sale of cigarettes) as well as some other variables. For the health educational aspect it will not be enough to record the reduction in smoking in a population, but also the effects of such a change in behaviour on the general lifestyle of the newly created non-smokers.

World Health Organisation Conferences

Most of the new developments in health promotion have been formalised in a number of reports, statements and declarations resulting from various WHO meetings. To trace these developments it will be useful to gain an insight into the most recent WHO conferences.

The WHO Health Promotion Conferences do not stand on their own. They are part of a wider movement towards Health for All and a new public health, as outlined in the Ottawa Charter for Health Promotion (see Appendix 1). They aim to highlight the progress achieved in the development of health promotion, to discuss strategies for action, and to develop consensus statements on the chosen subject area.

The World Health Organisation Health Promotion Project has developed ten principles to guide the preparation and process of conferences.

The World Health Organisation Health Promotion Conferences:

1. are firmly based in the overall developmental process towards Health for All;

2. reflect the philosophy of the Ottawa Charter for Health Promotion;

3. are held at a venue in a World Health Organisation Member State with a strong commitment to health promotion; if possible, the conference is linked to a major national effort in Health for All development that is launched on the occasion of the conference; this underlines and generates high-level political support and involvement; efforts are made to establish contact with the local people, so that they become aware of the debate and work of the World Health Organisation, and their interest in health promotion is increased; this depends on getting generous media coverage.

The Conferences:

4. are prepared in partnership with the host country; if possible, both government and non-government representatives develop the programme and conference style;

5. aim to ensure that participants in the conference have access to the health promotion experiences of the host country by setting aside a special day in the conference programme; this day is fully organised by the host country;

6. are working conferences, based on intense involvement by the participants who are given opportunities to debate and to exchange experience; most participants play an active role in the conference;

7. aim at multidisciplinary and intersectoral participation, including not only professional but lay and non-government representatives; at least part of the conference should be open to the general public;

8. aim to ensure supportive conference environments, that is, they are non-smoking conferences with opportunities for healthy activities and access to healthy food;

9. aim to give space in the conference programme for the development of informal networks and contacts;

10. aim to produce an outcome consensus document which reflects the participatory nature of the conference and which the participants can use easily in their everyday work on return to their home countries.

The Health Promotion Conferences are also a means of establishing closer contacts in health promotion between Regions of the World Health Organisation. The Australian venue of the Adelaide Conference (see Appendix 2) encouraged the building of regular contacts with the Western Pacific Region. These contacts will be intensified as a result of this Conference.

The Ottawa Conference

The First International Conference on Health Promotion met in Ottawa on 21st November 1986. It was influenced by the contributors from Toronto, who produced a paper "Toronto 2000" and declared it to be a "Healthy City". From this, the idea of healthy cities as special settings originated and was later extended to other settings.

The conference ended by producing a Charter for action to achieve Health for All by the Year 2000 and beyond (see Appendix 1).

The conference was a response to growing expectations for a new public health movement and the needs of industrialised countries, as well as other regions of the world. The Charter defined the health promotion activities as advocating, enabling and mediating. The health promotion action means building a healthy public policy, create supportive environments, strengthen community action, develop personal skills and reorienting health services. The participants of the conference pledged themselves to support health promotion and called for international action.

The Adelaide Conference

The Second International Conference on Health Promotion was held in Adelaide in 1988 and was concerned with the development of healthy public policies. The conference ended with Recommendations which defined the strategy for healthy public policy action (see Appendix 2).

The Recommendations defined "healthy public policy" as concerned for health and equity in all areas of policy including the accountability for the policy impact on health. The main aim of healthy public policy is to create a supportive environment which will enable people to lead healthy lives. It is a cross-sectoral endeavour to create a health-enhancing social and physical environment and allow people easier healthy choices reflected in their lifestyle. The value of health has been redefined to link economic, social and health policies into an integrated action characterised by equity, easy access and positive developments.

The Recommendations defined the following areas for action: supporting the health of women; food and nutrition; tobacco and alcohol; creating supportive environments; developing new health alliances; and the commitment to global public health.

The Sundsvall Conference

The Third International Conference on Health Promotion was held in 1991 in Sundsvall, Sweden. The main topic of the conference was the creation of supportive environments for health.

The conference produced a statement (see Appendix 3), which issued a call for action to everyone to participate in creating a supportive environment which should be taken up in all the communities, countries and governments. A part of the supportive environment deals with inequities and problems of poverty, as well as access to essential health care. One of the main issues raised at the conference was the achievement of global accountability for maintaining a health-supportive environment.

HEALTH EDUCATION

Following the Alma Ata Declaration and the differentiation between health education and health promotion, health education continued to be developed in the USA, whereas health promotion became the preferred choice in Europe, mainly due to the endeavours of the European Office of WHO. This does not imply that health promotion in Europe has completely neglected the health educational aspects, nor that the health education in the USA does not also address societal issues and does not use societal approaches. It is more a question of emphasis and of allocation of resources for research, evaluation, conferences, expert committees and documentation.

The most recent USA developments in health education should, therefore, be of interest to European audiences engaged or interested in this area of activity. These developments can be well summarised by looking in detail at an influential collection of essays from *Health Behaviour and Health Education, Theory Research and Practice* edited by Glanz, Lewis and Rimer 1990, Jossey-Bass, San Francisco and Oxford.

These developments in health education have been mainly concerned with the creation of a theoretical base for the activity. The models developed in this field have aimed at answering the question of **why** certain health behaviour does or should take place and why certain approaches are or should be effective in improving health and preventing disease. A close examination of the publications related to the different models shows that the question of **how** one should achieve the improvements has been largely neglected. The health education interventions within different theoretical frameworks have been taken for granted and mostly limited to the existing methods of traditional health education, i.e. from transmitting information to providing support for individuals for the improvement of their coping abilities. These facts should be borne in mind when considering the examples of various theories and models in health education derived from this publication.

MODELS OF INDIVIDUAL HEALTH BEHAVIOUR

Explaining Health Behaviour Through Expectancies
Health Belief Model
(Irwin M. Rosenstock)

In his article, Rosenstock analyses the development of the Health Belief Model (HBM) during the 1950s, based on Lewin's Field Theory (1935) and developed by the author and Hochbaum. The model tried to explain how individuals make decisions concerning health and what determines health behaviour. As a cognitive model it is concerned with people's opinions and postulates that people's behaviour will depend on their knowledge or awareness of the problem, their perception of severity and susceptibility, as well as on their perception of the likelihood of being able to reduce the health threat through an acceptable personal action. These perceptions can be summarised as perceived susceptibility, perceived severity, perceived benefits and perceived barriers. The model also recognises the possible influence of other variables such as, demographic, sociopsychological and structural as well as motivation and cues for action, which in specific circumstances can affect individual perceptions and influence health-related behaviour. In the last twenty years considerable progress has been made in further developing and refining the determinants of individual's health-related behaviour and ways to stimulate positive behaviour changes. Although the model is basically descriptive i.e. it looks at the levels of various perceptions and links them with behaviour, there have been some attempts to use it as a predictive instrument by measuring the levels of perceptions and predicting people's behaviour. The model, however, does not claim that by changing people's opinions (levels of perceptions) their behaviour will also change.

The model has received a number of criticisms which the authors tried to explain by stating that the model was never meant to be the one and only general explanation of health behaviour. The HBM was not able to define the relationship between the variables in terms of their positive or negative influence on desired behaviour. In some cases the high levels of perceptions are conducive to a desired behaviour (immunisation against influenza) whereas in others (prevention of cancers) the low levels of the same perceptions will increase the probability of certain behaviour taking place.

Bandura (1977) developed the concept of self-efficacy or efficacy expectation, as distinct from outcome expectation, and this is now considered to be an useful addition to the Health Belief Model. This concept is similar to HBM's perceived benefits and is defined as "the conviction that one can successfully execute the behaviour required to produce the outcomes".

Methods of intervention

The Health Belief Model was originally developed to explain health-related behaviour using cognitive variables. One of the ways to change cognition is to arouse affect, usually in the form of fear, by means of threatening messages. This approach is successful according to the Protection Motivation Theory (Rogers, 1975), which postulates that the most persuasive communications are those that arouse fear by enhancing perception of the severity of the problem, as well as likelihood of exposure to the event, and the efficacy of responses to that threat. The combination of fear and reassurance in persuasive communications is now generally accepted as a method of health education within the framework of the HBM.

The authors of the HBM recognise that there may be circumstances when the change in cognition need not necessarily change behaviour and other methods need to be applied. In an example, which applied the HBM to the area of reducing obesity among a group of children, the authors provided a set of instructions and a dietician provided them with weight reduction plan. In a influenza vaccination programme, the methods used depended on the target population. In one high risk group of patients in a Family Medical Centre the vaccination was offered by the staff. In another population group postcards were sent inviting them to participate. Depending on the contents of the message the effectiveness of the methods was defined. There are other situations, such as dealing with chronic diseases, where success will depend on enhancing self-sufficiency by developing specific tasks for specific aspects of health-related behaviour including development of specific skills. Developing awareness of specific situations in which efficacy may be low and rehearsing the desired behaviour may enhance self-efficiency in dealing with the problem. Other methods such as relaxation techniques to reduce anxiety, verbal reinforcement and even counselling may be effectively used to achieve the desired goals. These approaches may work on an individual level, whereas on a population level societal interventions may be more appropriate. As one can see, all these methods of intervention are not specifically related to the postulates of the HBM and could be a part of any health education intervention.

Health Behaviour as a Rational Process
Value Expectancy Theories
(William B. Carter)

Two important theories in the area of Value Expectancy Theories are: the Theory of Reasoned Action and the Multiattribute Utility Theory. A number of researchers applied the basic principles of these theories which apply only to behaviours that are under individual control. Behaviours that are dependent (compulsion) or restricted are outside the remit of these theories. The theories include most recent developments in psychology concerning the relationship between attitudes, beliefs and behaviour as well as in behavioural decision theories. Value Expectancy Theories are based on the concept of maximization, i.e. a person strives to maximise the benefits or expected benefits in the decision-making process.

The *Theory of Reasoned Action*, developed by Fishbein and Ajzen (1975) aims to predict a person's intention to perform a behaviour in a well defined setting. It assumes that behavioural intention is the immediate determinant of behaviour and that all the other factors are mediated through intention. Intentions are dependent on two sets of variables: the attitude towards the behaviour (including the belief that an outcome will occur and the evaluation about the outcome) and the influence of social environment (social norms and a person's perception of these norms or expectations of salient others about their action). The measurement of intention is based on the assumption that finding out the salient beliefs about the outcomes will be an important guideline for necessary health education interventions.

Multiattribute Utility Theory (MAU) predicts behaviour directly from a person's evaluation of the consequences or outcomes associated with the behaviour or its absence. The MAU Model (Keeney, 1982) predicts behavioural performance for a single person directly from his or her evaluation of consequences or outcomes and allows for identification of most influential consequences as seen by the actor. A further elaboration of this Model was the Hierarchical Multiattribute Utility Model, which ranks consequences according to their influence, thus breaking a complex multi-consideration decision problem into smaller and comparable units. The measurement of the MAU Model depends on a detailed content analysis of interviews which provides a taxonomy of issues and concerns, followed by individual evaluation of the subjective probability that a given consequence will occur if the behaviour is performed and the subjective value or utility given to that consequence. The stringent requirements for measuring subjective probability and utility can be bypassed by measuring personal beliefs related to behaviour in question.

Methods of Interventions

These Value Expectancy Theories provide a reasonable accurate predictions of voluntary health behaviour and the effectiveness of interventions aimed at change in behaviour will depend on their belief about being able to identify people's major concerns and expected barriers in their decisions about the change. The effectiveness of interventions will depend on their concentration on the most important issues in a person's decision-making process, which may be different for each person or for each issue.

Health education interventions will be successful if they are able to:

- understand the natural history of the target behaviour;
- identify salient and potentially modifiable cognitive and behavioural "causes" or determinants of the target behaviour;
- design and implement effective strategies to modify these determinants and enhance the practice of health protective behaviours.

The Value Expectancy Theories address the first two issues whereas the intervention strategy will depend on other theories related to health education interventions.

The Theory of Reasoned Action has been successfully applied in a number of studies concerning people's sexual behaviour such as the use of condoms, abortions, birth control and contraception. The MAU theory has been applied in predicting the uptake of influenza vaccination, birth planning decisions, cervical smear tests, and high risk sexual practices.

Causal Explanations Influencing Health Behaviour
Attribution Theory
(Frances Marcus Lewis & Lawren H. Daltroy)

Attribution Theory is based on the way people explain certain health-related events and the emotional and behavioural consequences of such explanations. The basic assumption is that people need to understand causes of certain events, which helps them to cope with them and manage them successfully. Such attributions can have positive effects by increasing self-esteem and reducing anxieties or produce feelings of hopelessness and motivational and cognitive deficits. Attributions can also serve as reasonably reliable predictors for outcomes of various change programmes.

Attribution Theory uses an information processing model, which enables the researchers to study the attributions people make either with respect to another person or some environmental factor. Studies have been concerned with the process, contents and the consequences of attribution for certain behaviour. They have been based on the assumption that people are motivated to explain, interpret and understand their causal environment. Such explanations are associated with personal or cognitive control.

Attribution Theory can be applied to health education in a number of ways:

- in the development of therapeutic relationship between the health care personnel and the patient;
- in the development of correct attributions;
- in the alteration of incorrect attributions;
- in altering the focus of attribution;
- in attributing characteristics to the individual;
- in the maintenance of perceived personal effectiveness.

A successful application of the Attribution Theory has been in the field of chronic diseases, especially following a heart attack. The way people explained why the attack occurred could be used to predict their future behaviour. Attempts to give the patients a scientific explanation did not always work and they preferred such explanations as "luck", "fate", etc. Some of the methods aimed at influencing people's attribution or explanations of certain events included written material and personal explanations.

It would, however, be wrong to assume that everybody engages in attempts to explain certain health related events. There is a certain percentage of the population which does not engage in such activities and for them it would be wrong to intervene by providing them with "right" attributions which they cannot use in their decision-making process, when they may prefer a degree of ambiguity in the case of conditions which cannot be controlled. Changing attributions in such cases may cause negative side effects, which need to be balanced against possible advantages of "right" information at any price. It is certain that attributions are very important for individuals, although it is not possible at this stage to decide which if any aspects of attributions can and should be modified and with what results.

Using Information for Action
Consumer Information Processing (CIP)
(Joel Rudd & Karen Glanz)

One of the basic characteristics of a cognitive model of health education is the process of transmission and integration of information relevant to health. Although it is known that accurate knowledge about a health problem and the ways of coping with it is not always sufficient to produce an action, it is still generally accepted that accurate health information about avoidance and management of illness is important.

Consumer Information Processing (CIP) Theory became popular in the late 1970's. It is derived from cognitive psychology and is a part of human problem solving and information processing studies. This work has been developed within the general framework of cognitive science and has been associated with attempts to develop artificial intelligence within computer science.

A relevant area of understanding CIP is the process of human problem-solving and the processing of information. This understanding is concerned with the processes as such, as well as with the methodology of measuring the information processing and decision-making activities. A theoretical explanation of CIP is to consider individuals as Limited Information-Processing Systems. This relates to the type of memory which is activated. It postulates that information processing occurs in short-term memory. There is a limited ability to transfer material to long-term memory and will be recalled only if it survives in the network of declarative knowledge. The assumption is that due to the limited nature of human information processing a cognitive technique will increase the utility of this limited information. One way of doing this is "chunking", which implies that individuals combine bits of information into more meaningful information units, which can then be utilised for decision-making. A problem associated with CIP is the way this process can be measured. There are a number of methods such as "verbal protocols", where the individual is asked to think aloud when making decisions, and "eye fixation measures", which measure eye movements with sophisticated instruments during the decision-making process. A more recent development is "matrix display methodology", where the individual is presented with a multidimensional matrix display of a large amount of information and is invited to follow it up by seeking more specific aspects of this information according to the interest aroused.

It can be concluded that the study of CIP requires professional expertise and often a laboratory setting. It is highly individualistic in its attempt to describe the on-going processes within the human mind in a decision-making situation. An important aspect of CIP is learning, which is also based on information processing. CIP has been associated with developments in communication theories and is aimed at understanding, predicting and developing intervention strategies in health education.

The criticism of this rationalistic and individualistic approach has resulted in special attention being paid to the role that affect plays in consumer behaviour and the more holistic environmental or systems approach.

The effectiveness of the CIP is dependent on the quantity and quality of information and the individual's ability to process it for the purpose of making decisions. There needs to be a differentiation between the process of transmitting information and the process of utilising such information in decision-making. There is some evidence that "too much" information can be counter productive in terms of individual ability to use it for making a decision. This is often the result of employing a number of sources of information such as advertising, labelling of products, word-of-mouth information, news reports and entertainment. This is especially true for health education information concerning lifestyles, nutrition, smoking, AIDS, etc.

The most attractive empirical and conceptual description of consumer behaviour within a CIP framework has been developed by Bettman (1979), who concentrated on such elements as "CIP capacity, motivation, attention and perception, information acquisition and evaluation, decision rules and processes, and consumption and learning".

The critical assessment of CIP as a means of explaining and predicting consumer decision with special reference to health behaviour has examined a number of different aspects, such as correlates of information, acquisition and use, minimum requirements for use of health information and policy issues in provision of health information.

Correlates for information acquisition and use have been included in the studies which examine the process by which individuals learn a particular type of information under a given set of circumstances. Key demographic factors have been used to explain the differences in predispositions to acquire and process information on a population level, such as socio-economic status and age. Another important factor affecting the interest level could be the extent of past experience of known risk status related to peoples' special health interests. Minimum requirements for the use of health information are considered to be: the availability of information about the products and the health services; the usefulness of information concerning the characteristics of a product, service or behaviour which will satisfy a consumer's needs; the information is processable within the time, energy and comprehension level of the client; it must be "format friendly", that is, strategically placed for the decision-making situation. Policy issues in health information provision are concerned with how much and what kind of information should be provided for the optimal influence on consumer decision-making. There is some evidence that too much information can create an "overload" and negatively affect decision-making. This has been questioned by some and now it seems that the increased amount of information can be positive or indifferent to consumer decision-making. Whereas the quantity of information does not seem to be decisive, the question of quality could be, although this aspect has attracted much less research. One can safely assume that the amount, type and channels of information will be manipulated by the providers to their greatest advantage.

Reference is made to two studies carried out concerning the application of CIP theory in health education: use of nutrition information in food choices and use of quality of care information in selecting health care providers.

The role of information is accepted as being important for health behaviour. There is not, however, sufficient data on the amount and quality of information that would be optimal for influencing positive health behaviour in patients and the general public. Because of this, the CIP theory should be considered within the more general framework of communication theories looking at the type of information as well as the environmental system within which such information is provided.

Perspectives on Intrapersonal Theories in Health Education and Health Behaviour
(Barbara K. Rimer)

In this article a summary is given of the various theories relevant to individual health behaviour, such as the Health Belief Model, Theory Of Reasoned Action, Attribution Theory and Consumer Information Processing Theory.

In addition to these theories a number of others of potential relevance are mentioned:

Protection Motivation Theory:

This emphasises the importance of cognitive processes affecting the changes in attitudes and behaviour along the lines of the Health Belief Model. The differences in the threat level of a message affect attitudes in the short-term and, therefore, this kind of information will be crucial for long-term changes in beliefs. One can assume that an action will be a function of "threat appraisal" and "coping appraisal". The theory also has similarities with the Social Learning Theory, in that it states that the likelihood of an action will be affected by internal and external rewards. In short, the protection motivation will be maximised when the threat is perceived to be severe, a person feels vulnerable and the response is considered to be effective and within the capacity of the person. The cost has to be acceptable. The application of this theory has been in the field of exercise, smoking cessation and breast self-examination.

Self-preservation Theory:

This views a person as an active problem solver whose actions aim at reducing the perceived gap between the existing state and the ideal or desired one. Behaviour reflects the cognitive representation of the current state and the desired state, includes plans for necessary changes and techniques for assessing the progress. The theory is related to the Attribution Theory and includes three stages cognitive representation of the health threat, the coping stage or action plan, and the appraisal stage, in which the person judges success in reaching the goal. The theory also includes an emotional component which may be different from the cognitive aspects of individual responses. It is considered to be of special interest in understanding patients' responses to symptoms. This is a new theory which has not been sufficiently operationalised and it is in the process of being tested.

The Transtheoretical Model:

There is a general assumption that processes of change are similar whatever the content of the change is (smoking cessation, weight control, etc.). The change process includes the following stages: contemplation, determination, action and maintenance. The model is circular, which implies that a person can enter at any point and proceed through the system. It is also important that any specific health-related change should be considered as part of more general and ongoing processes of change taking place in many other aspects of a person's life. These can be results of consciousness raising, self-reevaluation, self-liberation, contingency management, helping relationships, counter conditioning or stimulus control. All these processes are activated differently according to the type of problem related to change, although they share many common aspects, which make the transtheoretical model of direct use to practitioners. This model has also not yet been fully developed and operationalised. It could, however, provide a larger framework by integrating a number of other behaviour-related theories.

Relapse Prevention Theory:

Relapse is a major problem associated with any intervention aimed at behaviour modification or health actions. Maintaining the efforts to preserve change can be theoretically considered as different from the process of initiating such a change. It will therefore be necessary to apply different strategies for each aspect of change. Relapse Prevention Theory includes a variety of strategies aimed at preventing relapse. It is associated with the Social Learning Theory as applied to addictive behaviour and treats addiction as an "overlearned habit pattern". The method of reinforcing change is through self-management and self-control techniques. It also takes into consideration the role of beliefs and positive outcome expectancy. This theory has contributed considerably to the understanding of addiction and how to deal with it. Emphasis is given to the maintenance of change, which is different from initiating the change process. In this way, the addition of the Relapse Prevention Theory to a more general behaviour change programme can be very useful.

MODELS OF INTERPERSONAL HEALTH BEHAVIOUR

It is reasonable to assume that individuals do not live in a social vacuum and that their health behaviour will be acquired from "significant others" and that it will continue to be dependent on the interaction with others. To understand the processes which are involved in this influence, models have been developed which look at the results of this interpersonal interaction.

How Individuals, Environments, And Health Behaviour Interact: Social Learning Theory

(C.L.Perry, T.Baranowski, G.S.Parcel)

Social Learning Theory (SLT) has been developed to explain how individuals learn about the ways and means of preventing disease and managing both health and disease and how this can be modified or changed. It is based on the concept of interaction of behaviour and personal factors including cognition and environmental factors. The personal factors include the individual's ability to learn by observation and by analysing the processes and outcomes. This conceptualisation has been found to be useful for health education interventions which have concentrated on influencing cognitive elements for the purpose of changing and modifying behaviour.

The development of SLT has a long history starting in the early 1940s and has been consistently applied in various health education interventions. The main characteristic of this approach is to treat the individual as a "black box". Within this mechanistic approach, it postulates that the individual responds to external influences from others. The explanation of why certain behaviours are more frequent than others is based on the assumption that individuals have "drives" which create needs and motivate need satisfaction. The way to satisfy such needs is socially learned from others and will in turn stimulate similar behaviour in others.

The application of SLT related to behaviour has been based on two different theoretical explanations. One is based on the assumption that people learn through the influence of positive or negative "reinforcement" and one of the outcomes of such learning will be the development of a feeling that a person is or is not in control of events, expressed in terms of internal or external "locus of control". Whereas the internal locus of control describes a person who feels that he/she is in control of events, the external locus of control means that a person feels dependent on external factors influencing relevant events. Consequently, a person with an external locus of control will be more prone to be influenced by others, which may be an important element in designing health education interventions that use methods of assessing the health aspects of "locus of control" in individuals, which will be different according to previous experiences with relevant health issues.

The other theoretical explanation takes the approach of the acquisition of health behaviour beyond a purely behavioural explanation and emphasises the social elements. It questions the need for "reinforcement" in social learning and postulates that children learn by imitation associated with rewards, which may be indirect and not necessarily directly associated with the learned behaviour. This questions traditional learning theories and introduces the concepts of "self-efficiency" and "reciprocal determinism" in which environment, person and behaviour are in the process of constant interaction. This approach has been tested in a number of health education interventions, such as the reduction of risk from coronary heart disease. The importance of SLT for health education is due to its combination of cognitive, emotional and behaviouristic influences on behaviour modification. It also opens new perspectives for health education research and enables the utilisation of a number of psychological theories for the explanation of health behaviour.

The SLT has used a number of concepts always considered relevant to, and even dominant in explanations of health behaviour. These concepts, which have been developed in great detail, include: environment, situation, behavioural capability, expectations, expectancies, self-control, observational learning, reinforcements, self-efficacy, emotional coping responses and reciprocal determinism.

The "A Su Salud Project"

One application of the SLT was the "A Su Salud Project", a community approach to smoking cessation among lower-income Mexican-American families. The approach has concentrated on the stresses in life which may inhibit smoking cessation. A number of factors, included in the SLT, may inhibit the cessation or contribute to recidivism after stopping smoking. The main approach was aimed at creating social support in the hope of enhancing an individual's ability to carry out behavioural changes. This was achieved by using mass media to popularise methods of successful behaviour change by community members who were able to stop smoking. The second approach was to recruit several hundred volunteers who created networks of communication and disseminated the information about role models from mass media which served as reinforcers for behaviour modification. The third approach concentrated on counselling of families about the life events that make it difficult to consider the desired behavioural change as a priority. This was implemented by referring families to appropriate community agencies influential in dealing with stressful situations.

The anti-smoking campaign was carried out within a much wider framework based on the "six main killers" identified within the general mortality pattern of the community. Smoking was only one and the community members were aware of the main causes of mortality in their community. Mass media, therefore, targeted the six major causes and created an interest in the community for necessary changes. The programme was supported by provision of coping skills to enhance self-efficiency in dealing with these behaviours, and by means of reciprocal determinism created social support and individual skills in dealing with environmental factors contributing to the acquisition of this habit.

The first results showed that media modelling with social support is more effective that modelling alone, and that counselling was more effective among women than men in increasing cessation.

The Minnesota Home Team Study

The SLT has also been used in a programme aimed at improving children's eating habits, which targeted families with children in the age group 8-9 years old. The health education intervention aimed at using the concepts of the SLT within an appropriate educational package.

The intervention was based on a correspondence course lasting five weeks, consisting of mailing appropriate units to the homes of the children. Each unit contained instructions and material for a two to three hour set of activities to be carried out by the pupils and/or the parents. In each packet the pupils received a booklet describing the adventures of a set of characters related to healthy ways of life and games to enable the pupils to acquire knowledge and skills related to nutrition. There were different labels for food which the pupils should mix and match to achieve a healthy diet. The labels were supposed to be distributed around the house to be found so that they could be used for preparing simple snacks according to the provided recipes. There were sets of information about nutrition which could be stuck on the fridge. The pupils were allocated points according to the completion of different tasks and the highest score qualified them for a reward. The development of the material was based on several concepts from the SLT. These included methods for stimulating parent's participation, age related role models and the experiential learning method associated with the school work.

The evaluation was carried out on 31 schools which were randomly assigned to the four aspects of the programme: Home Team, Hearty Heart (school programme), combination of both or no programme.

The outcome showed the greatest behavioural improvement following the Home Team programme, although the Hearty Heart programme produced an increased level of knowledge among the pupils. The obvious conclusion is that the home provides the best environment for changing eating habits among children.

Social Support, Control and the Stress Process
(B.A.Israel, S.J.Schurman)

A considerable amount of research has indicated a link between stress and various physiological, psychological and behavioural factors. At the same time this research has found association between stressors and health. The research has also looked at a number of psychosocial factors, such as social support and control and found that they play a significant role in modifying levels of stress, thus improving health affected by stress factors. The model presented treats stress as a process in which individual and environmental factors interact to produce a variety of outcomes. This model has important consequences for health education since it postulates a comprehensive approach affecting a variety of factors at the same time. Dealing with such factors aims at reducing stress and thus improving health. One way of dealing with them, if they cannot be modified, is to enable individuals to cope with them and in this way reduce the effects of stress on health. The health education intervention will, therefore, depend to a large extent on strengthening social support and control as a means of reducing stress.

This comprehensive model will depend on the contribution of a number of theories from different disciplines. For example, systems theory from sociology and organisational psychology postulates a hierarchical ordering of biological, psychological and social levels or systems which are interconnected in their influence on stress. The systems approach means that any change in one of these systems will result in changes in other systems. The theory uses such concepts as status quo, homeostasis and equilibrium. The stress model postulates that the individual's perception of stress may be a result of, as well as a contributor to the source of stress through changes within the immediate and wider social environment of the individual.

The theory of the ecology of human development postulates an inter-relationship between the environment and behaviour and the social processes that mediate between them, which can produce stress and thus affect health.

The research related to stress has included many disciplines and approaches. The physiological model concentrates on the sympathetic nervous system ("fight or flight" response) and the pituitary-adrenocortical axis (general adaptation syndrome). Other researchers concentrated on various events which could produce stress. They produced lists of such stressful life events, i.e. events which needed a person's readjustment to reduce stress. Some research has looked at the role of cognitive appraisal in assessing objective events as stressful and came up with the recognition of the relative aspects of stressors, which implies that the same situation can be treated by one individual as normal whereas another individual may find it stressful. Research in the field of social psychology concentrated on occupational stress and stress related to physical and mental health. Three basic conceptual models were recognised: one includes the role of the environmental forces external to the individual, one that considers the characteristics of the individual in terms of internal reactions to stress (best known as type A behaviour), and an interaction model that assumes that occupational stress is the result of the interaction between workers and the characteristics of their work. Epidemiological studies have shown a close link between psychosocial variables and susceptibility to illness as a result of stress and social support. The latter is considered as a moderating factor in the reduction of stress.

Most of the studies carried out in the field of stress suffer from the same problem, i.e. how one can define the concept of stress. This methodological problem makes it difficult to compare research results or to reach a common agreement about the contribution of stress to health. In general there is an agreement that stress represents an imbalance between environmental demands and individual coping abilities. In this sense the definition of stress represents a description of a relationship which can be different in different situations and for different individuals.

Since stress is caused by stressors, that is the psychosocial and environmental conditions likely to produce stress, it is reasonable to attempt to define them. A number of researchers have tried to do this and have come up with a number of general factors, such as "major life events", which can disrupt normal activities and require adaptive responses; "daily hassles", which represent minor events liable to produce frustration and if numerous can be stressful; "chronic strains" such as overwhelming challenges, hardships and other problems in daily life, including for example poverty, unemployment, work overload, etc.; "cataclysmic events" or sudden disasters that require major adaptive responses, such as floods, accidents, war. imprisonment, etc.; and "ambient stressors", which are continuous in nature, such as chronic air and water pollution, continuous noise, etc. In addition to this differentiation of stressors, other indicators can be used in classification, such as the ease of recognition, the type of adjustment, the positive or negative value, the degree of control, the predictability, the necessity and importance, association with human behaviour, duration and regularity.

Another important factor is that of social support. This also represents a methodological problem since there is no general agreement of how it can be defined. Social support is often interchangeable with the concept of social networks. The latter has been the subject of a number of studies and has produced specific methodology and classification systems. The three main dimensions for study of social networks are their structural, interactional and functional characteristics. Social networks can, therefore, be considered as the main source of social support, associated with stress and stress control. Social support is a relational concept, with emotional, instrumental, informational and appraisal functions. These four functions of support may not always be independent in a real life situation. Other relevant aspects related to social support are the source and the quantity, as well as quality of support.

The third factor associated with stress is control, and here again there is no general agreement about its definition. There are many conceptual models of control, each one based on a different set of elements included in the definition (personal, contingency, cognitive, behavioural, existential, retrospective, decisional, processual, and social control). The interpretation of control relevant to the study of stress concentrates on external factors arising from the environment. Contingency control is, however, most relevant to health education. It implies that the individual perceives his/her reactions as being able to influence the stressors and thus affect the outcome. Relevant theories are social learning, locus of control, learned helplessness and self-efficacy.

It has been difficult to decide whether the act of participating or the outcome of participation are more dominant aspects of control. A number of studies in the field of working conditions and cardiovascular and psychosomatic consequencies, job dissatisfaction and depressions have tried to resolve this problem. For example, people who experience high levels of stress, but are also able to exercise high levels of control are less prone to cardiovascular diseases.

Taking into account the experience gathered from research into stress one can draw a number of guidelines for health education practice, one of which is to extend the number of indicators in evaluation to include other behavioural factors such as alcohol etc., in addition to a specific disease. The consequence of this approach is to include aspects of individual empowerment into interventions, as well as social and organisational situations which are beyond individual control.

The working environment is one area where interventions related to reduction of stress have been carried out. In addition to professional researchers, companies and unions are involved in such interventions. Some aspects of interventions are the encouragement of participation of personnel, and collaboration between the researchers and members of the organisation based on a learning process in which the workers learn about their own situation and the necessary action. This is achieved through the empowerment of the participants to control their own working life.

The methodological problems related to the lack of agreement in defining stress and its major components (stressors, support and control) should not reduce the attempts to deal with this problem which the state of health influences through action research and a multidisciplinary approach.

How Health Professionals Influence Health Behaviour : Patient-provider Interaction and Health Care Outcomes
(S.K. Joos & D.H. Hickam)

New developments in the delivery of health care have brought about a differentiation between the partners in this interaction. Patients are considered to be consumers and the various health care institutions are considered as providers within the framework of a market economy. This interaction is characterised by the disagreement between the two partners in the way they interpret health problems, appropriate treatment and expected outcomes. This disagreement in perception and expectation can affect patient satisfaction, compliance and resolution of the problem. Health care institutions as providers are not geared to meet all the new requirements, such as interviewing skills, estimation of the amount of information they provide and the patience required, and, therefore, have problems in resolving compliance of the patient. Patients as consumers are often reluctant to request information and express their needs. Poor health can be the outcome of a conflict due to bad communication between the providers and consumers.

Although the importance of this problem is recognised, there is very little research in this field and the existing research is mostly descriptive and observational. The existing research is not supported by theories and it concentrates mainly on physicians, with less emphasis on other health care professionals.

There are numerous publications reviewing existing literature on research into doctor-patient relationships. Early attempts used a social system framework and look at the roles of the interacting partners, the norms that regulate the role performance and the process of socialisation into those statuses and roles. One of the outcomes of such studies has been the development of the concept of the sick-role as defined by the rights and duties of the two interacting partners. There has been some criticism of the sick-role concept, since it is often considered to be applicable only to acute situations in which the patient is helpless. An improvement on the sick-role model has been the model of mutual participation, based on equality of both partners, which puts emphasis on the active role of the patient who treats him/herself and the physician provides only necessary support and help. This model is more appropriate for chronic illnesses. Another model, in line with conflict theory, describes the doctor-patient relationship, as a problem of adjustment of the doctor's expectations and the patient's willingness to comply. This model extends the system to include the lay referral system, which plays a very important part in influencing the patient's opinions about the problem and how to deal with it. The conflict is resolved by negotiation between the two sets of expectations.

The most recent theories relating to consumer-provider relationships are of a psychosocial nature. They look at the process of interaction as well as the influence others have on this process, including aspects such as cognition and information processing, reflecting on the quality of communication; the quality of interpersonal relationships, including the attitudes, beliefs, expectations and desires of the actors; conflict resolution and negotiation between the actors; and awareness of the influence of external social factors.

Most of the studies of the consumer-provider relationship (including the more limited doctor-patient relationship studies) concentrate on different issues such as the content of information passed between the doctor to the patient and the process reflecting the consumer and provider behaviour during the interaction.

In addition to numerous publications of such research, comprehensive reviews of such studies looking at common approaches and ideas have also been published. In general, the findings of the analysis of observational studies agree with the theoretical postulates suggesting that the positive effect on consumer care outcomes is achieved when the provider is able to establish rapport, encourages the consumer to express their point of view and is able to provide the necessary information. This is enhanced by good interpersonal skills and results in patient satisfaction and compliance.

In view of the limitations of observational studies, attempts have been made to carry out experimental interventions. These were aimed at the improvement of the communication process using two strategies: educating patients in ways of asking for information and teaching providers how to meet patient's needs. Assessments were based, on a variety of indicators, including the impact of interventions on behaviour and outcomes. The educational intervention for consumers included such skills as: formulating the questions; preparing them in advance by writing a list of questions; carrying out preparatory meetings simulating the interaction with the doctor; reviewing techniques for overcoming barriers; increased participation and sharing of information; and improvement of self-management of disease. Educational interventions directed towards the providers concentrated on teaching them ways of improving the recall of information transmitted to the consumers; on teaching them to understand the process of non-compliance related to the Health Belief Model; teaching them the skills of translating the professional terminology into lay language; and teaching them counselling skills related to certain addictive behaviours. The outcome of such interventions is based on a self-reinforcing argument: the more the patient participates in the interaction with the doctor, the more effective the doctor's interaction will be. A number of strategies have evolved to achieve this and they all seem to be concerned with the reduction of the gap between the perception and communication skills of doctors and their patients.

GROUP INTERVENTION MODELS OF HEALTH BEHAVIOUR CHANGE

In Europe, following the Alma Ata Declaration, a distinction was made between health education as the individual approach and health promotion as the community or population approach. In the USA this distinction is not so clear and there they use an extended model of health education which includes also the community and population approaches. The disadvantages of the European approach are the disregard of relevant developments in the individual or health education approach and the concentration on the community or health promotion approach. In the USA this has not been the case and there developments in health education have been accompanied by developments of the community approach as a part of health education. This has resulted in work being done on a number of issues related to community or population approaches as a part of the striving to improve health by individual behaviour modification within an environment which is conducive to health and supportive for individual health behaviour. These approaches are concerned with the functioning of groups, organisations, social institutions and communities and their role in the improvement of health of individuals and populations.

Improving Health Through Community Organisation

(M.Minkler)

The Community Organisation Approach, as interpreted by the author, is defined as "the process by which community groups are helped to identify common problems or goals, mobilise resources, and in other ways develop and implement strategies for reaching the goals they have set.". It is based on the concept of empowerment which enables individuals or communities to take control over their lives and their environment. It is assumed that community organisation is only possible where community competence or problem-solving ability has been enhanced in the process. The community must identify its own problems and should not be dependent on external agents. Although professionals may use some aspects of community organisation to mount a campaign, they cannot be said to be carrying out community organisation unless the community itself identifies that problem and wishes to solve it.

Historically speaking, the term community organisation was coined by American social workers in the 1800s to describe specific field activities characterised by the establishment of charity organisations and settlement houses for new immigrants and the poor. The social workers' efforts to coordinate this work were described as "community organising". There are some who dispute this description and maintain that there were others in addition to social workers who were engaged in similar activities, notably in the Populist Movement in the American South, which started as an agrarian revolution and developed into a political movement concerned with labour issues and with conflict as a means of change. In its early days, community organisation, as an activity of social workers, was concerned with people adjusting to social expectations and supported by social welfare. In the 1940s there was a change in the community organisation approach and emphasis was put on enabling people to help themselves instead of the change being achieved by an external agent.

Later developments in community organisation are characterised by the use of different models broadly favouring consensus and cooperation or either confrontation and conflict as a means of change. An example of the latter is the assumption that a community needs to be "disorganised" before it can be organised to satisfy the needs of its members. More recent developments of community organisation can be recognised in the civil rights movement and other similar movements directed towards social change. The US government reacted to these developments by integrating parts of it into their policies and promoting the concept of "community participation" in a number of social issues, including the provision of health care. An instance of this is the establishment in the 1960s of a community-based and community-controlled health centre in rural Mt. Bijou, Mississippi, based on a cooperative approach of landless farmers and including a public transportation system, training and education for future health workers and other aspects relevant to health. This centre is considered as "an ideal model" and has been the basis for the establishment of other community health centres.

Many international organisations have also been using community organisation and participation to improve the health and wellbeing of populations in many developing countries. The main changes in this field of activity follow the Alma Ata Declaration, which formally recognised the important role of community organisation and participation for the improvement of health. The Alma Ata Declaration states "that people have the right and the duty to participate individually and collectively in the planning and implementing of their health care". Emphasis is on participation and not on externally imposed programmes of improvement.

It seems obvious that the concept of community organisation is only viable in situations where one can identify "communities". There are many different ways of defining communities as social units. They are characterised by one of the following: "(1) functional spatial units meeting basic needs for sustenance, (2) units of patterned social interaction, and (3) symbolic units of collective identity". The ecological approach to the study of communities emphasises the characteristics of the population, whereas the social systems perspective emphasises formal organisations operating within a community. The interpretation of the meaning of "community" will influence the type of community organisation approach.

Although community organisation appears to be an unified approach, there are a number of typologies in existence, each emphasising different aspects of the ways of achieving a desired goal. One such typology differentiates between locality development, social planning and social action. Locality development stresses consensus and cooperation, while social planning is task-oriented and stresses rational empirical problem solving, and social action is task and process-oriented, including the empowerment of community members to achieve change through the redistribution of power and privileges. This classification system can be used to analyse a number of aspects of community organisation, such as goal categories, community structure, change strategies and tactics, practitioners' roles, medium of change, orientation towards power structure, boundary definition, assumptions regarding interests of community sub parts, and concepts related to client population and client role.

Bringing about change in a community, no matter which community model is preferred, includes some commonly shared practices such as: empowerment of the members of the community to achieve their desired goals; community competence in achieving these goals; community participation in this process; differentiation between problems and issues; and the need to create "critical consciousness" for the change to occur.

Examples of Intervention

An intervention has been carried out by health educators, supported by graduate students, among elderly residents of San Francisco's Tenderloin Hotels as a part of the **Tenderloin Senior Organising Project** (TSOP). One of the hotels was chosen for the initial work, in which an informal group of residents was brought together with the aim of identifying and tackling such issues as fear of crime, loneliness, rent increases and their own sense of powerlessness. A combination of organisational and educational approaches was used, based on theoretical postulates of a number of community organisation models, such as raising awareness through discussion, creating dissatisfaction with the present situation and choosing some initial problems which could be resolved relatively easily. Following the success of the first group, similar groups were established in other Tenderloin Hotels with each new group retaining its own character and uniqueness. As activities progressed, group members became aware of the need to extend their work outside their own group to a number of social institutions within the community. This approach resulted in the creation of coalitions between various hotel groups and became the Safe House Project, which included a number of businesses and agencies in the community. The issues were also extended from purely local ones affecting the hotel inhabitants to more general ones, such as the problem of hunger. This resulted in the creation of mini markets and breakfast programmes. The approach also included leadership training programmes and training for social skills in dealing with bureaucracies. The project is now run by Tenderloin residents who, despite their success, are faced with a number of problems such as power conflict, loss of people's interest in some issues, turnover of participants, etc. An inherent mistrust of external "experts" did not allow for an evaluation to be carried out, although there are many descriptive indicators which support the general view that the project has worked..

Another example to illustrate the community organisation methods applied by the health and social services practitioners is the **Minnesota Heart Health Programme,** which has applied the community organisation approach. The project represents a large scale community study involving approximately a quarter of a million residents of three communities and an equal number of controls in similar localities. The intervention included: "(1) developing and implementing coordinated community-wide health education strategies, (2) improving community health behaviour and reducing related risk factors, and (3) reducing the incidence of premature disability and death from cardiovascular disease. The focus of individual and community intervention has been in three areas: smoking cessation, detection and control of hypertension and changes in patterns of diet and exercise". The aim of the intervention was the development of a "community partnership" of health workers and community members.

Community organisation was, however, only one of the approaches used, the others being the mass media and the face-to-face education approaches. The researchers had a problem in differentiating between their scientific and community roles, thus raising the question of ownership of problems and responsibility. Each of the communities involved went through the stage of developing an increased community awareness of the heart health concept and the development of opportunities for practising behaviours related to the improvement of cardiovascular health. As the programme developed, the researchers gradually withdrew and the community members took over the programme, there was a set of outcomes such as developing an organisational structure, mobilising support systems and developing appropriate social norms and values. The initial system of external funding has also gradually diminished in importance with the community groups and support systems taking over the responsibility for activities aimed at improving community health.

The evaluation of the programme was concerned with the process of community organisation and the outcomes related to coronary heart diseases. The former has shown promising results in terms of community empowerment and community acceptance of the responsibility for continuing such programmes. The results of the health gain aspect are not yet available.

Diffusion of Health Promotion Innovations
(M.A. Orlandi, C. Landers, R. Weston & N. Haley)

One of the main aspects of health improvement is the development of new ideas, methods and resources. Public health has been mainly concerned with the application of epidemiological studies as a basis for examining individual influences on the reduction of mortality and morbidity through behaviour change. Although the knowledge of risk from certain diseases does exist, there are still whole populations engaging in behaviour which increases the risk from premature disability and death. There is a large gap between the existing medical knowledge and the lifestyles and practices of individuals. This has resulted in a number of public health studies of barriers to bridging this gap and the development of cost effective intervention strategies.

Within a whole range of health education approaches the diffusion theory plays an important part in translating new research findings into effective interventions. This chapter focuses on three key areas: " first, it reviews the concept of a generic diffusion system and notes some limitation of the classic diffusion model. Second, the chapter describes an alternative research framework that enhances standard approaches to both innovation development and diffusion planning by incorporating methods for increasing target group participation. Third, the chapter provides an example of this research framework in the form of a community-based health promotion study that utilises this approach during all phases of programme planning and implementation".

Diffusion is defined as "the process by which an innovation is communicated through certain channels over time among members of a social system. An innovation is an idea, practice, service, or other object that is perceived as new by an individual or other unit of adoption". Classical diffusion theory uses the communication process as a way of assessing the predictive validity of the movement from one innovation to another. It is also concerned with the most effective way of transferring solutions developed in test settings to real world settings.

Studies of diffusion of innovation originated from the introduction of innovations in the field of agriculture, which was later extended to the diffusion of a variety of practices and technologies, such as family planning, medical screening and the introduction of new pharmaceutical products. The amount of experience and insight gathered by the enormous number of studies has been synthesised in a number of publications. The main underlying assumptions are that diffusions depend on the scientific attributes of the innovation and the specific characteristics of the adopter. Based on the outcomes of such studies, some general ideas about successful medical diffusion efforts have been developed: compatibility of innovations with the existing system of the doctor; flexibility of the forms of application of an innovation; reversibility to the previous practices; relative advantage of an innovation when compared to previous and current practices; complexity of the innovations are directly related to adoption; cost efficiency of an innovation visible both overtly or being implied; and the risk associated with the adoption of an innovation. Different interest groups will have different roles in the adoption process, where one can differentiate between the resource system and the user system.

Recently there has been some criticism of the classical diffusion model, such as the treatment of innovation as a fixed package without regard to possible adjustments, the role of the resource system in influencing the diffusion process, and failing to recognise that the adoption is only one step in a much more complex process of achieving the desired goals.

If adoption of innovation is considered as a multi-stage process, then it is easy to recognise possible points of failure at each stage such as: innovation failure due to inability of the innovation to achieve the desired goal; adoption failure due to conflicting values and beliefs and lack of necessary resources; implementation failure even if the innovation has been adopted due to omission of certain components necessary for the implementation; maintenance failure which can result in loss of momentum, and ultimate failure of an adopted innovation.

In terms of health promotion one should differentiate between the development of innovations and their diffusion. Very often health promotion is mainly concerned with the latter and for this a number of approaches have been developed. One way of ensuring the success of diffusion is the "linkage approach", which depends on increased participation of the user group in all aspects of the innovation diffusion process. The process is composed of three sub-systems, the resource system, the linkage system and the user system. The linkage system represents the change agent in the area of interaction between the resource and user systems. The processes that take place within the linkage system are described by theories related to information exchange, community organisation, organisational change and social marketing. As one would expect, this approach requires the user system to define its needs and the resource system to satisfy those needs. This may not be directly relevant to the diffusion of innovations which have been developed independently and are subsequently "sold" to the user system.

The Mt Vernon CARES Project

An example of the application of the diffusion of innovation approach in health promotion was provided by the American Health Foundation, in their intervention aimed at cholesterol screening of the black American population in the Mt. Vernon community. A number of other institutions and organisation took part in the project, which lasted three years. It included the implementation of cholesterol education, screening and a referral programme for Mt. Vernon residents aged over eighteen.. The activities carried out in each year were: (1) community assessment and analysis of the findings, market research, physician education; (2) community education and recruitment of participants, dissemination of information, cholesterol screening and nutrition workshops; (3) cholesterol re-screening, nutrition education and evaluation of outcomes.

The project is in the early stages of development and there is no information about the final outcome. Positive signs of the development of new social processes within the communities and of the involvement of community members are, however, emerging. Developments within the linkage system are specially notable in enhancing the adoption of the innovation of screening services.

Mobilising Organisations for Health Enhancement: Theories of Organisational Change
(R.M. Goodman & A.B. Steckler)

There is a general agreement about the complexity of organisational theory, as a consequence of the complexity of organisations, which include the surrounding environment, organisational structure, management and the workforce. Organisational change can take place within each of these layers and there is some evidence to support the view that the greatest likelihood of successful health education intervention lies in a "multi-layer" approach. The change agent also needs to understand the ecology of organisations, in order to be able to produce change. Among the theories explaining various approaches to organisational change, two are presented here.

The Stage Theory of Organisational Change

This theory deals with the process of innovation within the organisations related to goals, programmes, technologies and ideas. The theory postulates that during the process of innovation an organisation passes through a number of stages, each one requiring specific strategies.

Historically, Stage Theory developed from two models: one dealing with factors resisting change and the other dealing with diffusion of innovation. A contemporary model of Stage Theory includes the following seven stages: (1) sensing of unsatisfied demands on the system; (2) searching for possible responses; (3) evaluation of alternatives; (4) decision on the course of action; (5) initiating action within the system; (6) implementation of change; and (7) institutionalisation of change. There is, however, no clear insight into how organisations move from one stage to another since most of the research has been concerned with processes within each stage. As an example, studies of stages in adopting innovation in a number of schools can be used to illustrate a number of different advantages and disadvantages.

One of the criticisms of Stage Theory is that it does not deal with what happens after an innovation has been institutionalised. There is evidence that many innovative programmes continue to evolve to meet new demands and so research is necessary into this process of renewal.

Organisational Development Theory

Organisational Development (OD) aims at improving organisational effectiveness through the contribution of behavioural sciences. Its goal is to improve organisational performance and the quality of work life through interventions affecting organisational processes and workers' behaviour.

OD developed from the 1930s "human relations" perspective characterised by the well known Hawthorne studies, which showed that the attention paid to workers is more important for an increase in productivity than any efforts in improving the working conditions or environment. This was followed in the 1940s and 1950s by the development of management studies related to organisational behaviour. Later work rejected the classical bureaucracy model in favour of the fulfilment of the needs of the workforce. This theory known as Theory X, postulated that management must exert control over the workers for them to comply with organisational goals. Theory Y became dominant as an alternative, postulating that work represents a natural human activity and that within a supportive environment the workers will comply with the management's requirements.

More recent developments in OD reflect interventions aimed at organisational design and technologies or its human processes. Emphasis is given to environmental influences and the possibility of transforming norms and values in entire organisations. This has resulted in attempts at developing specific OD Theories, which include Process Theory and Implementation Theory.

The criticism of the OD Theory includes the need for further development of Change Theory, as well as Implementation Theory. Some question the effectiveness of OD interventions that have not been tested in randomised controlled trials.

Integrating Tobacco-Use Prevention into School Systems

An example of the application of OD is an intervention related to the dissemination of "tobacco use prevention" curricula in schools. This was based on the Stage Theory. It included a four stage model with specific strategies for each stage: awareness, adoption, implementation and institutionalisation. The main contribution of the study was to combine the Stage and OD Theories by directing strategies towards multiple levels. The OD approach was adjusted to fit specific stages and to apply to different organisational levels. The project showed strength in its theoretical conception but had some problems in its application.

The role of the consultant was very important, especially in the area of problem identification, but the weakness in the application lay in the omission of an Action Research Model, so schools did not fully participate in diagnosing the problems.

A Team Approach to Patient Care in a Teaching Hospital

A group of residents at an urban teaching hospital undertook to improve the quality of patient care by strengthening the patient input. This could be achieved by creating teams consisting of patients, their families, physicians, nurses and aids. The experiment was initiated on one floor of the hospital to which team members were assigned with the permission of the hospital administration. The intervention lasted four months. OD consultants were employed to help with the formation of teams. They applied an action research strategy in order to identify perceived barriers to optimum patient care. Team meetings were held to discuss and remove these barriers, which included physicians' arrogance and poor communication, demoralised and intemperate attitudes of nurses and inconsistent support from attendance. The intervention was not very successful, with only one task force meeting being held, during which conflicts surfaced and the lack of motivation by physicians was noticeable. Some of the more committed members of the team became frustrated and acted on their own initiative by changing the configuration of patient accommodation for the purpose of facilitating team care. This resulted in more conflicts because of lack of consultation with the admitting office, with patients and their families and with hospital administration. One positive outcome was the increased communication between nursing staff, residents and interns. Due to their rotation, however, these benefits were of short duration and were lost when the new group of residents and interns came to work on that floor. This affected the general morale of nurses, which destroyed the team concept.

It is possible to identify a number of reasons for the failure of this case study, such as: hospitals are special organisations with a clearly defined hierarchy of statuses dominated by the physician; OD techniques require time, which was not available; rapid staff turnover limits the effectiveness of OD strategies if they are concentrated on one part of the hospital; and cultural constraints of hospitals may not allow for a collaborative diagnosis by consultants and clients.

Stage Theory deals with some of the problems highlighted in this case study by providing for appreciation, acceptance, adoption, implementation and sustenance to nurture innovations. Radical changes require time and the Stage Theory makes provisions for team development. It may also be necessary to take into consideration the differences between various group members and their statuses within the power structure.

Applying Social Marketing to Health Promotion and Disease Prevention
(W.D. Novelli)

Marketing is associated with selling financial, professional and personal services and, in the view of the public, it is associated with advertising, introduction of new products and various promotional activities. It is based on serious market research, product development, pricing and distribution strategies and financial analysis.

In the past, the elusive dream was to be able to sell ideas just like goods. To sell health as successfully as one can sell soap powder was thought of being desirable but impossible. The situation has changed, and today the principles of marketing are successfully applied to social issues and ideas. This is especially true of various health organisations of a governmental or voluntary character. The translation of marketing principles to service industry in general is not simple, however and requires special adaptation and adjustment.

One aspect of this adjustment is Social Marketing which is considered to be "the design, implementation and control of programmes seeking to increase the acceptability of a social ideal or practice in a target group(s)". The application of social marketing in the field of health may be motivated by the wish to increase the profit of the health care system with desired social and behavioural change as a secondary outcome, although there are programmes that have as a primary goal the achievement of health gain in the population. These include, for example, prevention of teenage pregnancy, stopping smoking, and reduction of obesity.

Marketing Theory is derived from theories of consumer behaviour based on social and behavioural sciences. Consumer behaviour theory tries to answer the question of why people make certain decisions, and what kind of decisions they make, as well as some other aspects of the decision-making process. In that sense, consumer behaviour draws on a number of scientific disciplines such as anthropology, sociology and social psychology, psychology and economics etc. These theories deal with the influences on the decision-making process, which include environmental factors, individual influences, information processing and actual decision-making.

Marketing is based on the theory of exchange, which differentiates between "buyer and seller" who participate in this exchange. In some exchange situations the elements are clearly defined, such as, for example, the case of the seller selling a product and the buyer buying the product and paying a price. In other situations, this exchange is more subtle as in the case of the seller selling an aspect of a lifestyle conducive to better health and the buyer having to buy it in the knowledge that its benefits may be recognised sometime in the future. Other theories contributing to understanding marketing are the study of consumer orientation, marketing tools and marketing integration or the "marketing mix" (including the 4 Ps, product, price, place and promotion).

An important aspect of the marketing mix is communication. This can be divided into a number of important areas such as, advertising, public relations, direct marketing, promotion and face-to-face communication.

The marketing process is of a circular character, with no specific entry point into the system. It includes a number of stages such as: analysis and assessment of needs; planning; development testing and defining of plan elements; implementation; assessment of in-market effectiveness; and feedback into renewed analysis.

Some of the problems that exist in trying to translate social marketing into practice are:

- the problems of analysing the market which includes the assessment of the consumer targets, and finding out relevant influences on consumer behaviour;

- the problem of market segmentation arising from the difficulty of dividing a market into homogeneous segments to be able to target marketing programmes at each key segment, which is especially difficult with social programmes where disregarding certain population segments could be interpreted as discrimination;

- problems with product strategy, which in the field of health is clearly defined in advance, whereas in commercial production it is possible to adjust the products to the desires of the buyers;

- problems of pricing strategy, which in commercial enterprises is based on maximising financial returns, whereas social marketeers are oriented towards reducing monetary, psychic energy and time costs incurred by consumers when adopting a recommended behaviour;

- problems in channel strategy which are not faced by commercial enterprises that can select intermediaries and distributors and monitor their performance, while social marketeers, may not be able to utilise and control desired intermediaries, such as physicians, media or community centres;

- problems related to communication strategy, which are more limited for social marketing due to the high cost of channels easily available to commercial enterprises.

Other problems are related to expectations of grant giving bodies which expect a specific type of appeal in preference to some other which could be more effective but not acceptable to them:

- problems related to evaluation, which is not possible in social marketing because the outcomes are not immediately quantified or obvious;

- organisational problems due to the existing tradition in many organisations and institutions active in the field of health who may not be ready to accept a radical change by introducing the social marketing model, this could be due to general resistance to change or to lack of technical assistance.

Metro Manila Measles Immunisation Campaign

An example from the Philippines illustrates the successful application of the social marketing model to the improvement of access of the population to basic health services, including the improvement of levels of immunisation against major childhood diseases. The programme, initiated by HEALTHCOM and funded by the US Agency for International Development, helped the Philippine's Department of Health to initiate a programme of health improvement using the social marketing model.

The programme included an initial review of past research related to immunisation; a survey of target mothers with children under one year old; interviews with mothers and staff members in eight health centres; a day-after recall test among target mothers to assess comprehension, recall on various diagnostic elements of television commercials; print and radio messages and television and radio advertising. The study produced positive results in terms of participation ín vaccination programmes and an increase in knowledge and awareness and an increased understanding of the immunisation process.

National High Blood Pressure Education Programme

Hypertension is one of the major health problems in the USA. The National High Blood Pressure Education Programme was established as a cooperative effort involving numerous partners. The aim was to reduce death and disability due to high blood pressure through professional, patient and public education.

The programme applied the marketing principles in the use of consumer research, audience segmentation, development of strategies and appropriate public messages. The programme began by raising awareness about the "silent killer" and the dangers of untreated hypertension. Following the public awareness about the dangers, screening programmes were introduced after which emphasis was shifted to the need for treatment.

The programme included education of the public and patients, as well as professionals. This simultaneous approach has been shown to be successful in shortening the time necessary to achieve results. In marketing terms, health professionals were selling the control of high blood pressure through the health care system, whereas the patients were buying the services provided.

The programme was successful insofar as at its conclusion 92% of the US adult population were aware that hypertension was a cause of heart disease and 77% were aware that high blood pressure increases the risk of stroke. In addition to increased awareness there is some evidence of changes in behaviour which were reflected in an almost 75% increase in visits to physicians for hypertension and a 20% increase of those treated for hypertension.

Media Advocacy:
Promoting Health Through Mass Communication
(L. Wallack)

Mass media shape our daily life, influence the way we think and behave, have enormous potential for influencing matters related to the health of a population as well as each individual. Although there is general agreement about the importance of mass media in health education, there is at the same time considerable disagreement about how and why they should be used. This disagreement is based on the poor understanding of the nature of the role that the mass media can play in health education.

Although we do not know why mass media work there are some areas where their function is clearly defined such as: in setting the public agenda; in stimulating public discussion; in conferring status and legitimacy on issues and directly or indirectly affecting our knowledge, lifestyle and possibly behaviour.

Health education uses basically two approaches in utilising mass communication systems to promote health. One is an enhanced public communication model, based on social marketing which integrates marketing principles and sociopsychological theories to achieve behaviour change goals. The second approach uses mass media to highlight socio-political issues and to redefine individual problems within a public health and social context. The outcome of this should be the development of "healthy public policies" and social-environmental change.

Although these two approaches share some common principles they are different in their underlying assumptions. Whereas public communication campaigns use individual-centred understanding of health as an absence of disease, the media advocacy approach is aimed at understanding of health as a result of external factors.

Media advocacy is a new concept, most closely related to the smoking control movement. This approach has also been used by consumer groups concerned with alcohol, nutrition and AIDS issues. It is defined as "the strategic use of mass media for advancing a social or public policy initiative". It uses a number of concepts from community organisation models such as empowerment, citizen participation and involvement in issue selection. The aim of media advocacy is to draw the attention of the population to certain issues, to redefine the framework of public debate and to increase public support for more effective approaches to public health problems on a policy level. It attempts to influence individual behaviour indirectly by focusing attention on the problem as a public health issue. Although the media coverage of health issues will enhance awareness and knowledge about health problems, media advocacy aims at stimulating public participation in the policy generating process. In other words, it shifts the emphasis from the individual problems to public responsibility for the existence of such problems.

A number of skills are required for media advocacy, such as research, "creative epidemiology", (the use of epidemiological data to attract media attention), issue framing and gaining access to media outlets.

Successful framing is another aspect of media advocacy. It implies that the issue should be framed in such a way as to be consistent with policy goals. It is important to use this skill appropriately, as is done in the corporate world of commerce.

Utica Alvin Ailey Protest

An example of the constructive use of media advocacy is the National Cancer Institute Project COMMIT (community intervention trial), aimed at protesting against the support that cigarette companies provide to the arts and thus purchase an "innocence by association" image for their products. The aim was also to reduce the number of heavy smokers through a community level approach by creating the awareness of smoking as a public health issue and not just an individual issue. One of the goals of the project was to reframe the community perception of cigarette companies from innocent corporate citizens to merchants of death. To achieve this a protest was organized against the Philip Morris cigarette company sponsorship of the local performance of the Alvin Ailey American Dance Theatre. The media event took the form of distributing pamphlets to theatre patrons. It was a carefully researched example of "creative epidemiology". The pamphlet was only marginally concerned with the health issue and the main thrust of it was to portray the company as the merchant of death. The outcome of this protest was gaining coverage in the local press. Another outcome was the activity of COMMIT to inform the media of any similar events sponsored by the tobacco industry which became a regular form of interaction with the media.

This media advocacy initiative was successful in gaining access to the media although there is no information about any actual changes in the activities of relevant tobacco companies.

DEVELOPMENTS IN THE UK

Introduction

The period following the Alma Ata Declaration has been characterised by the dominance of WHO EURO, which took the initiative in defining future trends in health education and especially the new health promotion approach. In the early 1980s it seemed that health education would have an important role to play, in view of the statements made by the then Director General of WHO, Dr Halfdan Mahler, and this was subsequently supported by Dr Ilona Kickbusch, then Director of Lifestyles and Health at WHO EURO, who later became Director of the Division of Health Promotion and Education, WHO Headquarters, Geneva.

In his introductory article for the new journal "Health Promotion" (Vol.1, No.1,1986), under the title "Toward a new public health", Dr. Mahler, wrote that ".....public health is in the process of change....(it) needs to move into positive and active advocacy for health. It needs to enable individuals and communities to develop their health potential.....Many endeavours have been undertaken in this direction in different forms all over the world. In industrialised countries, 'health promotion' has come to stand for many such activities. The World Health Organisation has fostered this development....".

In the "Introduction to the Journal" (Vol.1 No.1) Dr. Kickbusch, the Chairperson of the Editorial Board, wrote: ".....Health promotion is not a new and separate discipline, but a necessary and timely reconsideration of public health......The medicalisation of public health has led to expansive investments in diagnosis and cure with little emphasis on care or determined preventive action. The major social movements....have set health agendas but they have not managed to create a joint public health lobby to impose public accountability for health matters on those in power. A strong role for the public in health is all the more necessary because of the complex forces and interaction of political and economic interests.

That is why health promotion stresses the advocacy role towards the formulation and implementation of healthy public policy......Health promotion combines diverse and complementary methods and approaches. The approaches are selected to generate advocacy for health and to develop enabling strategies....The new public health lies between three spheres of action:

- the political sphere, which sets the parameters for healthy public policies which in turn influence the practice of health promotion and structure health access in everyday life;

- the social sphere, in which needs and wants are generated and expressed as demands towards the political and professional system;

- the public health sphere, with its twofold health promotion strategy of advocacy and support."

The concept of "new public health" thus needs to be seen as part of the new concept of "healthy public policies", which was the topic of the Second International Conference on Health Promotion, held in Adelaide in 1988 (see Appendix 2). Briefly, the position of WHO is that the "new" public health coincides with the new concept of "health promotion", which extends the traditional interpretation of public health to include the "advocacy" role.

New Public Health

In 1986, the U.K. Secretary of State for Social Services established a Committee of Inquiry into future developments in the Public Health Function and Community Medicine (known as the Acheson Committee). In its Report, the Committee looked at the present state of health and its major threats, with special reference to environmental health and communicable diseases. The Report was a direct response to the findings of two inquiries following recent outbreaks of communicable diseases: salmonella food poisoning and Legionnaires' disease. In this section, attention is drawn to those parts of the Acheson Report that directly contribute to the clarification of the concept of public health as it is at present interpreted in the U.K, as compared with the WHO conception.

The Acheson Report mentioned in several places existing dissatisfaction with the confusion in conceptualising community medicine and with the performance of some community physicians. It traced historical developments resulting in changes from public health to community medicine following the 1974 reorganisation of the National Health Service, and recommended that this trend be reversed and that there should be a return to the concept of public health. It even recommended "that the specialty of community medicine should in future be referred to as the specialty of public health medicine and its qualified members as public health physicians.....We invite the Royal College of Physicians and the Faculty of Community Medicine to consider the name of the Faculty in the light of this recommendation" (Recommendation 1,p.66).

The definition of public health adopted by the Report is "the science and art of preventing disease, prolonging life and promoting health through organised efforts of society", which recognises "that there are a multiplicity of influences which affect the health of the public".

According to its brief, the Report was concerned with "the future development of public health function" and, therefore, concentrated on the way public health should be organised, within the current institutional framework, with the following aims: (p.63)

- to improve surveillance of the health of the population centrally and locally;

- to encourage policies which promote and maintain health;

- to ensure that the means are available to evaluate health services.

In chapter four of the Report, dealing with the health services, local government and public health, a structure of the organisation of public health was proposed, including the establishment of a small unit within the DHSS, bringing together relevant disciplines and skills to monitor the health of the public (Recommendation 2, p.67). It also spelled out the responsibilities of the regional and district health authorities in the field of public health.

It was further proposed that the leader of public health on the District level should be appointed Director of Public Health. This person should be "a medical practitioner with special training in epidemiology and those environmental, social and behavioral factors which affect the balance between health and disease, in other words a consultant in public health medicine" (p.69). In regional health authorities such a person should be nominated Regional Director of Public Health.

There was a shortage of appropriately qualified persons for these jobs, and the Report recommended that Regional and District Health Authorities review their manpower requirements and amend their current training policies (Recommendations 16,17).

To meet these new needs for public health doctors, the Report recommended that the existing training bodies/institutions should "review their education and training programmes in the light of our recommendations and the need for renewed emphasis on public health issues" (Recommendation 30, p.73).

According to the Report this need for new education and training programmes demonstrated "the need for a strong national resource centre or centres, providing postgraduate education of the highest quality.....More generally we recommend that the relevant training institutions and professional bodies should discuss how to best achieve multi-disciplinary awareness and collaboration in the training of public health practitioners, including the possibility of establishing a school or schools of public health. (Recommendation 31, p.73). In addition there may also be merit at regional level in considering the school of public health concept in other locations bringing together existing departments."

Directly related to this was the Recommendation 33 (p.74) urging that "the representatives of RHAs, the Faculty of Medicine and the academic departments should undertake an urgent review of the requirements in the line of the general principles underlined".

It was also recommended that "RHAs, the FCM and the academic departments should organise a continuing education programme for all practising consultants in public health medicine and we urge health authorities to ensure that the public health doctors are encouraged to attend these courses" (Recommendation 38, p.74).

This new move from community medicine back to public health had been under discussion for some time, due to the dissatisfaction with the confusing conceptualisation and application of community medicine and the general trend to revitalise the image of public health. In the Report, the new image included the mention of "health promotion" and proposeed ".....that closer integration of the Health Education Authority into the work of the NHS at all levels.....early and close collaboration with RHA and DHA in nationally organising initiatives".

There was a difference between the way the Report described the new public health and the way it dealt with it in its recommendations. Reading the Report it is obvious that there was a distinction between the new concept of public health and the role public health medicine should play, the latter being only a small contributing factor in the more general concept of public health. Yet, the recommendations were limited to the role of public health medicine, without any mention of other contributing factors concerned with "the multiplicity of influences which affect the health of the public"; nor did the Report define the concept of health promotion, and, as far as advocacy is concerned, the Report was quite explicit: "We reject the view expressed in some evidence submitted to us that public health doctors, as public servants, have a duty or a right to advocate or pursue the policies which they judge to be in public interest independently of any line of accountability. The advisory function should be exercised by direct presentation of the issues to the health authority in writing and/or by oral presentation" (p.70).

Since the Report did not define the concept "health promotion", except to exclude the advocacy role of UK public health doctors, it could be assumed that in other respects the interpretation of this term coincides with that offered by WHO. This belief is reinforced by the fact that the Report explicitly stated under its "General Principles" the following : "The WHO has defined the range of targets to ensure "Health for All by the Year 2000". The U.K. Government has endorsed the WHO approach. Public health doctors can make a major contribution to setting and achieving such targets and to the evaluation of health services...." (p.65).

Since the U.K. Government was said to have "endorsed the WHO approach", but the Report categorically declined to accept the advocacy role of public health doctors, this issue requires further clarification.

The Concept of "Advocacy"

The question of advocacy is becoming important because it defines the political orientation of health promotion and health education. WHO EURO stated that "the new public health is identical with the new concept of health promotion which extends the traditional interpretation of public health to include the advocacy role". As we have seen, Acheson in his Report on "new public health" rejects advocacy as a part of the role of public health doctors as public servants who have different ways of intervening where they consider it necessary. Consequently it will be necessary to clarify the concept of "advocacy" in the hope that it could resolve the seemingly conflicting views of WHO and the Department of Health, which is probably due to the different interpretation of the concept "advocacy".

According to Cloward and Elman (1974) there are at least two basically different interpretations of the meaning of advocacy in the community sense. The concept was for the first time used to describe the events at 199 Stanton Street on New York's Lower East Side. In November 1962, a social worker from the Mobilisation for Youth Movement and an assistant moved into an unoccupied storefront at 199 Stanton Street and opened a shop. They called it the Neighbourhood Service Centre and over the door displayed a sign "Walk In". Many of the Stanton residents, 14% of whom were on national assistance, accepted the invitation. In this way a social worker, dissatisfied with the limitations of the case-work approach, started a community programme by moving into the community and helping the local population to solve their problems. The venture was a success and most of the problems presented had to do with people's relations with "Welfare" - the Department of Welfare and its officials. After working for some time and dealing with a large number of complaints, it became obvious that the majority of these had to do with the welfare officials not following the laws or regulations and thus causing problems for the recipients. The social workers tried to help people by informing them of their rights and advising them how to claim them. They saw their chief function as liaison between client and agencies; they did not yet realise that even these concrete activities would fail to resolve issues between the poor and the welfare state. There came the time when the social workers had to come off the fence and take sides. They found that they had to do more than refer, advise and counsel if they were to get results.

The social workers were forced to change their approach by their clients, who expressed their dissatisfaction by abandoning them. A new practice soon evolved, which came to be know as advocacy. An advocate in this context is one who intervenes between an agency of the government and his client to secure an entitlement or right which has so far been obscured or denied. To act effectively, an advocate has to have sufficient knowledge of law and of administrative procedures to recognise injustice when it occurs and then seek a solution in harmony with clients' interests. In practice, the social worker had to meet the officers at the welfare centre and negotiate a solution with them. Over time, that was found to be insufficient and they had to resort to threats of going a level higher if the officer did not provide the desired solution. In other words, they attacked as well as they defended. This often militant advocacy was always carried on with a calculated informality. The main reason that the people were drawn to the Centre, however, was that the social workers took sides and were willing to put themselves out to uphold their clients' rights under the welfare state.

After a year, it became clear that the indignation of social workers was not enough protection against injustices in the social welfare state, so the Centre established a free legal service, threatening the welfare with litigation. In this way, advocacy moved from intimidation to litigation . The welfare service was inclined to settle out of court to avoid creating precedents. The small number of cases that were taken to court created a great impression in the legal vacuum within the welfare ghetto. By 1963 MFY created another three centres. This specialised type of service could gradually be differentiated from those required for dealing with other problems for which the professional staff did not find enough time. The idea of recruiting support from community members to help with the work in the Centre turned gradually into true a community participation programme.

Another type of advocacy is described by Guskin and Ross in their article "Advocacy and Democracy: The Long View" (in Cox et.al. 1974). According to the authors, the last few years of urban crisis had generated a new concern about the citizens' role in the planning process. The complexity of issues and the growing sophistication of techniques in urban and social planning had made it impossible for community groups to participate effectively in the process, even given a chance to do so. They become easily manipulated, with the result that they became increasingly apathetic or frustrated and enraged with their impotence. From this perspective, the idea of planners who are advocates for certain deprived groups in the society gave rise to the concept of advocate planner, who has the expert knowledge and is concerned with promoting the interests of a threatened group or community.

The role of the advocate planner differs according to the ideological commitment of the person who takes on this role. Some advocate planners see themselves as agents of change of the existing system, some act as social scientists and collect data to support the demands of their clients, some act as community organisers to enable protest and community action, whereas some see themselves as liaison-contact persons mediating between the planning authorities and communities, which can result in reducing discontent by exchange of information and operating within the realities which are the objective conditions of life. The most salient value-orientation common to all advocate planners and the communities they serve is a strong belief in the participation of citizens affected in decisions that affect their lives, which gives a new meaning to community participation. Some see it as a right and as a way of increasing the effectiveness of a plan.

There seems to be a whole range of interpretations of the role of advocate planners and the way they will go about protecting the interest of the client population. The main ingredients, however, are the contribution of necessary expert knowledge and understanding of complex systems and sophisticated mechanisms, as well as ensuring a competent and effective community participation in the complex decision making process.

In some ways advocacy is related to the aims of a more general interpretation of health promotion, which also operates within the political, social, administrative and other systems, by encouraging effective community participation, resulting in active improvements in the environment and individual competence, thus creating a better life through better health.

"The Health of the Nation"

The reform of the NHS has been documented in a number of publications, of which the White Paper published by the Department of Health represents a cornerstone in the role of health promotion (see Appendix 4). The Secretary of State for Health, Virginia Bottomley, in her introduction to the summary of the Strategy for Health in England, (July 1992) states:

"The Health of the Nation" Green Paper, published in June 1991, stimulated an extensive public debate. More than 2,000 individuals and organisations sent in their views. Dozens of conferences, seminars and workshops were held. Newspaper and journal articles were written debating the issues raised.

Of course, many different views were expressed. But one thing above all was apparent: the very wide backing which the overall strategy set out in the Green Paper attracted. There was support for the need to concentrate on health promotion as much as health care; for the need to set clear and challenging targets - and not too many of them - at which to aim; and for the need for all of us to work together. These principles are essential if we are to make further significant improvements in the health of the people. The consultation showed that the time is right for the development of a strategic approach to health. It also confirmed the opportunities which exist.

The quality of the debate has revealed a common perception of what needs to be done. It has exposed the commitment which exists to make sure this is achieved. We are well placed to meet the targets set in this White Paper. If we succeed, the health of the nation will be substantially improved.

The Green Paper acknowledged our debt to the World Health Organisation's 'Health For All' strategy. I was particularly heartened by the warm welcome which WHO gave to our Green Paper. Now we will build on this, in a way designed to meet the particular circumstances in this country.

The priorities, the targets, the mechanisms and the action set out in this document speak for themselves. I should, however, like to emphasise four points.

***First**, there is a commitment in this White Paper to the pursuit of 'health' in its widest sense, both within Government and beyond. Within Government this reflects not only my role as Secretary of State for Health but also the responsibilities of my colleagues in other Departments.*

***Second**, the reforms of the NHS have made this strategic approach possible. the need to focus on health as much as health care has long been the ambition. The reforms have enabled us to make it a reality.*

***Third**, although there is much that Government and the NHS need to do, the objectives and targets cannot be delivered by Government and the NHS alone. They are truly for the nation-for all of us-to achieve. We must be clear about where responsibilities lie. We must get the balance right between what the Government, and Government alone, can do, what other organisations and agencies need to do and, finally, what individuals and families themselves must contribute if the strategy is to succeed.*

***Fourth**, this White Paper is not the last word. It is only the start of a continuing process of identifying priority objectives, setting targets and monitoring and reviewing progress. Over time new objectives and targets will be set, adding to or replacing those in this White Paper.*

This initiative is unique. It builds on achievements, both past and present. It proposes action and provides the focus for that action. Its ultimate purpose is to bring about further continuing improvement in the health of the nation."

The Patient's Charter

This document sets out the standards which the NHS is expected to meet in its care of the patients (see Appendix 5). In the Foreword the Secretary of State for Health, William Waldegrave, states:

"The rights and standards set out in this document form The Patient's Charter, a central part of the Government's programme to improve and modernise the delivery of the service to the public whilst continuing to reaffirm the fundamental principles of the NHS. The Patient's Charter puts the Government's Citizen's Charter initiative into practice in the NHS(DoH 1991).

Since it was set up in 1948, the National Health Service has been the envy of the world. Since then, it has grown immensely in capability. Every day, the doctors, nurses and other staff, who are the NHS, save lives and help patients overcome disabling conditions, in ways that would have been impossible forty years ago.

The Government believes that there must be no change to the fundamental principles on which it was founded and on which it has continued ever since, namely that services should be available to every citizen on the basis of clinical need, regardless of ability to pay, and that the service should in the future, as in the past, mainly be paid for out of general taxation.

The Government is also firmly committed to improving the Service - to creating a better National Health Service. This means a Service that:

- *always puts the patient first, providing services that meet clearly defined national and local standards, in ways responsive to people's views and needs. The Patient's Charter is a central part of achieving this objective by seeking to ensure everywhere the high standards of the best;*

- *provides services that produce clear, measurable benefits to people's health, with more emphasis than in the past on health promotion and prevention. The consultative document "Health of the Nation", which you can obtain from your local library, suggests explicit targets for improvements in health for the first time in England;*

- *is highly efficient, representing really good value for money, achieved through better management following the implementation of the proposals in the White Papers "Working for Patients" and "Caring for People";*

- *respects and values the immense resource of skill and dedication which is to be found amongst those who work for and with the National Health Service."*

The setting of standards for the NHS is very important for health promotion and health education since they will have to be reflected in the specifications which will define the expected outcomes.

SUMMARY

Part 1 provided a brief history of health education and health promotion HP/HE). It is an outline of what are in my view, based on four decades of work in the field, the most important issuues in the development of HP/HE.

The aim of this historical overview is to acquaint the reader with the complex pattern of development of health education, and later, health promotion. It is important for the reader to be aware of these historical changes and to be able to understand the most recent developments and changes.

The review traces the developments in health education and identifies the Alma Ata Declaration as a turning point in the approach to the improvement of people's health through the introduction of the new concept of health promotion. Today the circle has been closed, through the recognition of the importance of health education as well as health promotion as two sides of the same coin. This has been described here in the form of the organisational model, which deals with settings as systems and concentrates on consumers as individuals within these settings.

The difference in the developments in Europe and the USA needs also to be taken into consideration, so that each can benefit from the experiences of the other. In Europe it will be necessary to catch up on the developments in health education, whereas practitioners in the USA could benefit from the European experience in health promotion. The new organisational model is intended to bring together the two approaches.

PART 2

THE ORGANISATIONAL MODEL

INTRODUCTION

As we have seen, the developments in health promotion represent a change from an individual to a societal approach in preventing disease and promoting health. They are based on the Alma Ata Declaration, which has been adopted and implemented by the European Office of the World Health Organisation. The consequence of this change in emphasis has been the disregard in Europe of health education, representing the individual approach, which went on developing in the USA.

The concentration on health promotion has not been thought out and taken to its logical conclusion, with the consequence that the initial emphasis on societal forces has remained the main concern of the protagonists of this approach in WHO EURO. This is well illustrated by the contents of the various conferences and statements produced under the WHO EURO sponsorship which have been the main basis for past developments in this field (Pelikan, 1993).

Taking the health promotion model to its logical conclusion provides us with an interesting paradox. Health promotion, characterised by concentrating on organisations instead of individuals, has resulted in the recognition of a whole set of "health promoting settings", which are in fact organisations. It happens that most of these settings are part of the service sector, which is now strongly affected by the quality management movement based on the needs of the customers. Thus, the organisational model of health promotion comes back to individual consumers within an organisational framework. The needs defined by customers represent the "specifications" for the production process and regulate the relationship between the purchasers and providers of health services, which include also the prevention of disease and promotion of health. Since health education concentrates on the empowerment of individuals, it in turn becomes an important element of the organisational model. For this reason, this book provides the reader with an insight into developments in health education as well as health promotion, since anyone active in this field will have to take into account the most recent developments in both fields.

There is, however, another interesting twist to this story. Since the main protagonist (in terms of power and resources) of this new approach is WHO EURO, which is also an "organisation" one should examine its internal developments in order to be able to map out future trends. As this book is going to press, there has been an important change in WHO EURO, with the Director of Lifestyle and Health moving to the WHO HQ in Geneva. It is hoped that WHO EURO will accept the implications of the organisational model and will reintroduce health education as a viable method of promoting health and preventing disease.

NEW APPROACHES AND DEVELOPMENTS

INTRODUCTION

The tradition of health promotion and health education (HP/HE) has undergone a number of changes of which the most recent ones have been the distinction between the two activities and the application of the Ottawa Charter. One should, however, take into account that the Ottawa Charter as such is already out of date and that science in general is undergoing rapid changes which will consequently require an update of HP/HE to meet the new needs.

One of these changes in the field of science has affected the basic social science approaches. The traditional structural-functionalist approach was initially discarded in favour of a phenomenological approach, which emphasised the importance of personal experience as compared to population studies of processes and events only to be reinstated by accepting that in addition to personal experiences one cannot disregard the role of the structure of the system. This brought about the return of consideration being given to the social statuses and roles such as the "sick role" and the "at-risk role" when studying the behaviour of professionals and patients within the health care delivery system.

This was followed by the realisation of the importance of social influences on the personal perception of reality, with special reference to matters of health and disease. Accepting that the "reality" is socially constructed led some to believe that there is not something called "reality out there" and prompted them to accept an extreme relativistic approach. It is now accepted that reality is socially constructed, but once it is institutionalised it becomes the "objective" reality for individuals, with all its coercive powers and will be integrated by the individual as the "subjective" reality. This concept is useful for the understanding of social and cultural differences between population groups, which may appear to be contradictory and yet are able to coexist in a wider social context.

These differences can explain various health-related practices, which should be taken into account in any society but especially a multi-ethnic society.

Some new theoretical explanations and approaches have been developed that may enhance our understanding of a complex social world. Although they have not yet affected the HP/HE activities directly, the new conceptualisation of the problems promise to be highly relevant. For example, chaos theory postulates that even though the events may be unpredictable (or random) the system within which they take place could be predictable and measured. This is relevant to HP/HE since in the past it was maintained that it was not possible to carry out evaluation because there are so many uncontrolled variables involved and, therefore, it was not possible to predict direct cause-effect relationships. A chaos theory approach to evaluation is evenn more promising, since although it is still not possible to predict outcomes of individual events, the direction of the movements of the whole system may be able to be evaluated in terms of health gain of the individual members of that system. This theoretical approach has been enhanced by the development of the concept of fuzzy logic which represents a shift from the positivist approach of an "either-or" bivalent concept to a "multivalent" approach of "if this - then that", which takes into consideration a whole number of interactions. This approach has also a direct relevance to HP/HE activities since it is fully compatible with a "multi-sectoral" approach.

The new HP/HE developments depend on the possibility of defining and describing the interventions in terms of their effects on the consumers, including the concept of accountability, which will further require a sharpening-up of the methodology related to evaluation by including quality asseessment of the processes, as well as assessing the outcomes. This accountability can only be achieved if one takes advantage of the mentioned theoretical developments.

A summary of some of the most important changes and their consequence for the practice of health promotion and health education is given below.

THE PARADIGM SHIFT

It is generally accepted that the actions of scientists are governed by the way they perceive the reality of the problems they deal with, the solutions that are appropriate and the methods that are effective in solving a problem and reaching a solution. This perception concerning the problem, the solution and the method is known as a "paradigm". When the paradigm does not fit the objective reality, owinng to some new knowledge or a change in the environment, this can cause a "paradigm shift" or a change in the existing perception governing scientific thought (Kuhn,1970). It is for this reason that the recent dramatic changes, which are taking place, have resulted in a paradigm shift related to the conceptualisation and operationalisation of health promotion and health education interventions.

The Structural Approach

Humans can be described as "social animals" preferring to live in groups whenever possible. With increase in numbers, these groups manifest an increased complexity. Today we talk about societies, in which people live together and which have an internal consistency and order. These societies are prone to disruptions when the established order breaks down; the tendency is to attempt to re-establish order and bring things "back to normal", whatever the term normal may mean. One such major disruption was the French Revolution which resulted in major upheavals of the existing order. It prompted August Comte (1858-1917) to create a new scientific discipline and name it "sociology", with the intention of learning more about existing disorder and find ways of containing or reducing it. The practical aims of sociology attracted many followers of Comte who all contributed in different ways to the understanding of society, as a defined unit populated with people with specific needs and desires. They were all concerned with questions such as: What is the structure of a society? What are the parts of this structure? What are the relations between these parts? What are the mechanisms for stability and change? and What are the characteristics of people living in that society?

An important contribution of such enquiries relevant for the problems of health and disease was made by Talcott Parsons (1951), who used a structural-functionalist approach in tracing the career of people who become ill and seek medical help. Parsons built on the work of Sigerist (1929), who drew attention to the special position of a sick person in society. Parsons conceptualised illness as a social dysfunction and defined it as the state of disturbance in the 'normal' functioning of the total human individual, including both the state of the organism as a biological system and of his personal and social adjustments. To cope with such dysfunction, society provides for the integration of people who are ill by allocation of a special status with an accompanying role. Although Parsons was not primarily interested in the sick person, he used this example as an elaboration of "the major structural outlines of the social system from the action frame of reference". The concept of the "sick role", however, has contributed to the understanding of societal implications of illness and represented a major contribution to medical sociology. It included a description of the rights and obligations incumbent in the sick role as:

- the sick person is exempt from certain social responsibilities;
- he/she cannot be expected to take care of him/herself;
- he/she should want to and do everything to get well;
- he/she should seek medical advice and cooperate with medical experts.

Although illness as a special social status and role has been considered as useful in understanding the process of doctor-patient relationship, there were some who disagreed with Parson's definition of illness as "deviance" (Pflanz and Rhode, 1970; Beck, 1972; Twaddle, 1973). Others (Suchman, 1969) used Parson's idea to develop a career model of a person's acquiring the sick role which included the following steps:

- a healthy person notices certain symptoms;
- after assessing the meaning of the symptoms, he/she explores the reactions of the social environment to the idea of him/her taking on a sick role;
- if the reactions are positive and the symptom persists he/she will decide to go and seek medical help;

- the doctor will confirm the existence and the seriousness of the symptom and in this way will legitimize the sick role;
- after successful treatment the doctor will discharge the patient who will relinquish the sick role and will take on the well role.

Within the framework of medicine in general (includinng curative as well as preventive aspects), the concept of the "sick role" was not considered to be adequate by itself. This resulted in the development of the concept of the "at-risk role" (Baric, 1969, 1975), which was more appropriate for the needs of preventive medicine and health education.

Neofunctionalism in Post-modern Societies

With the demise of communism in Eastern European countries and the spread of market economy and democracy, the Eastern European countries have been faced with the need to replace their Marxist theoretical explanations with those prevalent in the West. This change in the general ideological orientation has also been reflected in the interpretation of human behaviour in illness and health. As a consequence a number of sociologists have been engaged in the revival of some, if not all, of the theories developed by Parsons (Robertson and Turner, ed., 1991).

One of the articles in Robertson and Turner's book is by Frank (1991), who writes about Parsons' sick role in the post modernist light. The term post-modern chronologically follows what has been know as modern society. Giddens (1990) describes 'modernity' as the specific forms of life and organisations which developed in Europe from the seventeenth century onwards and which spread out into the rest of the world. Today, at the end of the twentieth century, there is a generally shared feeling that the world is entering a new period, which is characterised by sufficiently distinctive changes to merit the new label of "post-modern".

The two main characteristics which according to Frank explain what is understood by "post-modern", are a specific time period and a specific style. In relation to medicine, post-modern *time* is characterised by increased effectiveness of medical care in terms of technology and cost; increased government involvement and patient awareness of scarce resources; and relegation of ethical problems to "resource management" decisions. The *style* is characterised by the "deconstruction" approach, which is another way of saying that the idea of a grand unifying theory of society is discarded in favour of breaking down the historical events into discrete units, which may or may not be related but which, when understood, can still throw light on the whole.

The reassessment of Parsons in the light of post-modernism is mainly concerned with his writing about the concept of health. Health can be conceived off as a state or as a resource. The Parsonian post modernist conceptualization favours the latter. It stems from Parsons' description of the 'sick role' which, as already explained is not only a state of the organism but an institutionalised role. A role is defined as the action aspect of a social status and as such defines the mode of interaction between the incumbent of that role and the social environment. In one of his last writings, Parsons (1978) treats health "as a symbolic circulating medium regulating human action and other life processes.... (It is) the teleonomic capacity of an individual living system...to maintain a favourable, self-regulating state that is a prerequisite of the effective performance of an indefinitely wide range of functions". Health as a 'capacity' constantly circulates and can be considered in terms of 'income' and 'expenditure' in the process of acquisition of other resources.

Illness (which is the obverse of health) is not only a physical but also a social dysfunction. It requires society to deal with it in a way that will reduce as far as possible the negative consequences of such a dysfunction. This is achieved by allocating the individual a 'sick role', which includes a set of rights and duties aimed at regulating the adjustment of the individual to social expectations. For an individual, the 'sick role' compensates for the loss of health as a necessary medium for social interaction, by making clear that illness is not the individual's fault and exempting him/her from ordinary daily obligations and expectations. In a sense, it provides the individual with special conditions for social interaction with a 'reduced medium for interaction' at his/her disposal.

This reinterpretation of the sick role within a modernistic framework makes the concept again acceptable as well as useful in the interpretation of the interaction of a sick person with the social environment, which also includes the healing professions.

The Phenomenological Approach

Understanding the society in which we live depends on the way the society is envisaged and studied. The study of society has undergone many changes. One relatively recent approach has been to examine society from the perspectives of people living in it. The structuralist approach fell into disrepute because it was concerned with the abstract characteristics of the social system and disregarded the people living in it. This new way of studying society became the "phenomenological" approach, which has been well described by one of its initiators (Schutz, 1964), using as an analogy the role of a "stranger" who enters a society and tries to learn more about, it as compared to using the knowledge advantage of locals who live in it.

This approach treats the cultural pattern of a society as a social phenomenon, which will be differently perceived by the "sociologist" coming from outside and the "actor" who lives in that society. Whereas the former will try to be objective and classify observations in a neutral way, the latter will observe the society as a field of actual and potential actions and will think about it only as far as this is relevant to him/her. This kind of observation is characteristically centred on the observer and will encompass areas which are within his/her "relevance" parameters. These areas may not be linked and may differ in intensity and scope. One could say that this kind of knowledge is in scientific terms (for a sociologist) incoherent, partially clear and not free from contradictions, whereas for the actor it is sufficiently coherent, clear and consistent for him/her to be able to survive in that society.

This way of thinking is functional as long as there are no disruptions in the social life, the body of knowledge received from parents and education remains consistent and meets the needs of the everyday life in that society and this knowledge is shared by other members of that society. The continuity of this knowledge may be interrupted by a change in any one of the parameters mentioned which will result in a "crisis" and will demand a reconstruction of the existing body of knowledge.

The idea of a "stranger" entering a society for the purpose of study illustrates the limitations the stranger will face, because he/she will be able to observe only what is here and now and not be able to understand the historical background of such observations. A member of a society, by taking a scientific approach to the observation of his/her own society will have the advantage of "objective" scientific methods as well as of understanding the historical background of the observations made. In this sense the "phenomenological" approach is basically a humanistic approach, which looks at social phenomena in terms of their human meaning.

Social Creation of Reality

Within the tradition of a phenomenological approach, sociologists have tried to examine the concept of "reality" as it is perceived by the members of a society. Although the domain of philosophy, the sociology of knowledge has been concerned with this concept under the assumption that reality is relative and socially constructed (Berger, Luckmann, 1967).

The relative character of reality is based on the assumption that there is an "objective" reality, in which a person lives, and a "subjective" reality, or the individual perception of this objective reality.

The social construction of reality is reflected in the objective reality into which a person is born and in which a person lives. This objective reality is composed of numerous practices which are tested through trial and error and, when shown to be functional, come to be shared by the rest of the society and become institutionalised. These shared practices are transmitted from one generation to the next by means of secondary socialisation within formal or informal settings and become a part of the legitimised knowledge of that society.

Individuals are considered to have inborn needs or drives, which, as opposed to instincts, do not come with programmed ways of satisfying them. These have to be learned by the child in the form of socially accepted ways of satisfying them. Once the child learns the "rules" defined by the objective reality, these rules become internalised as a child's subjective reality. This process is known as socialisation.

Socialisation thus ensures the continuity of values and norms of a society, perpetuated from one generation to the next. These represent the objective reality of that society which may be different from some other society.

In case of a paradigm shift, the objective reality (including the complex of norms, values and beliefs) will change and the individual will have to adjust the subjective reality to the new objective reality by means of resocialisation.

If one looks at the developmental process of an individual going through different stages of growing up and maturing, it becomes obvious that it will not be possible for that individual to internalise, during primary or secondary socialisation, all the values and norms associated with the changing statuses/roles within a life time. The adjustment to different statuses/roles will take place through the process of anticipatory socialisation. In that sense socialisation is the process of learning how to meet social expectations associated with different statuses and roles an individual will have during a life time.

One can conclude that a person's feeling of what is real and what is right will be culture-specific and will reflect the values and norms of a specific cultural or social group. Nevertheless, although reality is socially constructed or human-made, once it becomes institutionalised as the objective reality of a society it will provide a fixed framework of social expectations and values for individual members of that society. Differences occur in the degree of individual success in internalising it as his/her subjective reality. In other words, there is a generally shared objective reality in a specific society within which a variety of subjective realities are possible.

The New Science of Chaos

A relativistic approach to reality and individual perception of it, combined with a phenomenological approach to the study of a society, is bound to create a feeling of uncertainty and insecurity.

This has been reflected in the discussions about evaluation of health promotion and health education interventions. The argument is that it is impossible to evaluate an intervention, which is exposed to so many influences most of which are beyond the control of the intervention as such.

The present methods of evaluation, utilising the scientific rigour usually applied to research methods, deal with population studies of change as the result of a health promotion and health education intervention. The data are acquired by questioning individual members of a population group (target population) and the inferences are made by aggregating the data and using traditional statistical theories applied to the distribution of events and the significance of its relationships. To achieve this, it is necessary to simplify the individually collected data so that they can be aggregated and compared. This approach is obviously opposed to the phenomenological approach, which lays great importance on the experiences of individual members of a social group, which cannot be truly reflected if they are reduced to a quantitative measure for the purpose of aggregation and comparison.

The uncertainty associated with research and evaluation in the field of health promotion and health education can benefit from the recent scientific developments in the area of research methodology. A similar problem of uncertainty has had to be faced by scientists working in the field of particle physics, where the unpredictability and randomness of the behaviours of various particles did not fit the classical model aimed at the predictions and generalisations of the research findings. The main preoccupation of these scientists has been the discovery of natural laws which would provide a picture of order and regularity in nature. The tendency has been to discover the ultimate goal which is a grand unifying theory of the universe and which still eludes us. In their research scientists have been confronted with a number of irregularities, disorder, discontinuities and erratic events (chaos) which they considered as puzzles to be disregarded in their quest for order and predictability.

In the 1970s, a group of scientists in the USA (mathematicians, physicists, biologists, chemists) turned their attention to this disorder and tried to find connections among irregularities (Gleick,

1987). When they started looking they found a surprising order in the chaos of the observations they recorded. Following these first developments a new movement grew up, using the shorthand label of "chaos" theory, which is influencing the basics of present scientific thought. At present, there is an abundance of conferences, journals, university departments, dedicated institutes and funds for the study of this phenomenon. It has also developed a new methodology, using computers and of graphic imaging, and a new language ("fractals, bifurcations, intermittencies and periodicities, folded-towel diffeomorphisms and smooth noodle maps" p.4/5) describing the new elements of motion. Gleick says: "Chaos is a science of process rather than state, of becoming rather than being" (p.5).

Whereas in physics the complexity was "simple minded" and the forces involved (i.e. the fluttering of a leaf in the wind) could be described by one set of mathematical equations, there were other systems like in biology where one could find much richer forms of complexity, which included intrinsic changes and adaptive qualities. Here, the concept of chaos was found most useful. The traditional scientific approach had endeavoured to discover regularities, patterns, consistencies and predictability, whereas the new approach using the concept of chaos accepted that it is not possible to know all the facts and those available are only approximations of the real situation. The scientists accepting chaos theory were satisfied if the consequent results could be of the same level of approximation.

Traditional scientists working with a linear model, expected results to be commensurate with causes. This is not always the case, as shown by the so called "butterfly effect", which illustrates the interconnectedness of every system and raises the possibility that a flutter of butterfly's wings in a Brazilian forest could cause a storm in Texas.

The new ideas related to chaos theory provide a new look at systems and their operations. It is assumed that it is possible to have an ordered system which consists of random parts and that even if it is not possible to predict the exact position of each part one can predict the trends of the whole system. The theory challenges some of the prevailing beliefs such as:

- Simple systems behave in a simple way. Now we know that simple systems can manifest complex behaviour.

- Complex behaviour implies complex causes. Now we know that complex systems can give rise to simple behaviour.

- Different systems behave differently. Now we know that the laws of complexity apply universally and are not dependent on the system's constituent parts.

This change is only gradually permeating through the research fraternity, who are becoming aware of the possibilities of explaining some complex system and the need for finding new explanations for some of the systems they were studying. Chaos theory is now applied in addition to the original fields of meteorology and particle physics, to evolution, economy, biology, population studies, astronomy, etc. One of the fields of special relevance to health promotion and health education has been the study of information systems and the application of information technology.

The Theory of Fuzzy Logic

The idea of positivism using the "scientific method" has been questioned and criticised by many. Its main problem is that it cannot deal wtih meaning. Since positivism demands clear statements of "truth", based on experimental testing or mathematical proof it became the monopoly of "pure" scientists who treated any statements by "empirical" scientists lacking such characteristics as "non-truths". Under this category one can subsume statements about beauty, values, God, morals and any other which cannot be "disproved" (Popper, 1945), either experimentally or mathematically, i.e. in fact all the theoretical constructs with which most social sciences operate.

Many of the scientific fraternity realised that by setting such strict positivist rules they limited their own area of influence and what is more, within that limited area they had to accept that regularity and predictability are only one aspect of interpreting the world and that in their analyses they had been disregarding many anomalies, irregularities and inconsistencies.

This is where the theory of *fuzzy logic* joins chaos theory in the interpretation of the world, nature and the universe. It tries to help people to accept uncertainties and integrate them into their thinking and their technological products. The Japanese have been pioneers in the application of fuzzy logic to such product as camcorders, TV cameras, etc., and have taken leadership in the development of commercial machine intelligence. While the West is only now considering the various possibilities, the Japanese have already passed the $ 1 billion mark in investments in this field.

Fuzzy logic questions the positivist belief in dichotomies expressed in such opposing concepts as 'right - wrong', 'black - white', 'good - bad', etc., and postulates that there are many situations and events which fall in between into a so called grey area. Kosko (1993), gives a good historical background, citing the philosophers responsible for the prevailing thinking, and argues that this "bivalence" cannot meet the expectations arising from the new developments of modern science. "The fuzzy principle states that everything is a matter of degree...Fuzziness has a formal name in science: multivalence. The opposite of multivalence is bivalence or two-valuedness or two ways of answering a question: right or wrong... the indeterminacy (of the fuzzy logic) defines a continuum, a spectrum between 0 and 1". A statement can be placed on any position in that continuum, such as for example "nearly right".

The theory of fuzzy logic is thus an attempt to help us to deal with a world which is full of contradictions and uncertainties and be able to plan our lives and our existence as if we knew exactly what should and could be done. This applies to programmes for health as to the rest of life. One should, however, add a caveat in the sense that the "fuzziness" related to the picture of the world does not lie in the characteristics of the world but is the result of human limitations and fallibility in interpreting it. There will also be cases of "fuzzy semantics" rather than fuzzy logic, which is yet another issue..

This fuzzy approach initially met with strong resistance in the academic world. Its progress can be attributed to the commercial world, where machines were produced with fuzzy logic which enabled them to deal with such concepts as "cool temperature" or "slow speed", enabled them to learn from experience and let them grow their own rules from examples. It enables the machine to deal with theoretical constructs (cool, slow, etc.) by using sensors which carry out a set of measurements which in different combinations will give different commands. For example, a fuzzy washing machine will measure the load, the fabric, the density of dirt in water, etc., and adjust the washing process in terms of temperature, speed, amount of washing powder, etc. The same applies to a fuzzy TV set which checks and adjusts each picture for maximum colour and focus. It is consistent with the shift from digital computers programmed to act sequentially to neural networks and smart artificial intelligence machines programmed to learn before acting, based on parallel computing.

An illustration, which can serve as an example of the application of this kind of thinking can be derived from the latest developments in genetics. Most social and other researchers use sex to classify a population into males and females. There seems to be no question about how to allocate a human being into one of the two biological categories either based on the observation of appearance or verified by observing the genitalia of a person. Within this clear distinction of sexes, anomalies such as homosexuality, transvestism etc., are recognised, which are usually considered as behavioural deviation from the norm and have been disregarded, for example, in the majority of epidemiological studies. This has also been reinforced by genetic studies of humans, which biologically clearly distinguished between females as having two X chromosomes whereas males have an X and a Y chromosome. It has, however, been known for some time (Dobson, 1994) that the differentiation is not always so clear. A condition known as Androgen Insensitivity Syndrome (AIS) which occurs in one of every 50,000 women is responsible for the situation that women with AIS are genetically males and have XY and not XX chromosomes. These female children are born with a female body and partly female genitalia (without ovaries, fallopian tube or uterus). They will not be able to have children. Some may need vaginoplasty if their genitalia are not fully developed. In any case it is a very traumatic experience for both the parents and the child born with this condition.

This raises the question of how does fuzzy logic work in practical classification. If one compares a bivalent system (0 and 1) to a multivalent system with a great number of places between 0 and 1, (as the grey area between the black (0) and the white (1) positions), one can conclude that a machine will be more accurate (with a higher machine IQ) the more of these grey area positions are included into the rules that govern machine performance. One should add to this the role of knowledge (based on expertise) in defining these points in the grey area as well as the accuracy of sensors which will enable the machine to detect each of those positions on the 0-1 continuum.

The conclusion should be that the successful performance of an intelligent machine, as well as that of the health promotion and health education programmes will depend on the accuracy of knowledge base, the amount of data collected, the sensitivity of sensors in collecting the data and, finally, how well all this has been integrated into the rules programmed into the "machine", which in this case is represented by a health promotion and health education intervention.

Implications for HP/HE

Rapid changes in science and technology have been reflected in the new developments that are taking place in HP/HE. The reason for this lies in the fact that HP/HE is only now developing specific appropriate theories and have been drawing on existing theories derived from social and behavioural sciences as well as from medicine. These new HP/HE theories have been responsible for the changes in emphasis from health education to health promotion, and now back to a combination of health promotion and health education within an organisational model.

Recognition of the importance of social structure in affecting the way the health issues have been approached has brought about a renewed interest in social roles and norms, with their associated expectations. The study of doctor-patient relationship, the status of the patient, the social expectations associated with the at-risk role, the way society treats and provides for endangered population groups (children, elderly, chronically ill) as well as the institutionalisation of new forms of prevention (screening) and treatment (transplants), all have influenced the way HP/HE has been developed.

Other new developments, such as the concept of chaos and fuzzy logic theory have not as yet been fully integrated into HP/HE. They have, however, opened new doors for the planning and evaluation of HP/HE, through showing that it is possible to use a systems approach in human affaires, even if the behaviour of all individual parts cannot be predicted. Benefits can also be derived through by paying more attention on the system even if one cannot control all the parts, and by being forced to define the various theoretical constructs (needs, benefits), for the purpose of evaluation and meeting the requirements of accountability.

DEMOGRAPHIC CHANGES

One of the most dramatic changes in our conceptualisation of the world around us is associated with the increases in numbers of people and the physical and social conditions in which they live. The most recent population studies (UN Fund for Population Activities: Annual State of the World Population Report, 1994) estimate the present population as 5.66 billion and growing at an annual rate of 94 million people. These predictions indicate the need for some dramatic adjustments in health promotion and health education interventions.

Population

The rapid increase in global population is of deep concern to most countries and professionals and has brought about a spate of world conferences and meetings. One such world-wide conference was organised in 1991 by the Royal Swedish Academy of Sciences and the Swedish Council for planning and coordination of Research in Stockholm, Sweden. This was followed in 1992 by an international conference on "Population Growth, Resource Consumption and a Sustainable World" organised by the Royal Society, London and the US National Academy of Sciences, and the UN Population Conference in Cairo in 1994.

In 1993 a group of 15 academies organised a Population Summit of the World's Scientific Academies (Graham-Smith, 1994) held in New Delhi, India, and attended by representatives of a great number of academies throughout the world. It produced a joint statement signed by 60 academies from various parts of the world. The topics included dealt with the complex reality of the situation; linkages between population, natural resources and the environment; demographic transition in a gender perspective; and family planning and reproductive health.

Growth

The "population explosion" term alludes to the fact of rapid growth of the earth's population (10 million population 10 million years ago; 100 million population 2000 years ago; 2.5 billion population in 1950; 5.66 billion in 1994).

The reason for this accelerated growth is the decline in infant and child mortality, combined with the existing high birth rates, which leads to exponential increase. Since it is not acceptable to keep infant and child mortality rates artificially high as a means of population control, the only other solution is a reduction in high birth rates. This can be achieved by reducing the present high birth rate of 3.3 children per woman to 2.1 children, which would result in the total population increasing to 11 billion people by the end of the 21st century. If the reduction is even higher, for instance to 1.7 children per woman, the total population by the mid 21st century would be 7.8 billion. On the other hand, if fertility does not go down below 2.5 children per woman, by the end of the 21st century, the population would peak at 19 billion by the year 2100 or 28 billion by the year 2150. In many countries, the growth of the population has been dramatically reduced by lowering the fertility rates to a level which has resulted in a halt of population increase ("demographic transition"). Other countries, however, still have high fertility rates, which offset individual successes, and which result in a high increase in the overall population growth.

The reduction of fertility rates will depend on understanding and being able to control the factors associated with high fertility rates. These have been found to be associated with a number of cultural factors (preference for large families due to value of children as a potential labour force or source of security for parents in old age, and preference for male offsprings to the extent of introducing hidden infanticide of new born girls or abortion of female foetuses), economic factors (poverty, low education and status of women), and social factors (high infant mortality, deficiencies in the reproductive health care services, availability and acceptability of contraception). Reduction has, however, been most notably associated with increased income per capita, increased life expectancy and an increase in women's education and employment.

Sustainable growth

The recent increase in concern with rapid population growth has been strengthened by present space exploration ("we went to the moon and discovered the earth"). It created the awareness that "the spaceship earth" is a planet with a limited supply of basic resources necessary for human survival (unpolluted air, fresh water, food and shelter) and that there is an optimum and a maximum number of people which the planet can support, in short, that there is a danger that population growth could outstrip the available food and energy resources. A further concern is that even the existing limitations of the planet to sustain human life are not fixed but are being eroded by various human activities (destruction of the ozone layer, over-utilisation of fresh water and sources of energy, destruction of food producing land, pollution of seas, etc.).

The consequence has been the understanding of the interdependence of *population growth, environment and the resource consumption.* The survival of the human species on earth does not, therefore, depend only on lowering the numbers, but also controlling the use of limited resources available and slowing down, if not stopping altogether, the destruction of the environment.

Family planning

One important factor in this tripartite equation is the control of population growth through family planning. This implies deciding on the desired number of children and spacing their arrival in a family. A great number of national and international programmes concerned with family planning have been carried out in the past, based on different assumptions, using different methods and producing their share of success as well as failures.

The role of health promotion and health education has been varied, ranging from completely depending on it to practically ignoring it. In India, at one time, the whole Ministry of Health was changed into Ministry of Family Planning. On the other hand, on a global level there is not sufficient collaboration between the Health Promotion and Family Planning services.

The role of women

The old assumption that "he who owns the means of production controls the system" may have helped in differentiating between the owners and the work force, but does not necessarily hold in case of women and their fertility. Women may own "the means of production" but in most cases are not in control of the process because of the cultural, social, economic and legal pressures on them to produce or not to produce children.

Family planning programmes have mainly concentrated on the provision of various methods of contraception without being able to change the conditions under which women (and men) could and would use them. In the words of the Director General of UNICEF "family planning could bring more benefits to more people at less cost than any other single technology available to the human race". This can only have a hope of success if some of the following issues are addressed:

- cultural and social norms in favour of planned families and acceptance of smaller families;

- elimination of gender-based inequalities, sharing of sexual decisions between genders, changing women's expectations in terms of family numbers and empowering them to be in control of the reproduction process;

- availability of general as well as reproductive health services which will provide contraceptive facilities as well as ensure the health of the woman and the child;

- the provision of resources and mechanisms for the achievement of the necessary changes;

- reconsidering the role of government coercion and social control in favour of the development of positive attitudes to planning families.

These expectations represent a new challenge for health promotion and health education as an integral part of the family planning and population policy movement.

Environment and Habitat

Another factor in the tripartite equation represents the maintenance of an environment fit for humans to reproduce and live in. There is a fear that the increased numbers of people will produce an ever-increasing demand on the environment, as well as contribute to its gradual destruction.

The most important examples of the destruction of the environment can be found in areas where, owing to the need for arable land, mass destruction of forests is taking place. NASA has been monitoring the spread of destruction using satellite pictures of earth at night and measuring the areas of forest fires. For example, in the South American area of Rondonia, on one day (9.9.1983), there were 2,500 ongoing fires which could be observed from satellite pictures. A similar study carried out by the Smithsonian Institute in Bidlat, Peru, found on one sampled tree in the rain forest 5000 different species including 48 different species of ants. One can conclude that the rain forest is "the nursery of life" with its enormous variety of species. This indicates that the existing estimate of approximately 5 million species on Earth is not accurate and that the more likely number is probably 50 million. One can imagine the extent of destruction if one considers the fact that in the area between Panama and Mexico a 2000 mile strip of forest has been gradually destroyed with at present only 2% of the forest remaining.

Another important example of environmental destruction is rapid urbanisation. This is especially relevant to the way people live and congregate in expanding urban settlements. So far, the health promotion and health education approaches, together with government policies, have not been successful in contributing to the solution of these problems.

This arises because of the new situation relating to the settings in which people live and are active. The community approach, aimed at influencing people's lifestyles and derived from rural experiences, was useful at a time when most of the world's population lived in rural areas (70% in 1950), and towns were few and small, retaining most of the characteristics of a "rural" community. The new projections as far as life on earth in the year 2000 is concerned indicate a radically different picture. It is estimated that 75% of the world population will be urbanised, with 20% of them likely to be living in towns with over a million population. The number of cities with a population over 5 million will increase from 7 (1950) to 57 (2000), with 42 of them in the Third World. Twenty five cities are likely to have a population of over 10 million of which all but three will be in the South.

The Mexico syndrome

We are now faced with the new phenomenon of a *"mega city"*. The best example is Mexico City, with a population of 30 million, from which the label of "the Mexico syndrome" has originated. The methods of health promotion and health education in this new situation will have to take into account the qualitative and structural characteristics of such "mega cities". It is already possible to see that the problems facing us are due to the following changes: complete dependence of large masses of population on the provision of basic services (water, energy, food, transport, work, waste disposal, communication, education, health care, etc.); exaggerated inequalities among population groups; the special subcultures in specific fringe areas near towns, inhabited by squatters and known by different names in different parts of the world; the different priorities according to the severity of problems facing the population; different systems and modes of communication between authorities and such population groups; and the ability of these population groups to utilise the services and communicate with service personnel.

Inner city developments

A special case in most of such large conurbations is the rapid decline of inner city areas. Here, the most deprived population groups live under squalid conditions, in poverty and suffering from unemployment, disease, crime and deterioration in their competence to cope with the problems they face. These are also the areas with highest levels of air pollution, afflicting the people living there and especially the children. The National Environmental Technology Centre at Harwell, Oxfordshire monitors air pollution in British cities and has revealed that the five worst polluted cities are Sheffield, Newcastle, London, Manchester and Belfast. The five cities with cleanest air are Strath Vaich (Ross and Cromarty), Lullington Heath (Sussex), Ladybower (Derbyshire), Cardiff (Wales) and Stevenage (Herts.). The indicator used to measure air pollution is the level of nitrogen dioxide (NO2) and its main source is the car exhaust (Ryan & Reeve, 1994).

In the UK over the last twenty years the Department of the Environment has increasingly focused on urban policy concerned with the problems of urban development in general and inner city problems in particular. Recently an Inner City Research Programme has been conducted to evaluate the processes and outcomes of such a policy. The results have been published (DoE, 1994) in a report on "Assessing the Impact of Urban Policy".

The aim of this study was to examine the impact of the central government urban policy in England over the last 10 years. There have been a number of discontinuities due to changes of government policies during that period. The study was mainly concerned with the Action for Cities (AfC) package. This dealt with 57 Urban Priority Areas (UPA) and had four aims, which indicated the ways the government believed living conditions could be improved:

- to encourage enterprise and new business, and help existing businesses to grow stronger;
- to improve people's job prospects, their motivation and skills;
- to make areas attractive to residents by tackling dereliction, bringing buildings into use, preparing sites and encouraging development, and improving the quality of housing;
- to make inner city areas safe and attractive places in which to live and work.

The indicators used in the assessment of government urban policies included the relationship between expenditure and socio-economic outcomes, such as long and short term unemployment, new firm formation, and residential attractiveness for the purpose of retaining or attracting young people (25-34) into the area.

The study produced a number of well documented findings, concerned with the positive as well as negative outcomes of the government urban policies: *"Across a whole set of targeted places and in the smaller areas within some of the conurbations, public resources appear to have made an impact on turning-around aspects both of economic and residential distress in urban areas. But in the most deprived areas - and especially in the conurbation cores and areas of high unemployment - policy has not been able to make significant inroads....However, to set against this, within virtually all the authorities in the three selected conurbations (Greater Manchester, Merseyside and Tyne and Wear) there is consistent evidence of increasing polarisation between the worst and the best areas. Despite the positive overall impacts, there are therefore strong suggestions of continuing decline in the worst areas. From this one might draw the conclusion that people-targeting, as against place-targeting, needs to be given greater weight than now".*

The conclusions of the study reinforce the view that "throwing money at problems" is not the answer. The suggestions include the need for coordination and participation through the creation of effective coalitions of partners or 'actors', and for the development of structures and mechanisms which would facilitate this collaboration, as well as concentration of power in local authorities and development of coherent programmes and sharing of resources.

Resources

The third factor in the tripartite equation is the availability of natural resources necessary for sustaining human life. The two main resources on which human life depends are globally circulating ground water and the agroecosystem. Both are in danger, owing to the rapid increase in population and the pollution-derived degradation of land. It appears that the water scarcity will become acute in 2025 unless a proper ground water management policy is implemented. Expanding agriculture is the main reason for deforestation and destruction of many species dependent on that habitat. It is estimated that 30,000 species are destroyed every year.

The result is the growing difference between the rich North and the impoverished South, and this gap is increasing.

The main reason for the degradation of the environment is the increased demand on food, which is closely linked with population numbers and available arable land. Another reason is industrial expansion, which uses water and land to dispose of its by-products, which are increasing in proportion to the increase in production and consumption. The fact that humans have mastered the food production technology and at the same time there are areas suffering from famine, indicates that the production of food is not always directly related to the consumption. As a result of inequelities in distribution, transport and commerce, there are areas which cannot produce enough food to feed the indigenous population and on the other hand there are farmers subsidised by government not to produce food or even to destroy existing food surpluses.

In summary, not only increasing population numbers are limited by the existing resource potentials of the earth, but even more by the political systems affecting the production and distribution of food, land tenure, credit system, prices and exchange rates, tax policies, agricultural extension programmes, excessive government controls and civil wars.

In addition most land is privately owned and local inheritance systems will influence the size of the family and preference for male offspring.

POLITICAL CHANGES

Introduction

This changing picture of the world we are, and will be living in, requires a radical rethinking of the responsibilities, services, competencies, resources and influences related to health and disease in a population. The new political developments have seen a radical change in the distribution of power and the introduction of new economic systems in a large part of the world. Some new problems include moral disintegration of whole societies, insecurity, unemployment and poverty, collapse of authority, displacement of refugees, migration of the working force, and growth of nationalism with resulting military conflicts. The present body of knowledge about the problems and the mechanisms which characterise such populations is limited and there is a nearly complete ignorance about feasible and effective solutions in general, especially those dealing with health problems.

Health promotion and health education can play a very limited role in reducing or solving such problems, in comparison with all the other forces and institutions at the disposal of a society. Even such a limited role will need to be effectively carried out, and, for this health promotion and health education will need to produce a scientific grounding of their methods and approaches as well as include a high degree of accountability to the consumers.

Most of HP/HE activities have been criticised as being concerned with middle class populations in industrialised societies well provided for by adequate resources and catered for by a developed health care system. The new demographic studies are showing new trends which include a high population density, the development of mega cities and highly populated settlements on the fringes of towns, as well as inner city conditions of life riddled by poverty, conflict and all kinds of discrimination (racial, sex, age, etc.). There is also an ever increasing number of unemployed and a prevalence of bad living conditions of the elderly. In addition to all this there is an increasing population migration with associated problems of displaced refugees, immigrant workforce and social dislocation of whole populations due to radical political changes and/or military conflicts. Government policies aimed at reducing the strains caused by urbanisation and inner city degradation have not produced the expected outcomes. The result has been a change in the character of problems facing HP/HE. This has been matched with the changes in the responsibilities laid onto HP/HE following the new models and approaches resulting from the Alma Ata Declaration and the Ottawa Charter.

The Family

The dislocation of whole populations due to political, military or economic reasons has placed a heavy burden on the family. The extended family is breaking up. This is partly the effect of the economic migration of the younger generation, arising from famine and search for food in numerous refugee camps; wars and forcible relocation as a result of "ethnic cleansing"; unemployment and the need to follow the employment market; and new trends in the family lifestyle with the increase in the numbers of mobile one-generation "nuclear family" and single parent families.

Writing about the family in the UK, Iley (1994) paints a picture of the type of family that TV viewers most identified with and have selected as their preferential model. It is a one-parent family, with the mother at the centre, economically independent and looking after the children at the same time as earning her living. The father is absent and a boyfriend is present (occasionally). The man in the family has become a non-essential extra. The family lifestyle has changed, with the mother being the main earner, the meals are not cooked at home and take the form of ready-made food eaten when convenient.

The Information Pack "One plus One" (Mattison et.al, 1994) produced by the Marriage and Partnership Research Charity is highly informative in describing the problems associated with modern marriage and their resolution. According to the available data the marriage rate in Britain has dropped dramatically. Between 1971 (68.5 per thousand) the marriage rate has halved by 1991 (36.3 per thousand). In spite of this considerable reduction in marriage rates, Britain has the highest marriage rates in Europe (following Portugal). This has been mainly explained by people marrying later as a result of a number of factors, such as the acceptance of premarital cohabitation, greater acceptance of parenthood outside marriage, increasing numbers of women in work and the influence of high divorce rates. The high marriage rate in Britain could also be due to the high rate of remarriages (in 1971 one in five marriages was a second or subsequent marriage compared with 36% of remarriages in 1991). Another factor which could influence the reduction in marriage rates is the cost of the wedding, which on average in South East England can amount to approximately £8,000 per marriage.

There is a radical change in the way marriage as a research subject is currently treated by social scientists. The traditional approach of looking at marriage as an institution has been changed to looking at marriage as a relationship. This change in the scientific approach to research in marriage has not been matched by the perception of marriage by the partners, who still tend to think of marriage as a desirable institution.

Another reason for the drop in marriage rates could be the increased rate of cohabitation. Of the couples marrying today, 58% have lived together before marriage. This has also been reflected in the number of births occurring outside marriage, which in 1992 was over 30%. There have been some indications of the relationship between cohabitation and divorce. In the UK, couples who married in the 1980's after having lived together were shown to be 50% more likely to divorce within five years of marriage.

It can be predicted that four out of ten marriages are likely to end in divorce. Research into divorce used to look at the type of person whose marriage was most likely to end in divorce, whereas now it is realised that modern marriage as such is the problem. The risk factors likely to cause divorce are listed as: marriage under 21; divorced parents; living together before marriage; if it is a second or subsequent marriage; and if the couple are in social class four and five. Most divorces occur between five and nine years after the wedding, and 72% of divorce petitions are filed by women. In the UK, the average age of divorcing men is 38 and divorcing women is 36 years of age. The trend, however, is that divorces are occurring earlier and earlier in marriage. The greatest increase has been in marriages lasting between 0 and 2 years. The legal reasons given for divorce in the UK are, in most cases, "irretrievable breakdown", which must include one of these five preconditions: adultery; unreasonable behaviour; two year desertion; two year separation with consent from the respondent; five year separation with or without consent. The most predominant factor quoted by women is "unreasonable behaviour", whereas by men it is most likely to be "adultery". Adultery was in 1990 responsible for 38% of divorces. This is due to the fact that 86% of British people rate being faithful as very important for a successful marriage and 83% say that extra marital affairs are always or nearly always wrong. This information relates to cases of adultery known to both partners, whereas there is no reliable information about the frequency of undetected adultery. A confidential study came up with an estimate that anything between 25% and 75% of married people have had an extra marital affair at some time in their lives. There is also some evidence that this is more likely with cohabiting partners than with married ones. There is also some evidence that not all detected adulteries lead to divorce. There is a difference between men and women in their reaction to the occurrence of adultery, although one should differentiate between the use of "adultery" as a reason for divorce and the actual prevalence of the event.

There is growing evidence that men and women often regret their divorce. One study showed that half of the men and one third of the women would have preferred to stay married and 10% of divorced couples stated that they both regretted it. One reason for this may be a very low percentage (2%) of married couples who seek help from a marriage guidance counsellor in the case of marital problems. They are more likely to seek help from their immediate and wider social environment, which does not necessarily contribute to saving the marriage.

Divorce has been seen as having a serious impact on the health of divorced couples, as well as on their children. A study of the stressful events caused by disruption showed that divorce is top of the scale compared to other event such as separation, change in financial status, children leaving home, trouble with in-laws, change in living conditions, etc. Divorce has also been found to be a very costly event for the people involved, their employers and the state. In 1992, £3.4 billion was spent as a direct consequence of divorce, including welfare payments, legal costs, health care, absenteeism, expense of moving house, and cost of running two separate homes..

Parents and Children

In many cases the children are a part of a "four parent" family with stepfathers and stepmothers included, or they may live in a one-parent family, with, for example, an independent and self-sufficient mother, spending the week with the mother and the weekend with the father. Children learn to cope with this conflicting situation by manipulating the two systems.

Disruption of the family, as an environment in which children grow up and are socialised into existing values and norms, has been linked to the growing crime rate among children. In addition to a few well publicised cases of murder and even rape committed by children, the number of small crimes is on the increase (Miles, 1994). The number of youth crimes has soared by 54% in the last 10 years, a large proportion of which is stealing and damage to property.

There has been a noticeable fall in the number of children born per woman in the UK (Mattison et.al, 1994), from 2.43 in 1971 to 1.80 in 1992. The event of parenthood affects marriage in a number of ways and is experienced differently by men and women. In both cases, marriage satisfaction drops during the period of pregnancy and early parenthood. The effects of these changes can be reduced by improving communication and increasing the support from family and friends.

The relationship between parents and children is affected by the increased probability of employment among women with children. This fact, however, does not change the expectation that women should carry the main share of household tasks. It has been noted that women spend 34 hours per week on shopping, cooking and cleaning whilst men spend only 13 hours on average. Even in households where both partners work women usually carry the main share of housework. This implies that women in full time jobs have 10 hours less leisure time per week compared to men. This does not change when women are not employed, since they use that time for household tasks.

Society in general is showing concern for the problems associated with childhood and children. The UN Convention on the Rights of the Child represents an attempt to improve the lifestyle of children, which is at present threatend by the existence of child labour, homeless children, child abuse, and children as war victims.

In the UK, the Government is attempting to solve some social problems with a number of Charters which define the legal rights for various population groups. Within the Citizen's Charter the Government has published the "Parent's Charter" (DoE, 1994) which states the legal rights of parents in the area of children's education. The Charter set the standards as:

- new rights to information on how schools are performing;
- better arrangements for inspecting them;
- clear National Targets for Education and Training - for schools and colleges, employers and the Government.

The choice available to parents has also been expanded such as:

- new types of schools;
- more rights for parents; improvements for parents of children with special needs;

The National Targets are concerned with the improvements in children's educational achievements and emphasises the right of every child to have a free of charge access to a school between 5 - 16 and a college place between 16 - 18 years of age.

The parent's right to information includes:

- a report about the child;
- regular reports from independent inspectors;
- performance tables for all the local schools;
- a prospectus about individual schools;
- an annual report from the school's governors.

While at school, the child has a right to a broad and balanced education based on the National Curriculum. The child will be tested at the ages of 7, 11 and 14 and will be awarded certificates of achievement. The Charter makes provision for maintaining discipline in schools with appropriate punishment for bad behaviour. The parents have a right to influence the way a school is run and have access to complaints procedures if something goes wrong.

A formal statement of the rights of parents in relation to the education of their children has helped to clarify many areas of potential conflict and has laid the responsibility squarely on the parents' shoulders.

The new UK educational opportunities have, however, been better utilised by girls than by boys (Hymas et al. 1994). The trend of empowerment of women and their self-sufficiency has been reflected in the opinions and achievements of school children, when boys and girls are compared. The girls, especially in single-sex schools, have achieved better results than boys at all age groups and in most of the subjects, some of which have in the past been considered as a male domain. At present there is a major problem in education concerned with how to deal with underachieving boys who make the majority population in special educational units dealing with persistent truants and underachievers.

Health Issues

The changes in the numbers of people, in their living and working conditions, and in the values and norms which regulate their lifestyle have also been reflected in the changes in disease patterns in a population.

One of the most spectacular changes accompanied the population explosion in the early 19th century in Britain, when the population increased from under ten million in 1801 to twenty-three million in 1875 (Ministry of Health, 1966). This increase was paralleled by rapid urbanisation and industrialisation, with the resultant overcrowding in towns and high mortality from infectious diseases. In 1839 Farr showed that death rates in London were 50% higher than in rural areas. Further inquiries showed that death rates were not evenly distributed in the towns and that they were much higher for certain parts of London than others. Observations of the distribution of death rates brought about a better understanding of the spread of infectious diseases; the original blanket assumption that it was due to the overcrowding and unhealthy living conditions in towns as compared with the "healthy" life in the countryside gradually gave way to the assumption that the main blame lay on bad housing conditions in towns. The result was the development of public health services, which focused on the building of sewer systems, water supply, sanitary facilities, food control, isolation of patients and vaccination against smallpox. It also prompted local authorities to spend vast amounts of money on rehousing people from slum areas.

These sanitary measures reduced the death rates to a certain extent, but the rehousing schemes did not meet with the expectations. In 1933, M'Gonigle (1936) carried out a survey among 710 rehoused inhabitants in Stockton-on-Tees, comparing them with those who stayed in their old houses. He found an increase in deaths from infectious diseases (measles, bronchitis, pneumonia) as well as heart conditions among the rehoused population. This finding shook the belief that bad housing is the main cause of higher death rates in towns and suggested that the main cause was poverty. The rehoused people were faced with increased expenditure on furnishing and keeping up with the higher standards of the new environment. Today, however, London has a lower infant mortality rate than Wales and the North, a fact which brings us full circle in the distribution of higher mortality rates: from rural to urban areas, from the residential areas of a town to slums, thence back to rehousing areas and finally being located in the rural areas of the under-developed parts of the country.

Discoveries of the causes of infectious diseases and the ways of preventing them resulted in the rapid development of preventive medicine and public health. Although a large part of the problem of high death rates could be got under control by legislative measures and public works (for example, through improved water supplies and sewage systems), further advance depended on such measures as vaccination. It soon became obvious that public participation in vaccination and people's allocation of limited financial resources to improve nutrition depended on information, motivation and readiness for action on the part of the individual as well as on the nature of his social environment. This realisation resulted in the development of health education as a part of public health and preventive medicine.

Another important aspect of the rapid change in medicine was the shift in the causes of morbidity in the present century, from infectious to chronic disease, that is, from diseases strongly influenced by social conditions to diseases largely dependent on individual behaviour. There were many reasons for this, including the discovery of the causes and the consequent successful treatment of infectious diseases, the raising of general standards of living, the provision of adequate community health facilities, better medical care for ill people. These developments resulted in the steady lowering of death rates for such diseases as tuberculosis, pneumonia and enteritis, while there was a steady increase in death rates from such diseases as coronary heart diseases, cancer in general and lung cancer in particular. This implies that whereas, previously, preventive medicine was concerned with mobilizing the support of large segments of the population in communities for various sanitary measures, it became more concerned with the behaviour and actions of individuals, through trying to influence their living habits, diet, smoking patterns, and lifestyle. The result has been a change of emphasis within the health education services from the widespread dissemination of information to an interest in individual decision-making.

This emphasis on the individual has also been due to a shift in responsibility for individual health. In the past, the uninformed individual reacted to symptoms of various diseases and then sought medical help, if and when available, or, on the other hand received services such as the installation of running water or a sewer. Today, with the vast amount of information about risk factors and early signs, he/she is supposed to undertake certain actions long before the onset of obvious symptoms such as pain, a rash, or raised temperature. In other words, the doctor-patient relationship has greatly changed: we have today a health care delivery system offering services and advice, and a client population with full responsibility for seeking this help and advice as well as protecting their own health and preventing the occurrence of disease. From the point of view of health education, it has meant that the population should be informed about health threats and early signs of diseases, made aware of their susceptibility and told about ways of avoiding the dangers.

The often quoted change from infectious to chronic diseases has now been superseded by a return to infectious diseases, some of which are old and started to re-emerge, whereas others are new. Among the re-emerging old diseases are those associated with malnutrition and starvation, wars and atrocities associated with enemy activities and bad living conditions. Some new ones are associated with substance abuse and sexual practices. This changing picture of health threats challenges HP/HE to conduct interventions that are not only related to personal factors but also are strongly under environmental influences.

The Department of Health continues to endeavour to improve health care delivery. The Patients Charter which provides standards for the delivery of care and emphasises the rights of the patients (see Appendix 5) is an important aspect of the Charter movement.

The new situation has, however, not been matched by appropriate developments in social and behavioural sciences. There are no tested theories which would explain how people survive and cope with these new challenges and what mechanisms could be used for HP/HE interventions. In many cases HP/HE will not be able to afford to wait for other disciplines to come up with an answer. Thus, HP/HE practitioners are facing a challenge to develop their own theories and approaches for the purpose of meeting these new needs. These attempts are described in the next section.

The often quoted change from infectious to chronic diseases has now been superseded by a return to infectious diseases, some of which are old and started to re-emerge, whereas others are new. Among the re-emerging old diseases are those associated with malnutrition and starvation, wars and atrocities associated with enemy activities and bad living conditions. Some new ones are associated with substance abuse and sexual practices. This changing picture of health threats challenges HP/HE to conduct interventions that are not only related to personal factors but also are strongly under environmental influences.

The Department of Health continues to endeavour to improve health care delivery. The Patients Charter which provides standards for the delivery of care and emphasises the rights of the patients (see Appendix 5) is an important aspect of the Charter movement.

The new situation has, however, not been matched by appropriate developments in social and behavioural sciences. There are no tested theories which would explain how people survive and cope with these new challenges and what mechanisms could be used for HP/HE interventions. In many cases HP/HE will not be able to afford to wait for other disciplines to come up with an answer. Thus, HP/HE practitioners are facing a challenge to develop their own theories and approaches for the purpose of meeting these new needs. These attempts are described in the next section.

Implications for HP/HE

One of the most promising developments for the future of HP/HE has been the change in the political climate concerning health in general and HP/HE in particular, as one of the ways to improving it.

These changes can be traced on the international level through the new policies and strategies promoted by WHO, in the form of conferences, workshops and expert committee meetings and seriously facing the problems of increasing HP/HE effectiveness, efficiency and accountability.

In the UK, this political change has taken the form of the Government's commitment to HP/HE, expressed in a number of documents and charters. The reorganisation of the NHS reflects this new interest in HP/HE, demonstrated by the provision of resources to pay the members of the NHS for their HP/HE work.

This new opportunity has been met by increased efforts of the HP/HE services to improve their methods and increase their participation in a multi-sectoral approach to the improvement of people's health. Such efforts as a change of emphasis from problems to settings seems promising but needs to be evaluated to see whether all the optimism and expectations will be realised.

NEW DEVELOPMENTS IN GENETICS

Recent important changes in the science knowledge base for health promotion and health education have been associated with the developments in genetics and the resulting understanding of the causation of diseases (Watson, 1968, Harsanyi & Hutton, 1983 Brown, 1989, Dawkins, 1989, Jones, 1993;). This has changed existing concepts, differentiating between environmental and personal factors contributing to illness, by accepting that the contribution of each factor varies. In some diseases the environmental factors are dominant, whereas in others personal factors, including genetic makeup, predetermine the presence or absence of the risk from a disease.

Historical Events

The present dramatic changes in genetic science represent a qualitative change in the knowledge base of the study of human reproduction and inheritance. There is no doubt that humans have for a long time been aware of the close resemblance of offspring to their progenitors, although in some societies the link between sexual intercourse and conception was not recognised. The domestication of animals allowed for greater understandding of selective breeding. There was, however, a long time gap between the awareness of the contribution of both sexes to the process of reproduction and the full understanding of the process. Greek philosophers were very interested in the inherited characteristics that later formed the basis of the studies of heredity. Explanations were linked to the existing knowledge about the human body and reproduction. Later advances in the understanding of heredity were hampered by the idea of "spontaneous generation", propagated in the Middle Ages, which assumed that living organisms could arise spontaneously or even from non-living matter. This came to be rejected in 17th century following an experiment, with two jars with pieces of raw meat, of which one was sealed and the other open to flies. Only the open one produced worms, as one would expect today, whereas then it was a sensational discovery.

The discovery of the microscope enabled scientists to see things that could not be seen with the naked eye. One such discovery was the human sperm, although it took another 200 years before the female egg was observed, which is not surprising since it is microscopically small and relatively rare in a female. These important discoveries did not, however, contribute to the understanding of the laws of heredity.

It fell to a monk, Gregor Mendel, to lay the foundations of modern genetic sciences by deriving the basic principles of inheritance from his breedinng studies of peas. In 1860, Mendel the identified "genes" as carriers of specific characteristics; each gene has two alleles, one of which is dominant and the other recessive; and Mendel was able to see the relationship between presence of forms of genes and how they were expressed externally (genotype and phenotype), which can be described in mathematical laws of combinations through generations. In Mendel's view: 1) hereditary traits are governed by genes and do not blend together; 2) one allele of a gene may be dominant and the other recessive; 3) each adult organism has two copies of each gene, one from the mother and one from the father; 4) different alleles are distributed in the sperm and egg randomly. These laws of heredity , although important made little impact and had to be subsequenly rediscovered by Morgan (1900).

The invention of the microscope enabled scientists to observe things not seen by the naked eye. With the widespread scientific use of the microscope there were practically daily discoveries of new organisms, such as bacteria and among others also the composition of the sperm and the composition of the human cells. Looking at a cell through a microscope one could see the nucleus and in it the chromosomes. Reproduction happens when cells divide. During that process chromosomes duplicate and divide, with the copies becoming a part of the new cell. This cell division is called mitosis, and each cell receives exactly the same number of chromosomes. Cells of different species have a different number of chromosomes (for humans 23 from the mother and 23 from the father, i.e. a total of 46 chromosomes; a mosquito has 6, a cabbage 18, a dog 78, a cat 34, etc.). Sperm and egg cells have only half of the chromosomes called gametes. When they combine they produce a complete cell with 46 chromosomes, which are matched so that they form 23 homologous pairs.

Understanding of the behaviour of chromosomes concentrated the attention once again on heredity and Mendel's laws. Scientists repeated the experiments and obtained similar results. They linked the idea of chromosomes with that of genes and decided that each chromosome must have a great number of genes to carry all the instructions necessary for forming a complex organism. Each human cell has two sets of chromosomes; homologous pairs of chromosomes were actually seen and thus became actual physical objects instead of the abstract qualities that had earlier been used to explain hereditary qualities passed from one generation to another.

Historically speaking (Connor, 1994b), it took some time before the understanding of heredity was linked to chromosomes. Despite Mendel and Horner, a Swiss Ophthalmologist, who showed in 1876 that colour blindness is inherited, work on chromosomes in 1880s was not linked to inheritance. Morgan, who had repeated Mendel's research, went on to show in 1911, that genes are strung along chromosomes and are the agents of inheritance. In the same year, Wilson discovered that the gene for colour blindness lies on the X-chromosomes. This was the first success in mapping the place of a gene within a chromosome. In 1927, Muller demonstrated that genes can mutate if exposed to x-rays.

Discoveries continued and increased knowledge of the mechanism of inheritance. In 1944, Avery showed that genes are made of DNA and not proteins. Although Herrick, in 1910, discovered the disease sickle-cell anaemia, it was Pauling, who was able to show that sickle cell anaemia is a molecular disease arising from a defect in the structure of haemoglobin.

DNA became a major interest for researchers. In 1950, Chargaff showed that DNA carries specific instructions for making proteins. These studies of DNA continued until, in 1953, Watson and Crick were able to construct the double-helix structure of DNA. Following this discovery, new research findings in this field accelerated, with new results being published every few years.

In 1959 a link between DNA and the synthesis of protein was established. This was experimentally achieved in 1960 by using the genetic code.

The success of genetic research depended to a large extent on the availability of technology necessary for studying DNA. In 1973, scientists assemble a "tool-kit" for cutting and splicing DNA in the test tube and became the basis for future genetic engineering. In 1979, Bodmer and Solomon first proposed the use of 'markers' to map human genes, in 1980 Sanger unravelled the chemistry of the DNA message.

The Present Situation

The most recent findings in the study of genetics have been developing unevenly. Whereas more is known about the chemistry of chromosomes and genes, their existing and potential behaviour is only partly understood. The traditional model of the genetic mechanism has been replaced by a dynamic model which shows many strange properties of genes.

Rennie (1993) has summarised the new developments which continue to unfold. The traditional model was simple inasmuch as it recognised the basic processes of DNA replication, which included the transcription of DNA into messenger RNA, which in turn translated the information into a peptide. The dynamic model of replication is more complex and includes the reorganization of DNA, transcription and reverse transcription resulting in the primary RNA transcript, which when processed produces an alternative splicing product, an edited RNA product and the messenger RNA, which is translated into a peptide. Another interesting discovery has been the 'jumping' gene, or the ability of genes to change locations on the DNA through the influence of certain environmental factors. This change of location can also occur if some genetic material is transmitted from one DNA to another. This type of 'jumping' genes represent a mutation, unknown until recently. Another mutation occurs when genes expand or balloon in size, with tragic consequences. Such mutations have been associated with some inherited forms of mental retardation, as well as with some forms of muscular dystrophy. The whole subject of mutations has become highly politicised through the discovery that environmental influences can influence mutations as a part of the natural selection process. This 'directional' mutation has raised many questions and is highly controversial, although it has received support from some existing research in this field. Added to all this, the processes of 'splicing', 'editing' and other processing that occurs in the transmission of instructions suggests that the process is highly complex and that new aspects will continue to be discovered. The conclusion must be that there is still a lot more to be learned and that the genetics' story is only at its beginning.

One could summarise the present situation as representinng a highly volatile field of rapidly increasing knowledge about genetics in general and the role the genetic makeup plays in the health of individuals. This new knowledge, due to its rapid development, does not allow for the ensuing problems to be accompanied by institutionalised solutions. In such a situation the role of health promotion and health education is very difficult. The question is whether people in general have a right to be informed about this new knowledge even if there are no institutionalised norms which would indicate how this knowledge can be used in daily life. This problem is even more acute if one takes into consideration the ever increasing number of applications of this knowledge in daily life, as can be seen from following chapters.

Mapping the Genetic Code

The most significant advance that will have direct effects on health educatioon and health promotion is gene mapping.
The great investment of scientific and financial resources as well as the respectability of the subject matter (demonstrated by the number of Nobel Laureates) has made mapping the genetic code big business. This is in contrast to the doubts many people initially felt, in view of the so-called "science" of eugenics, based on misunderstood genetics, which underpinned genocide in Germany in 1930s. The international medical community is now aware of the importance of this subject for genetic engineering as well as the early discovery and treatment of a number of diseases for which so far there had been no cure. In 1984, Robert Sinsheimer proposed the establishment of an institute with the enormous task of "reading" all

the 50,000 to 100,000 genes or 3 billion letters of the human genetic blueprint. This idea became reality in 1989, with the establishment of the Human Genome Project under the directorship of Dr James Watson the co-discoverer of the DNA structure for which he and Dr Francis Crick received a Nobel Prize. The task of the Human Genome Project has been to map all the estimated 100.000 human genes by the year 2005. An amount of $3 billion has already been allocated and the work is being carried out by a number of scientific institutions and universities, making it a true international effort.

The general idea that this project is too important and too large to be limited to one institution led to widespread international cooperation, many institutions and many scientists becoming involved in the search for links between certain human characteristics and the genetic makeup of the individuals. The early idealistic view soon became contaminated by the vested interests of countries and individuals, arising from the enormous power and commercial benefits from controlling such discoveries. Consequently, the question of patenting the discoveries was raised and at present many patents have been registered in different countries.

In the early days mistakes were also made by certain scientists. A good example is the British discovery of a process that led to the development of a diagnostic testing procedure used universally in immunological diseases. In 1975, the MRCs Caesar Milstein discovered the monoclonal antibody process, which they did not patent. This was later patented in the USA with profits of hundred of millions of dollars which have served to finance their biotech industry. In 1992, this issue caused Dr Watson to resigne from the Genome Project having been accused of conflicting interests, since he was both the Director and held shares in biotech industry.

At present the research is continuing but participants are said to be protecting their interests by publishing the results of research in scientific journals which recognise the authorship of the researchers who in turn are patenting their discoveries. An interesting practice has been "protective patenting", where sequences of DNA are patented although there is no knowledge about their role, in case one day something of interest will be discovered on that sequence. This also jeopardised the data base that would include all the information about genes so far, which should be constantly updated with new discoveries. Since the British Medical Research Council has so far patented more than 2000 sequences of human DNA, Italy, Germany and France have refused to include their research findings into the British data base (New Scientist, 11.4.1992). This practice has been condemned by the Human Genome Organization and a number of governments, but the MRC is taking this course because the National Institutes of Health in the USA are.

The Genome Project

To understand the enormous task lying ahead of the researchers involved in mapping the genetic code (The Genome Project) it may be useful to remind ourselves that each chromosome has a full set of genes (approx.100,000) which entail all the information necessary for building a human organism.

Although each chromosome has a full set of genes not all of them are activated which enables the differentiation of genes associated with different cells in the body (cells of the brain, the bone, the liver, the muscle, etc.) Each gene has a whole set of components (thousands of them) which define the character of the gene. Only recently a British and an American scientist (Roberts and Sharp) received the 1993 Nobel Prize for Medicine or Physiology for their discovery of "DNA junk", i.e. that about 90% of the DNA does not produce any proteins, does not, therefore, send any messages and can be considered as junk.

At present there are very few genes which have been directly associated with a disease (such as sickle cell anaemia) and in most cases only the gene products, such as proteins, can be associated with certain diseases. These are called "markers" and it is hoped that ultimately the Genome Project will identify markers for all the 6.000 diseases for which there is some evidence about their genetic associations. This can, however, only be achieved by breaking the code of all the genes in a human chromosome.

This very cursory description of the way the genes operate and the way they will eventually be coded should help the understanding of what is involved and what can be expected from the Genome Project. The genetic makeup of an individual can either be the cause of a disease (e.g. cystic fibrosis) or a predisposing factor which can bring about a disease if triggered off by certain external factors (e.g. certain cancers). The outcome of this genetic work will be revolutionary for medicine in all its aspects and will redefine the existing role of health promotion and health education.

Genetic Screening

The result of the new insight has been the development of methods for genetic screening. This is expected, ultimately, to make possible the classification of a high risk population and explain the relationship between environmental, behavioural and genetic factors as contributors to certain diseases and health threats. It will also enable an individual to obtain his/her own genetic profile and be aware of the personal risks as well as the risks for their progeny. At present, hundred of markers have been identified as being associated with certain diseases and this number is rapidly growing, with new markers being discovered on practically a monthly basis.

Genetic Treatment

As one would expect, once a person with a genetic fault has been identified, the next question is what can be done about it. This has resulted in the development of genetic treatment which consists of exchanging the faulty gene with a "normal" one.

In his article Wilkie (1992) describes such a procedure applied, in 1990, to a 4-year old girl in Cleveland, Ohio. She received, by transfusion, a gene transplant to correct a dangerous flaw in her immune system known as severe combined immune deficiency (SCID). Her prospects were limited due to the danger of dying from any of the many possible infections. There is, at present, also the hope that a similar procedure will be possible for the sufferers of cystic fibrosis, for which the responsible gene was identified in 1989. The tests of transplanting genes in animals with such a condition have been successful.

In the UK a similar case has been reported by Hall (1993) when Doctors at Great Ormond Street hospital, London carried out a gene transplant on 8 months old Carly Todd from Lennoxtown near Glasgow who is suffering from a deficiency of the immune system resulting in the system not producing the enzyme Adenosine Deaminase or ADA necessary for the full development of the immune system. Without it Carly is vulnerable to all infections which a normal baby would be able to fight off. Carly's brother had already died from the same condition.

Genetic Engineering

Genetic treatment is an aspect of genetic engineering, which through manipulating genes alters the genetic makeup of a person. The attraction of genetic treatment lies in its simplicity (Newell, 1990). Dr Jon Wolff of the Department of Medical Biochemistry at the University of Wisconsin discovered a simple way of introducing new genes into a human body by simply injecting the new genetic material into the muscle of the patient. The body takes care of correcting the genetic shortcomings causing certain diseases or sensitivity to some diseases.

Genetic engineering has other aspects, includingis the creation of new, or the modification of, certain strains in a species. Americans have developed four new strains of mice. The first one is known as the "oncomouse" patented by Harvard University. It is susceptible to cancer and useful for studies of that group of diseases. Other mice strains develop enlarged prostate glands, cannot develop a fully functional immune system, or produce beta interferon a virus attacking protein. in their milk.

Genetic Fingerprinting

The possibility of identifying the genetic makeup of a person has also led to genetic fingerprinting which is based on the fact that each person has a unique genetic makeup. This method of identifying persons by their genetic profile has many applications, as in detection of crime and identification of culprits, in paternity suits as well as in developing a data base of each person's susceptibility to certain diseases. The technique developed by Jeffreys, professor of genetics at Leicester University, has been applied in a number of court cases (especially in case of rape) and helped in the identification and conviction of the culprit This method has more recently been challenged by a number of scientists who question the level of probability attached to the guilt of the accused which can differ according to the statistical method used.

Another reason for questioning the validity of genetic evidence in courts is due to the reliability of the tests used. Lightfoot (1994) reports on the quashing of the conviction of a rapist accused of raping two Manchester students on the strength of genetic evidence produced by a private firm who bought the patent for the procedure and is engaged in genetic fingerprinting. The problem arose when the laboratory used a special gel for its tests. The success of this appeal may open the floodgates for questioning the convictions of more than 600 people a year, as the result of these tests.

The level of reliability of genetic fingerprinting for the purpose of medical records raises a number of ethical and legal questions. Labelling a person as carrying a predisposition to a certain disease may influence that person's chances of getting a desired education, a preferred job, getting married and having a family, getting insurance cover, etc. All this could happen to a person who appears at the time to be perfectly healthy and normal in every respect.

This outlook opens a new perspective for health promotion and health education and gives a new meaning to their methods of enabling, advocating and mediating. Some of the relevant issues are presented in the following chapter.

The Law and the Ethics

The explosion of knowledge related to genetics has already raised new problems. The urgent need to solve these problems becomes obvious if one takes into account the fact that the knowledge is the basis for a multi-billion dollar industry which needs to be regulated. At present, there are various bodies that deal with the legal and ethical aspects of the consequences of spreading and implementing this new knowledge including the Nuffield Council on Bioethics and the Brussels based Senior Advisory Group on Biotechnology. Some of the topics being considered are:

- the ownership of and the right to use the new discoveries, i.e. the position of a gene on the DNA chain which is associated with a certain disease or health risk;
- the ownership of the procedures and technology for research, screening and engineering of genes;
- the ownership of information resulting from screening and testing for the purpose of developing a genetic profile of an individual, including the right to use such information and the duty to disclose it;
- the right to have access to genetic interventions related to eugenic issues such as sex, appearance, intelligence, artistic abilities and any other characteristics which will be without any doubt discovered to be genetically influenced;
- the right to develop new organisms by genetic engineering, the utilisation of the same and their release into the environment;
- the stakeholders' share in the profits from marketing the genetic information and interventions;
- the existence and ownership of a local, national and international data bank of genetic information on individuals and populations;

Ethical questions have already been prompted by this new knowledge. There is, however, no general agreement about who should provide the answers, or even who should control the provision of answers and related decisions. Some of the issues have already emerged and many more will emetge in the future, such as:

- testing before marriage and disclosure of genetic information to the spouse;
- the testing of the unborn child and the right to abort it in case of a genetic problem;
- the testing of people for insurance purpose;
- the requirement of a genetic profile when applying for as job;
- the right to disclose genetic information by the doctor or some authority;
- the duties related to the disclosure of information by individuals;

In view of the way the situation is at present developing, there is no doubt that different countries will produce legislation to regulate the whole field of genetic research, technology, information and all the different aspects of its application. All these legal and ethical questions will, however, be shaped by the interests of an international multi billion dollar industry and may not be what the world needs.

A major concern already is that genetic screening will produce a new 'underclass' of people who are not suitable for certain jobs or who have a higher than average risk from specific diseases. They may be excluded from the normal economic activities or discriminated against in terms of marriage and having children. This type of screening is already being carried out in the USA (Trofimov,1993), and the fear is that it will soon spread into Europe.

Patenting the Discoveries

Closely related to the legal and ethical issues of the results of new genetic knowledge is the question of ownership implied by patents. It gives a person the exclusive right to royalties from anyone who wishes to use such discoveries.

A patent (Watts,1994) can be registered with respect to a specific discovery, for example the gene associated with cystic fibrosis (taken out by Universities of Michigan and Toronto). A patent can be registered on a sequence of DNA without knowing its exact function (protective patenting) or even on a whole chromosome (in USA a patent has been registered for the Y chromosome). Some of patents have been on parts of DNA without knowing exactly what their biological function is, whereas others have been registered on parts which are still under research without any knowledge what the outcome of such research will be.

Another area is the patenting of genetically engineered new organisms. Americans have patented four new strains of genetically engineered mouse.

The discussion about patenting new discoveries in the field of genetics was in the beginning limited to new technological inventions used in this field. The patenting of parts of the DNA which is now taking place may seem to be a subject for academic discussion until one realises what the practical implications are of such a practice. At present there are institutions that own certain genes in our bodies, and anyone who wishes to carry out research, or any other intervention on such a gene must pay royalty to the owners. Since most patents have been taken out by government institutions or commercial enterprises the question arises about the rights of the owners as well as about the possible misuse of such ownership. In conclusion one must say that the present dilemma related to patenting has resulted in many of the patents not being registered or still being the subject of litigation and appeals.

Implications for HP/HE

The increased knowledge about our genetic makeup and the association between certain genetic characteristics and diseases carries a clear message for the future role of health promotion and health education. The conclusion is that the former should concentrate on creating positive environmental (physical and social) conditions conducive to health maintenance and prevention and treatment of disease and health risks, whereas the latter should concentrate on individuals to enable them to understand the meaning of new knowledge and to cope with the consequences of their genetic makeup and the environment in which they live, and which has implications for their health and wellbeing.

Awareness

New developments in genetics, which have as yet not been fully understood or considered, will have enormous consequences for the practice of health promotion and health education. At present most of the information about the new developments is transmitted through the daily press, radio, TV and weekly magazines. The information presently transmitted can be differentiated according to the contents into a number of categories:

General information

One trend has been the transmission of general information about the meaning of genetics and the issues involved. There have been many introductions to genetics for laymen. Outstanding examples include the series of lectures on the topic in the 1991 Reith Lectures, given by Dr Steve Jones, from which his book on genetics emerged (Jones, 1993).

Another example was the Sunday Times Nobel Laureate lecture, given by Nobel Prize winner Dr Karry Mullis, a chemist from California, who had invented a method of replicating molecules of DNA (Ryan,1994). In his lecture he painted a rosy picture of the future, thanks to genetic discoveries which would not only help humans hopefully to banish all the 6.600 hereditary diseases, but would also be able to reproduce chunks of DNA material of famous people like pop stars and sell it to their fans. A more serious aspect of Dr Mullis's work was his discovery of the possibility of reproducing strands of DNA, which permitted the development of the HIV test, as well as techniques in forensic science to identify criminals, and the better understanding of evolution through the study of the migration of our ancestors. It also opens the way for genetic surgery for the replacement of defective genes.

Discoveries

A great number of articles in the media are devoted to reporting the most recent advances in genetic research. These articles have reported on discoveries or a better understanding of the association of certain genes with certain diseases and their location within the DNA (cancer in general, breast cancer, lung cancer, colon cancer, liver cancer, arthritis, HIV, Alzheimer's disease, asthma, Huntington's disease, cystic fibrosis, etc.).

Screening

Another topic of interest for the general population is that of screening for genetic disorders or sensitivities which could have profound consequences for their daily life. In addition to reports of new technology and methods of screening, the media have concentrated on the issues of ethics arising from such practices. One important aspect has been the right of insurance companies to require a genetic profile of a person before calculating the premium. The other has been the right of a person "not to know" their genetic profile or to have to disclose it to anyone. This could have implications for marriage and parenting, which are questions of ethics that need to be addressed by the society. The ability to screen an unborn baby for possible genetic defects raises the problems of abortion and the question of whose right it is to make such a decision.

Genetics and behaviour

The new discoveries in the field of genetics have not been limited to disease and health risks. Some researchers are expressing their concern about the final outcomes of the Genome Project, which is bound to come up with knowledge on the genetic anatomy of *human intelligence* (Wilkie,1992b). At present research has shown that levels of human intelligence are linked with breast feeding (Hunt, 1992) along with a large number of other environmental factors. If, however, there are genetic associations with intelligence and if one links it with the existing methods of pre-natal genetic tests, the future of a child's upbringing and education, if not survival, will be affected, even if one does not want to contemplate the more sinister aspects of eugenics or selective breeding of future generations. This goes beyond the old arguments of nature-nurture in human intelligence.

An even more controversial issue has been the report that scientists for the first time have hard evidence of a genetic basis for *homosexuality* (Connor, 1993a, 1994) located on the X chromosome which men inherit from their mothers linked to the sexuality of gay men. The reaction in the USA caused discoverer Dr Dean Hammer, at the National Cancer Institute in Washington to make a promise to fight against any testing of the population for a "gay-gene". This would be possible if he patents his discovery and does not permit anyone to develop a test for this trait.

The genetic base of behaviour has been further broadened by scientists' finding a specific genetic mutation associated with *aggression* (Connor, 1993b). Han Brunner, the leader of the research team at the University Hospital in Nijmegen, Holland, found that a defective gene seem to cause a build-up of natural chemical messengers in the brain of the male carriers which led them to overreact in an aggressive manner. Although the finding needs to be taken with great caution since it is based on the results of only one Dutch family where learning difficulties and bouts of aggressiveness have been diagnosed through several generations, other scientists believe that this finding could have important implications for future exploration of behavioural disorders in humans.

Drug abuse has also not escaped the attention of geneticists. A test through using human hair (Bennetto, 1994) has been commercially developed. It permits drug abuse within the last few weeks to be established, as compared with the urine test which is effective only for the last few days. It also distinguishes between different types of narcotics and when they were taken. The test has been available in the USA since the 1980s and has been used to check on addicts under treatment. In UK some companies have applied the test to their employees. The Tricho-Tech clinic based at the Cardiff Medicentre plans to offer tests in sports and to meet any similar requirements.

Nutrition

The proposed new approach to nutrition, called "Genetic Nutrition" (Simopoulos et al., 1993) shows the impact of genetic research on human life style. Nutrition is a very important and popular topic for health promotion and health education and forms a part of any intervention associated with a number of diseases, of which coronary heart disease is one instance. The authors are critical of the existing "public health" approach, which is concerned with collective recommendations for the entire population and are in favour of a more selective, informed process that will take into account individual genetic differences related to the absorption and metabolising of nutrients and the expenditure of energy. They provide a method of assessing one's own "genetic heritage" by developing one's own medical family tree. This should indicate which diseases are not likely to develop because the genetic blueprint shows that they are not a part of the genetic makeup, and those that may develop because of genetic predispositions. It should also call attention to the real dangers that are programmed into the genetic blueprint, which will indicate the need for the prevention or postponement of negative consequences. .

Interpreting the news

On the one hand, there is a general optimism about the dawn of new predictive health care and on the other there are grave doubts about the practical meaning of the present state of research for people's health (Turney, 1994). The present argument is that owing to "sloppy reporting in the media...competition between scientists and the institutions that fund research; commercial promotion of gene testing", the public has difficulty in understanding the practical implications of the research findings concerning risk and the behaviour of genes. Turney refers to the case of the genetic base of breast cancer. When, in October 1990, Mary-Claire King (University of California, Berkeley) first engaged in this research, scientists knew of the existence and the rough location of the relevant gene, BRCA1. Due to the misconception that one gene causes a single disease, there is the danger that people will consider BRCA1 as *the* breast cancer gene. This is however only partly true. BRCA1, if not working properly, can cause cancer. A team led by Deborah Ford at the Institute for Cancer Research in Surrey, suggests that a woman carrying the altered gene runs a 80% risk of breast cancer before the age of 70. If argument is now turned around and examined from the point of view of the incidence of breast cancer, then only 5% of cases are caused by a faulty gene inherited from the patient's parents and only half of these are due to BRCA1. There are women with breast cancer who do not have the altered gene. The scientific explanation of this situation assumes that BRCA1 represents only one stage in a complex process leading to breast cancer. Thus, even when the BRCA1 gene is finally "discovered" it will require further research to untangle the processes of breast cancer development. Even if tests are developed to establish the risk, at this stage very little can be done to improve women's chances of survival.

THE NEW WHO APPROACH

Health in General

The definition of health agreed by the Member States of the World Health Assembly (1948), describing health as a *state of physical, mental and social wellbeing* and not just absence of disease, had mostly been disregarded until the Alma Ata Declaration (1978) revitalised it and drew the attention of the world to its full implications.

A brief summary of the relevant points agreed upon at Alma Ata are:

- health is a basic human right; it is the duty of each government to ensure a state of health for their people;

- the promotion and protection of the health of the people is essential to sustained economic and social development and contributes to a better quality of life and to world peace;

- health is the most important world-wide social goal; its realisation requires the coordination of many other social and economic sectors in addition to the health sector;

- people have a right and a duty to achieve health; the right should be expressed through community participation in health planning and management; the duty, through the acceptance of responsibility for one's own health;

- existing gross inequalities of the health status of populations, particularly between developed and developing countries as well as within countries have become politically, socially and economically unacceptable, and the situation, therefore, is of common concern to all countries;

- primary health care is the key to attaining this target as part of a development in the sphere of greater social justice.

The Alma Ata Declaration states that the goal of all the member countries should be the achievement of *"Health For All By The Year 2000"*. The World Health Organisation undertook the task of developing a Global Strategy and Regional Strategies as guidelines to member states to enable them to develop their own national strategies and undertake the necessary actions to do their best to ensure the achievement of the stated goal. The achievement of this goal includes measures for health promotion, disease prevention, diagnosis, therapy and rehabilitation.

Defining health as one of the basic human rights and charging the government with ensuring its even distribution raises a number of questions which have to be answered not only by the health care system but by all the other institutions in the country. For this purpose WHO emphasises the need for a *"multisectoral approach"* and provision of adequate *primary health care*. There is still some confusion in the interpretation of the meaning of primary health care and attempts have been made to differentiate between primary health care and primary medical care. Some interpret primary health care as the first contact with a health problem usually in the context of the family and followed by either self-medication or the decision to seek medical help by activating the primary medical care system. Others still interpret primary health care as the first contact with the medical services. To clarify this issue WHO produced a report of a Working Party on "Analysis of the Content of The Eight Essential Elements of Primary Health Care" (WHO 1981), which defines the four levels of primary health care:

- home level;
- communal level;
- first health facility level; and
- first referral level.

In terms of improving health the first two levels of primary health care depend on the "competence" of individuals and families to assess the situation appropriately and accordingly reach a decision followed by an action. The second two levels, which include the first contact with the health care system and being referred to specialist services deal with the availability and utilisation of the health care system and compliance with the prescribed behaviour within the framework of a legitimised sick or at-risk role.

Inequalities in Health (Education)

One argument, put forward (Baric, 1989), is that health education, as currently practised, is not a means of reducing inequalities in health, but, on the contrary, contributes to the perpetuation of such inequalities.

This paradox arises because of the general approach used in health education, which does not differentiate between the specific needs of various population groups. Although methods are used which aim to ensure that the message reaches all the population groups concerning most prevalent health problems, the contents are not necessarily appropriate for the needs of different population groups.

In most cases, health messages are constructed using logical arguments based on scientific data. This assumes that there is no difference in decision-making processes according to social class and educational level of the consumers. Thus, middle class values are often unthinkingly transmitted by middle class public relations specialists and health education agents.

Since this issue has not been raised so far, it has not been considered in the evaluation of existing health education interventions and there are no data which could support or disprove this assumption.

This highly charged concept of "inequality" is a visible or latent concern in almost all social programmes. The feasibility of creating equality is often taken for granted. In relation to inequalities in health as a specific field of common concern, the general interpretation is moderated by a number of qualifications.

The first qualification is that not all people are born equal in terms of health. Studies of congenital disorders (Carter,1976, pp.1-12) indicate that a percentage of newly born babies will have congenital disorders, which will reduce their life expectancy and quality of life if they survive. The second qualification is that, even if born healthy, not all the newly born babies will have an equal opportunity to stay healthy. Studies (Townsend et.al., 1982, pp.54,55) have shown considerable differences in disease prevalence and causes of death according to family background, geographical location, social class and educational level of the members of the family into which a child is born. The third qualification is that, when these children are adults, they will not have an equal opportunity of staying healthy and alive. Studies have shown that mortality and morbidity in a population are particularly influenced by the occupation, education and social class of individuals.

For example, the Black Report on "Inequalities in Health" (Townsend et.al. 1982, pp.41,55,206) examined this issue and stated that the best indicator of inequalities in survival and health is occupational class (social class). Using this indicator, the Report showed the differences between social class V (manual workers) and social class I (professionals) in morbidity and mortality as well as utilisation of health services. This difference exists for both sexes and all ages. A class gradient can be observed for most causes of death in favour of social class I. The Report ended with a statement that this inequality cannot be explained in simple terms and that it is the result of a complex interaction of many factors. The Report went on to produce a whole range of recommendations for measures necessary to reduce this inequality.

There are two distinctive issues here which need to be addressed. One is the improvement of people's health in general and the other is the reduction of inequalities in the rate of this improvement among different population groups. As the Black Report states, even when there is a general improvement in health these inequalities persist among different social classes.

At present, there is a differentiation between health promotion and health education. Since health is considered to be a function of external and personal factors, health promotion represents a mediating strategy between people and their environments, synthesising personal choice and social responsibility in health to create a healthier future (WHO,1984). Health education, on the other hand, is concerned with the raising of individual competence and knowledge about health and illness, about the body and its functions, about prevention and coping; with raising competence and knowledge to use the health care system and to understand its functions; and with raising awareness about social, political and environmental factors that influence health. The main difference, therefore, is not so much in the aims, but in the levels at which these are carried out (Baric,1985).

The current approach in health education is concerned with building up the self-reliance of people in looking after their own health, supported by the appropriate utilisation of health services. It depends heavily on cognitive models that postulate that people need accurate information to make an educated decision about their own behaviour and actions. If the decision is not appropriate then they are to blame. This "blame the victim" approach allows the formal health education system to abandon responsibilities for health in general as long as it is seen to provide information that is accurate, timely and accessible to everyone (evaluation of effort).

The present confusion concerning HIV, listeria and salmonella infections is a good example. The formal health education system is waiting for experts to define in each case the cause of infection so that advice can be published for people in general, with special reference to high risk groups. Once the publications have been distributed, the responsibility will be on individuals to follow the advice given. The present confusion is about the medical advice to be given (the contents) and not about the health education methods used to achieve the reduction of the infection.

The main reason for the perpetuation of inequalities in health by means of health education is not due to the methods used, but to the way the contents are being presented. The drafting of a message is usually based on the most recent medical knowledge about a health threat and its causation. The causation is mostly expressed in terms of probability whereas the solution is presented in absolute terms. Thus the contents, which usually include advice for behaviour modification or an action, are based both on the credibility of the scientific source and the assumption about the existence of consumer's "free choice" in selecting the "logical" way of reducing the risk or avoiding a disease.

There is a considerable amount of theoretical work which seriously questions these assumptions. The effectiveness of the advice given will depend on *the timing* of the message. Studies of the socialisation process (Baric et al., 1978) distinguish between the acquisition of knowledge and attitudes according to age groups and the character of the situation within which socialisation takes place. *The arguments* used in explaining the message will be differently perceived (Suchman,1965, pp.1-16) according to the social class and educational level of clients and in terms of their "cosmopolitan" or "parochial" orientation to the health services and the arguments used in the interpretation of the advice given. It has been shown that the interpretation of "scientific facts" is a learned skill and that people without advanced formal education depend more on the legitimation of information by the members of their social network than on "scientific" arguments. The description of the threat in terms of *probability* will also have different outcomes according to studies carried out in the field of people's behaviour in uncertainty. It has been shown that ordinary people, as compared to scientists, cannot accurately assess the given probability and use instead their personal feelings (faith, luck) as guidance for action (Baric,1979,pp.173-184).

Consequently, an evaluation of the existing methods and contents of health education messages should provide an insight into the perpetuation of inequalities in health by means of health education which treats the target population as a homogeneous group capable of understanding, accepting and operationalising the information provided.

The "Progressive" Approach

The recent political changes in Europe and some other parts of the World have created new demands on health promotion and health education, as a part of the general efforts to reintegrate Countries of Central and Eastern Europe (CCEE) with the rest of Europe. The problems inherent in these countries are poverty and deprivation, unemployment, lack of basic foods and commodities, disorganised infrastructure, inadequate health service and distorted values and norms. The extent of the problems has forced the WHO to shift the emphasis from health problems to people who have health and other problems. In the health promotion and health education jargon this is known as the shift from a "problem-based" to a "settings-based" approach. The acute character of the problems has resulted in the recognition of this imperative need to shift the emphasis from studying the problems to testing the solutions.

There is a current discussion about the best forms of help for the "new" Central and Eastern European Countries (CCEE). The assumption is that what they need are knowledge and skills in tested methods for a speedy solution of their problems, including new resources, improvements in existing ones as well as resocialisation of the population for coping with new values and social expectations. This is a very general description of their needs and is not easily operationalised. This is even more the case with new approaches being developed, which are shifting the paradigms related to health once again. The Alma Ata Declaration (1978) has stated that "health is a basic human right", which represents an important value orientation but is at the same time so general that it cannot be implemented in practice. In 1993, the US President Clinton presented to the Congress a health package which promised to take health care into the 21st Century. It took the Alma Ata Declaration a step further and states that not only health is a basic human right but that there is a right to *"universal health care"*. This was a proposed new addition to the American Constitution which at present pledges a right only to life, liberty and the pursuit of happiness. The slogans describing this new move stated for example "health care that is always there" and "health care from the cradle to the grave". It was described as a new "progressive and activist" approach (not to be confused with socialism) based on market forces and competition and at the same time providing security to everyone, but met with great opposition and had to be abandoned in its original form.

The consequence of the new WHO development will be the need to reappraise existing health promotion and health education approaches to fit the new system with its different values and institutions. A new *"progressive health promotion and health education"* approach may be widely accepted in the 21st century. It will require new research and the testing of new models, as well as retraining and resocialisation of many who have so far been involved in these activities or who should be involved as a consequence of this new approach.

Problems and Solutions

Existing practice in health promotion and health education depends, as we have seen, on etiological and epidemiological studies for the definition of problems combined with the application of generally accepted methods of solution. This has been shown to be inadequate in the present situation. There are many reasons for research and testing of new solutions and interventions, inlcuding:

- the demand for effectiveness and efficiency;
- the need to take into account ethical issues;
- the limitations due to available resources;
- the inclusion of new information and communication technologies;
- the professional involvement requiring theoretical justification for recommended procedures;
- the redistribution of resources in favour of studies concerned with the solutions;
- the accountability of the agents carrying out interventions, including monitoring, evaluation and auditing.

The best way to carry out this research and testing is through concentration on the settings approach.

The "Settings-based" Approach

The traditional approach so far has been to concentrate on a health problem and try to improve or solve it. Even when the intervention has been defined by location (e.g.North Karelia), the approach was still problem oriented (e.g. CHD).

This kind of "problem-based" approach has influenced the epidemiological and etiological studies that have produced data related to a specific problem (e.g. distribution of leukaemia in a population; distribution of lung cancer in smokers). The advantage of such an approach has been the easy access to epidemiological and etiological data for health promotion and health education interventions. The disadvantage of such an approach has been the inability to identify a target population for the intervention necessary for the solution of the problem. The compromise has been to select a problem and to limit the intervention to one population group (e.g. smoking in pregnancy). The limitations of such a compromise is that it requires constant readjustment of the target population as the insight into the epidemiology of the problem improves (e.g. AIDS and homosexuals, drug addicts, heterosexuals, the general population) or as the aetiology of the problem changes (e.g. CHD and cholesterol in diet).

The WHO answer to the new situation has been to change the emphasis from the traditional "problem-based" approach to a "settings-based" approach. This approach starts from a target population and plans interventions for a population in different settings relevant to that population:

- it recognises that any population group will have a number of health problems and, therefore, does not limit itself to one problem;

- it also accepts that the health problems present in that population group are the consequence of the functional relationship between the environmental and personal factors associated with that population;

- it considers the interaction between these two groups of factors as being reflected in the lifestyle of that population;

- it takes into account the fact that the different aspects of a person's lifestyle are associated with the different setting in which that person lives, reproduces, learns, works, utilises different services, enjoys leisure, etc;

- it treats each of these settings as a system which is characterised, for example, by a certain structure, norms, participants, communication, interaction and values;

- it recognises that each of these settings is a part of a wider systemand is interdependent with other parts of the system, in terms of providing services or mounting interventions.

The WHO Priorities

The WHO EURO defines its activities within the framework of the Ottawa Charter (see Appendix 1). Within this general framework, WHO EURO has been successful in supporting the development of the movement concerned with various health promoting settings. The present concern of WHO EURO is the support and initiation of the development of healthy public policies in member states, especially using the settings framework.

Implications for HP/HE

It is only now becoming obvious how radical are the methodological consequences of a shift from a problem based to a settings based approach in health promotion and health education. The consequence has been the emergence of an "organisational model", with implications for a focus on new partners in a health promotion interaction.

In the past, people working in health promotion and health education have been concerned with health problems, their management and prevention, and have had as their counterparts the members of the medical and paramedical professions. The health professionals associated with health problems are engaged in providing health care and in preventing diseases. In dealing with these health professionals, people engaged in health promotion and health education learned their language and accepted their value system. The application of this "medical model" included the concepts of treatment and care, of prevention and coping, of rights of the patient, and of purchasing services for "health gain". Medical professionals have a code of conduct and a professionally controlled code of ethics which governs their relationship with the patients. The patients have certain rights and obligations, for example, as defined by the "Patient's Charter" (see Appendix 5). People engaged in health promotion and health education find themselves in a sensitive position when entering into this "doctor - patient" system and have to adjust their conduct to the ethics governing a medical intervention.

The switch from problems to settings has produced a new set of partners for people engaged in health promotion and health education. These new partners are the members of the management team in a "setting". They are the main decision makers, in a position to declare their setting as a "health promoting institution". They operate with a "management model" based on theories associated with the behaviour of organisations and behaviour in organisations, either explicity or implicitly. Managers have a different set of values and loyalties and a different language. Whereas the medical profession is motivated by the provision of services to clients (patients), managers are mainly concerned with the advancement of the interests of the organisations they manage. The interests of clients are once removed from the managers and become a consequence of the successful operation of the organisation which is being managed.

The shift from a "medical model" to a "organisational model" has had important implications for the methodology employed in health promotion and health education. The traditional methods employed in health promotion and health education interventions are also undergoing changes as a result of the new situation and new developments.

The method most commonly associated with a "medical model" is concerned with the amount and quality of population participation in interventions initiated and carried out by health care professionals. It is based on "community organisation", which is now better known as "community participation", and aims at regulating the relationship between the providers and consumers of health care. In its traditional form it postulates that the members of a community should be actively involved in any changes related to health (and any other community issue). This can be achieved by approaching the community through the "gate-keepers" or the "key-persons", who are expected to accept and promote the innovations in that community.

The community development model was first developed by agricultural extension workers in promoting innovations in agriculture and was initially applied in rural communities. Subsequently it was translated, with some success, to urban situations, where the agents of change went to a great length to establish the existence of "communities" (e.g. a high rise block of flats; a school; a factory; a deprived town district; etc.) equivalent to those in the rural situation.

The shift from communities dealing with problems to treating communities as settings that should accept and carry out health promotion has given the "community participation" method a new meaning. The traditional approach based on "gate keepers" is at present undergoing fundamental changes as the result of empirically collected knowledge and the changing world situation (Baric, 1990b). The change lies in the emphasis given to the role of the agents of change. It has been shown that "selling" programmes by external agents through "gate keepers" can produce short term changes, but without any lasting effect on that "community", and that any benefits are lost once the external agents withdraw their support from the "gate keepers".

The revised "community participation" approach based on an "organisational model" treats a community as an organisation and looks at its structure as well as at the function of the managers within that organisation. It has changed the emphasis from "gate keepers" supposed to be the natural leaders of a community to managers who are appointed and paid to run an organisation. One function of the managers is to provide a healthy environment for the members of that "community", to integrate health promotion into the policy and strategies employed in the running of that "community" and to enable networking with similar "communities" as well as to create "healthy alliances" with other "communities" (organisations) in that area. The members of that "community", with the help of the external agents, are expected to gain competence in improving their own life through change, in accordance with the organisation's accepted rate of change and the available resources.

THE ORGANISATIONAL MODEL

INTRODUCTION

The argument of the previous section is that the change from a problem-based to a settings-based approach in health promotion requires a shift from a medical to an organisational model.

A historical review of health promotion and health education shows the different changes that have occurred in the past. The most recent changes in health promotion have, however, been in the shift from a "problem" to a "settings" based approach. The result has been the development of the concept of a "health promoting institution" as the setting in which people live, work and play. In simple terms this means that *we look at a population within a particular setting and find out what kind of health problems they are exposed to and what kind of health needs they experience and deal with them by means of health promotion and health education.*

To be successful in applying a "settings" approach it is thus necessary to change the emphasis from a "medical" to an *"organisational"* model. This represents the structures and the functions of organisations or settings and provides a theoretical background for the understanding of individual activities within such "settings" or "organisations". A consequence of this innovation has been the need for people engaged in health promotion and health education to become acquainted with organisation theories, as well as with the set of values and language used by the members of such organisations.

This section represents an attempt to familiarise the reader with these new concepts, theories and terminology, which are a basic prerequisite for the successful introduction of health promotion and health education into these new settings. It distinguishes between the theories associated with organisations and theories associated with people's behaviour within organisations.

SETTINGS AS ORGANISATIONS

The settings in which people live, work and play can be of different kinds and different levels of complexity, from a nuclear family to an international corporation or a national army. All these settings can be defined as organisations, which *represent a social entity, recognised by its structure and functions.* A health promotion and health education intervention using a settings approach should, therefore, be aware of the main results of the study of organisations.

There are many definitions of an organisation, most of which agree in principle but differ in the emphasis given to various components. For example, Robbins (1990) states: *"an organisation is a consciously coordinated social entity, with a relatively identifiable boundary, that functions on a relatively continuous basis to achieve a common goal or set of goals".*

In other words, an organisation represents a group of people (social entity), who consciously coordinate their activities (management) for the achievement of common goals (function) on a more or less permanent basis. It is characterised by a set boundary which defines who is a member of that organisation and who is not. The relationship between members is defined by implicit or explicit contracts (norms) which represent the structure of that organisation.

The **structure** of an organisation is composed of statuses/roles associated with the goals (function) of that organisation. Status denotes a position within a structure, whereas a role denotes the performance of the incumbent of a status. In other words, status and role are two aspects of the same thing. The structure and the function jointly represent the "character" of an organisation. Depending on the type of an organisation, the structure will manifest different degrees of complexity represented by the number and arrangement of statuses/roles. It will involve different levels of formalisation of these statuses/roles, and it will differ in the degree of centralisation or decentralisation of power in that organisation. There are two main types of organisational structure: the vertical and the horizontal. A *vertical* organisational structure is more common and represents a model of "top management", "middle management" and the executive or work force. The *horizontal* model aims at simplifying the channels of communication by reducing the number of people in top management, excluding middle management where possible, emphasising the importance of the work force and allowing for a more direct contact between the decision makers and the decision executors.

The distribution of *statuses/roles* represents the "design" of an organisation which is undergoing constant changes according to the new demands and conditions affecting the achievement of an organisation's goals. It is a well known fact that the most common method of solving an organisational problem is by means of "reorganisation" or changes in the design, which may provide personal satisfaction to the management, and a feeling that something has been done about the problem without necessarily solving the problem.

Organisation as a System

Organisations represent a very attractive subject for study, especially since most of them are associated with commerce and industry and are, therefore, supported by ample financial resources. This is reflected in abundant literature on the subject (for example Robbins,1990; Dawson,1992; Scott, 1992; Kast & Rosenzweig,1985; etc.).

Historically speaking, it is possible to trace the evolution of approaches to the study of organisations according to the conceptual framework used by the researchers. Robbins (1990) uses the description of this evolution prepared by Scott (1978) and describes four distinct types of approaches:

Type 1 This conceives of organisations as mechanical devices to achieve goals. It concentrates on the achievement of efficiency in the internal function of the organisation; (main contributors were: Taylor,1911; Fayol,1916; Weber, 1947; Davis,1951).

Type 2 This conceives of organisations as closed systems and emphasises the informal relations and non-economic motives operating within organisations. Organisations are not thought of as well oiled and perfectly predictable machines. The informal associations, friendships and relationships are also important for success in achieving organisational goals; (main contributors were: Mayo,1933; Roethlisberger & Dickson, 1939; Barnard, 1938; McGregor,1960; Bennis,1966).

Type 3 This is based on rationality and sees organisations as a means of achieving certain goals. Size, technology and environmental uncertainty are seen as major factors on which a successful structure will depend; (main contributors were: Simon, 1947; Katz & Kahn, 1966; Woodward, 1965; Perrow, 1967; Thompson, 1967; Pugh, Hickson, Hinnings & Turner, 1969).

Type 4 This represents the current approach in which the social perspective is strongly represented, but within an open-system framework. Structure is not the result of management intentions, but an outcome of struggles for control within organisational coalitions. (main contributors were: March & Simon, 1958; Pfeffer,1978, 1981).

It has to be realised that there is no generally agreed upon classification of various research approaches and that each author will have a slightly different way of seeing the matter. For example, Scott (1992) suggests that one can recognise three different perspectives in studying organisations:

Organisations as rational systems

This view considers organisations as instruments for the achievement of specific goals, based on the technical or functional rationality of the structure, by organizing actions in such a way as to produce maximum efficiency in goal achievement. The language employed in such an approach includes such concepts as information, efficiency, optimisation, implementation and design. Another set of terms, such as constraints, authority, rules, directives, jurisdiction, performance programmes and coordination, indicate the cognitive limitations of decision-makers and imply that the rationality has clearly defined limits. Two main characteristics, are considered to make a contribution to the rationality of the organisational action, goal specificity and structural formalisation. This approach is characterised by a number of writers, including

Weber, who at the turn of the century was the earliest to develop a theory of bureaucracy and whose work was later translated from German into English (Weber, 1968); Taylor (1911), who wrote about scientific management; Fayol (1949) who produced an administrative theory; and Simon (1976) who produced a theory of administrative behaviour;

Organisations as natural systems

Theories using this approach look at organisations as collectives and accept the goal specificity and formalisation as characteristics which differentiate organisations from other types of collectives. They also emphasise the importance of some characteristics shared with all social groups, such as goal complexity and goal specificity. The achievement of goals depends not only on formal, but also on informal structures, and thus are affected by formal role descriptions as well as by the personal attributes which the members of an organisation possess. Some of the main contributors are: Mayo (1945) who represented the Human Relations School and carried out, the now classic "Hawthorne" experiments; McGregor (1960), who emphasised the difference between the rational system management theory (theory X) and the human relations approach (theory Y); Barnard (1938) examined organisations as cooperative systems; Selznick (1949) promoted an institutional approach emphasising the fact that organisations "have a life of their own", which needs to be taken into account; Parsons (1951) developed a social systems theory and defined the needs that an organisation must meet if it is to survive (adaptation, goal attainment, integration and latency).

Organisations as open systems

The concept of an open system implies that there is an interdependence between the organisation and the environment within which it operates and on which it is dependent. The systems approach to organisations examines them as *cybernetic systems* (including feedback as a self-regulatory mechanism); as a *loosely coupled system,* which means that some elements are weakly connected to others and are capable of autonomous actions; as *hierarchical systems,* which are a fundamental feature of complex systems and are defined by differences in status and power. The main contributions have been in the development of the *systems design* (for example Mintzberg 1979), in a pragmatic and applied way; and *contingency theory*, Galbraith (1973), which is based on two assumptions i.e. that there is no one best way to organize and that any way of organizing is not equally effective. Organisation depends on the environment within which it is carried out; the stress is on *information processing*, Weick (1969) developed a *social psychological model* of organising instead of a model of organisations; his emphasis is on organising through information processing. It tries to resolve the conflict between the open system perspective and individual participants and the relationships among them.

One should emphasise that these three perspectives are not exclusive, but coexist and build on each other. They are characterised by attempts to integrate them into more general approaches. Some contributors to this attempt are, for example, Etzioni (1964), who developed a *structuralist* model, trying to combine both the natural and the rational systems approach to the analyses of the central issue of power; and Thompson (1967), who tried to *integrate* the three perspectives within a "levels" model, by arguing that organisations strived to be rational, although they are natural and open systems.

Another summary of the various approaches to the study of organisations is given by O'Donnell (1992). He draws a distinction between *formal and informal* organisations, with special reference to bureaucratic organisations. In addition to traditional organisational theories, he mentions the *social action and interactionism theories,* which argue that it is important to realise that people seek to make their roles and activities within organisations as meaningful as possible. *Conflict* theorists raise issues of power, control, domination, exploitation, legitimation and various other forms of conflict, including class conflict. The latest approaches to the study of organisations include the tendency called "Thatcherism", a special attempt to introduce elements of the free market into the public sector and to strengthen managers at the expense of professionals.

The understanding of settings, through using the research findings concerned with organisations, can be enhanced by considering the enormous amount of research done on the *meaning of work,* as one of the main processes taking place within a setting. This area of study covers the various models and theories related to production within general political orientations such as capitalism, communism, post-capitalism, etc. O'Donnell also mentions various attempts to theorise about the experience of work, including the *social action* approach and the concept of *alienation.* The major issue, however, is *unemployment* and the role of *trade unions and strike actions.* Considerable attention is given to the development of professionalism and *professions,* including such criticism as that made by Illich (1975), a well known critic of professionalised knowledge, who maintained that often the professional ideology functions primarily in the interest of professionals despite its supposed concern with standards and quality of service. Another type of criticism comes from *feminist* ideologists who explore the exploitation and disadvantages of women in various working situations. Closely related to the study of work and unemployment, are the studies of *leisure* which some theorists consider to be highly influenced by work patterns.

Organisational Change

Organisations are a part of and operate within a world that is constantly changing. This implies that to survive and be successful, organisations must either be in a position to control the outside world or to adjust to the necessary changes (March, 1981). A common approach to organisational change is based on a cognitive model of decision-making which does not always apply in real life. The model of organisations as open systems seems to be more appropriate. Change within such a model depends on a number of *"imperatives"* in the management of change (Dawson, 1992), which include: elements of rationality and irrationality; relationship between decision and action; variable participation in decision and action from people in different position in the structure; and processes of learning and creativity.

Change effected in an organisation can be usually traced to a felt *"need"* by its members, which can be based on rational or irrational arguments. The rational arguments may be associated with the changes in the environment (market, technology, product image, etc.), whereas the irrational arguments usually reflect the wishes of the change agents who may believe that an organisational change may solve the internal problems facing the organisation.

There is, however, no doubt that the survival of an organisation will depend on its *adaptive powers* to meet the new situations. This is the area of interest of the many "organisational development" theories and practices (Clark and Krone, 1972) which have resulted in a variety of programmes addressing the topics of communication, problem-solving, decision-making and conflict resolution.

More recent work on changes in organisations is associated with the idea of organisational learning. The concept of a *"learning organisation"* (Pascale, 1990) treats organisations as open systems and is based on the assumption that, similarly to individuals, organisations can also learn. Organisations can be thought of as using the "experiential learning method" and thus, learn by doing, through experimenting and adjusting, through a feed-back mechanism that provides the management with indications about the outcomes of introduced changes. Schien (1985) advocates a "double loop learning" method, which, in contrast to the single loop learning method, is open to outside influences, involves participation of all members and encourages creativity. Once the importance of the organisational potential to learn has been recognised, a number of different learning approaches can be developed. The emphasis now is on open-minded, creative learning management styles.

In the light of the "Health Promoting Settings" there is a need to rethink the necessary organisational changes. Existing organisational changes could be sufficient in a setting where people intend to start some HP/HE activities, such as for example, to introduce the HP/HE subject matter into a school curriculum. The creation of a "Health Promoting Setting" will require more fundamental and radical changes in the structure, role definition and the culture of the organisation. This need has been recognised by management experts and there are at present new labels for radical new ways of managing change and coping with the restructuring of organisations. One such approach deals with the need to *"reengineer the setting"*. The idea of reengineering is having a big impact in industry. It represents a new development in organisational change (Hammer & Champy, 1993), and means starting over instead of tinkering with the system or making incremental changes. *"Reengineering is the fundamental rethinking and radical redesign of business processes to achieve dramatic improvements in critical, contemporary measures of performance, such as cost, quality, service and speed"*. Hammer and Champy published their ideas in the form of a "Manifesto for Business Revolution". The key word in their definition is "process". They suggest that the managers should concentrate on the process instead of the tasks, jobs, people and structures. This new approach has been adopted by a number of large companies (IBM Credit, Ford, Motor and Kodak) and seem to produce some visible advantages and results. The process aims to meet contemporary demands of quality, service, flexibility and low cost. Some of the characteristics of the necessary change are:

- several jobs are combined into one;
- workers make decisions;
- the steps in the process are performed in a natural way;
- processes have multiple versions;
- work is performed where it makes most sense;
- checks and controls are reduced;
- reconciliation is minimised;
- a case manager provides a single point of contact;
- hybrid centralised/decentralised operations are prevalent.

The outcomes of these changes result in the following:

- work units change from functional departments to process teams;
- jobs change from simple tasks to multi-dimensional work;
- people's roles change from controlled to empowered;
- job preparation changes from training to education; performance and compensation shifts from activity to results;
- advancement criteria change from performance to ability;
- values change from protective to productive;
- managers change from supervisors to coaches;
- organisational structures change from hierarchical to flat;
- executives change from scorekeepers to leaders;

All of this is possible because of the growth and application of information technology, which is envisaged not as an improvement in the existing ways of storing and retrieving information but as a revolution in utilising information for creative thinking and the management of organisations to create preconditions for continuous change.

There are various guides to practical application of these changes including the one that has been published by Morgan (1993) describing models for conceptualising the ways of achieving radical change. Morgan gives practical examples in the form of six different models which should enable a company to locate itself in one of them and apply the necessary steps for a radical change.

Another example of current innovations is promoted by the American guru Tom Peters (Golzen, 1994), who uses another notion of "virtual companies", borrowing the idea from "virtual reality". His idea for the future is a company model which is project-directed and fully concentrated on the process. It implies small flexible companies which will be able to fill niches in the market and will be dissolved once such needs have been satisfied. It will also imply a complete loss of any job security resembling construction companies, which employ workers for a project and have only minimal number of permanent staff. The idea of company loyalty will be replaced by professional loyalty to one's peers and colleagues, as in the film industry. The emphasis is on networking which will produce a list of experts for different jobs who can be selected if and when necessary. The problem of the great number of empty office blocks may be a blessing for the reduction of wasteful commuting. This approach to work is consistent with the ongoing transformation of work practices.

Organisational Goals

Other recent developments reflect the changes in social and cultural studies in Europe, defined as "post modernism". Theorist of post modernism challenged positivist conceptions and substituted interpretation for explanation. They have only just begun to turn their attention to organisations and available studies are limited.

This new conceptualisation builds on the work of Foucault (1977), Marcuse (1964), Habermas (1971), Derrida (1976) and Moi (1985). All approaches agree, however, that the main purpose of an organisation is to achieve some defined goals. Therefore, the concept of "organisational effectiveness" is considered to be the main concern of any organisation theory and a part of any study of organisations. In operationalising this concept, it is clear that the definition of "effectiveness" will depend on the indicators and criteria used. Researchers have used different approaches in the study of effectiveness, but overall they can be described in terms of four main approaches (Cameron, 1984):

Goal attainment. The indicator is the level of attainment of the set goals. It, however, requires specific and well defined goals which are measurable.

Systems approach The indicators are related to the processes associated with the acquisition of inputs, processing and producing outputs. It requires a causal relationship between inputs and outputs.

Strategic constituencies approach The indicator is the level of satisfaction of expectations of those constituencies in the environment on which an organisation depends for support and existence.

Competing values approach this groups the various indicators into three models: the human relations model (emphasis on a cohesive and skilled workforce); the systems model (emphasis on flexibility and ability to acquire resources); and the rational-goal model (emphasises the need for existence of specific plans and goals and high productivity and efficiency).

Since the choice of indicators and criteria will vary according to the individual who carries out the evaluation of an organisation, it is clear that the definition of "effectiveness" is subjective, although most definitions will include goal achievement, maintenance of the life cycle of the organisation and a successful relationship with the environment in which it operates and on which it is dependent. These would be part of an answer to the question whether an organisation is effective or not.

Organisational Structure

The question, *why* an organisation is effective is difficult to answer. The structure of an organisations is sometimes considered the most important factor affecting the effectiveness. The concept of the structure is like the blue print of a system. A structure is the way a whole is constructed including the supporting framework and the essential parts of that whole. In terms of organisations, Kast and Rosenzweig (1985) define structure as "the established pattern of relationships among the components or parts of the organisation". This can be considered as the static element in understanding organisations as systems. The dynamic element in the understanding of organisations is its function, which cannot easily be separated from the structure. Function is considered to be the mode of action by means of which an organisation fulfils its purpose. If the structure of an organisation represents the relationships between its parts, then *the consequences of these relationships can be defined as the function* of that organisation. In the study of organisations, the structure and the function represent two different aspects (static and dynamic) of the same system.

The study of the structure seems, therefore, to be the best way to understand and explain an organisation, which has been used by many researchers in this field. Robbins (1990), as mentioned before, lists a whole lot of variables which are used in the study of the structural dimensions of an organisation: administrative component; autonomy; centralisation; complexity; delegation of authority; differentiation; formalisation; integration; professionalization; span of control; specialisation; standardisation and vertical span. Robbins concludes that many of these variables represent in fact three basic dimensions for the study of an organisation, i.e. complexity, normalisation and centralisation.

Complexity

"It refers to the degree of differentiation that exists within an organisation" (Price, Mueller, 1985). The complexity of an organisation is closely associated with its **size**. The classification of an organisation according to size usually depends on the number of full time employees. This number has to be interpreted according to the existing norms for different functions. A shop with 100 employees would be classified as large (if the norm is 10), whereas a car factory with 100 employees would be classified as small (if the norm is 1000).

Blau (1970, 1971) maintains that size is the most important determinant of structure. He carried out a study of fifty three autonomous state and territorial employment-security agencies, including twelve hundred local agency branches and three hundred and fifty headquarters divisions. He found that although increasing size promotes structural differentiation, it does so at a decreasing rate.

The Aston Group (Pugh et.al,1969) also found size to be the major determinant of structure. They looked at forty six organisations and found that the increase in size was associated with greater specialisation and formalisation.

This "size imperative" has been explored by many other researchers who came to the same conclusions. There has, however, been criticism of the size imperative by a number of researchers who carried out a secondary analysis of the studies in favour of size imperative. Argyris (1972) analysed Blau's data and questions his measures as applicable only to civil service organisations, which have budget limitations, distinct geographical boundaries, predetermined staff sizes and are influenced by regulations. He concludes that size may be associated with structure but one cannot say that it is causally related. Other researchers also criticised the size imperative in terms of causality but not in terms of the relationship of one with the other.

Taking into consideration the great number of studies in this area, one can conclude that size is associated with complexity, with formalisation, as well as with centralisation. There is still the unanswered question concerning the size itself, i.e. when is big big? This debate produced a number of sidelines of which the best known is "Parkinson's Law" (1957), which states that work expands so as to fill the time available for its completion and argues that there is no relationship between the work to be done and the number of people who are supposed to do it.

The understanding of the role played by the size of an organisation is very important for health promotion and health education operating within an organisational model and associated with the settings approach. The fact is that most studies concerned with the relationship between size and structure have been carried out in big government departments or big companies; but in most of industrialised societies at least a third or more of organisations can be described as small and employ between three and five employees. It, therefore, seems most probable that a large part of health promotion and health education activities will be conducted in small organisations. The question is then whether the existing organisational theories apply to small organisations. Robbins (1990) thinks that it does and argues that small businesses also depend on the appropriate structural design, although they may face different problems and priorities.

The structural variables developed in organisation theories are of lesser importance to a small business manager because of the limited range of variations resulting in a minimal degree of horizontal, vertical and spatial differentiation. Most small organisations are characterised by low formalisation and high centralisation, with less internal specialisation. Specialist services are usually bought in, if and when required, such as for example, accountants, solicitors, doctors, etc. The structure tends to be flat and the vertical differentiation, as well as spatial differentiation, is small. Other aspects which are of reduced importance in small organisations include management conflict, resistance to innovations and changes in organisations' culture, owing to the fact that small organisations are usually young and have no great sense of history of tradition, which results in easier achievement of change if necessary.

There are certain issues which are of greater importance for small organisations than for large ones. They include the question of control and accountability, efficiency, and environmental dependence. Control is usually achieved through direct supervision and observation. Efficiency is more easily achieved because of less slack time, which is a characteristic of situations with a great number of employees. This, however, means that there is less tolerance for inefficiency and the emphasis is on the right structural design. The environmental dependency of small organisations is reflected in their need to obtain supplies from outside, having to face competitors directly and having to constantly argue financial resources. In this way, small organisations are different from large ones in terms of their concerns and priorities, although they depend on the same variables within their structure as the large organisations. It is important to realise that small organisations are not just scaled down large organisations, but that there is a qualitative difference between the two.

The **differentiation of complexity** can be horizontal, vertical and spatial:

- **Horizontal differentiation** refers to the units in an organisation and their similarities and differences in performing the organisation's tasks. An important aspect of horizontal differentiation is the degree of specialisation within each unit, which can in more general terms be described as the level of "division of labour" in an organisation. Some experts in organisation theory (OT) refer to this as "functional specialisation". If the individuals are differentiated instead of their work, then it is called "social specialisation". The complexity of a structure depends on the degree of specialisation within an organisation. The more the work is differentiated, the more complex the mechanism will be for interaction and control of such activities. Specialisation leads to departmentalisation, which enables an organisation to coordinate the activities which have been horizontally differentiated.

- **Vertical differentiation** refers to the hierarchical levels in an organisation. An organisation, as was mentioned earlier, can be, in terms of its vertical differentiation, "tall" with many levels of hierarchy, or "flat" with only few levels of hierarchy. This is closely related to the "span of control" or the number of subordinates under the control of a manager. This has to be considered in terms of the total number of employees in an organisation. The larger the number of subordinates under one manager, the smaller the number of managers. This can be cost effective but can affect the productivity of the organisation.

- **Spatial differentiation** refers to the division of functions as well as the division of labour in an organisation, where different functions are located at different places. The common situation is the division between the production and sales departments in an organisation. This also includes the differentiation between branches of a company which can be located in different towns or even different countries.

These three approaches to differentiation are represented in different combinations in real life situations. It is impossible to draw a rule about which combination is most effective. The one decisive element in it is the "complexity" of an organisation. High complexity has consequences for communication, coordination and control systems and will depend on the expert knowledge of the incumbents for the achievement of a high level of effectiveness and efficiency.

Normalisation

Normalisation refers to the degree to which jobs within the organisation are standardised (Robbins, 1990). A high level of normalisation of a job in an organisation implies that the incumbent has very little scope in decision making, since this is all defined by regulations, which are a sign of normalisation. These regulations will cover the job description and the procedures relating to work processes. With low normalisation, the employees have a wide range of choices and independence in performing their jobs.

There is an ongoing discussion among organisation experts as to whether the rules have to be written or not to become formal. In other words, the study of organisations using the level of normalisation in the description of the organisational structure, can consider either the explicit or implicit rules. The study of explicit rules uses "hard" data, whereas the study of implicit rules uses attitudes as internalised organisational norms. One indicator of the level of normalisation could be the flexibility of a job description, ranging from defining the job to defining the expected outcome (sales representatives). Another indicator could be the level of professionalization of a job. Workers with no professional status have to comply to the rules laid down by the organisation in which they work, whereas professionals entering an organisation acquire the rules of their expected behaviour during their professional socialisation, before they join the organisation. The normalisation process in an organisation, if the expertise is not "bought from outside", will have to take place within the organisation. This can take many forms, such as the selection procedure for employees, the job description, as well as written rules, established procedures and general policy statements. This can be accompanied by certain rituals, which can accompany promotion from one status to a higher one ("obtaining the key to the executive washroom"). The degree of normalisation within a structure will depend on size and specialisation in an organisation.

Centralisation

Centralisation refers to the degree to which the decision-making process is concentrated in one place, one position or one person within an organisation. A low concentration reflects the decentralisation within an organisational structure. The traditional way of measuring centralisation by using as an indicator the amount of power concentrated in one position, one person or one managerial level, is now being replaced by access to information as an indicator. This is the result of the spread of information technology within organisations and individual access to centrally stored data through personal computer links.

The study of organisations as systems has looked at their structures and the important aspects within those structures. Organisations include goal orientation, which means that they have a certain purpose; they represent a psychosocial system which consists of people interacting in a face-to-face or group situation; they are technological systems where people use knowledge and technology to fulfil their goals; and they depend on the structure as a means of regulating the interactions of people in the system.

Implications for HP/HE

The change from problems to settings required an organisational model since the settings were considered as organisations with the consequence that many of the existing beliefs needed to be modified or changed. The organisational model was meant to expand on the existing health promotion activities which have been concerned with the adjustment of environmental factors to provide legitimation and support for individual adjustment.

The main problem, however, has arisen when the settings are a part of the service industry. The organisational model has had to take into account the needs of the customers expressed in terms of health gain. This has meant that the organisational model needed to set the aim of producing appropriate environments for individuals and at the same time enabling individuals to make best use of these positive environmental factors.

The application of an organisational model in HP/HE requires the understanding of the latest developments in the study of organisations, their structure and function as well as mechanisms for change. These issues are new to a great number of agents engaged in traditional HP/HE.

PEOPLE IN ORGANISATIONS

As we have seen organisations are systems in which people perform to achieve a certain purpose or goal. The exploration of people's actions in organisational situations is known as the study of *organisational behaviour.* The term is here being used in the strict sense, concentrating on individuals and their behaviour. Sometimes management theorists use the term loosely, to refer to organisation theory, structure and function as well. The difference is between behaviour in organisation and behaviour of organisations.

Organisational behaviour involves some psychological concepts, such as perception, motivation, learning and personality. It also includes concepts from social psychology, such as groups, their formation, structure, social control and effectiveness. An important area included is the study of the impact technology has on individuals working lives. Another broad area includes the study of management, decision making, conflicts and the distribution of power.

For the purposes of this part, it will be convenient to differentiate between two aspects of organisational behaviour, that of management and that of the workforce.

Management

The relationship between the structure and the management of an organisation has been the topic of many studies, resulting in a number of schools of thought and theories.

Theories and Approaches

The first writers in the field of management have been subsequently labelled as protagonists of the so called *"classical management theory"* (Pugh, 1991), included the writings of a number of people prominent in the management of various successful organisations and enterprises. They wrote about their experiences in terms of guidelines or suggestions for others to follow.

The actual term *"management science"* is closely associated with the establishment of The Institute of Management Sciences in 1953 (Kast and Rosenzweig, 1985), and has been gradually recognised as a discipline in its own right, although there is still a considerable overlap with operational research and decision theory.

Although these writings were based on personal experiences of the writers, they did not have a common theoretical background.

Lussato (1976) has nevertheless identified and named some common concepts: the *scalar concept* sees enterprises as composed of units at various levels in a sequence from superior to inferior grades with an appropriate grading of authority from top to bottom; the principle of the *unity of command* suggests that every person in an enterprise has only one superior from whom he or she receives commands; this principle also includes the concept of *unity of direction* which means that the commands follow a defined path from top to bottom; the *exception principle* indicates that delegation should be maximised with people who actually carry out the work being able to make decisions as often as possible; the *span of control* concept is concerned with the optimal number of subordinates under each manager; the concept of organisational *specialisation* is concerned with the differentiation of activities in an enterprise according to their objectives, processes, clientele, materials or geographical location.

The scalar concept is well illustrated in the organisation of the church, which, like any other enterprise, has a clear definition of authority from top to bottom with the exception that the origins of this distribution are scribed to divine intervention. An example of span of control can be found in the organisational structure of the army, where the number of individuals under one command are strictly limited.

A major development in organisation theory was the work done by Max Weber at the turn of the century, who developed the *bureaucratic model*, which although an important contribution to sociology, has been widely applied in the study of large scale complex organisations. Weber's work is recorded in many of his publications which at that time were published in Germany and later published in the UK, (see Weber 1968).

Frederick Winslow Taylor (1911) is known for his management innovations concerning efficiency, standardisation and discipline. He is considered to have started the movement concerned with management efficiency. In 1914 Henry Fayol, a French mining engineer built on the ideas of Taylor, and developed the *administrative management theory* (Fayol, 1916). He and a number of other authors believed that their principles of management had universal value and could be applied to most organisations. Their advice was concerned with how to allocate tasks, control the work being done, and motivate and reward those doing it. Fayol drew on his personal experience in his development of a general theory about management, in which he classified organisational structures and developed principles for organisation administration.

Economic theories, also concerned with business organisations building on the concept of "economic man" i.e. an ideal type who has all the information and is able to carry out rational choices, also had an influence. Economists have contributed to the understanding of how market forces affect the structure and design of organisations and have been concerned with competitive strategies in individual industries, which reflect on business policy and strategic management.

The development of the concept of *public administration* based on Weber's bureaucratic model examined the experiences from various public agencies. There was an attempt to develop principles of administration based on the developments in the field of management. The dominant concept was the separation between policy making and administration, with the latter being concerned with the implementation of government policies.

In the study of behaviour in organisations two strands are discernible: the behavioural sciences approach and the management sciences approach. The first draws on the theories and methods of *behavioural sciences.* Early developments used a traditional behavioural sciences approach (Berelson and Steiner, 1964), adopting a positivist, scientific approach to the study of human behaviour in organisations, employing empirical evidence collected in a "scientific way".

This approach was supplemented by the qualitative descriptive approach of Elton Mayo (1945), whose work on the "Hawthorne effect" began the human relations movement in industry. The Hawthorne observations of workers showed that attention to human needs, no matter what form it took, improved productivity. This highlighted the human aspect of the workplace. This was followed by a number of other writers who extended the idea of "industrial humanism" to other situations. Another important contributor was Rogers (1942), who developed important insights for organisation theory and management practice through his client-oriented therapy and counselling methods. Moreno (1953) contributed to the study of organisations through his sociometric method of analysing human relationships within groups. Lewin (1935) with his field theory and group dynamics also provided a basis for understanding of organisations as groups.

The accumulation of studies in this field and the use of the *operational research* methods gradually brought about the recognition of a special field of organisational development, which also included *human resources management.* The latter was initially concerned with the two main tasks of managers i.e. productivity and the quality of work life.

The opening of markets in the 1980 s and the inclusion of partners from the Far East changed the rules of the game insofar that the existing strict descriptions of the organisation design had to be modified. The new approach known as the *"contingency approach"* which had been developed in the 1960 s, and which followed the classical management theory and the human relations theories, was faced with the task of meeting these new needs. The general idea underlying this new approach is the recognition of the fact that people carry out work within certain environments, including cultural environments, and that the adjustment of people to that environment will be contingent on the prevailing circumstances. Hunt (1979, p.189) states: "contingency theory refers to attempts to understand the multivariate relationships between components of organisations and to designing structures piece-by-piece, as best fits the components. This approach rejects earlier theories of universal models for designing formal structures and argues that each situation must be analysed separately".

Management as an Activity

The second development affecting the study of people in organisations is management theory. Management in general refers to the activity of people exercising authority over the activities and performances of other people. In a formal sense, management is carried out within a structured organisational setting, directed towards aims and objectives through the efforts of other people using systems and procedures (Mullins, 1992).

Being a manager may be interpreted as performing a certain *function* or as occupying a certain *status.* These are very general interpretations which can often be overlapping and are interchangeable.

There is also often a confusion over the meaning of "management" as compared to "administration". In fact in some languages management is translated as administration (French). The term "management" is now widely accepted; "administration" is interpreted as a part of the management process.

The common *activities* of management include planning, organizing, command, coordination and control. Another interpretation of management treats it as a social process, which includes judgement and decision in determining plans and in using data to control performance; and guidance, integration, motivation and supervision of the personnel carrying out the operations.

There are many definitions of the *tasks and contributions* of managers, which involve most of the concepts mentioned earlier. They can be summarised as: setting objectives, ensuring that they are carried out by means of motivation and development of human resources, and controlling the outcomes. A good description of the concept "manager" was given by Brown (1974), who describes the manager as a person who has more work than he can do himself and has to delegate some of it to others, for whom he is accountable to higher authorities.

Another recent development in the manager's role is *"just-in-time"* planning, which refers to obtaining stocks of raw materials and parts necessary for production, where lengthy warehousing is replaced by the delivery of materials and parts just when they are need. This reduces capital investment and forces the producer to establish long-term relationship with the provider of raw materials or parts.

An important aspect of the manager's activitiy is concerned with *personnel* policy. This includes the selection and assessment of personnel, within a successful organisational structure, by defining the roles and securing optimal conditions for work. This role includes manpower planning and employment, salary and wage administration, education training and development, welfare, health and safety services and industrial relations.

Another managerial status is that of a line manager, who is in charge of a department or unit, generally responsible for the production process, essential for the achievement of the goals of the organisation. Line managers are part of a complex management structure and have a clear role definition including power and accountability.

To be able to achieve relevant tasks a manager should, according to Mullins (1992), have the following *attributes*: technical competence, social and human skills including decision-making, and the ability to conceptualise problems and to see them in all their complexity.

Managerial Behaviour

The background to the study of the behaviour of a manager is derived from theories as a part of organisational behaviour and especially concerned with *motivation*, of which the most important and best known is Maslow's (1943) hierarchy of needs. This was adjusted by Alderfer's (1972) modified need hierarchy model and expanded by Herzberg's (1974) two-factor theory and McClelland's (1962) achievement motivation theory. Motivation is considered to be reflected in the direction and persistence of action and explains why one continues with a particular course of action in the face of difficulties and problems. Mitchell (1982) describes four common characteristics which underlie the definition of motivation: motivation is typified as an individual phenomenon; it is usually described as intentional; it is multifaceted and the purpose of motivational theories is to predict behaviour.

McGregor (1987) builds on Maslow's hierarchy of needs model to argue that there are basically two different managerial approaches, related to managers' attitudes towards people. **Theory X** is based on the traditional assumptions about organisations, which accepts the following generalisations: the average person is lazy and has an inherent dislike of work; most people must be coerced, controlled, directed and threatened with punishment if the organisation is to achieve its objectives; and the average person avoids responsibility, prefers to be directed, lacks ambition and values security most of all. The central principle of Theory X is direction and control through a centralised system of organisation and the exercise of authority.

Theory Y is at the other extreme of the continuum. It is based on the central principle of integration of individual and organisational goals. It assumes that work is as natural as play or rest, and people will exercise self-direction and self-control in the service of objectives to which they are committed; commitment to objectives is a function of rewards associated with their achievement; given the right conditions the average worker can learn to accept and to seek responsibility; the capacity for creativity in solving organisational problems is distributed widely in the population; and the intellectual potential of the average person is only partially utilised. Whereas in Theory X motivation occurs only at the physiological and security levels, in Theory Y, motivation is assumed to occur at the affiliation, esteem and self-actualisation levels of Maslow's hierarchy of needs.

A third example is **Theory Z** exemplified by management style in the Japanese culture (Ouchi, 1984), which emphasises the need to manage people in such a way that they can work together more effectively. Theory Z organisation includes: long-term employment, often for a life-time; relatively slow process of evaluation and promotion; development of company-specific skills and a moderately specialised career path; implicit, informal control mechanisms supported by explicit formal measures; participative decision-making by consensus; collective decision-making but individual ultimate responsibility; broad concern for the welfare of subordinates and co-workers as a natural part of a working relationship and informal relationships among people. The best known UK application of Theory Z is in Marks & Spencer's (Tse, 1985).

A more recent management orientation known as **"total quality management"** (Walton, 1989) has been derived from earlier work on quality by Deming (1986) and is sometimes known as the "Deming" approach. Deming served as a consultant to Japanese industries, where he developed the concept of total quality control as compared to the usual end-of-the-line inspection. The general idea is that each stage of production process is separately assessed and adjusted. In this way, the quality of the end product is assured through assuring the quality of each stage of the production. This method was reintroduced into the United States from Japan, following the enormous success that it has achieved in terms of the quality of Japanese industrial products. There are many companies in the United States who now apply this method of quality control with success, and it has transformed the cultures of the organisations.

As one would expect, the crucial role of the manager(s) in an organisation has attracted researchers from many disciplines. For our purpose, it is of interest to note the ways managers are assessed. Langford (1979) identifies four broad groups of *criteria* used in the studies of managerial effectiveness, which include:

- the managers work - decision-making, problem solving, innovation, management of time and handling information;
- the manager himself/herself - motivation, role perception, coping with stress, seniority and average salary grade for age;
- the managers relationships with other people - subordinates, superiors, peers and clients; handling conflicts and leadership role;
- criterion of general effectiveness - allocation of resources, achieving purpose, goal attainment, planning, organizing, coordinating, controlling.

Within this general framework, a number of authors have developed various *instruments* for the assessment of managers, emphasising one or more of the mentioned areas of enquiry. Among the most quoted authors are Blake and Mouton (1985), who developed a Managerial Grid with two principal dimensions (concern for production and concern for people); Likert (1961), whose System 4 Management includes the principle of supportive relationships, group decision-making and high performance aspirations; Drucker (1968), who developed the Management by Objectives (MBO) approach, which is often used to describe a style of management which attempts to relate organisational goals to individual performance and development through the involvement of all levels of management. It includes the following principles: the setting of objectives and targets; participation by individual managers in agreeing about objectives and criteria of performance for each unit; and review and appraisal of results. Reddin (1970) developed a three-dimensional model of managerial behaviour, covering task orientation, relationship orientation and management style, as the combination of the two.

The Workforce

The study of people at work has been the concern of a wide range of scientific disciplines, including politics, economics, sociology and psychology. Each of these scientific disciplines has looked at the problems people meet at work from a different angle and developed models and theories to explain them. Whereas the study of management started from a wide range of premises and tended to converge to a recognised subject of management studies, the study of the workforce developed in exactly the opposite way. Starting from psychological interpretations such as motivation, it has diverged into a whole set of different models and theories. The contributing studies are briefly described below:

- **Political sciences** examine various ideologies, such as capitalism and communism, in describing working conditions and the relationship of workers to the means of production. It also examines the development of the trade union movements and their implications for protection of workers' interests. Of special interest here is the concept of conflict and the consequences of strike actions as a means of establishing workers' rights.

- **Economics** looks at the relationship between production and consumption and has developed various economic models, related to labour in both planned and market economies. Of special interest is the problem of unemployment and its consequences for the workforce.

- **Sociology** looks at the societal level of work and the relationships within working organisations, as we have seen earlier in examining the issues related to organisation structure and behaviour. It looks at work as a part of society and treats the industrial revolution as a pivotal point in human experiences at work. It pays special attention to development of professions and bureaucracies. It examines social stratification based on occupations and looks at the norms governing the expectations associated with different statuses.

- **Psychology** examines human experience at work and raises the problems of perception, motivation, learning, personality, alienation, deskilling, fulfilment, and the consequences of unemployment. It looks at the role definition associated with various statuses and role performance in terms of conformity and deviance. It is also concerned with the formation of groups and group functioning.

- **Medical sciences** cover the health of people at work and the effects of both work and unemployment on health. The specialisms of occupational health and safety at work are concerned with the working environment and conditions of work, problems of absenteeism and prevention of accidents. More recently it has taken on some special issues, such as smoking in working premises and the protection of non-smokers from passive smoking, as well as the issue of women's rights at work and the problem of sexual harassment. The health care system in the UK, and even mores so in Europe has developed a special health service at work regulated by a number of laws and directives concerning the conditions of work and people's behaviour and supported by occupational health specialists and health and safety officers. The service offers preventive health screenings of employees aimed at the detection of various risk factors. The larger enterprises cooperate with the health service in developing healthy menus in canteens and providing the employees with facilities for exercise and sports.

Management Sciences

The management sciences have concentrated on the study of the performance of the workforce (Mitchell and Larson, 1987). The classical theorists believed that the difference in performance was associated with differences in workers personality traits and abilities. Since this could not fully explain the differences in performance, the behavioural scientists came up with the idea that personal satisfaction produces high performance even under most difficult conditions. They soon found out that even very satisfied workers could manifest variations in their productivity. This failure of explanation was followed by the assumption that future performance could be predicted on the basis of past performance. The outcome was that a worker with a good track record would be rewarded by promotion to a new position. An exaggeration of this assumption came to be called the "Peter Principle" (Peter & Hall, 1969), which states that by applying this criterion to promotion means that people will be promoted until reaching the level of their incompetence, since without a good past performance no promotion should have taken place. The absurd conclusion from this assumption is that all the jobs (especially the top ones) are at present occupied by people who reached their level of incompetence since they have not been further promoted. Although this principle is very simplistic, it served to illustrate how unreliable an indicator past performance could be for future achievements.

The contingency approach to performance effectiveness postulates that it depends on the proper match between the worker and the job. The job of the management is to ensure that the right people are doing the right job under the right conditions. The outcome of such an approach has been the development of appropriate methods for the selection of personnel, based on an appropriate job analysis, and followed by an appropriate performance appraisal and reward system.

Job Analysis

If the idea is to match individuals to jobs, then it follows that it will be necessary to know precisely what the job is and what kind of demands it may put on the worker who is supposed to carry it out. The methods of job analysis vary, but usually depend on the collection of information by observation, statistical analysis of various measurements and by interviewing others who already perform that job. The job analysis forms the basis for the job description and should be used in assessing the applicants. This description is usually accurate in technical details but does not touch on the sensitive issues which may differentiate a successful from a poor performer. To compensate for this shortcoming, researchers have been developing increasingly more sophisticated methods of measurement. This includes *professionally developed questionnaires*, which cover all the aspects considered to be relevant to job performance. Another research method uses the *critical incident technique*. Workers are asked to describe incidents which lead to a good or a bad performance. The analysis of the answers provides a behavioural description of a good and a bad performer. On the basis of characteristics that could include behaviour, skills, knowledge and abilities, it is possible to identify the attributes a successful applicant should have. It should be noted that such a job specification should not be allowed to fossilize, and should be regularly updated to include all the new developments associated with the organisation and the expected performance. Carrying out a job analysis is, therefore, a skilled activity and requires certain knowledge and skill in collecting and analysing information. Special skills are required for making inferences on the basis of the information collected, useful in the next step, in personnel selection which is the selection of candidates.

Candidate Assessment

This will depend on how successful the job description was, on the recognition of individual differences in personal characteristics of the applicants, and the selection of those which are pertinent for the job performance. The methods of assessment of candidates include a number of approaches:

The most common is the **interview** which is aimed at providing the employer and the candidate with a personal experience of learning as much as possible about each other. There are a number of different guidelines for conducting interviews and emphasising various pertinent points which should be included. The employer makes a judgement based on the way the candidate performs at the interview, which becomes a part of the employer's decision-making process. The interview usually includes an aspect of the candidate trying to sell him/herself to the enterprise and the employer trying to sell the enterprise to the candidate. In this way, it should be considered as a two way process of interaction. It can take the form of an *unstructured interview* which is a loosely organized conversation, or a *structured interview* which consists of a predetermined set of questions set by the employer. Sometimes the employer may use the *stress interview,* which is aimed at testing the candidate under difficult conditions. Other forms include a *group interview*, where the candidate is a member of a group of candidates, or a *panel interview*, where the candidate is interviewed by a number of representatives of the employer. There is considerable literature on how to conduct interviews, including specific methods, interpretation of responses and assessment of candidates. It also includes considerations given to possible *errors* derived from the disagreement of assessors, prejudice of the employer and personality traits of the candidate which may appear in the interview but may not be relevant for the job. A lot of work has been done on the communication process during interviews, with special emphasis on non-verbal communication. The final assessment of the candidate is usually performed on a subjective level since there are no agreed standards that could be applied. It is also carried out in the context of availability of other candidates as well as the requirements of the job. All these potential errors indicate the need for the interviewer to be professionally skilled in carrying out the interview and also in making inferences from the available information. Structured interviews have the advantage of ensuring that all the candidates are asked the same questions, which will provide comparable answers.

More recently, the assessment of candidates has also included **psychological tests.** These can aim at assessing the candidate's mental abilities, muscular and motor coordination, personality traits and physical and sensory capacities. Job descriptions will define which of the tests are appropriate. Each of these areas of enquiry includes whole sets of different tests that could be appropriate depending on the preferences and the skills of the interviewer. It is important to ensure that the chosen test is assessed for *validity and reliability,* with special emphasis given to predictive validity. This is very important if one considers that most of the tests measure some trait, and the score of this measurement is then interpreted by the interviewer as appropriate or inappropriate for a particular job. *Predictive validity* refers to the ability of the test to accurately predict performance for a particular job. Finally, it should be noted that most of the tests can only be obtained and applied by professional psychologists to avoid misuse and misinterpretation.

As a result of the complexity of job requirements it is sometimes beneficial to use **assessment centres** for the selection of job applicants. Such an assessment centre usually combines a whole variety of methods combined into an evaluation package. The information gathered can be used for selection, promotion, training and development of employees. An assessment centre usually includes a number of professional assessors able to administer complex tests and other assessment tools, which is not usually available in a company or organisation. The assessment usually takes 1-3 days and candidates' performance is rated by themselves, their peers, and the assessors. All this information is used to predict the future performance of a candidate. Existing literature suggests that the predictive value of this assessment method is considerable and the results are satisfactory. It is especially appropriate for the selection of middle and higher levels of management personnel. The problems for the company in using such assessment centres is mainly the high cost, which is another justification for the company to use it only for highly paid jobs. The problem for the candidate is the danger of being stigmatized if they do not perform up to an expected standard and they may be labelled for life as inappropriate for certain jobs.

The increasing variety of assessment methods implies that not one of the existing ones is satisfactory. A new, recently developed approach, is the use of **work samples**, i.e. simulation of situations which closely correspond to the actual work situation in which a candidate is tested and assessed. The main assessment judges whether the candidate's performance in a *simulated exercise* will accurately reflect the performance in a real life situation. For some jobs such as typists this has been a standard method of testing, whereas for some other jobs it has been dependent on the development of appropriate technology, such as flight simulators, etc. The most popular work sample technique for managers is known as an *"in-basket" test*. It includes placing the most characteristic items of a manager's job (memos, invoices, etc.) in an in-basket and asking the candidate to play the role of the manager and deal with this in-basket material.

In addition to various methods appropriate for the selection of candidates it may be necessary to provide the candidate with the possibility of a making realistic assessment of the job in question. The method developed for this purpose is **job preview**, which provides the candidate with all the necessary information about the job and an opportunity to become personally acquainted with other people working on the same or similar jobs in the company. This method has been shown to be very successful in allowing the candidate to develop a realistic picture of the job in question and is reflected in the low turnover of the workers participating in this process.

Performance Appraisal System

The assessment of the performance of employees depends on the precision of a job description, which should include the expectations concerning their performance, but also depends on the motivation of workers, associated with the existing reward system. Methods of assessment can take many different forms, the outcome of which will influence the administrative decision related to promotion, transfer, dismissal, wage and salary administration and bonus pay. Assessment will also be used as the indicator for various employee development programmes.

Appraisal techniques can include measures of *volume or quantity* of output, which can be assessed against preset standards associated with a specific job. They will include the assessment of *quality* as indicated by spoilage, rejected items, or any other indicator of failure; and can also include measures of *lost time,* through absenteeism or tardiness; and involvement in *training and promotion* can also be included if it is appropriate for a certain position. In jobs which do not have generally agreed upon standards of performance the assessment will have to be done on the basis of *subjective judgments* of supervisors or assessors. This subjective assessment can be based on some absolute standards or by comparison with other people.

The **instruments** for assessment are many and usually include a set of questions with the possibility of ranking the answers (i.e. from exceptionally good to poor). Instruments which use absolute standards are based on previous job assessments. They often include a *check list* of various behavioural patterns or actions which are then rated. These instruments can be more sophisticated by including weighted check lists and behaviourally anchored rating scales.

The **problems** associated with performance assessment are usually due to errors made by the raters, such as the *"halo error"* which implies that the raters tend to prefer people who are similar to themselves. Some other errors include leniency, strictness, and central tendency. Some raters tend to place the respondents at the positive end of the scale *(leniency)* or at the negative end of the scale *(strictness)*, whereas some tend to place everyone in the middle of the scale *(central tendency)*. The other error which can occur is due to *single criterion* problems. This implies that the ratings can suffer either from deficiency or from contamination. A rating will be *deficient* if it does not cover all the relevant aspects of a person's performance or *contaminated* if it covers aspects that are irrelevant for the job. If one accepts that any rating can to a certain extent be deficient or contaminated, it will be necessary to use more than a *single indicator* if one wants to avoid this error. Thus there is an advantage in using multiple performance measures.

Some errors arise from differences among jobs and among the raters. It is possible that one supervisor consistently rates people unusually high. This implies that some will merit the label "*tough judge*", whereas others will be known as an "*easy touch*". This can be avoided by setting objective standards and carrying out statistical analysis of the outcomes, which produces a weighting of one set of ratings compared to another.

Performance assessment is important not only for the employer but also for the employees. Through the mechanism of *feed-back*, the employees can be informed about their performance so that they can adjust. The outcomes of assessments suggests the need for counselling, additional training, addressing the problem of motivation, or the adjustment of some other environmental or behavioural factors. Most promising, however, is to allow the employees themselves to participate in the development of assessment instruments.

Since performance assessment is part of a more general *evaluation process*, it is necessary to consider the questions of who is doing the evaluation, how often it is carried out, its ethical and legal aspects, the recording of outcomes, and the consequences of such an evaluation. All these issues confront management and are very often a topic of interest for trade unions.

Systems of Reward

One of the main reasons for performance assessment is to provide information associated with the distribution of rewards or punishments. The *reward* mechanism is a very important aspect of the motivation of employees to fulfil expectations or even exceed them. The *punishment* aspect can operate positively or negatively, depending on the general situation in the organisation, the situation on the job market in general and the form the punishment takes.

Most jobs include two types of rewards. The *intrinsic* rewards are considered to be a part of job performance and they are expressed in terms of personal satisfaction, feeling of competence, self-fulfilment etc. The *extrinsic* rewards are considered to be a part of the formal reward system and include pay increases, promotion and some other "benefits", such as unemployment compensation, disability insurance, hospital benefits, private health and security benefits, retirement and life insurance, special employee services, meals and transportation, and compensation during vacations, sick leave, jury duty and lunch time. Most of these benefits, however, are not strictly limited to performance but are associated with specific position or type of job and serve as a general motivation for people occupying these positions. Only pay and promotion rewards are linked to performance and are distributed according to certain preset standards. In some organisations both the intrinsic and extrinsic rewards are in operation and, where they are not sufficient, a special system of bonus rewards is introduced. This bonus system is directly linked to performance.

A simple system of reward is the *piece-rate* system, where everybody knows what the norms are and when they can expect bonuses. The problems with this are associated with productivity being dependent on environmental and technological factors, in addition to the personal motivation of workers.

Where people work in *groups*, the reward system must reflect this situation and provide a mechanism for rewarding the groups as a whole. There are many different ways of doing this, profit sharing being an extreme example.

More recently developed systems of reward, include "*cafeteria-style compensation plans*", where the employee is told about the total amount of pay and reward appropriate to him/her and can choose which part of it he/she will receive in cash and which in other various benefits. Another new reward system is the "*skill-evaluation plan*", which rewards employees for every newly acquired skill. The advantage of this is that workers may move between different jobs and increase the flexibility of the interpretation of the job definition. This also has implications for the selection of employees who may, in such a system, be appointed with fewer qualifications or skills but can be promoted as they acquire new skills during their stay in the organisation.

The *problems* with a performance based reward system are mainly associated with the equity of the system, the level of aggregation at which performance is measured, salary versus bonuses, and the confidentiality of the pay and rewards.

Policy Implications

The acceptance of an organisational model in health promotion has important implications for the health promotion policy. The acceptance of this model will have a number of important consequences, such as:

- the change from a problems to a settings approach will require a change of emphasis from a medical to an organisational model; the accent is on the *change of emphasis* and not the abandonment of the medical in preference to an organisational model;

- the inclusion of an organisational model into health promotion, which was in the past dominated by a medical model, represents a major change in the conceptualisation of the activities, choice of methods and evaluation of outcomes; this, however, *does not mean that one can disregard the medical model* as it will ultimately be required to solve the problems facing health promotion;

- it implies a *change in the partners* with whom the initial contact is being established, i.e. from (problem-related) medical and paramedical professionals to (settings-related) management and administration personnel;

- the consequences of the change of emphasis from problems to settings are most obvious in the *area of budgeting*; instead of money following the problems (cancer, AIDS, accidents, etc.), it will now be targeted at settings (schools, hospitals, communities, families, etc.); the settings budget is expected to provide the necessary resources for dealing with all the major problems facing the population within that setting;

- the new partners within settings *have a specific value system, special language of communication, highly specialised aims and objectives*; they operate in different systems, with characteristic power structures and hierarchical decision-making processes; they apply different models based on appropriate theories and use specific approaches and methods for evaluation; the consequence of including an organisational model into health promotion will be the revision of the curricula for teaching health promotion to include topics related to organisations and management;

- an important aspect of the organisational model is the *concept of accountability,* which is expressed through the mechanism of auditing; the inclusion of the organisational model implies that the health promotion activity will also be subject to auditing, even if, for various reasons, it was able to avoid evaluation in the past.

Summary of Policy Implications

WHO EURO has provided the impetus for the change of emphasis from a problem oriented (medical) approach to a settings (organisational) approach. It has provided, by means of expert committees, workshops, publications and statements (including charters) the justification for this change of emphasis. So far, this has been limited to a very successful campaign concerned with "selling" the idea, which is now being accepted by most health promotion institutions and agents. The survival of this radical change will depend on WHO EURO continuing to develop these efforts by integrating them into their policy.

The next steps to be taken, in order to adjust health promotion policy to this new situation can, therefore, be summarised as follows:

- it will be necessary to take steps to **adjust the existing conceptual framework** of health promotion to include the organisational, as well as the medical model; this will require the inclusion of the existing organisational theories and management methods into health promotion interventions, as well as the development of new ones relevant to looking at problems within their settings. Some of the new areas for consideration are:

  i) *organisations as systems*; their structure, their mechanisms and their processes; effectiveness; technology; power structure; productivity; relation with the environment;

  ii) *people in organisations;* management theories; responsibilities and goals; motivation; status and role; group dynamics; leadership; conflict and change; consumerism;

  iii) *accountability*; the concept of self-assessment and evaluation; the concept of auditing and social responsibility; health gain as an indicator; control over negative or undesirable side-effects;

- it will also be necessary to **clarify the difference** between the existing practice of health promotion in a setting and the new concept of a "health promoting setting". This will need the definition of standards required for the achievement of the status of a "health promoting setting"; these standards should include the following three preconditions:

  i) *creation of a healthy working and living environment* for the participants in that setting;

ii) *integration of health promotion into the daily activities of that setting;* and

iii) creation of conditions for the setting to *reach out into the community* (social and physical environment) and by means of networking and healthy alliances promote the spread of this concept to other settings;

- any policy statement should include the **distinction between the role definition** of the health promotion specialist and the role definition of other agents who are expected to be active within the framework of a multisectoral approach for the improvement of health in a population. This implies revising the existing curricula for the purpose of complementing the competence of health promotion specialists in dealing with other professions and settings, as well as the integration of health promotion knowledge and skills into the training programmes of other professions within their own settings;

- the emphasis given to health promotion reflects the scarcity of **empirical studies** related to the application of various concepts and approaches included in practical health promotion. It is still often the case that innovations are promoted due to their ideological or commonsense value without any empirical evidence of their consequences. The clarification of the role of health promotion as compared to health education is of vital importance and should be reflected in intervention studies which monitor and evaluate both health promotion and health education aspects.

Strategy Implications

Practitioners in the field of health promotion are facing problems in finding out how to implement this new approach into their daily practice. Whether they are involved full time or treat their work as an integral part of some other professional activity, their knowledge base does not include the recent developments in organisation and management theories. In this new situation there is, therefore, the tendency to fall back on old health promotion theories and practices which have been shown to be inadequate in dealing with new partners and in achieving the newly set aims. There is an urgent need to devote time and resources to the detailed development of new strategies for the implementation of this "new" health promotion. The strategy briefly outlined in the previous section is expanded below.

Adjusting the Conceptual Framework

The radical changes taking place at present in health promotion are primarily reflected in the new ways of thinking about health in general and health care delivery in particular. To achieve the acceptance of this new thinking, the strategy should include support for, as well as initiating measures to bring about changes in the conceptual framework of health promotion. This should include:

- **theoretical work** aimed at integrating the existing knowledge base concerning organisations and management into the subject of health promotion; this can be achieved by supporting intervention studies; by enabling the exchange of knowledge and experiences between experts from health promotion and organisation and management areas; and by supporting the publication of literature dealing with the integration processes and outcomes;

- **training and education** will require the reorganisation of curricula for existing educational ventures in health promotion and planning of new ones, to deal with the new needs of the extended field of consumers of such ventures; this can be achieved by consultations with people responsible for the organisation and execution of various health promotion education programmes; expert committees and workshops on this topic; publication of programmes and exchange of experiences; and by evaluation of the outcomes;

- initiating and supporting **intervention studies** associated with the new developments in this field for the purpose of testing and verifying the different methods and approaches; this can be achieved by introducing an intervention study element into existing developments (healthy cities, health promoting hospitals, schools, enterprises, etc.) and promoting new studies in this field; by insisting on evaluation of the existing and new ventures; by creating a mechanism for auditing the activities based on this new approach; and by providing outlets for exchange of experience.

Defining the New Concept

The application of the new concept of "health promoting settings" will depend on the ability of those concerned to understand the difference between health promotion in a setting and a health promoting setting, and their willingness to change from the former to the latter. The strategy should include:

- exploitation of the **interest and motivation** among people in certain settings, in this pioneering stage, and ensuring that the settings comply with the preconditions for the recognition of a "health promoting setting". This can be achieved by demonstrating the advantages arising from such an important step, which should be more than just the prestige and benefits from being the "first" in a country or a region; by creating a pressure group within a setting which will recognise the benefits from the creation of a "healthy working environment" and will provide the impetus for the continuation of such a movement within a setting; by utilising the social pressure from networks of similar settings that have already successfully acquired such a status; and by creating pressure groups within the community which will represent the consumers' interests and needs and take responsibility for the continuation of this process;

- ensuring that health promoting settings comply with the **preconditions** for the acquisition of such a status, which include (a) creating a healthy working environment for staff and consumers, (b) integrating health promotion into all the activities within the setting, and (c) ensuring outreach from the setting into the community. This can be achieved by commitment within a setting to undertake such activities; by a detailed analysis of the undertaking in terms of its feasibility; by requesting that within each setting, a set of intervention studies is undertaken for the purpose of developing and testing the approaches most suitable for a specific setting; by providing professional advice and consultancy to settings if and when requested;

- developing mechanisms for **monitoring and auditing** of the activities within a health promoting setting. The purpose of monitoring these activities is to ensure that the initial enthusiasm of the management arising from the promise of a recognised status, will not dissipate and be lost over time, as a result of encountering possible obstacles and difficulties. Auditing is an integral part of assessing the performance of any organisation (setting) and will automatically be extended to health promotion activities, if and when they become a part of the general settings' activities. This can be achieved by using the existing auditing mechanisms or establishing new ones; by including health promotion into the existing auditing procedures for a setting; by creating data banks of information relevant to auditing; by promoting the idea of evaluation of the various intervention studies; and by raising the competence of the members of a setting as well as of relevant bodies in the community, concerning the tasks of evaluation and auditing.

Redefining the Role of HP/HE Agents

The inclusion of most of the members within a setting in health promotion activities requires a wider definition than usual of the role of health promotion "agents". The rapid increase in the body of knowledge and empirical case studies relevant to the practice of health promotion has resulted in a proliferation of educational ventures in this field. These range from one-day seminars to 5-year programmes of research work leading to a doctorate, which are on offer in numerous educational institutions. In some countries, this has resulted in the recognition of appropriate professional qualifications in health promotion, which may or may not lead to the recognition of health promotion as a profession in its own right. The arguments for professionalising the activity are based on the nature of health promotion work, which deals with clients whose interests can only be protected if the interaction is within "professional" bounds. The arguments against creating a "profession" of health promotion are based on the need for a multisectoral approach and the full participation of all the members of a "setting" in looking after themselves and others in that setting.

The redefinition of the role of health promotion agents can be achieved by:

- **revising the curricula** concerning the teaching of the subject matter of health promotion and striking a balance between the theories related to organisations and management, medical topics, and health promotion approaches and methods. This can be achieved by encouraging intervention studies, which will enable each professional group within a setting to work out their needs according to the aims of their work and the best learning methods according to their expectations; it will involve consultations with the existing teachers of the subject matter; it will require preparation of new teaching material; it will require the adjustment of qualifications to the needs of various professions; and it will be necessary to develop a theoretical base for teaching this extended curricula on an academic level;

- the newly revised curricula will depend on the **definition of the "educational product"**. For this, it will be necessary to explore the potential health promotion aspects of many professional roles and redefine them in that light. This can be achieved by allowing various professionals to explore their own capabilities and needs within the planned intervention studies in various settings; by discussions and agreement with educational institutions offering various professional qualifications, to integrate health promotion into their existing curricula; and by reaching agreement on shared standards for qualifications in health promotion;

- the concept of **accountability** needs to be introduced into health promotion activities, together with the appropriate auditing. This can be achieved by defining the settings approach as a "people-based" approach, and examining people's rights and duties related to health matters; by including into auditing the possible negative, as well as positive outcomes; by accepting the new concept of "green auditing" and applying it to health promotion interventions; by organizing expert committees, workshops, seminars and meetings of a multi-professional and multi-occupational nature to discuss these issues; by publicising the behavioural norms concerning health promotion activities, as well as sanctions for the deviants; and by using existing or developing new mechanisms for evaluation and auditing of health promotion.

Summary of Strategy Implications

It is not easy to redefine an activity, that was not well defined to start with, and one that has achieved recognition only in health promotion circles, whereas other professions often consider it to be either a part of their work (anyway) or basic common sense (using the cognitive model).

In summary, however, the strategy in spite of existing difficulties, should develop two approaches:

- use the ensuing upheaval arising from the switch of emphasis and **raise the standard of expectations** related to health promotion in general. This can be achieved, as already mentioned, by means of intervention studies, which are a precondition for the acquisition of a recognised "health promoting setting" status. They should provide a theoretical basis, which has so far been limited as far as the practice of health promotion is concerned. This has been the main cause of doubt about health promotion's credentials as far as the other "more respectable" professions were concerned. Once this theoretical base has been provided, it will be relatively easy to include the subject matter into the curricula of other professions. Due to the socialisation effects of professional training, the new generations of the various professions involved will accept health promotion as a "normal" part of their activities together with other aspects of their professional practices;

- use the existing "pioneering" spirit to recruit as many different settings into the movement, and **set strict standards** for the achievement of recognition of the desired status of a "health promoting setting", thus raising the value of the status and not allowing it to be achieved "on the cheap". This will require a clear distinction between "health promotion in a setting" and a "health promoting setting". This, in fact, represents the qualitative difference between the existing and newly recommended practice.

These procedures should shape a viable strategy for the introduction of new health promotion strategies. In summary, it can be stated that in many instances and for many problems, the new approaches of health promotion are the only available solution.

HEALTH PROMOTING SETTINGS

INTRODUCTION

As has been show the concept of health promoting settings represents a new phase in the developments of health promotion and health education (HP/HE) following the Alma Ata Declaration and the Ottawa Charter. These developments are crucial in providing a basis for the requirements within a health promoting setting (a hospital, a school, an enterprise, etc.).

It is important to realise that the concept of a health promoting setting goes beyond traditionally defined HP/HE activities since it uses a systems approach and a holistic treatment of daily activities. It also extends the setting's activities into the community by means of healthy alliances aimed at satisfying client's needs reflected in their health gain.

The application of an organisational model in HP/HE within a setting puts new demands on HP/HE. These are mainly concerned with accountability of the staff in using HP/HE in their interactions with clients. Accountability requires the evaluation of the activities through the application of quality assessment within a Total Quality Management model.

The issues raised here represent a challenge to HP/HE experts. This is due to the fact that HP/HE has, in the past, been mainly concerned with studying problems and treating solutions in a commonsense way. To meet the standards and specifications required by quality management, new research into HP/HE solutions will be required. For this reason a commitment to creating a health promoting setting includes intervention studies aimed at testing and validating HP/HE solutions used in meeting clients' needs, as has already been stressed.

The Settings Approach

It is interesting to note that, in Europe, developments in health promotion have already resulted in a shift of emphasis from health problems to the settings in which people with such problems live, work and play. Most of these settings are organisations and form a part of the service industries, which means that they are concerned with providing services to individuals. Consequently, if one takes the settings approach to its logical conclusion by introducing any organisational model, it will be necessary to use both health promotion as a means of creating a healthy environment and health education as a means of enabling people to achieve lifestyles conducive to health. In other words, the differentiation between health promotion and health education can be shown to be a theoretical artefact, which cannot be strictly applied in practice.

We should be aware that a setting is a part of a system with specific tasks carried out within a defined structure by a defined set of professionals and auxiliary staff. This implies that the **emphasis should be on the setting** and that we should be able to explain to the setting's management and staff, in a language that they will understand, how health promotion and health education can contribute to the improvement of the achievement of their task.

It is necessary to **distinguish** between **health promotion in a setting** and the **"health promoting setting"**. Within every setting dealing with clients, certain aspects of health promotion are carried out as a part of normal care for clients. The "health promoting setting" represents a qualitative innovation, since health promotion becomes an integral part of the general climate in the institution, part of the way the setting is managed, and part of the extended care provided for clients, which includes their social and physical environment and mobilises other community and professional services as a part of this extended approach to care.

The setting, as a system, can be considered to have an **"input"** (clients), a production **process** (care and treatment) and an **output** (health gain of clients). The main variable in this equation is the difference in clients according to their readiness and competence related to coping and the management of their health problems (input), resulting in a difference in the health gain (output) provided the process is standardised and optimised (i.e. the best available). To explain the contribution of health promotion and health education within this framework, one can use the analogy from the field of education where the concept of **"value added"** has been most successfully applied. This represents the gain from the educational process, achieved by students with poor entrance grades (input), when they get high grades at the end of the educational process (output), as compared with the expected high achievement of the students with high entrance grades. By analogy, one can say that health promotion and health education contribute to the "value added" of the clients with low levels of competence and readiness on entering the setting, which enables them to achieve levels of health gain at the end of the process equal to those of any other clients.

The Organisational Model

Although the introduction of health promotion and health education within a setting can produce "value added" to the outcome, in helping the clients, the concept of a "health promoting setting" represents a qualitative difference in the services provided.

It will be important to keep in mind that a setting has a clearly defined role in the community and within the health care system. The introduction of the concept of a "health promoting setting" can only mean that such a setting **should carry out its predefined tasks as well as enlarge its role within the community, under the assumption that health within the setting could be improved by the introduction of health promotion and health education,** within the three parameters set:

- creating a healthy working and living environment;
- integrating health promotion and health education into daily activities;
- outreach into the community in the form of health promoting alliances.

The success in introducing a "health promoting setting" will depend on the changes which are required for such a transformation. These will include, in the first place the complete change in the style of management of the setting. The management changes will be necessary in relation to the following key areas:

- customer satisfaction;
- quality;
- people growth;
- organisational climate;
- innovation;
- productivity;
- eeconomics.

The new style of management for success in these key areas is known as **"total management".** It requires a basic change in the corporate climate, a horizontal instead of a vertical organisational structure, change from a "conveyor belt" to a "group" production approach, full participation of all employees (in "quality" and "health" circles), interchangeable roles within working groups, total quality management, etc. In other words it will be necessary to "reengineer the corporation" (Hammer & Champy, 1993) with respect to health.

The creation of a "health promoting setting" is a **new venture** which has no precedent. This fact will affect the role of the **consultant** and the link of the setting with an academic institution, necessary to complement the lack of specific expertise among staff in the field of HP/HE, as well as concerning research and evaluation. The consultant cannot be expected, nor should attempt to provide "ready made" prescriptions of what should be done and how it should be done and evaluated, but provide ways and means for the **staff in the setting** to mount intervention studies for the purpose of **finding out their role** in health promotion and health education and validating the experiences for transmission to other settings.

The consultant, as an expert in HP/HE, should, however, enable the staff to use a selection of HP/HE **methods** related to the aims of each intervention. These aims differ according to the nature of the work in each department and consequently methods will be specific to each aim. The available methods should be selected on the basis of a differential diagnosis and should be appropriate for influencing normative behaviour as well as influencing decision making processes and the acquisition of routinised behaviour. The methods used will in turn be reflected in the objectives of the intervention, expressed in terms of specifications and will require special evaluation approaches.

The novelty of the venture is also the reason for creating **"pilot"** settings, which should provide empirically tested methods of producing health gain for the clients, and thus contribute to the body of knowledge of health promotion and health education.

The consequence of such an approach will be that **evaluation will not be concerned with health promotion as such, but with the activities in the setting** and the role of health promotion and health education in achieving the expected health outcomes within the given framework.

A setting, as a part of the health care system, is accountable for its activities and their consequences. Each setting has, therefore, a **well developed system of quality management** and is being **audited by external professionals (medical and financial).**

Quality management varies according to the character of the setting. In the case of a setting where health promotion and health education are treated as separate projects for specific client groups, a general method of quality assessment will be sufficient. In case of a "health promoting setting" where health promotion and health education are integrated into all its activities, it will be necessary to introduce the **"total quality management"** model of quality assessment. There are, however, different opinions about the contribution of TQM to performance within a setting. Some complain that this requires disproportional amounts of bureaucratic and administrative activities, which can be a considerable burden on small and medium sized settings. Others have found that TQM can only be effective if it is a part of a **"total management"** approach, which will guarantee a change in the corporate culture and will achieve the full benefit from the systems based approach of TQM.

The inclusion of health promotion and health education into setting activities, within a purchaser/provider relationship, will require the provider to develop new **"specifications"** for services as a means of quality assessment.

A **pilot** "health promoting setting" has an additional role, to provide a **"benchmark"** for the quality of activities within settings. Its role will also include its efforts to meet the standards required for **"certification"** by a recognised body (BS5750, etc.) which can be more generally applied throughout the network of similar health promoting settings.

Once health promotion and health education become an integral part of the overall activities within the setting, the auditors will need to take them into consideration when auditing the work of the setting. This implies an **extension of the auditing remit** to include health gain, as well as environmental influences ("green auditing"), through health promotion and health education, in addition to the existing examination of the setting's financial and professional activities. Of course, these new functions cannot be audited by traditional accountancy-trained auditors.

Establishment of a recognised "health promoting setting" will result in some drastic changes in that setting. Change in **culture** will be the most difficult thing to achieve. It includes such topics as:

- belief that the improved product should be "sold for the same price as before", which implies that the change should be "resource-neutral";

- conviction that the improvement can be achieved within the existing manpower and technical resources;

- experience with the selling of the product as a part of a niche in the market may change the image either because of the increased cost or slowing down of production.

Change in **attitudes** of the managers and the workforce will include:

- commitment of top managers to quality assessment procedures;

- working for quality themselves and not delegating it to lower managers;

- achievement of commitment of all the personnel involved in the process from top manager to he worker on the shop floor;

- willingness of workers to take on responsibility for quality and also for the documentation of the quality of their products;

- in terms of the process, each stage is characterised by the nature of the end product/raw material as it passes from one worker to another during the production stages; the question is whether the workers will be willing to check the quality of the product as it enters into their working process and refuse it if it does not meet the specifications.

Communication among the various levels of the employees could be a problem because of the different types of educational background. Those with lower levels of education may be dependent on verbal communication, whereas those with higher levels may be better able to deal with written communications.

Another problem may be the time necessary to carry out the **documentation** involved in quality management. Small enterprises may not be able to find time without affecting productivity.

It will be necessary to distinguish between the process of meeting **standards and defining the specifications**. Whereas the standards for quality management are defined by the BSI, who will provide accreditation and carry out auditing, the specifications of the product will have to be defined by the management in terms of a cost-benefit analysis in relations to the existing benchmarks in the line of production in the real life situation.

In the transitional stage, when the consumers are not specially sensitive to whether the producer has quality management or not, it may seem that the extra efforts required for meeting the standards resulting in certification are not justified. This obviously will not be the case when quality management becomes a necessary method of production if the setting wants to stay **competitive** and survive in the market place.

To sum up, the aims of HP/HE within an organisational model are defined by the Ottawa Charter as:

- enabling;
- mediating;
- advocating.

It will be necessary to realise that the "organisational model" operates on three levels:

- background work;
- implementation on the organisational level;
- implementation on the consumer level.

The methods used to achieve these aims are reflected in the objectives set for each aim. They can include a whole range of interventions: from individual counselling to community participation in actions; and from transmitting information to changing social norms and values.

The evaluation of HP/HE is an integral part of the organisational model and in line with the concept of accountability, using quality as one of its main indicators. The implications of the requirements of the organisational model are reflected in the reconsideration of some basic interpretations of the evaluation procedures.

CREATING A HEALTH PROMOTING SETTING

The nature of a "health promoting setting" has been discussed. In this section, the way in which a setting is created is explored. It requires a set of activities, which can benefit from the "community participation" approach.

Creating a Movement

The basic assumption underlying the new settings approach is that each setting can be considered as a "community". Consequently, a "health promoting setting" should be treated as a "community", and a pilot intervention should use the same stages of the intervention as in any other community setting.

The importance of external factors in promoting healthy life-styles, as well as the self-reliance and self-determination of people in a community setting, can be taken into account through the following planned activities:

- a mass media campaign should be designed with the aim of popularising the idea of "health promoting settings" and should explain the commitment and involvement of a setting in creating a healthy environment, with healthy people living and working there;

- it is important to obtain the support and cooperation of representatives of national, regional and local authorities as well as those of the health care system, who should be identified with this movement; to achieve this, a set of meetings and consultations with the leaders of such settings should be organised;

- the HP/HE team, including the members of an academic institution participating in the activity, should produce supporting literature, reports and explanatory texts to back-up the activity;

- meeting with representatives of local press and mass media should be organised to devise a campaign programme to popularise the movement;

- a background document should be prepared explaining the general principles as well as details of procedures related to the commitments being made within the setting.

Participation of the Setting

It can be expected that the outcome of a mass media campaign will be the creation of interest among people in certain settings to participate in the movement and take on commitments associated with declaring themselves as part of a "health promoting setting".

A meeting with the interested representatives in the settings should be held to explain the commitments and work out a detailed plan of action.

The participating academic institution should organise a workshop for the settings representatives, with the aim of enabling them to carry out the commitments and to raise their competence through providing them with skills necessary to achieve improvements in their setting.

To achieve these aims the workshop should include the following objectives:

- knowledge about the administrative processes involved in attracting support for settings programmes;

- knowledge about the power structure in the setting, as well as the decision-making processes involved in taking on and fulfilling commitments concerning participation in the "health promoting setting" movement;

- knowledge about collecting and interpreting information about local problems as well as about available solutions;

- information about proposed intervention, the methods used and the indicators that should form the basis for evaluation;

- management skills in running a programme of this kind.

At the end of the workshop participants should be able to take on definite commitments and be able to carry them out.

Following the acceptance of the commitments, a second thrust of publicity should include information about participating in the setting and the leaders involved in the process. It should indicate that a systematic monitoring has been introduced and that the public should regularly be informed about progress as well as the problems encountered and the ways of solving them.

Initiating a Health Promoting Setting

The question usually asked following a lecture on health promoting settings is "and what am I supposed to do on Monday?". This is known as the "Monday Syndrome" and is experienced by most of the managers who contemplate making the changes within their organisations in order to make them into a health promoting setting. Some of the practical actions are set out below:

The Introductory Stage

The whole process usually starts with an expert visiting a setting and having discussions with the top management. This may be at the request of the management or initiated by experts from the health promotion and health education services. The discussion should include:

- a brief description of the concept of a health promoting setting;
- exploration of the potential and actual needs of the organisation;
- the potential benefits for the organisation from such an initiative;
- the necessary commitment of the management;
- the steps in the process of becoming a health promoting setting.

The Pre-Commitment Activities

Once the idea has been accepted in general terms by the management, it will be necessary for them to hold discussions with the employees to secure their approval and commitment. The employees should be aware of the following:

- what is involved in terms of the benefits for the organisation;
- what benefits will accrue to the employees;
- their commitment to integration of HP/HE into their work;
- the need for introduction of a Total Quality Management system or of extending the existing QMS to include HP/HE indicators;
- participation in a needs-assessment exercise;
- mechanisms for monitoring and evaluation.

Many of the ideas raised in the discussions may be new to some managers and most of the employees. Therefore, once the commitment of the organisation has been made, the employees should be informed about the arrangements for the provision of detailed information and skills, in the form of training programmes.

The Post-Commitment Stage

The approval of the staff will provide a basis for the full commitment of the management, who will be expected to produce a **"policy statement"** about the new character of the organisation.

The policy statement needs to be cleared with **the purchasers** of the services so that the planned activities meet the purchasers' expectations and fit the criteria they use when deciding on where they will purchase the necessary services. The discussions with the purchasers serve as a motivation for them to undertake the task of developing **specifications** for the services they intend to purchase. These specifications will serve the health promoting setting, in its provider role, to adjust the aims of its HP/HE activities to meet these specifications.

Following the commitment of the management and employees to the transformation of their organisation into a Health Promoting Setting, and following the discussions with the purchasers of their services, but before the actual intervention takes place, it will be necessary to carry out a **survey** to collect the necessary data base for all the activities that should follow.

The Intervention Programme

The provision of a workshop has already been discussed earlier. After representatives complete the workshop and return to the setting, they should organise a meeting with local staff, some of whom should have an active role in carrying out the programme. The aim of this meeting is to ensure a multisectoral participation and involvement in the programme;

The outcome should be the creation of a team, with the following tasks:

- to identify the local problems and rank them according to priority in which they should be tackled using the criteria of seriousness, distribution and potential for successful solutions;

- the guiding principle in selecting the problems should be the achievement of an "optimal" instead of a "maximal" improvemen; the optimal improvement is defined as the improvement within the constraints of the problem and the available resources;

- to assess the necessary resources including those locally available; to devise methods and procedures in attracting outside support if necessary; to discuss the methods of approach, adjust them to local needs and possibilities, and to make a role distribution among the setting's staff;

- to carry out the programme;

- to ensure a continuous monitoring, evaluation and feed-back mechanisms for the duration of the programme;

- to design and pretest indicators, criteria and instruments for evaluation;

- to ensure continuous flow of information to the mass media about the progress of the programme, the problems encountered and the ways they are being solved.

At the end of the trial period, a more general assessment of a number of such programmes in settings should be made and lessons should be drawn from the shared experiences;

The settings participating in this programme can be used as outlets for field training programmes, according to their various teaching programmes.

The final assessment of the intervention programme should be made according to the improvements achieved, its usefulness for the field training of students, and the outlook for long-term attempts of these settings to deal with their problems and satisfy their felt needs, within the principles of self-reliance and self-determination.

The interim, as well as the final reports, should serve as documentation of empirically tested methods within the framework of the new interpretation of the meaning of "community participation" in the "health promoting setting" movement.

DESCRIPTION OF A HEALTH PROMOTING SETTING

Introduction

Once the preliminary organisational commitments have been undertaken, people in settings will have to define their aims and objectives. The character of the setting will define in greater detail the appropriate aims, objectives, indicators, methods and criteria.

An aim describes *what* is intended to be achieved, while an objective defines *how* this aim is to be achieved. Indicators describe what is considered to be the appropriate way to measure the achievements related to the institution's performance.

Each objective is followed by a description of the health promotion and health education methods that should be used in achieving the set aim, by means of each specific objective. The character of work performed by staff and the services offered to clients will define the specific methods appropriate for the achievement of each aim. The methods available can be differentiated according to the expected outcomes and should include: enabling, mediating and advocating for the health gain of the staff and clients.

The evaluation of the achievements will depend on the validity and reliablity of the methods used for each objective. These should not be confused with the validity and reliability of the research instruments. (validity refers to whether the instrument actually measures what it is intended to, and reliability refers to the repeatability of results from an instrument by different researchers). Validity of HP/HE methods will indicate the possibility or probability of the achievement of a specific aim through the chosen objective and the methods used. Reliability of a HP/HE method will indicate the level of success or failure in a general application of chosen methods associated with the objective for the achievement of a specific aim. The assessment of the achievement will depend on the criteria used for validating the success or failure of the intervention.

Aims and Objectives

A health promoting setting is characterised by a set of general and specific aims. These are set out below:

General Aim 1: Creating a Healthy Environment for Staff and Clients

This general aim operates on the settings level and is concerned with the character of the setting, the working environment it provides for staff and clients as well as the internal and external relationships among the staff, among the clients and between staff and clients.

Specific Aim 1.1: creating healthy working conditions

Objective 1.1.1: Securing a healthy working environment
Indicator.1.1.1.1: Level of safety at the work place
Method (enabling, mediating, advocating):
Evaluation (criteria):

Objective 1.1.2: Ensuring satisfactory working arrangements
Indicator 1.1.2.1: Level of complaints by staff and management
Method (enabling, mediating, advocating):
Evaluation (criteria):

Objective 1.1.3: Ensuring job satisfaction of staff
Indicator 1.1.3.1: Level of motivation and turnover of staff
Method (enabling. mediating, advocating):
Evaluation (criteria):

Objective 1.1.4: Meeting the needs of the clients
Indicator 1.1.4.1: Level of need satisfaction of clients
Method (enabling, mediating, advocating):
Evaluation (criteria):

Specific Aim 1.2: proper accommodation for staff and clients

Objective 1.2.1: Ensuring proper accommodation for staff
Indicator 1.2.1.1: Level of staff satisfaction
Method (enabling, mediating, advocating):
Evaluation (Criteria):

Objective 1.2.2: Ensuring proper accommodation for clients
Indicator 1.2.2.1: Level of complaints by clients
Method (enabling, mediating, advocating):
Evaluation (Criteria):

Objective 1.2.3: Ensuring appropriate commuting facilities
Indicator 1.2.3.1: Level of complaints about commuting
Method (enabling, mediating, advocating):
Evaluation (Criteria):

Objective 1.2.4: Ensuring alternative accommodation
Indicator 1.2.4.1: Utilisation of alternative accommodation
Method (enabling, mediating, advocating):
Evaluation (Criteria):

Specific Aim 1.3: availability of healthy nutrition for staff and clients

Objective 1.3.1: Assessment of existing nutritional values
Indicator 1.3.1.1: Meeting standards for healthy nutrition
Method (enabling, mediating, advocating):
Evaluation (Criteria):

Objective 1.3.2: Provision of a healthy diet
Indicator 1.3.2.1: Selection of food on offer
Method (enabling, mediating, advocating):
Evaluation (Criteria):

Objective 1.3.3: Improvements in the catering system
Indicator 1.3.3.1: level of competence of catering staff
Method (enabling, mediating, advocating):
Evaluation (Criteria):

Specific Aim 1.4: prevention and treatment

Objective 1.4.1: Prevention of health threats for staff
Indicator 1.4.1.1: Changes in health behaviour of staff
Method (enabling, mediating, advocating):
Evaluation (Criteria):

Objective 1.4.2: Prevention of health threats for clients
Indicator 1.4.2.1: Changes in health behaviour of clients
Method (enabling, mediating, advocating):
Evaluation (criteria):

Objective 1.4.3: Utilisation of preventive services by staff
Indicator 1.4.3.1: Level of utilisation
Method (enabling, mediating, advocating):
Evaluation (Criteria):

Objective 1.4.4: Utilisation of preventive services by clients
Indicator 1.4.4.1: Level of utilisation
Method (enabling, mediating, advocating):
Evaluation (Criteria):

Objective 1.4.5: Improvement of service provision (treatment, teaching, production, etc.)
Indicator 1.4.5.1: Level of negative outcomes (complaints)
Method (enabling, mediating, advocating):
Evaluation (Criteria):

Specific Aim 1.5: care and relationships

Objective 1.5.1: Improvement of relations between staff
Indicator 1.5.1.1: Level of conflicts & discriminations
Method (enabling, mediating, advocating):
Evaluation (Criteria):

Objective 1.5.2: Improvement in staff - client relations
Indicator 1.5.2.1: Level of conflict & complaints
Method (enabling, mediating, advocating):
Evaluation (Criteria):

Objective 1.5.3: Improvements of relations between clients
Indicator 1.5.3.1: Level of conflicts
Method (enabling, mediating, advocating):
Evaluation (Criteria):

Objective 1.5.4: Improvement in client satisfaction
Indicator 1.5.4.1 Level of satisfaction of client needs
Method (enabling, mediating, advocating):
Evaluation (Criteria):

General Aim 2: Integrating Health Promotion into the Daily Activities of the Setting

This aim operates on the staff-client level, and takes into account the fact that the structure of most settings is composed of a number of units which can be called departments, workplace, production units, subjects, clinics, outlets etc. Each of these "units" has a separate management structure, specific aims and different people working in it. The integration of health promotion into the daily activities of a setting will, therefore, have to be carried out for each of these units separately and the outline presented here should be applied in planning the integration of health promotion for each unit.

Specific Aim 2.1: consideration and satisfaction of the health needs of the staff

Objective 2.1.1: Ensure that the staff avoid risk creating behaviour
Indicator 2.1.1.1: Level of smoking, obesity, exercise, and other risk creating behaviours
Method: (enabling, mediating, advocating)
Evaluation (criteria):

Objective 2.1.2: Ensure that staff utilises preventive services
Indicator 2.1.2.1: Level of utilisation of health check-ups, cervical screening, etc.,
Method (enabling, mediating, advocating):
Evaluation (criteria):

Objective 2.1.3: Ensure that the staff working conditions are compliant with reduction of risk at work

Indicator 2.1.3.1: Level of stress, accidents, conflicts, etc., measured indirectly and directly

Method (enabling, mediating, advocating):

Evaluation (criteria):

Objective 2.1.4: Ensure the general health of the staff

Indicator 2.1.4.1: Level of utilisation and timing of curative health services

Method (enabling, mediating, advocating):

Evaluation (criteria):

Specific Aim 2.2: consideration and satisfaction of the needs of the clients

Objective 2.2.1: Ensuring the health aspects of services and/or goods provided for clients

Indicator 2.2.1.1: Level of health hazards associated with the client population

Method (enabling, mediating, advocating):

Evaluation (criteria):

Objective 2.2.2: Ensuring the client's awareness of health risks and available solutions

Indicator 2.2.2.1: Level of client competence in avoidance of risk to health

Method (enabling, mediating, advocating):

Evaluation (criteria):

Objective 2.2.3: Ensuring the client's competence in dealing with existing health problems and health risks

Indicator 2.2.3.1: Level of client's competence

Method (enabling, mediating, advocating):

Evaluation (criteria);

Specific Aim 2.3: assessing and meeting the needs of the immediate social environment

Objective 2.3.1: Ensuring the social support from the client's immediate family and relatives

Indicator 2.3.1.1: Level of support, type of conjugal roles, type of family cycle of development

Method (enabling, mediating, advocating):

Evaluation (criteria):

Objective 2.3.2: Ensuring the social support from client's colleagues at work

Indicator 2.3.2.1: Level of support from colleagues at work

Method (enabling, mediating, advocating):

Evaluation (criteria):

Objective 2.3.3: Ensuring the social support from client's reference group, friends and neighbours

Indicator 2.3.3.1: Level of support

Method (enabling, mediating, advocating):

Evaluation (criteria):

General Aim 3: Initiating and Participating in Community Developments

This general aim operates on the settings level and is concerned with the settings position and interactions within the community.

Specific Aim 3.1: initiating and promoting the "health promoting setting" movement in the community

Objective 3.1.1: Popularising the "health promoting" status of the setting in the community

Indicator 3.1.1.1: Amount and content analysis of the publicity given to the setting in media

Method (enabling, mediating, advocating):

Evaluation (criteria):

Objective 3.1.2: Public meetings for representatives of other settings to learn about the concept of "health promoting settings"

Indicator 3.1.2.1: Attendance rate, comments and commitments of the attending representatives of other settings

Method (enabling, mediating, advocating):

Evaluation (criteria):

Objective 3.1.3: Workshops for representatives of other settings interested in becoming a "health promoting setting"

Indicator 3.1.3.1: Attendance rate, level of satisfaction and learning achievements, level of commitment

Method (enabling, mediating, advocating):

Evaluation (criteria)

Specific Aim 3.2: networking with other similar health promoting settings

Objective 3.2.1: Creating and/or joining a local network of similar health promoting settings (e.g. hospitals)

Indicator 3.2.1.1: Extent of the local network

Method (enabling, mediating, advocating):

Evaluation (criteria):

Objective 3.2.2: Creating and/or joining the national network of similar health promoting settings

Indicator 3.2.2.1: Extent of the national network

Method (enabling, mediating, advocating):

Evaluation (criteria);

Objective 3.2.3: Creating and/or joining the international network of similar settings

Indicator 3.2.3.1: Extent of the international network

Method (enabling, mediating, advocating):

Evaluation (criteria):

Specific Aim 3.3: creating healthy alliances with other health promoting settings on a local, national and international level

Objective 3.3.1: Establishing mechanisms for cooperation with other health promoting settings on a local level (e.g. hospitals, schools, services, enterprises, prisons, etc.)

Indicator 3.3.1.1: Extent of the cooperation with other settings

Method (enabling, mediating, advocating):

Evaluation (criteria):

Objective 3.3.2: Establishing mechanisms for cooperation with other health promoting settings on a national level

Indicator 3.3.2.1: Extent of cooperation with other settings

Method (enabling, mediating, advocating):

Evaluation (criteria):

Objective 3.3.3: Establishing mechanisms for cooperation with other health promoting settings on an international level

Indicator 3.3.3.1: Extent of cooperation with other settings

Method (enabling, mediating, advocating):

Evaluation (criteria):

The Survey

All these activities related to planning and carrying out HP/HE in a setting will have to be based on information about the existing situation as well as the needs and potentials within the setting. This is especially valid for the initial policy statement which should be produced by the management, approved by employees and validated by purchasers

This policy statement as well as all the other activities will be based on a survey carried out in the organisation with the support of external experts (consultants or academic institutions). The survey will include the following areas of inquiry (based on the example of a survey carried out by a Health Promoting Hospital):

Base Line Information

AIM 1: to establish the needs of the patients in relation to their utilisation of hospital services; to achieve this aim the study will have the following objectives:

Objective 1.1: to explore the ways and reasons for patients' attending different hospital units;

> *Indicators 1.1.1*: records of admittance and referrals;

Objective 1.2: to explore the "patient career" as a part of the treatment;

> *Indicators 1.2.1*: records on duration of stay; types of treatment; access to specialists;

Objective 1.3: to explore patient satisfaction with the outcome of treatment;

> *Indicators 1.3.1*: statements of patients about the satisfaction of expectations; objective and subjective expectations;

AIM 2: to describe the internal structure of the hospital as a means of satisfying patients' needs; to achieve this aim the study will have the following objectives:

Objective 2.1: to define the organisational structure, power structure, role definition and role relationships, professional expertise of the hospital;

> *Indicators 2.1*: the management structure; the role definition; the role relationships;

Objective 2.2: to explore potential conflict areas and possible resolutions within the hospital staff, as well as between the staff and the patients;

> *Indicators 2.2*: survey data on conflicts between the staff and staff with patients;

Objective 2.3: to explore the available technology as well as accommodation for staff and patients within the hospital premises as a means of satisfying patients needs;

> *Indicators 2.3*: opinions of staff about technology and existing accommodation;

AIM 3: to describe the links of the hospital with other institutions, the community and the environment; to achieve this aim the study will have the following objectives:

Objective 3.1: to explore the means and the level of financing of the hospital and its activities;

> *Indicators 3.1*: information about the available resources related to the needs for running the hospital; potential shortcomings;

Objective 3.2: to explore the relationship between the hospital and the DHA, FHSA and other community and voluntary bodies;

Indicators 3.2: descriptive data about these relationships with the assessment of them in terms of expressed expectations;

Objective 3.3: to explore the interaction between the hospital and the wider environment in terms of the provision of services, sources of employment, utilisation of transport, and sources of waste disposal and other aspects of potential contamination;

Indicators 3.3: data on any negative assessments of the hospital activities affecting the environment;

AIM 4: to describe, in addition to treatment, the preventive and promotive activities relevant to the successful treatment of patients; to achieve this aim the study will have the following objectives:

Objective 4.1: to explore the existing preventive services on offer;

Indicators 4.1: information on the existing preventive services;

Objective 4.2: to explore the existing health promotive activities;

Indicators 4.2: information on the existing health promotion activities concerning the behaviour of staff and patients;

Objective 4.3: to explore the links between the hospital and other preventive and health promotive actions in the area;

Indicators 4.3: information about existing links;

AIM 5: to explore with the hospital staff the possibility of undertaking a commitment to become a "Health Promoting Hospital" within the WHO conceptualisation of the requirements for such a commitment; to achieve this aim the study will have the following objectives:

Objective 5.1: to explore the felt needs of the staff and possibility of meeting their requirements;

Indicators 5.1: survey data on the needs of the staff; exploration of existing mechanisms for satisfaction of those needs;

Objective 5.2: to explore the necessary resources to meet the existing shortcomings within the provision of hospital services;

Indicators 5.2: data on existing and required resources for provision of hospital services;

Objective 5.3: to organise a workshop for members of the hospital staff and other relevant institutions (DHA, FHSA) for the purpose of establishing a joint commitment for collaboration and support in this endeavour.

Indicators 5.3: curriculum for workshop for the hospital staff;

Information for the Intervention

AIM 6: the creation of a "Health Promoting Hospital" movement in the hospital; to achieve this aim the study will have the following objectives:

Objective 6.1: the self-selection of members of staff who will undertake commitments and carry out role definition and task distribution among its members;

Indicators 6.1: list of members and their commitments;

Objective 6.2: the organisation of training ventures for staff concerning their commitments;

Indicators 6.2: timetable for training venture;

Objective 6.3: provision of skills for monitoring and evaluating the progress of the intervention as well as the changes within the hospital;

Indicators 6.3: content analysis of training ventures concerning the skills necessary for evaluation and monitoring;

AIM 7: the planning and provision of health promotion and health education ventures as a part of the normal activities of a "health promoting hospital"; to achieve this aim the study will have the following objectives:

Objective 7.1: planning of tasks for each subgroup formed in the hospital;

Indicators 7.1: list of subgroups; lists of tasks for each subgroup;

Objective 7.2: definition of indicators and criteria for the evaluation of each health promotion and health education venture;

Indicators 7.2: list of agreed indicators and criteria for evaluation;

Objective 7.3: carrying out the planned tasks;

Indicators 7.3: data on each health promotion/education activity carried out within the hospital; assessment of each activity using the set indicators and criteria;

AIM 8: integration of hospital health promotion and health education activities into the overall activities of the "health promoting health care system"; to achieve this aim the study will have the following objectives:

Objective 8.1: collaboration with the existing activities of the Health Promotion Unit of the DHA;

Indicators 8.1: data on collaborative activities;

Objective 8.2: collaboration with the existing activities of the FHSA;

Indicators 8.2: data on collaborative activities;

Objective 8.3: integration of all these activities into the health promotion and health education activities of the health care system in the district;

Indicators 8.3: District Health Authority programme on health promotion and health education; data on hospital aspects of these activities;

Information for Post-Intervention Activities

AIM 9: to carry out the monitoring of the intervention study; to achieve this aim the study will have the following objectives:

Objective 9.1: developing computerised instruments for monitoring the ongoing activities within the intervention;

Indicators 9.1: computerised instruments in place;

Objective 9.2: application of instruments for monitoring the activities;

Indicators 9.2: daily check of usage of instruments;

Objective 9.3: analysis of data collected by means of the monitoring process;

Indicators 9.3: checking reports of the analysis;

AIM 10: to carry out the evaluation of the intervention; to achieve this aim the study will have the following objectives:

Objective 10.1: evaluation of the health promotion activities within the intervention study;

Indicators 10.1: checking the evaluation methods and reports;

Objective 10.2: evaluation of the health education activities within the intervention study;

Indicators 10.2: checking the evaluation methods and reports;

Objective 10.3: evaluation of the outcomes of the intervention study in terms of staff satisfaction and improvements in the health of the patients;

Indicators 10.3: checking the results of the evaluation;

AIM 11: the auditing of the intervention in terms of staff and patient satisfaction of the expressed needs; to achieve this aim the study will have the following objectives:

Objective 11.1: establishment of existing professional and social norms related to the aims of the intervention;

Indicators 11.1: checking the changed norms;

Objective 11.2: measurement of intervention outcomes in terms of the established professional and social norms;

Indicators 11.2: checking the intervention outcomes;

Objective 11.3: definition of areas where the existing professional and social norms need reinforcement or change;

Indicators 11.2: list of sensitive areas.

The Intervention

The first step in the transformation of a setting into a health promoting setting, based on the information collected by the survey, will be a series of **meetings** of management and staff to find out who is willing to undertake which activities, to carry out a role definition of the agents and explore their needs in terms of further training programmes.

The role distribution will provide **names and tasks** for individuals willing to take an active part in the development of the necessary structure for HP/HE in that setting. These tasks will include:

- establishment of a *working group* composed of representatives of management, employees and clients aimed at carrying out the daily activities related to the new commitments; these daily activities will include the development of an effective communication system with the aim of sharing information with all the employees; the establishment of a training programme for management and employees with a specially adjusted curriculum in the subjects such as HP/HE, TQM, networking and alliances with other institutions in the community for the purpose of mobilising help and support, which may take the form of expertise and resources;

- establishment of *working sub-groups* within sections or departments in the setting, in order to carry out the activities on a local level; depending on the structure of the setting it may be necessary to decentralise the activities and delegate tasks to sub-groups with the same agenda as that established for the central working group;

- establishment of *Health Circles* at each work place, which can be the same as the Quality Circles if they exist, with the aim of enabling full participation of all staff in these activities; these are expected to take on the responsibility for actual HP/HE work since they will be at the interface with the clients;

- introduction of mechanisms for the *monitoring and evaluation* of HP/HE activities following the principles of the Total Quality

Management approach; in the case where such a system does not exist and the size of the setting justifies it, such a system will need to be introduced; in the case of small settings where such a system may be too great an administrative burden for the small number of employees, a monitoring and evaluation system may be introduced, using the same principles as TQM, but without all the necessary administrative documentation;

- where there is a plan for the setting to apply for *membership* of a national and/or international network, or even for the recognition of a "pilot" status, it will be necessary to establish a certain number of intervention studies within the framework of the activities of its various departments or sections; there are preconditions set by such networks which will be different for different types of settings, and which will have to be integrated into the daily activities of the setting and into the programmes of different working groups in that setting;

- even if there is no plan for the setting to acquire recognition the working sub-groups will have to develop *specific programmes* of activities adjusted to their special needs and opportunities.

A Guide to Writing a Protocol for an Intervention Study

The following summary guide may help in drafting an initial protocol for an intervention study. This is, however, a very short summary of a process which will need to be tailored and expanded to meet the requirements of differing kinds of research.

It is, therefore, recommended that appropriate academic or other research support is sought before proceeding too far with project planning.

Outline of a research proposal

The Health Promoting Settings are required to meet a number of conditions to be recognised as a 'pilot' or 'model' Health Promoting Setting. One of these conditions is to carry out at least five research projects within that setting.

These research proposals should be based on the principles that apply to intervention studies. This arises because they should provide an opportunity for members of each setting to acquire the necessary knowledge and skills in health promotion and health education and, through the intervention study, find out for themselves the best ways of fulfilling the principles on which a health promotion setting is based. These are: creating a healthy working environment integrating health promotion into daily activities, and initiating and/or enabling creation of networks and alliances within the community.

The main issues that a research proposal for an intervention study should address are set out below:

Description of the situation/problems

It is envisaged that the intervention studies within a health promoting setting will choose topics based on the activities of various organisational units, problems, professional services, or some other unifying issuc. Thc rcsearch proposal should describe the way the main topic of the intervention study fits into the general setting framework. It should also describe the main characteristics of the topic in general (drawing on other people's work and publications) and more specifically, the characteristics of the topic within the setting. It should, in addition, describe the relationship of the chosen topic(s) to the work of other settings and services within the community.

Description of the study

- *aims of the study:*

  the aims of the study should define the working hypotheses and the expected outcomes of the intervention;

- *objectives of the study:*

  the objectives of the study define the way of achieving the set aims. In an intervention study one should differentiate between objectives of the study in general and the specific objectives of the planned intervention:

  i. the general objectives will describe the ways the study will be conducted in relation to the main study aims(s); they should be based on general principles of applied research;

  ii. the specific objectives of the intervention will link its activities to the expected outcomes of the study; they should be based on the theories and practices of health promotion and health education;

- *methods:*

  the description of the methods should cover both the research methods associated with the study and the intervention methods associated with the set objectives:

  i. the research methods should cover the descriptions of the establishment of the baseline information, definition of the indicators and criteria, the measurement of changes and inferences based on the set aims and objectives;

ii. the intervention methods should describe and justify the achievement of planned changes, develop mechanisms for monitoring and measuring them, as well as making inferences on the basis of research outcomes

- *resources:*

  the proposal should include a detailed analysis of the resources required for the study and for the intervention:

  i. the study will require recurrent, as well as non recurrent finances, equipment, external help, etc.;

  ii. the intervention will require external help, learning material, workshops, equipment, help for data collection and analysis, etc.;

- *timing:*

  the proposal should be divided into phases relevant to various activities within the intervention study, as well as the total planned duration of the study.

Monitoring and evaluation

Every planned intervention study influences the overall corporate image of the setting, as well as the specific aims stated by the study. The evaluation should, therefore, include:

- *setting changes:*

  evaluation of the effects of any intervention study on the corporate image of the setting should include:

  i. collection of baseline information concerning the structure and role distribution within the setting, with special reference to health promotion and health education topics;

ii. definition of indicators and choice of criteria for monitoring and evaluating organisational changes, which can be directly or indirectly related to an intervention study;

iii translation of indicators into instruments for measuring changes;

iv choice of methods for monitoring and collecting information related to the process and outcome of changes;

- *intervention aims:*

  the evaluation of a specific intervention depends on the establishment of aims and objectives, measuring their achievements and making inferences; this is a part of the research design and it will be used also to throw light on the achievements of the intervention study, within the framework of the three main preconditions associated with the recognition of a health promoting setting, as mentioned earlier;

- *effects on the community:*

  the evaluation should also include the monitoring and recording of the influence of an intervention study on other similar settings within the community (networking), as well as on other settings and organisations involved in health promotion and health education (healthy alliances); for this purpose the evaluation should include:

  i. baseline information about other relevant settings in the community and their activities in the field of health promotion and health education;

  ii. description of existing, and creation of new, mechanisms for the interaction between various settings in a community;

  iii.establishment of changes within the existing community structure and community services provided by various settings and organizations following a health promotion and health education intervention.

Management, accountability and reporting

The intervention study should be placed within the general health promotion structure of the setting concerned and have a defined managerial and executive structure related to the study.

The study should be subject to peer evaluation and auditing. It may be necessary to create mechanisms for this purpose, if such do not already exist.

The reporting should take into account the preservation of confidentiality concerning the patients involved in the study and allow for reporting any possible adverse effects of the intervention, with the view of protecting the patients' rights and interests.

EXAMPLE: A WORKSHOP FOR STAFF IN A SETTING

Creating a "health promoting setting" through self-care and self-determination, involves, in the first phase, the popularisation of a movement concerned with declaring certain settings as "health promoting", and the actions of settings in achieving such improvements. The second phase includes the raising of competence of staff in a setting and/or representatives in four major areas: **initiating, organising, managing** and **evaluating** the setting's activities.

This example of how to organise a workshop offers a blueprint aimed at raising the competence of staff in a setting and representatives. It should be organised by the participating academic institution.

The participants of the workshop should be management and professional staff of settings who have shown an interest in participating in this movement. They are expected, after attending the Workshop and learning about the requirements for this involvement, to take on the commitment to participate in the movement.

This movement is based on a similar concept of "health promoting health care system", developed in some European countries, and already spreading, with a number of settings declaring themselves as "health promoting settings".

The background qualifications of the participants will be different, from highly educated professionals to management experts and administrative staff.

The teaching programme of the workshop is divided into four modules: initiating, organising, managing and evaluating a setting programme.

Workshop Module 1: Initiating A Programme

The **aims** of this module are to enable the participants to become familiar with and competent in "selling" the idea of declaring their setting as a "Health Promoting Setting" to the people living in that community, by emphasising the advantages and presenting the realistic contributions expected from each community member and setting staff.

At the end of the "initiation period" the setting should have established a "working team", examined the existing problem and selected the priorities in preparation for the development of the "organisation programme." The stages of the "initiating" process include:

The "Softening" Process

Initiating a setting's activity requires the support of the setting's staff,expressed in their active commitment to certain activities. To achieve the general acceptance of the idea of declaring a setting "healthy", the first step should be the discussion of the idea and its implications with individual staff members of the setting. This should create awareness of the possibilities as well as responsibilities associated with such a commitment. The individuals should be chosen for their influence, possible opposition, control of resources, etc. At the end of this process, the idea should be known in the setting and the staff should have had the opportunity to sound out the "significant others" whose opinions they value and respect.

The part of the Module 1 covering this stage in the process should enable the participants to acquire skills in "directive interviewing", i.e. individual conversations with the aim of acquainting a partner with the idea and sounding out their opinions and possible objections.

The content should include information about raising issues, listening to opinions, providing arguments, answering questions, as well as about the way of conducting an interview (introduction, questions and answers, conclusion).

The method of acquiring this knowledge, as well as skills, related to interviewing should include simple explanation of the major points, supported by numerous illustrations and followed by practice in the form of role play.

The assessment should include the expression of confidence by the participants, the opinions of their partners and the external observers, as well as the assessment of the supervisor.

Mass Meeting

Following the general preparation, the initiating process should include the organisation of a mass meeting of the setting staff. This can be a special meeting or a part of an existing mass meeting. The organisation includes the following stages:

- the advertising of the meeting, including the title, the time, the place, the agenda and the speakers;

- the agenda should include the clarification of the concept, the outline of advantages and possible disadvantages and the role distribution of potential participants;

- the "questions and answers" period should be allowed sufficient time for clarification of any issues and constructive treatment of any objections;

- the outcome of the meeting should be the acceptance by people within the setting as a whole to undertake the commitment and enter into the exploratory process of finding out in reality what this commitment implies;

- the follow-up should sound out individuals according to the role definition presented as part of the agenda, and organise a meeting with the members who agreed to participate actively in attempts to improve the "life" of the setting, which could also include health issues.

The part of the Module 1 covering the organisation of a mass meeting should enable participants to acquire skills in planning, advertising, organising, leading and participating in such meetings. The contents should include information about attracting attention and using mass media; the considerations to be taken into account when planning a meeting (place, size of the auditorium, seating arrangements, acoustics, lighting, chairing and running a meeting, presentation of speeches, leading a discussion, answering questions, dealing with troublemakers, and getting a commitment or opinion by sounding out the participants). The method of acquiring this knowledge and skills should include some general advice, a task and role play. The assessment should include the subjective feelings of the participants and subsequent evaluation of the meetings organised by the participants.

Forming a Working Team

The individuals concerned with the issue and willing actively to support the movement who come to the smaller meeting following the mass meeting, should be concerned with the following topics:

- forming "working teams" in various parts of the setting from among all the people interested;
- distributing the tasks among the members in relation to the organisational programme;
- taking on the task of studying and defining the problems in the setting.

The part of Module 1 dealing with forming working teams should enable the participants individually to approach different members at the mass meeting, recruit them for a working team and distribute tasks among them. The contents should include the understanding of the rationale for building such a team, familiarity with the general problems of the setting, the skills in collecting and storing information, ability to assess the potential contributions of each member, gaining their commitment and setting the task of objectively establishing the problems in the setting. The method should include some simple explanations about team leadership; practical skills in collecting and storing data, data analysis, and presenting the findings in an interesting and relevant way; these skills should be acquired during the work on tasks and practical examples. The assessment should be based on the preparations for the next mass meeting and reaction of the staff to the presentations; it should also be based on the choice of priorities and the level of commitment of the staff.

Second Mass Meeting

Once the work of the teams has been completed, they should call another mass meeting to discuss the findings and inform all the setting staff about the progress made towards organising certain activities. The outcome of this meeting should be a general agreement of the setting about the priority of problems according to their seriousness and feasibility.

The part of Module 1, dealing with organising the second mass meeting, should enable the participants to learn from the experiences gained during the organisation of the first mass meeting and avoid most of the mistakes made. The contents should include ways of critically analysing the outcomes and possible improvements. The method should include the simulation process in the form of tasks, where the participants get information about an imaginary meeting and carry out the exercise of improving on it. The assessment should be based on the outcome of the exercises as well as on the level of confidence expressed by the participants. A long term assessment should include the evaluation of the second mass meeting.

Programme Planning and Organisation

These preparations should produce a programme of future activities and Module 2 deals with its planning and organisation.

Workshop Module 2: Programme Planning and Organisation

Once the general idea of commitment has been understood and the staff have expressed their readiness to participate in this "movement", the **aims** of this module are to enable the participants to become competent and confident in drafting a programme for action, testing it with the general staff of the setting and producing a final organisational and operational programme for action.

The first step in planning and organising a programme for action should be to make a diagnosis by examining the causes and prescribing relevant solutions. The "medical" diagnosis should be available from the medical profession and it should include medical "causes and solutions". For a HP/HE intervention it is necessary to carry out a differential diagnosis with the emphasis on "health promotional/educational solutions".

One should take into consideration the fact that the activities of a "Health Promoting Setting" should include the problems of the staff working in the setting, the problems of the patients using the setting and the community within which the setting is located. The solutions to the problems in each of these areas should be adjusted to the needs and possibilities of each one. The success of such a simultaneous set of activities in these interacting areas should require a mechanism for coordination, evaluation and feedback. The main steps to be discussed in the workshop can be envisaged as follows:

Commitment

The implementation of the chosen solution should require the agreement and commitment of the institution, the patients and the community concerning certain required actions. This commitment can include resources, working time, expertise, services etc. It should be defined by the nature and the character of the solutions prescribed.

Tasks

Once the general commitment within the setting has been gained, the next step should be to specify the solutions in terms of activities. These activities should then be distributed in the form of task-distributions, for settings, and role definition, for individual members of each setting.

Action

Getting the whole programme underway will require actions on the part of the participants in the setting, following the task distributions and role definitions. These actions will have to be synchronised to achieve maximum effectiveness.

Coordination of Activities

Synchronisation of activities will require a mechanism for coordination as well as close cooperation of all the actors involved.

The task of such a mechanism for coordination of a programme will depend on the management skills of the teams, and this is the aim of Module 3.

Workshop Module 3: Management of the Programme

The **aims** of this module are to enable the participants to acquire knowledge about issues involved in management of a programme as well as skills in carrying it out.

The main objective of management is to *coordinate* the various planned activities involving members of the setting and their patients. This coordination is vital for *simultaneous actions* to take place.

Some of the solutions will depend for their success on the *synchronicity* of actions, such as for example in changing norms, values and opinions of the members of the setting and the patients.

The management of the programme should also include synchronising commitments within the setting as a whole and among its different parts, their acceptance of specific tasks and roles, as well as the adjustments of their actions with the aim of supporting and reinforcing each other.

Success should be evaluated. This is dealt with in Module 4.

Workshop Module 4: Evaluation and Feedback

The **aims** of this Module are to provide the participants with an understanding of the need for and the skills necessary for evaluating a programme, as well as making use of the feedback mechanism for the adjustments and corrections of the programme. This Module should clarify the distinction between the traditional evaluation process and the new evaluation adjusted to the needs of a "health promoting setting", which implies including the quality assessment procedures.

Evaluation should be included in the planning stages of a programme. To achieve a successful evaluation, the following preconditions should be met:

- the programme should have its aims and objectives defined in a measurable way; measurement requires a set of indicators, defined by criteria for assessment and translated into instruments which can be used to carry out the measurements; in terms of quality assessment, the programme should have a set of specifications for the expected outcomes, agreed upon by the purchasers, providers and consumers;

- the programme should be divided into steps or phases, and each one should require a specific evaluation of the achievement of each sub-aim or sub-objective;

- the programme should include a mechanism for utilising feedback information and adjusting the programme accordingly;

- in terms of a "community" type action in a setting, the phases involved are:

  i. *commitment:* It will be necessary critically to assess the commitments undertaken within the setting as a whole as well as by the individual members; these should be synchronised and should be supportive as well as specific; they should also be relevant to the aims of the programme; any problems noted at this stage should be fed back into the system and corrected before the next phase is undertaken;

ii. *tasks and roles:* It is important to distinguish between the general and specific aspects of commitments; the specific commitments will make task distributions and the role definitions possible; any problems due to the mismatch between the institutional tasks and individual role performance should be fed back into the system and adjustments should be made;

iii. *actions*: Evaluation should link the commitments undertaken with the distribution of tasks and roles and the actions carried out; it should also link the actions monitored with the actual achievements in terms of programme aims; since a number of actions and activities will be carried out within the framework of the programme aims, each one should be assessed separately; the feedback mechanism should enable corrections and adjustments over time, since action in a setting represents an ongoing programme and continuous activity as part of changing the life style in the setting.

EVALUATION, QUALITY ASSESSMENT, AUDIT

INTRODUCTION

A new approach to evaluation is considered to be necessary in the UK because evaluation in HP/HE programmes has tended to lag behind the development of evaluation in general. The concept of accountability, employing objective measurements of progress, has, for example in USA and Canada, resulted in evaluation being included in most government and other institutional programmes. Consequently, models and methods have been greatly improved and refined (Rutman,1984). The concept of metaevaluation (evaluation of evaluation) has also been introduced, as a part of auditing the evaluation programmes themselves. With the integration of evaluation into most of programmes, the number of evaluative studies has increased, resulting in the creation of a professional body of evaluators in the USA.

The new settings approach, based on an organisational model, has specific requirements concerning the assessment of the processes and outcomes of the interventions. This assessment will require the concept of quality assessment to be taken into account in settings where HP/HE are integrated into other activities. In the case of health promoting settings, however, the total quality management approach will be required as a special case of HP/HE interventions.

The introduction of the concept of auditing requires a distinction to be made between auditing and evaluation. In general terms, *evaluation aims at assessing success or failure in achieving stated aims/objectives, whereas auditing measures the outcomes against certain predetermined standards.* Although HP/HE have at present no agreed standards, there have been attempts to reach a consensus, as for example during the WHO Consultation on Ethics and Health Promotion (WHO,1989), when a set of ethical considerations for the practice of HP/HE were proposed. In most cases, however, the practice of HP/HE is measured against some general standards. For instance, HP/HE in educational settings is measured with respect to the rights of parents, pupils and the professional conduct of the teaching staff.

Auditing applied to evaluation studies, critically examines the models, the methods and the interpretations of results, using a set of agreed-upon standards, such as for example, an acceptable degree of scientific rigour.

Metaevaluation is concerned with the assessment of evaluation methods used in a whole range of programmes. It is of special interest for governmental and other bodies, which are engaged in providing funds and support for interventions and other programmes.

EVALUATION

The practice of HP/HE within the framework of "health promoting settings" will require new models and different standards, supported by evaluation that differs in kind from the existing cost-benefit analysis approach. The model presented here takes these new demands into consideration by examining the planning and management aspects and including for the first time the concept of "audit" as a special aspect of evaluation. It explores the requirements for a comprehensive monitoring, evaluation and auditing of this approach as a part of a wider health promotion and health education programme.

The comprehensive model for evaluation of activities concerned with this type of intervention serves as a tool for the planning, management and auditing of HP/HE programmes. It uses a systems approach and a modification of community participation methods for the set aims.

The three aspects of a programme, planning, management and auditing, are set out below and the various methods used for each aspect are examined.

Planning

The planning process requires the following: the definition of aims based on established needs; the setting of appropriate objectives reflected in the methods of intervention; securing the necessary resources (personal and material); and meeting the requirements for the evaluation of the programme.

The Needs

In HP/HE, as in any other area of planned change, the planning process starts with some initial and often firm notion about the desired outcome, which is based on the assessment of the needs of the client or target population. This idea about the outcome can be either objectively assessed or subjectively assumed by the change agents. The integration of evaluation at this early stage contributes to the objective assessment of "needs", by encouraging planners to measure them in the target population and, thus, link them to "outcomes". If this link is not established, then the measurement of "need satisfaction" as the outcome of an intervention in the target population will be merely an unsupported assumption, since it was not established that these "needs" existed in that population in the first place.

It should be assumed that people have a whole set of different needs, and that there are institutions and services, which individually cover most of these needs. For example, the health care delivery system is responsible for the satisfaction of health needs in a population, whereas the educational system, including its settings, is primarily responsible for the satisfaction of the population's educational needs. It is, therefore, important to establish which of many health needs can be satisfied directly in a "health promoting setting" now the setting can support the activities of the existing health care system.

Aims and Objectives

The integration of evaluation at the planning stage will also contribute to clarity in the definition of the aims and objectives of the intervention. *Aims* represent the intended outcome of an intervention. *Objectives* represent the activities which are planned to achieve the desired aims. This clarity can be achieved by establishing the necessary causal relationship between the aims and objectives and between the intervention and the outcome. It will not be possible to assess the outcomes of an intervention if the aims against which the objectives can be evaluated, have not been defined, or if the causal relationship between the aims and objectives has not been established. This can be done as a part of the intervention or can be assumed to exist if such a relationship has already been established..

If establishing and utilising causal relationships between aims and objectives becomes a part of the evaluation process, then in order to operationalise it will be necessary to define the *indicators* for the measurement of success or failure. These indicators include *criteria* relating to the achievement of the aims through the chosen objectives, which need to be translated into appropriate *instruments* for use in any measurement exercise. Thus, the integration of evaluation in the planning stage requires planners to be precise in what they aim to achieve and to account for the associated objectives.

An educational "health promoting setting" programme, could define aims in terms of the expected outcomes, such as the increase in self-sufficiency of the staff and the pupils, the creation of mechanisms for participation of parents, teachers and pupils in the decision making process, improvements in the environment (setting and external), and improvements in the health of the pupils and staff. The achievement of these aims can be judged through chosen objectives, such as increase in knowledge, social skills, motivation, success with the adherence to the educational programme.

Indicators

Indicators specify the evidence that will be used to find out whether a selected objective achieved a stated aim. The relationship between aim and objective is usually based on existing scientific evidence about the effectiveness of an objective in achieving an aim, tested in similar situations with scientific rigour, or, as is more often the case in health promotion and education, views about the relationship are based on "common sense". Integration of evaluation in this stage should encourage the planner to examine the existing evidence ("scientific" or "common sense") as to the causal relationship between the stated aim and the chosen objective.

In the example used, indicators could include the level of concern for health issues in the setting, the involvement of staff and pupils in health improvements, absence due to illness, and general information about morbidity (and possible mortality) arising from different causes (avoidable and unavoidable).

Criteria

Criteria represent the units that will be used in the measurement of the contribution of a certain objective to the achievement of a defined aim. They also include a value judgement about the measured level of achievement.

In the example mentioned, one aim could be to raise the awareness of people involved about the health needs relevant to the setting environment. The decision of the evaluator will be concerned with how to measure the different aspects of "awareness" to be able to establish the presence or absence of it in terms of the planned activity. This will, furthermore, require a decision about how to measure the different levels of different aspects of "awareness" to be able to establish the "minimal" and "optimal" as compared to the "absolute" level, which can then be used as a measure of success or failure.

Instruments

Once the indicators have been chosen and criteria for their measurement and assessment have been agreed upon, the planner will have to translate them into instruments to be used for the collection of relevant information or data. There is a whole set of different forms, which such instruments can take, from structured questionnaires and "aide mémoires" to diaries and scaling methods. The value judgement about the expected levels of change, as compared with those observed, will be important for the analysis of data and the justifiable inferences.

In our example of measuring changes in people's awareness about the health issues and the desired changes in behaviour, it would be necessary to develop an "aide mémoire" for an intensive study of professional opinions about the threat and the solution and a structured questionnaire to establish the level and character of knowledge in the target population, as well as the reported types of behaviour. This could be refined by adding certain scales (for measuring attitudes etc.), or other more precise forms of measurement, such as, for example, scales for measuring health needs, deprivation and locus of control related to decisions. This would provide base-line data against which one could measure any changes, following the planned intervention.

Evaluation will only be possible if the aims and objectives are defined clearly enough to allow for the selection of appropriate indicators and criteria. One should also mention that the instruments chosen for the establishment of base-line data and the measurement of change should be tested for validity and reliability before use.

Management

The management of a programme of intervention can benefit from a *formative* evaluation approach which monitors the programme in its different phases. This is characterised by a *feedback* mechanism, which examines each stage of the programme execution, feeds the findings back into the programme and allows the management to adjust the next stage in accordance with the findings from the previous stage.

The first factor that formative evaluation will have to consider is the *availability and utilisation of resources.* The questions to be asked will include the assessment of the adequacy of planning the allocation of the necessary resources and their appropriate utilisation.

The second factor to be considered is the *role definition and role performance* of the agents and institutions involved in the execution of the programme. This will provide an opportunity to monitor their performance and allow for any required adjustment or compensation. At this stage additional training could be a part of the necessary adjustment.

The third factor will be the *reaction of the population.* Those affected should be cooperatively involved in the execution of the programme, depending on the intervention methods used. The established objectives will be reflected in the methods used. Formative evaluation at this point should indicate whether the set objectives and methods are appropriate for the achievement of the stated aims.

Each of these factors, if taken into consideration in each stage of the execution of a programme, will provide the programme executives with invaluable information about the way the programme is developing and about the possible changes in the direction in which the programme is progressing.

QUALITY MANAGEMENT

Since a settings approach treats settings as organisations and uses the knowledge base developed by organisation theories and management sciences, the same organisational principles apply to the assessment of health promotion and health education (HP/HE) within a setting.

Whereas the evaluation of any intervention aims at assessing the achievement of the defined aims of that intervention, quality assessment looks specifically at the quality of procedures used in the achievement of the stated aims as well as the quality of the final product. This requires a clear definition of aims, objectives, indicators and criteria, as well as the translation of these into instruments which can be used to measure the achievements. If the aims of a HP/HE intervention within a setting are defined as the achievement of the needs satisfaction, of the clients or consumers with the health gain as the end product, combined with the issue of quality, then the evaluation becomes an instrument for the quality control of a HP/HE intervention, as well as a measure of health gain by the client or consumer.

The management sciences have devoted considerable attention to the question of the quality of products, in terms of quality management, quality assurance and quality control. Introduction of the concept of quality into the evaluation of HP/HE activities adds a new dimension to the existing approach of evaluation, which has so far mainly been concerned with positive changes in the level of risk from a specific health threat and measurable improvements of health of the consumer. To understand the implications of such an innovation in evaluation, it is necessary to understand the various aspects of quality management. These include the setting of standards, which need to be met if people in the setting wish to obtain a formal certification of its quality assessment system, including specifications and procedures that will serve as the basis for measuring the interventions and their outcomes.

Quality

The British Standards Institute (BS 4778: Part 1: 1987 / ISO 8492:1986) defines quality as **"the totality of features and characteristics of a product or service that bear on its ability to satisfy the stated or implied needs"**.

Other authors have added their own iddeas about quality such as "fitness for purpose" (Juran, 1988); "zero defects" (Crosby, 1984); "mistake proofing" (Shingo, 1986); "focus on problem of variability" (Deming, 1986); "cause and effect" (Ishikawa, 1976); "routine optimisation of the process" (Taguchi, 1981).

Quaility can be summarised as a continuous effort to improve performance and its outcomes based on the needs of the consumers, which provide them with a product or service that meets their needs at an acceptable price.

The Quality Task

Seting up a quality system addresses the questions of short-term and long-term goals. The short term-goals will provide the means of achieving day-to-day results, reflected in the quality of the products or services provided, whereas the long-term goals ensure continuity and reliability of quality products or services. It should answer the questions such as "are we achieving what we set out to achieve?" and whether the needs and expectations of consumers are being met.

To achieve this it is necessary to set "quality tasks", which will include:

- identifying the customers;
- establishment of their needs and expectations;
- setting up specifications and procedures;
- agreeing on and testing the means of delivery;
- documenting the necessary procedures;
- training the staff;
- evaluating and reviewing the whole process and outcomes.

It is necessary to distinguish between internal and external "customers". The external customers are the beneficiaries of services. The internal customers are the employees of the institution that provides the services who, according to their role definition, are part of a process in which they receive as well as produce certain materials or services.

The establishment of the needs of customers will depend on their role definition in the process. External customers will be interested in the outcome, whereas the internal customers will be interested in the support for the achievement of their specific tasks. Effectiveness in defining needs will depend to a large extent on the process of communication between the providers and consumers. The communication process may break down for a number of reasons, such as inability to express oneself and not knowing exactly what the needs are. This can also happen if the needs are clearly defined but the providers can not meet them due to lack of expertise or resources. It is, therefore, very important that any evaluation within the framework of quality takes into account the processes at the "interface" between the suppliers and consumers, whether internal or external. This requires building up an assessment system which will monitor the quality of communications at such interfaces.

The Quality Chains

The interaction between internal suppliers and consumers within a setting can be envisaged as a "chain" composed of a number of links. Since a chain is only as strong as its weakest link, the examination of the links in each chain of the production process will contribute to the assurance of the quality of the services or the product. Any break in the chain will have a knock-on effect on the whole process. This means that even a small mistake could be generalised and give the whole setting a bad reputation.

To ensure the effectiveness of each Quality Chain, it will be necessary to repeat the requirements mentioned in the Quality Task for each Quality Chain. This implies a realistic and effective definition of specifications and procedures for each Quality Chain. It also requires, for the purpose of quality assessment, the introduction of appropriate and accurate methods of monitoring, based on standardised documentation.

The Quality Circles

Quality Circles are composed of individual employees or Quality Chains, who join together in a group with the aim of ensuring the quality of the service or the product. This they can achieve by providing support to the members of the Circle and sharing in the tasks and responsibilities related to the production process.

The general idea behind a Quality Circle is that the members of a group share responsibilities by abolishing the job demarcation lines and becoming interchangeable with each other in performing certain tasks. It also implies that the members stand in for any absent member so that the group performance does not suffer. Within a Quality Circle members address all the problems that arise in addition to production, such as the quality of the service or the product, the personal problems of a member or any health issues which could affect a member's productivity and thus put the burden on the rest of the group. Another important aspect of the Quality Circle is its educational component, i.e. members take on the responsibility to educate and train one another or to provide members with time for training and thus raise the quality of the production process of the whole group.

Quality Assurance

One can describe Quality Assurance as including all the activities and functions concerned with the effort of ensuring the quality of a product or a service. These should include:

- a formal system of monitoring and evaluating quality;
- a set of specifications based on the existing resources and consumer needs;
- well tested procedures to ensure the meeting of the requirements set by specifications;
- a total integration of quality control into all the aspects of the production process;

- a total commitment of the top management to implement the requirements of Quality Assurance.

The basis for Quality Assurance is established by the standards set by national and/or international bodies recognised as certifying bodies for Quality Assurance systems in various settings.

Standards

One should, however, differentiate between "standards" and "specifications or procedures". The standards have acquired a specific meaning in terms of quality assessment and denote the preconditions that have to be fulfilled when introducing a quality management system in order to qualify for certification by one of the several certifying bodies. **Specifications are concerned with defining the type and quality of the actual product; standard practices and procedures define the quality of the processes involved in the production of the product to which the specifications will be applied.** In that sense, they should be a part of any evaluation no matter whether the quality assessment has been certified or whether evaluation uses only the principles of quality assessment as a part of the general evaluation approach. In other words, standards for quality assessment will be equally applicable to the production of large or small cars if that car manufacturer wants to gain certification of their quality assessment system. Regardless of the presence of a quality management system, the type of car to be produced will depend on the specifications of the product, whereas how it should be produced will depend on the procedures and standard practices for the achievement of acceptable type and quality for that product.

It is important to note the difference between quality assessment as a formal system and the evaluation of an intervention based on the principles and methods of quality assessment of a service. Some settings (i.e. hospitals, schools, etc.) may already have an existing quality management system, that has been certificated; other settings (such as small enterprises, general practices, or dentists) may not have such a system. Furthermore, such a heavily bureacraticised system will not be suitable for such settings. In either case, the accountability of HP/HE will be achieved by examining the quality of services provided, which can be done either by utilising the existing quality management system or by ensuring that evaluation uses the same indicators and criteria as the quality assessment in operation.

For this purpose, it is necessary to consider the question of specifications and procedures. In most institutions (firms, services, etc.), there already exist explicit or implicit specifications related to the their activities. These need only to be examined and translated into measurable entities in order to be usable for quality assessment. There are, however, new situations, production lines or services, for which there are no agreed specifications and quality assurance here needs to start by producing accepted specifications for that activity. Health promotion and health education are such newcomers in this field that the quality assessment of the HP/HE services requires the development of specifications and procedures as a basis for the evaluation of these activities.

In general terms, quality is assessed according to the level of satisfaction of clients' needs and expectations, which are reflected in the market forces.

Once the idea of "quality" has been clarified, it is necessary to describe the way it can be measured. It is obvious that there is no general way of deciding the level of quality of a product or service. It is necessary to establish the specifications against which the quality will be measured and the procedures or standard practices which are expected to produce the set specifications. There are three sets of sources from which one can derive criteria to be used in defining the specifications for a product or a service, if such specifications do not already exist:

- stakeholders - which implies the investigation of the expectations and opinions of the major institutions, groups and/or individuals involved in the production and consumption of the product or service;

- the benchmark approach - which refers to the comparison of the quality of the product or service under investigation with the quality set by the "leaders" in the field, generally recognised for their excellence and success;

- consumers - who have the possibility to vote with their feet, ie. prefer those services which best meet their requirements.

Stakeholders

In health promotion and health education, the stakeholders can be identified according to the setting in which these activities are being carried out. In general terms, the stakeholders will include the representatives of the owners or the government system to whom the setting is responsible, the employees working in the setting and the consumers affected by the products an/or services provided by the setting. Their contribution to the definition of specifications can be already noted at the time of establishing the service, or in the case of a new service or a new aspect of existing service, the specifications can be clarified by carrying out surveys and in-depth discussions to see the specifications aimed at in the provision of those services, as well as expectations concerning the quality of services provided or received.

The NHS has been concerned with quality related to the provision of health care to the patients. The expectations have been defined in the **"The Patient's Charter"** (see Appendix 5), mentioned earlier, which covers patient's rights, national charter standards and local charter standards . Each service is expected to produce its own set of standards (or specifications) within the framework of the Patient's Charter. It should, however, be noted that the term "standards" in this document is synonymous with our interpretation of "specifications", since NHS institutions are not required to have their quality assessment procedures certified by an outside body and are not, therefore, required to meet the kind of "standards" required for certification.

Benchmark approach

The opinions of the stakeholders can be complemented by looking at the quality of services provided by the "leaders" in this field. Frequently, an institution provides exemplary services, which could then serve as a specification of the expected quality of such services in general. To be able to use this kind of "benchmark" in other situations one would have to know what is being provided, how it is being provided, and what the outcome is, as well as why this approach has been successful. The institution serving as a "benchmark" would consequently have to carry out detailed monitoring and evaluation of their activities to be able to provide the answers to the above questions.

This has been achieved in some settings such as those of the health promoting hospitals. There are at present 20 pilot health promoting hospitals within the European Network of HPH. They are expected to monitor and evaluate their activities so that they could serve as a "benchmark" for all the other health promoting hospitals which intend to join the European Network.

Consumers

Since HP/HE, as an integral part of the activities in most health promoting settings, is an innovation and does not have precedents (compared to HP/HE in a settings), there is practically no consensus as between stakeholders and customers about the specification of HP/HE procedures and expected outcomes.

At present, there is no general agreement as to the exact meaning of the concept "health gain" which is given as the aim of most health promoting settings. It is also not clear how one can best differentiate between customers' needs and wants. Some attempts have been made to define "needs" in objective medical terms, whereas "wants" are preferences that the customers would like to have satisfied although it may not always be possible. For example, a patient may "need" an operation although he/she may not "want" it. The same applies to certain behaviours and actions, such as smoking, which a person needs to give up but may not want to.

One has to take into account that the popularisation of the "health promoting setting" will have important consequences for the expectations of the consumers. It will, therefore, be necessary to monitor these dynamic changes and upgrade the specifications accordingly.

Specifications

The evaluation of a HP/HE activity, based on the monitoring of quality of the services and outcomes, will depend on the success of the process of defining the specifications against which the quality will be measured.

Specifications should be defined in a positive way, that is, they should state what the product should be. This applies to the product in each stage of the process of production as well as to the end product. Specifications cannot be described in terms of wishful thinking or hope about the end product. For example the product of a HP/HE intervention should be described as "a non-smoker", "a person on a healthy diet", "a pupil not engaging in risk taking behaviour", "a person using condoms", "a person able to recognise symptoms of a certain disease", "a mother able to look after her child", "a worker using protective clothing" etc.

One should bear in mind that most of the settings (schools, hospitals, general practices, etc.) already have implicit or explicit specifications about their end products. The problem at present is how to complement the existing specifications with new ones related to HP/HE aspects of their work. The attempt to do this may be a daunting task and require considerable support from an external consultant.

Defining specifications

One way of defining specifications is to ask the people involved to describe their vision of the end product. The *stakeholders* (i.e. WHO, Department of health, etc.) have tried to achieve this by setting targets which, however, are only applicable to populations and not individuals. Many of the targets set by the Department of Health can only be met by means of a strong input of HP/HE, such as for example their target B1 "To reduce the death rate for breast cancer in the population invited for screening by at least 25% by the year 2000". The problem is that such population targets cannot be used as ready-made specifications for a setting, which, in this case, is engaged in offering breast screening services. The role of HP/HE in achieving this target is clear: getting women to attend the screening clinics. The specification for a HP/HE intervention in this case would be to use effective procedures to motivate women to attend such services and the quality of the end product would be measured by the willingness of the women to attend, their positive attitudes to the preventive measure on offer and their ability to cope with the results from such a test.

For the *members of a setting* (management and employees), this is not always easy, since there may not be a general agreement about what the end product should look like. In HP/HE interventions, this may not be all that clear: should a patient after being cured, leave the hospital as an established non-smoker? Or should a discharged patient only be made fully aware of the risks from smoking? Should a mother with a new-born baby pass a competence test concerning the feeding and the care of the baby before being discharged? Or should she only be made aware before discharge that there is a body of knowledge regarding the care of the new-born baby and where she can obtain it?

Asking the *customers* may be even more disappointing. They may have a different image of the setting and what to expect from participating in its activities compared to the stakeholders and the members of such a setting. They may want to get a quick relief from pain or discomfort and may not want to be forced to change their behaviour or modify their actions at the same time. A survey of customers or potential customers may, therefore, produce a "wrong" specification or at least a specification which is not comparable to that derived from the survey of stakeholders or members of the setting.

Reaching a consensus

When HP/HE was concerned with problems (cancer, CHD, AIDS, etc.), evaluation was much easier since a reduction in the incidence and prevalence in a population was a good indicator of HP/HE success or failure. With the shift to settings, such population indicators are not useful and new indicators based on new specifications are required. As we have seen, these do not as yet exist and need to be developed. The method of developing them cannot be based on surveys of those involved and more precise methods of approach will be necessary.

The quality management approach provides some helpful ideas as to how this can be achieved. In this process, the role of the consultants needs to be emphasised. They should be experts in quality management as well as in HP/HE.

An indication of a method of approaching the development of specifications can be derived from the quality management approach. The quality management approach requires a clear policy statement for each setting. In this policy statement, the role of HP/HE should be clearly defined, in terms of the specifications which will serve as the base-line for the measurement of the quality of the end product. All those involved (stakeholders, members and consumers) need to be in agreement about the policy and the derived specifications.

The issue at present is, therefore, to devise a new policy for a setting, which is based on the new settings approach of HP/HE and uses quality as the measure of success or failure. The basic policy of the new settings approach has been defined as creating conditions for a change in the culture of a setting which should include, in addition to immediate tasks within the setting, wider considerations relevant to the consumers. A health promoting setting is, therefore, required to address the following issues:

- creation of a healthy working environment;
- integration of HP/HE into its daily activities;
- outreach into the community.

These three areas of activity of a health promoting setting should represent the main concerns of the specifications for HP/HE activities in that setting.

If one now recalls the main aim of a setting as the "health gain" of the consumers, in which HP/HE need to play an important role, then the specifications for the setting will be different from those for a HP/HE intervention. This differentiation is necessary for the clarity of the defined specifications and the measurement of the expected achievements.

Total Quality Management

The concept of "total quality management" has been very influential in terms of quality assessment. It was developed by Deming and is sometimes known as the "Deming Management method" (Walton, 1989). It was developed by Deming shortly after the second World War, when he acted as a consultant to the Japanese industry and commerce, in order to help them carry out a successful renewal of their economy. Today, there is no doubt that this was successful, if one considers the dominant position of Japan in world trade and economy. In the West, many countries have studied Japanese success and discovered that it was of an American origin. This renewed interest in Deming and his work in Western countries, which has now spread through many companies and enterprises that attempt to emulate the Japanese methods based on Deming's principles.

Thc basic idca promoted by Deming is very simple, although at the time it was highly original. Deming postulated that the economic success will depend on the quality of goods. At thc timc, immcdiatcly following the war, it was a sellers' market and it was possible to sell anything that was available. Deming foresaw that this would change and that in a buyers' market the quality of goods would be decisive.

Stating that "quality sells the product", Deming examined the production process as a system, into which he included the supplier and consumer as well as the production process. This was new and proved to be critical for the success of quality control. In line with this approach, Deming maintained that one person's "raw material" is somebody else's "end product", and that one person's "end product" is the consumers' "raw material". In this way, a **production unit** is composed of suppliers' raw material, the process of production and the end product aimed at consumers. It is, therefore, logical that quality assessment should include the quality of the raw material, the quality of the production process and the quality of the end product.

A **production line** is a system which can include a number of production units. Quality control applies to all the stages within each unit as a part of the production line.

The indicators for quality assessment will be given by the needs of the production process and the needs of the consumer. Deming did not rely on asking consumers about their needs and emphasised that the producer should lead in the definition of consumers' needs by anticipating new developments and possibilities in a specific production process.

Acting as a consultant for a great number of years, Deming accumulated valuable experience on how successfully to carry out the required and often radical changes in an enterprise. He learned that the only way to achieve transformation is to **involve top management** and encouraged them to learn about the elements of their commitment before they take it on. A radical transformation will only be possible if the top management is behind it. This was tested in a number of situations where Deming acted as a consultant and where his approach produced direct profits for the enterprises.

The Deming theory of management control is of special interest to those involved in the evaluation of health promotion within an organisational model, since it has been tested and proved successful. The application of a tested model in health promotion would represent an innovation, since most of the models and approaches in present use are justified only on the grounds of arbitrary preference or commonsense, without any proof that they work.

Deming postulates that ensuring the highest possible level of quality in a product will require the selection of the best available "raw material", the most appropriate "method of production", and a detailed knowledge of the "needs" of the consumer. The inclusion of resources and the consumers into the model of production is an innovation that has resulted in considerable gains in industry and commerce. The adjustment of this approach to the needs of health promotion could represent an improvement of the existing method of evaluation in this field.

AUDITING

The concept of auditing is new to the practice of health promotion and education. According to Hudson and McRoberts (1984), auditing originated at the time "when the first property owners left their affairs in the hands of overseers, who were then required to account for their handling of the properties". To avoid misrepresentation of the situation by the overseers, the owners employed independent third persons to check on the situation - to carry out an audit. This is how the profession of auditors evolved, with all its surrounding procedures and protocols.

Hudson and McRoberts also report on the auditing of US programme evaluation activities and mention a study carried out by the US General Accounting Office for the year 1980. Although out of date, the study illustrates the extent of the development of auditing as well as evaluation activities. The study found that the total amount of resources devoted to programme evaluation in that year was approximately $177 million, covering 2362 evaluations.

Audit and Evaluation

In many cases it is impossible to differentiate between an audit and summative evaluation and the two terms are sometimes used interchangeably. It is, however, important to differentiate between each activity. *Evaluation* is defined by WHO as the systematic and scientific process of determining the extent to which an action or set of actions was successful in the achievement of predetermined objectives (aims). The definition of *medical audit*, given by the Royal College of Physicians (1989) illustrated how it differs from evaluation. It is "the sharing by a group of peers of information gained from personal experience and/or medical records in order to assess the care provided to their patients, to improve their own learning and to contribute to medical knowledge". An audit is thus carried out against certain set standards, which can be legally or professionally defined or may be shared by the peer group. Whereas evaluation looks at the achievement of aims, audit examines the upholding of predetermined standards and the accuracy of the information provided. For example, a financial audit will look at the appropriateness of the presentation of accounts in the light of current practice, and a medical audit will examine a medical intervention against set professional standards. (It is worth noting that a recent confusing use of "audit" refers merely to checking the existence of something, for example, as for "an audit of the resources in the department". This is not the sense in which it is used here.)

The introduction of the concept of "audit" into the evaluation of HP/HE activities faces the problem of the very small number of professionally defined specificiations against which a HP/HE intervention could be measured. This arises because HP/HE does not have a professional status, with a theoretically based body of knowledge, a code of ethics and a professional organisation to safeguard the conformity of the practitioners to professional norms. There have been attempts to professionalise HP/HE, with the consequent risk of creating a new professional elite. These attempts are in conflict with the WHO initiative for a "multisectoral" approach to the practice of HP/HE.

At present, efforts are being made to increase the professional responsibilities of HP/HE interventions, without creating a new profession. This has been reflected in the introduction of "accountability" for the outcomes, by using cost-benefit analysis as a part of the evaluation process. The introduction of "auditing" will extend accountability to expression in qualitative as well as quantitative terms, and efforts are being made to come to an agreement about at least some shared specifications.

One such effort has been "The Consultation on Ethics and Health Promotion" held in Tampere, Finland, in December 1987. The published document (WHO,1989) states: "In discussing ethics and health promotion, we are not concerned with passing moral judgement on the policies, behaviour or moral judgements of others, but rather with understanding which principles, practical criteria and decision-making procedures are appropriate to the exercise of professional responsibility in health care and in health promotion activities in particular". Fundamental ethical principles in health care apply also to health promotion and are concerned with beneficence (or non-maleficence), justice, and respect for others.

The principle of *beneficence* (to do good rather than harm) has been taken to imply several kinds of moral duty - the duty to protect the vulnerable, the duty of advocacy and a general duty to care. The principle of *justice* relates not only to punishment and compensation for harm done to individuals or the abuse of political power and public resources, but more fundamentally to distributive justice or the requirements of universal fairness, i.e. non-discrimination against and equal opportunity for individuals, and equality of outcome for groups. *Respect for others* has been interpreted to mean not only respect for the life, dignity and bodily integrity of the individual, but also respect for the autonomy and rights of the individual, e.g. the right to know, the right to privacy and the right to adequate care and treatment.

It appears that although HP/HE is not a recognised profession, the existing number of generally agreed specifications justifies the introduction of auditing as a qualitative aspect of evaluation.

Elements of audit

There are certain common characteristics shared by any type of audit, such as:

- *the client:* can be a person, an institution or an organisation which owns, or is responsible for, some function or activity, and being unable to exercise close control over it, will depend on reporting or accounting from others;

- *the auditee*: the person or a group of people who are responsible for certain actions or activities which will be audited;

- *auditor:* the person or a group of people with a recognised expertise or professional status who will carry out the audit on behalf of the client;

- *the criteria:* or standards are the basis for comparison of stated against expected achievements. These can be legal (theft, embezzlement etc.) or professional (not to harm the patient, provide adequate education, etc.).

Establishment of specifications

The main problem facing the attempt to audit a HP/HE intervention is the establishment of specifications against which the outcomes will be assessed. There are two different kinds of specifications, which can be applied in auditing: the personal and social specifications.

Personal specifications

The personal specifications against which a HP/HE intervention can be assessed will include two main areas:

i) Rights and duties

Each individual in a society has certain basic human rights of which health is one. This has been recognised by the WHO Constitution and serves as general standard against which various interventions can be assessed. In addition each individual has a set of rights and obligations allocated according to the social position that individual has in a society. An individual's perception of such rights will be the basis for the personal assessment of the effects of an intervention or of the provision of necessary services.

ii) Needs and wants

Each individual has a whole set of needs and desires or wants against which an intervention can be assessed. In some cases these needs are specific to an individual, whereas in other cases they may be shared within a certain culture. Fulfilment of these needs and wants will colour the individual's satisfaction with the available services or the outcomes of an intervention. One can distinguish between the needs and wants by considering the needs as objectively defined, whereas the wants represent subjective preferences and desires, and may not be objectively justified.

Social specifications

A social group can only function if its members are allocated certain positions or statuses and roles which define their expected behaviour or actions. This role performance is defined by norms or social expectations, which include a set of rights and duties associated with each status. An individual can have several statuses and play several roles, which are jointly described as a role set. This role set will have attached a whole set of different norms. These norms can serve as specifications for the assessment of an intervention and its outcomes.

A value system in a society denotes the broader specifications which, when related to the actualities of social life, can give rise to complexes of institutionalised norms. Norms can be defined as shared expectations in a population relating to a certain social position, behaviour and actions. Most of the activities concerned with the preservation of health and the management of disease are regulated by a whole range of institutionalised norms defining the behaviour and actions of the healing profession and their clients.

The measurement of social expectations or norms are of the utmost importance since the norms will be the main standard against which an intervention can be audited. The most important thing to remember when measuring social norms is to distinguish between the concept of a norm and the individual perception of that norm. Furthermore, one should include the measurement of the various characteristics of the norm, such as historicity, legitimation and sanctions, which together can be described as the basis for the norm's coercive power.

Audit scope

Reporting on US auditing activities, Hudson and McRoberts (1984) found that each study had a different focus, but that they covered three broad areas of concern: auditing the organisation and management of programme evaluation activities; programme evaluation measurements and reports; and reporting and using programme evaluations.

Medical Audit

A medical audit can use many techniques, such as peer review, large scale surveys and cost-quality analysis.

Assessment and analysis of a general practitioner's practice have been carried out sporadically for centuries and the standards set by experts have been used to measure a doctor's performance. The Working Party of the College of General Practitioners now recommends that "medical audit should quickly become established practice for all physicians" and the College has established an Advisory Committee on Audit to keep the subject under review.

The medical audit should measure the quality as well as the quantity of care. The problem arises when the opinions of patients about quality differ from those of physicians, and at present the specifications used are based on the professional norms defined by the professional organisation.

A characteristic of a medical audit is that patients are protected by anonymity and the reporting physician must preserve the confidentiality of reports to avoid any danger of documents used in audit being employed in legal proceedings.

Educational audit

Assessment and analysis of teaching practice have been carried out sporadically for centuries and the specifications set by experts have been used to measure a teacher's performance. Educational audit can use many techniques such as peer review, large scale surveys and cost-quality analysis.

Educational audit should measure the quality as well as the quantity of teaching and learning. This is not easy because the opinions of pupils/students about the quality may differ from those of teachers, and at present the specifications used are based on the consensus of peers.

There are three main categories of teaching and learning activities, which can be measured:

- *structure,* which includes the quantity and type of resources available;

- *process,* which is what is done to the client, and includes consideration of the ways teaching has been performed, what methods were used and the participation of the clients (pupils/students). Measures of process have to assume that the activities under review have been shown, by credible research related to teaching and learning methods, to produce an acceptable outcome;

- *outcome*, which is the result of teaching procedure. This includes measures of acquisition and retention of knowledge, acquisition of skills, ability to operationalise the knowledge and skills, and to carry out the designed role performance related to the educational programme.

Meta-evaluation and Meta-auditing

Since evaluation is a recognised activity it can also be audited. This is also known as meta-evaluation or evaluation and the auditing of evaluation components of different programmes (Cook et al.1978).

Although numerous grant-giving bodies support research and interventions, at present there is little attempt to carry out a meta-evaluation of such programmes. One could think of a number of reasons for this lack of interest in the standards of evaluation included in the programmes that these bodies finance or carry out themselves. An excuse often heard is that HP/HE "cannot" be evaluated because of so many variables to control. With the introduction of auditing into HP/HE, such excuses need not be accepted since any intervention can be assessed against certain generally agreed upon specifications related to the interests of the consumers.

SUMMARY

This second part of the book has dealt with the central topic of health promotion and health education (HP/HE). It has described the new approaches based on the WHO settings approach and the organisational model.

The development of this new approach reflects the changes in the scientific thought and the way subjective reality has been restructured to reflect our changed objective reality. The objective reality has changed largely because of the demographic changes, including the increased number of people in a society, the change in the age structure of a society, the changes in the location of most of the population which moved into towns, and the changes in the structure and values relevant to families.

Our attitude to disease and health threats has been radically changed as a result of the new developments in genetics. People have moved from the "blame the victim" approach to the "blame the victim's parents" approach. These new developments have also contributed to a move towards the resolution of the long-standing argument about the "nature-nurture" balance in the attitudes and behaviour of humans. The Genome Project promises to produce a complete blueprint of human genetic code and discover the association between specific genes and specific diseases an health risks. Dealing with this new problem area will require an extended screening service, together with the HP/HE contribution to the utilisation of such services and support for people to cope with the new knowledge and the new "at-risk" status based on their genetic inheritance. At present there is considerable confusion about the interpretation of genetic screening results, through lack of rcliability or thc translation of results in terms of causality instead of probability.

The outcome of this paradigm shift has been the development of a new HP/HE approach. Most work in this area has been carried out by the various groups and institutions commissioned by WHO EURO, who has the leadership role in this field. This has resulted in the shift of emphasis from problems to settings, that is the institutions in which people live, reproduce, work and play. Since such institutions can also be considered to be organisations, the logical consequence must be the introduction of an "organisational" model of HP/HE.

This new organisational model has introduced some radical changes to the HP/HE practice. The theoretical background has had to be extended to include organisational and management theories, which have not so far been a part of the standard HP/HE curricula. It is obvious that the new partners in health, the management, are operating under a different set of values and are motivated by a different set of goals. Their involvement in HP/HE is usually only partial and temporary, existing until the organisational aims have been achieved. The involvement of the workforce within organisations in HP/HE activities has thus required a commitment which has been much greater that previously accepted.

The main change, however, has been the distinction between the concept of "HP/HE in a setting" and a "HP/HE setting". Whereas the former represents existing practice, in the form of the integration of HP/HE into a setting as a separate activity with specific aims (screening, vaccination, prevention of CHD, giving up smoking, etc.), the latter is a new concept and requires the change in the culture of settings and the commitment to HP/HE by the management and all the employees, with the aims of creating a healthy working environment, integration into daily activities, and outreach into the community.

There is a special process which HP/HE needs to initiate for the purpose of popularising the idea of HP/HE settings, explaining the concept of a HP/HE setting, and helping various interested settings to initiate the changes and become a recognised HP/HE setting. There has to be an understanding of the potentials and needs of a setting.

This can be obtained by means of a survey. The data from such a survey will indicate potential problems as well as the existing resources within a setting. Bringing about the change will require additional training of the management and staff of a setting. A workshop can be planned, which could include four modules dealing with the most important aspects of initiating, integrating, monitoring and evaluating the work of a HP/HE setting.

An important consequence of the introduction of the organisational model is the change in the evaluation approach. Traditional evaluation has been concerned with assessing the achievement of the aims of a programme. Evaluation within an organisational model is based on the assessment of the quality of the processes involved as well as the quality of the end product. The theory of quality management and assessment is a new topic for most of the traditional experts in HP/HE and will require planned in-service training programmes. To assess a HP/HE setting, quality assessment procedures may not be adequate and a more far-reaching Total Quality Management (TQM) approach may be needed. Even if a setting is not sufficiently large to justify the administrative efforts required by TQM, the TQM principles will be most appropriate. It should, however, be kept in mind that even the TQM model in management is being at present supplemented by new developments of which HP/HE should be aware and which it should take into account when applying an organisational model in practice.

The reorganisation of the NHS has changed the way services are managed and run. The new differentiation between the purchasers and providers of services has had important consequences for HP/HE services. These have in the past been considered as providers of HP/HE and have developed expertise in this area. They are now a part of the purchaser's system and are expected to be involved in the development of specifications for the services which they are expected to purchase. Within the new organisational model the providers are the managements and employees of different settings. HP/HE should be an integrated part of their activities. The specifications for those activities should be based on the health gain of the consumers, who should be actively involved in the planning and implementation of such services.

This new organisational model requires a differentiation among the evaluation, the quality assessment and the auditing of HP/HE activities. Each of these has specific requirements and uses different indicators and criteria. This requires a very precise approach to planning and execution of HP/HE activities, this in turn needs a clear statement of the aims and objectives, description of the indicators and the decision about the criteria for the evaluation of the processes and outcomes.

All these new developments are now spreading throughout Europe, with the encouragement by WHO EURO of the establishment of European Networks for specific types of settings (hospitals, schools, etc). This is the subject of the next part of this book.

PART 3

CASE STUDIES

INTRODUCTION

HP HEALTH CARE SYSTEM
HP GENERAL PRACTICE
HP HOSPITAL
HP DENTAL PRACTICE
HP SCHOOL
HP COMMUNITY SERVICES
HP VOLUNTARY ORGANISATIONS
HP ENTERPRISE
HP COMMUNITY

SUMMARY

INTRODUCTION

The switch to a settings approach is of a recent origin and the newly created "health promoting settings" are few in number and have not been operating long. There has hardly been enough time to evaluate this development. It is still the case that most health promotion and health education is only partially and opportunistically integrated into various settings.

The transition of a setting into a health promoting setting includes three stages: *ground work, implementation on the organisational level, and implementation on the client level.* Most new health promoting settings have more or less successfully completed the first two stages (Grossmann & Scala, 1993), but it is still necessary to find out how the process is working on the client level before one can pass any conclusive judgement on the movement.

At present, there are European networks of healthy cities, health promoting hospitals and health promoting schools. There are also initiatives in the UK to explore the possibilities of creating similar institutions, such as "health promoting general practices", "health promoting general dental practices", "health promoting community care system", "health promoting voluntary organisation", "health promoting prison" and others.

The limitations of experience should be taken into account when considering the case studies of health promoting institutions presentedd here. At the same time, the limited number of such institutions does not reduce the importance of the introduction of an organisational model into HP/HE nor the extension of evaluation to include quality assessment measures. The current change from problem orientation to a settings approach that is taking place implies using an organisational model, as has been shown. The radical change in organisations needed to produce "health promoting organisations" is a gradual process. It takes some time and probably a number of modifications until it is generally accepted. The encouraging signs are, however, that compatible organisational and management models are gradually having an impact on many organisations, and they offer a favourable climate for health promotion and health education. HP/HE developments should take place simultaneously with organisational changes and be a part of them, since organisations can hardly be expected to undergo radical changes twice. The cases presented in the following section provide good examples of the problems related to the introduction of the organisational model into various settings without a parallel change in the organisational management of such settings.

The movement initiated by WHO EURO, which changed the emphasis from problems to settings and resulted in creating "health promoting settings" has spread into many areas of human activities. There are health promoting settings within the health care system itself, as well as within the various organisations and services in the community. The former include among other general practices and hospitals, whereas the latter include schools, community services, and enterprises.

Although the changes in emphasis from problems to settings are a recent development, in the UK this has been fully supported by the Government and is reflected in the most recent Government papers concerning the reform of the NHS (see Appendices 4, 5, 9 and 10).

The planning and organisation of health promotion and health education (HP/HE) within an organisational model have some general features that can serve as a basis for the programme as well as the framework for the intended activities:

1. The difference between health promotion and health education as two different but complementary aspects of improvement of health and prevention and management of disease should be clearly stated:

- health promotion is mainly concerned with the creation of a favourable environment (physical, social) for maintenance of health and prevention and management of disease;

- health education is mainly concerned with individuals and groups, and has the purpose of enabling, advocating and mediating in their adjustment; it should help them to cope with their living conditions, lifestyles and practices with the aim of enhancing health and preventing and managing disease.

2. The distinction made in the provision of health care between purchasers and providers has changed the role of the various health authorities and fund holders who as purchasers have an important duty to ensure the best possible care by defining appropriate specifications. The providers, who are now dependent on purchasers instead of on Government budgets, are required to meet these specifications and compete for contracts, by ensuring the high quality of their services.

3. The development of the role definitions of purchasers and providers is a dynamic process which is undergoing constant improvements and changes. These are based on experimentation with different ideas and the need to face the consequences of various changes, which may not have been envisaged at the outset.

One such consequence has been the radical change in health promotion arising from the introduction of the organisational model, and the need to rediscover health education as a neglected complementary aspect of health promotion. The need for inclusion of health education is the result of implementing the organisational model in the service industry, which deals with individual customers and needs individual solutions to the health problems, including the reduction of health risks and achievement of health gain.

4. The new overall approach to HP/HE is based on the shift of emphasis from problems to settings; settings are considered as organisations which implies the application of organisational and management theories into the HP/HE planning and quality assessment into evaluation;

5. The new organisational model of HP/HE provides two variations:

- HP/HE within an organisation or the "integrative" approach (i.e. inclusion of certain HP/HE programmes based on specific health problems);

- creating a health promoting organisation (i.e. organisational restructuring relevant to undertaking the following commitments: creating a healthy environment, integrating HP/HE into the process and outreach into community in the form of networks and alliances).

6. The new organisational model of HP/HE operates on three levels:

- ground work;
- implementation on the organisational level;
- implementation on the consumer level.

7. Each of these three levels can be identified with the phases of implementing HP/HE within an organisation and can be further subdivided into a number of stages, which are set out below:

PHASE I: GROUND WORK

This phase is concerned with work at the top administrative and managerial level of a setting, where the decisions are being made about the implementation of the HP/HE programme in the organisations. It can be divided into following stages:

Stage I:1 Consultations

The top management of a setting will have to be convinced that the planned programme of HP/HE is necessary, feasible and promising in terms of health benefits for the consumers/clients and financial benefits for the setting. These managers should, therefore, be well informed about commitments and possible outcomes as well as the necessary requirements. The decision should be made about whether they wish to engage in such a process and on which level. This should be, as an integration exercise or as an approach to creating health promoting settings, or both.

The outcome of this consultation should be the creation of a Programme Team, which has the task of initiating the necessary developments and keeping top management informed.

Stage I.2 Base line studies

Once top managerial level has agreed that a HP/HE programme is desirable, it will be necessary to establish which problems are to be faced and solved by such a programme.

For this purpose it will be necessary to collect information, using a case study approach (qualitative analysis) and a survey approach (quantitative and secondary data analysis), of the setting and their health problems.

Stage I.3 Publicity

Depending on the decision made by the top management of the setting it will be necessary to publicise the movement among staff.

Stage I.4 Recruitment Programme

The outcome of this ground work should be the implementation of the programme. This will depend on the facilitators (health consultants) who should enable appropriate programmes to be carried out. The health consultants should meet the following criteria:

- knowledge about health problems (causes and solutions);
- knowledge and skills in people and resource management;
- knowledge and skills in HP/HE methods.

Stage I.5 Workshops for Health Consultants

The selected health consultants should have an opportunity through workshops to learn more about this specific programme and exchange opinions and produce suggestions for its improvement. They should also have an opportunity to update their knowledge in areas in which they do not feel fully competent.

PHASE II: IMPLEMENTATION ON THE ORGANISATIONAL LEVEL

This phase includes the Programme Team's approaches, directly or through the appointed health consultants, to various organisational units which have volunteered to participate in the programme. This will include the following stages (applicable according to the size of the organisation):

Stage II.1 Explanation of Commitments

Each organisation's top management will have to be briefed about the character of the programme (either the "integrative" or "health promoting setting" model) and be invited to prepare consultations with their line managers and employees.

Stage II.2 Role Distribution

The members of the setting and the management need to decide on a number of issues for the implementation of the programme including the following:

- establishment of needs and the selection of topics according to the needs of the employees;
- role distribution among the members of the Health Circle;
- development of a time table for the plan of action;
- development of a feed-back mechanism for adjustments of the programme.

Stage II.3 Workshop for Staff

The implementation of a HP/HE programme in a setting will require certain expertise which is best obtained by attending a workshop. In case of smaller organisations a workshop could be organised for the members of a number of them at the same place. A sample programme for such a workshop has been presented earlier.

Once the organisational preconditions have been met it will be necessary to implement the programme.

PHASE III: IMPLEMENTATION ON THE CONSUMER LEVEL

This is where the actual HP/HE work takes place. It can take a number of forms and the stages can run consecutively or simultaneously according to the needs and available resources.

Stage III.1 Plan of Action

According to the established needs the plan of action will include the following:

- selection of topics and preparation of background material;
- selection of methods according to the topic;
- monitoring and evaluation.

Stage III.2 Implementation

The implementation of the plan of action will include the following:

- the time table, membership, place and the programme of action;
- expert support and relevant material;
- mechanisms for evaluation;

Stage III.3 Evaluation and Feed-back

The evaluation will be carried out using the principles of Total Quality Management already discussed in detail earlier.

THE HEALTH PROMOTING HEALTH CARE SYSTEM

The aim of this chapter is to provide the background to the field reports on the creation of various health promoting settings. The experiments have taken place within the framework of the movement initiated and supported by the WHO EURO, and their European Networks for various types of health promoting settings.

In the UK, the movement has been implicitly as well as explicitly recognised in the many documents published by the Department of Health, in which health promotion and health education are presented as the basis for any health improvements, as well as supported by the recommended structural changes within the health care system.

The NHS reform

The reform of the National Health Service is described in the document "Health of the Nation" (HMSO, London, 1991) and includes ideas presented a year earlier in the document "Working for Patients" (HMSO, 1990). The "Health of the Nation" document represents a departure from the "medical" model of provision of health care. It states that the strategic role of the Department of Health is to monitor and assess the health of the nation and take the action necessary, or ensure the action is taken, to improve and protect health.

Emphasis on health instead of disease is reflected in many different places in the document, such as for example in the attempt "to develop a health strategy for England" as well as in stating that the responsibility of District Health Authorities is "the health of its people". The new development represents the concentration on the "health" role of a person, which is the focus of prevention, coping and empowerment in terms of decision-making. The document is, therefore, "progressive" since it to some extent reflects new trends in social and health sciences.

The policy objectives emphasise the need to identify the main health problems, not only through epidemiological statistics, but also identifying the felt needs of individuals and the means of satisfying them effectively.

The document emphasises health promotion and disease prevention and the need to redress the balance between prevention and treatment which has until now enjoyed a privileged consideration. The document, however, fails to explain what is meant by "health promotion". It appears to be identified with the provision of information to the population in general and patients in particular. This is of special importance since the document recognises the complexity of factors influencing health, such as genetic inheritance, personal behaviour, family and social circumstances and the physical and social environment. In international HP/HE it is generally accepted that health promotion is responsible for the improvements in "external" factors, whereas health education is more concerned with personal behaviour and family competence. This distinction is not made in the document, and there is a possibility that the "health promotion" recommended there will remain dependent on "cognitive" models, concerned only with improvement in knowledge and access to information.

The document is also "progressive" in terms of recognising the importance of a multisectoral approach in looking after the health of a population. In a very positive way it refers to the contributions and responsibilities of a number of relevant sectors, in addition to the health care system, such as the Department of Environment, Department of Transport, the Chancellor of the Exchequer, Home Office, Ministry of Agriculture, Fisheries and Food, Department of Education and Science, Department of Social Security, Department of Trade and Industry, Department of Energy, Employment Department and Health and Safety Commission, as well as local government, industry and commerce and the voluntary sector. It places emphasis on community participation and responsibility concerning health care services. The effectiveness of such a recommendation for multisectoral action will depend on the development of an appropriate mechanism for community participation, in addition to mechanisms for the "scrutiny of performance and outcomes". This implies that in addition to local and voluntary organisations, mechanisms should be developed for the mobilisation of population resources, and increasing their competence in decision-making processes, which are decisive for the effectiveness and efficiency of the health care system.

The health strategy for England, however, reverts to the old "problem-based" approach within a "medical" model and lists the causes of morbidity and mortality, areas of potential improvements and of potential risks to the health of a population. It does not mention the need for improvements in the physical and social environment, which are also contributory factors to ill-health and premature death. It is now recognised that air and water pollution, nutrition, working conditions, unemployment and social as well as geographic differences can affect the health of a population. Although the document stresses the need for the adjustment of services to the available resources, it does not tackle the differences in resource distribution between preventive and curative medicine.

The document emphasises the new role in health promotion and health education given to the District Health Authorities and the Family Health Services Authorities, as well as the service providers such as General Practitioners and Hospitals. It also emphasises the need for the quality control of activities carried out by the health care system, which also includes the need for evaluation and audit by independent and professional bodies.

HP REGIONAL HEALTH AUTHORITIES (HP RHA)

The new role of Regional Health Authorities as purchasers of health services has been reflected in the tasks facing the RHAs and their contribution to the national strategy for health, these include:

- providing a strategic framework which is agreed and shared by purchasers of health care, which takes account of both national objectives and targets and the particular needs and priorities of each region;
- supporting purchasers in developing and producing local strategies and the production of purchasing plans which translate regional and local priorities into action;
- providing a focus for collaborative working on a region-wide basis;
- agreeing standards for improvements in health jointly with FHSAs, DHAs and GP fund holders against which performance in achieving health objectives can be monitored;
- providing an active link between national, regional and local health programmes and support activities, including those of the Health Education Authority;
- encouraging innovation and research.

In relating the new role of RHAs to the WHO strategy, the most important aspect would be for RHAs to develop the NHS activities within the framework of the WHO "Health for All by the Year 2000" policy and the targets set by WHO to achieve this aim (WHO, 1984). In order to do this, RHAs would need to provide the initiative for the DHAs and FHSAs in the implementation of the NHS Reform and produce standards for the assessment of such achievements.

The most recent developments (June 1994) indicate the possibility of abolishment of RHAs and the decentralisation of the whole system, by giving the fund holders purchasing power and expecting them to set specifications for the providers of services.

HP DISTRICT HEALTH AUTHORITIES (HP DHA)

The main shift in the DHA role has been from being concerned with disease to becoming responsible for the health of the local population. Their role in health promotion and health education has changed from providing services to purchasing a comprehensive range of high quality health care services to meet the needs of the local population and to achieve optimum health outcomes. The DHA is required to participate in planning health promotion and disease prevention services in addition to services for diagnosis, treatment, care and rehabilitation.

Each DHA's responsibility, to complement those of Family Health Services Authorities, will include:

- collection, analysis and interpretation of routine and ad hoc information about the health of the population, and preparing annual reports which analyse current problems affecting health;
- agreeing priority areas for targeting effective service interventions to those populations most at risk and for assessing the impact of services;
- working with local communities in promoting and maintaining health locally;
- collaborating with others on the development of joint policies and strategies for health promotion and disease prevention, including with FHSAs on primary care, and with local authorities over wider public health issues such as environmental health, outbreaks of food poisoning and accident prevention;
- making specific recommendations for achieving health outcome objectives which relate to the purchasing of services by the DHA, as well as pointing out action required by other organisations to help improve the health of the population.

The fact that the DHAs' purchasing of services should be based on the expectations of consumers as well as the needs of the local population, implies that the DHAs should have the ability to assess these needs in a valid and reliable way and translate them into specifications for the purchased services.

At present, there are attempts to improve the methodology of discovering such needs through surveys aimed at "listening to people" and recording their needs. The information collected is assessed by the DHAs according to priority and available resources, and acted upon accordingly. The main problem with such an approach is that it is a slice in time and does not take into account the dynamic character of population needs. It also limits the participation of the population in the decision-making process to providing information.

In its circular "DHA Project: Views of Local People", the NHS Management Executive (draft document October 1991) recommends, among other things, that the emphasis should be on "involvement not consultation: need to develop a process of on-going involvement rather than one-off consultation initiatives", and further on: "Key responsibility of DHA to encourage local people to be involved in the purchasing process".

To ensure the involvement of local people it will be necessary to establish mechanisms for people's participation in the decision-making process within DHAs. Such mechanisms should operate through some formal body created specifically for this purpose. Participation should present an opportunity for the constant updating of information about "people's needs", directly derived from the participants. The joint decision-making process should ensure that the population contributes to the choice of priorities within a situation of limited resources, and accepts the limitations. There needs to be a constant feed-back concerning the consumer satisfaction. In addition to information from the participants, the DHA should establish mechanisms for recording and collecting information about people's needs and opinions directly from the providers of services (hospitals) or indirectly (GPs opinions about hospital services). The verification of the representativeness of information collected can be achieved by specific surveys.

Information collected from the population as well as the consumers should include monitoring the respect for patients' rights, as well as the standards of services as defined in the "Patient's Charter" (Dept. of Health, HMSO, December 1991). For this, the RHAs and the DHAs should produce indicators, criteria and instruments, as well as the methods of data collection, storage and utilisation.

HP FAMILY HEALTH SERVICES AUTHORITIES (HP HSA)

Within the NHS reform, there has been a change from the Family Practitioner Committees to Family Health Services Authorities. The new role of the FHSAs is described as:

- developing, with DHAs, joint health profiles of the local population, agreeing priorities and setting targets, and contributing to annual reports by Directors of Public Health on the health of the population;
- targeting cash-limited resources, in conjunction with DHA resources, at areas of greatest need and assessing the impact of service developments;
- establishing consumer groups to contribute to the planning process;
- establishing joint planning arrangements and contributing to joint working with DHAs and Local Authorities, voluntary groups and community groups;
- agreeing joint policies for the service and health programmes shared with DHAs, such as immunisation, child surveillance, cervical and breast cancer screening, health education, and the care of elderly people;
- encouraging and supporting multi-disciplinary team working and training in primary health care;
- funding facilitator services to enable them to introduce and support organisational change within general practice, including the adoption of minimum standards for screening, audit of records etc.
- supporting family health practitioners in developing high quality, consumer-responsive services which meet local needs.

The establishment of the new Family Health Service Authorities has been accompanied by new contracts for GPs and dentists (DoH, 1989, DoH, 1990). These have stimulated a lot of discussion prior to acceptance and signing of the contracts by the GPs and dentists. The changes concerning their health promotion and health education role have been radical, since for the first time the GPs and dentists are being paid for this kind of work.

This work has mainly taken the form of payments for reaching certain targets, such as immunisation and vaccination and cancer screening. To achieve these targets the GPs have had to resort to health promotion and health education methods, with the aim of increasing the utilisation of these services by their patients. The contract made also provision for GPs to provide their patients with "health promotion clinics". These had to be registered and approved by the FHSA and had to fulfil certain conditions such as being held in a specific place at a regular time and have a minimum of 10 patients each.

This innovation has prompted some FHSAs to contract for research projects to examine specifications for such clinics and acceptable methods for persuading the patients to utilise the services on offer.

Such a study has been carried out in Salford, UK. The results have shown shortcomings and indicated better ways of approaching patients. For example, persuading patients to use immunisation and vaccination services has concentrated on selling such services, through emphasising the benefits. It has disregarded the fact that most patients could not identify with the benefits since they had never seen most of the diseases against which they were supposed to protect their children. Selling the health threat before selling the protective measures might have improved the uptake. The study of the uptake of cancer screening services has drawn attention to the conflict between the need to reach certain targets and the rights of the patients to refuse such preventive screening activities. The study of the existing and potential health promotion clinics has also shown that there are two types of clinics: those concentrating on the problems (asthma, diabetes, etc.) and those concentrating on the methods (counselling, advocacy, etc.). The study showed that the GPs have specific needs and require an update of health promotion and health education knowledge and skills, for themselves as well as for the other members of the health care team. The FHSA has to reach agreement on the specifications for the assessment of such clinics before approving payments.

Other studies have been carried out to discover how effective this very costly exercise has been in terms of patients' health gain. An article by Peter Pallot in the Daily Telegraph (19th July 1993) under the title

"GP's £200m health drive 'is a flop' ", has or should have sent ripples throughout the health promotion community. The new approaches initiated by WHO seemed logically to provide for patients needs in order to improve their health. In simple terms: "shift from the medical problems to the people if one wants to help them improve their health". That is exactly what happend through focusing on various settings, including that of general practice. This treated the practice population as a target, found out about their needs and tailored programmes to meet them. The new contract signed by GPs in fact gave them a paid opportunity to offer their patients services intended to change their behaviour and life style, prevent disease and improve health. The patients made use of this offer and a whole range of health promotion clinics were organised and paid for.

The article mentioned reports on two studies, one costing £1.5m and the other £1m, which found that the GP activities in the form of health promotion clinics, costing £200m and raising the GP income on average by £2,400 each, have not been successful in meeting the expectations concerning the improvements in the health of the patients. The predominant method was individual counselling and advice given to the patients by the practice nurse. The article stated that a "fundamental rethink" was necessary if the White Paper targets were to be achieved.

The "rethink" mentioned should lie in the direction of supporting research and intervention studies concerning health education methods, their effectiveness, efficiency, and possible side effects. The first steps have already taken place through the rediscovery of the importance of health education and through concentrating on the quality assessment in health promotion, including the health education methods employed in health promotion programmes.

The health promotion and health education aspect of GPs contracts has been recently changed. At present, the GPs can register their health promotion and health education activities according to the type of services provided in three different bands and are paid accordingly. (For details see GP Case Study). There is also a possible change in that DHAs and FHSAs may be joined into one purchaser unit. This will require a redefinition of their responsibilities and competences with special reference to health promotion and health education.

THE HEALTH PROMOTING GENERAL PRACTICE

Introduction

The reform of the NHS as described in the White Paper "The Health of the Nation" and reflected in the new contracts between the GPs and the NHS, made provision for the GPs' role in health promotion and the way they should be paid for such activities. In the first instance the GPs' payment was linked to targets concerning the immunisation and vaccination as well as screening programmes; it was followed by their receiving payment for health promotion clinics attended by a minimal number of their patients.

The present situation is that the GPs play two roles: as fundholding purchasers of services from other setings and as providers of primary care to the patients. In the latter role, they can register for health promotion activities within three bands and are paid according to the band for which they have registered. GPs, in all the three bands, are expected to have relevant information about the target population in the practice, develop plans for reaching those in the target population who do not come to the practice and carry out health promotion aimed at patients in the target groups.

- band 1 (developmental) includes the advice to the patients about smoking;
- band 2 (mainstream) includes the implementation of a health promotion programme for tackling coronary heart disease (CHD), including smoking, diet and exercise;
- band 3 in addition to the activities concerning CHD, health promotion should address at least one other problem of national or local priority.

AN HP GENERAL PRACTICE (HPGP)

The concept of a "health promoting general practice" (HPGP), represents the new organisational model approach encouraged by the WHO. It involves the practice as a whole in HP/HE activities, including staff, patients and members of the immediate and wider community. The assessment of activities is based on quality management; it uses indicators related to the health gain of the patients and reflect the specifications required by the purchasers.

The formal recognition of a general practice as a "health promoting general practice" requires the GP to undertake the commitment to fulfil the following conditions:

- creating a healthy working environment;
- integrating HP/HE into all the practice activities; and
- establishing links (alliances) with other relevant institutions in the community for the benefit of the staff as well as the patients.

Creating a healthy working environment

The GP should make certain that the premises, working conditions of staff, working hours, appointment system, personal relationships, records etc., are conducive to a healthy and satisfying ambience in which the staff work and interact as well as see patients and provide services for them.

Integration of HP/HE

The services provided to meet the needs of patients can be distinguished as medical, psychological and social, or a combination of some or all of these. The medical services deal with the symptoms presented and medical conditions diagnosed; the psychological services deal with emotional states of the patient which may but need not be directly related to the medical condition; the social services deal with the patient's interaction with and support from the social system within which the patient lives, works and plays.

Both, medical and psycho-social services include an important contribution of HP/HE. Within the medical services, HP/HE are concerned with the raising of the patient's competence and enabling the patient to cope with the health problem, and with strengthening the patient's compliance with the prescribed treatment, in order to become well as soon as possible. Within the psycho-social services, HP/HE is concerned with dealing with the emotional problems of the patient, such as anxiety, animosity, anomie, andf so on, as well as advocating patient's rights and mediating between the patient and the social system, including working, learning and living conditions.

Outreach into the community

A successful GP will need to establish networks with other GPs either directly or through the Family Health Services Authority (FHSA) and to enter into alliances with other institutions and services in the area. This is in agreement with the new role of a HPGP which operates with a "career's" model of the patient's role. This implies that the GP takes into account the various characteristics of patients during the first contact with the practice, and continues to monitor their progress when they leave the practice and either return back to the community or enter another service due to referral.

In addition, the GP may be required to help a patient to solve some social problems for which the GP will have to mobilise the support of other institutions and services in the community. This "outreach" into the community enables the GPs to carry out their mediating and advocating role.

PRACTICAL IMPLICATIONS FOR AN HPGP

An organisational model applied to the activities of an HPGP suggests that an HPGP will operate on three levels: ground work level, practice (organisational) level and patient (consumer) level. Using this conceptual framework, activities can be analysed as follows:

The Ground Work Level

To create an HPGP a GP will have to undertake a number of practical steps:

Exploration

The impetus for considering the transition of a general practice into an HPGP can come from outside or from within the general practice. External suggestions may come from the new settings approach, which is now being popularised in the professional as well as the popular press, as illustrated by examples of some health promoting settings such as a "healthy city" or a "health promoting hospital". There are also movements identified with certain organisations (WHO, NHS, HEA, etc.), which are looking for volunteers within certain settings (schools, hospitals, enterprises, etc.) to initiate and undertake pilot projects in that area. The members of certain general practices (managerial and/or professional) may have established contacts with such movements and may initiate such an activity within their own general practice.

Current experience with certain health promoting settings such as hospitals, enterprises and schools, suggests the need for expert advice in this process. This arises from the fact that the members of a general practice are experts in management and specific professional activities but need advice on the health promotional and health educational aspects of such a dramatic change.

It is, therefore, considered to be advisable in this first phase of exploration, to have discussions with health promotion experts, which will enable the management as well as professionals and other staff of the general practice to become aware of the commitments expected from staff of a HPGP.

Consultation

No matter where the initiative comes from, it will still be important to establish contact with a HP/HE expert and enter into preliminary discussions about the requirements, processes, obstacles, and any other aspects of such an important transition. The HP/HE consultant should describe the contents as well as outline the methods of fulfilling the expectations from a HPGP. The consultant should be able to answer any questions and clarify any doubts which may arise, provide information about the time scale, planning procedures, methods of assessment, possible networking with other similar HPGPs, required resources and sources of possible support.

The consultation should take account of the internal structure of the general practice, which can be divided according to activities, professions, subject matter, work practices, etc. The members of Eech of these "units" should have an opportunity to find out what is involved for them in such a commitment.

This consultation can include several activities:

- personal communication with the management and/or staff of the general practice;
- provision of information by means of written material, attending national and/or international meetings and interaction with other general practices;
- organisation of a workshop for the management and staff of the general practice, where such topics as principles of health promotion and health education, planning, evaluation, and operationalisation should be discussed.

Commitment

As in the case of any other health promoting setting, there are certain preconditions that the management of a setting needs to fulfil. In the case of a Health Promoting General Practice, the manager or the GP will need to become acquainted with these requirements, discuss them with the members of the practice and take on the commitment to fulfil the necessary conditions. These include:

- acceptance of the Ottawa Charter;
- development of a healthy working environment;
- integration of health promotion and health education into daily activities;
- outreach into community (networks and alliances);
- planning and execution of intervention studies in main areas of activity;
- evaluation in the form of quality assessment of the services provided;
- in-service training programmes in health promotion and health education for the practice staff.

It is important to realise that health promotion and health education activities should be "resource neutral", that is, they should be carried out within the existing resources of the practice.

When a practice is recognised as having a "pilot status" it will have to make special efforts to monitor its activities and produce documentation, which can serve other practices in carrying out a similar transformation. In this case the pilot practice should receive additional support, in the form of resources and advice, to enable them to carry out such monitoring activities.

Recognition of the status of a health promoting general practice should enable such a practice to join the National and European Networks of Health Promoting General Practices. This includes a number of additional commitments, such as participating in the business meetings of the Networks, organising workshops, publishing progress reports, but offers the advantage of being able to share experience.

The original idea of providing "health promotion clinics" for patients has been modified as a result of the introduction of programmes of activities designed to meet the needs of the population registered in each practice. From the five key areas proposed in the Health of the Nation document (CHD and stroke, cancers, mental illness, HIV/AIDS and sexual health, and accidents), health promotion in general practice concentrates on the first area, on that of CHD. The CHD activities are differentiated according to content and range. They include some general obligations and have specific commitments within three bands of services.

A practice will undertake the following general commitments:

- to obtain relevant information about target groups in the practice population;
- to have plans for reaching those in the target groups not presenting at the surgery;
- to carry out health promotion interventions aimed at patients in the target groups.

A practice will undertake the following commitment within bands:

- band 1: (developmental) starts with giving advice to patients about not smoking;

- band 2: (mainstream) implements a health promotion programme for tackling CHD, covering smoking, diet and exercise;

- band 3: implements a health promotion programme for CHD and at least one other national or local priority condition.

Chronic Disease Management (diabetes and asthma):

Practices are expected to develop an organised programme of care for patients with diabetes and asthma. For each of these diseases the practice will have to undertake certain commitments:

- a practice register;
- a call and recall system;
- education for newly diagnosed diabetics or asthma patients;
- continuing education for diabetics and asthma patients;
- individual management plan;
- clinical procedures;
- professional links;
- referral policies;
- record keeping;
- audit.

Training:

Health professionals offering the diabetes or asthma CDM programme should be able to demonstrate that they have special training, which they can obtain by attending special courses or in some other way.

Reporting and monitoring

The practice will be required to provide information on the number of patients with either non-insulin dependent or insulin dependent diabetes who have received an annual review and information about the clinical audits conducted.

Monitoring can take two forms:

- by the practice, including information on compliance in the practice report; a 10% sample of diabetes patients is checked for a management plan; a questionnaire is given to the patients to check their understanding of their disease; or

- a clinical adviser may visit the practice to check records against the submitted protocols.

The new role of GPs in health promotion and health education places new demands on the FHSAs as purchasers of these services. The latter are expected to develop specifications for these services and to provide training programmes for the staff working in general practices. To be able to do this, they will have to support and initiate research into tested methods before they can expect GPs successfully to provide the services required.

The Practice Level

Once the preliminary discussions and examinations of the commitments have been successfully completed and the practice decides to continue with the process of transformation, it should undertake certain activities affecting the practice and the people working in it. This represents the activity on the organisational level and creates the preconditions for improved services for patients.

The Method

The method of transforming a general practice into a Health Promoting General Practice has not yet been fully developed, nor has it been tested in a real life situation. The process needs help and support on different levels:

- the management team of the general practice can benefit from advice from external consultants in different areas of activity such as the transformation process, the health promotion and health education methods and approaches, as well as in Total Quality Management; this can be provided directly or in the form of workshops and other forms of in-service training;

- the staff of the general practice will need advice and help in establishing a set of intervention studies in different areas of activity for the purpose of finding out for themselves where and how their health promotion and health education activities could best benefit the patients and contribute to their health gain, using a differential diagnosis approach;

- the general practice as a whole will need to complement or update their data base with appropriate systems for data collection and retrieval related to the health promotion and health education activities concerned with establishment and satisfaction of patients' needs for the purpose of maximising their health gain and minimising any undesirable side-effects.

The final commitment of a general practice to declaring itself as "health promoting" should follow a series of consultations between the management, the professionals and the staff of that institution, together with representatives of the consumers of the services which the institution provides (patients, community members, etc.).

This commitment should include the establishment of mechanisms for close interaction between the members of the general practice, for monitoring the processes and evaluating outcomes. It should be formalised by a plan of action.

These mechanisms should include the nomination of a member of the practice as the Programme Manager and the creation of a Project Support Centre (PSC) within the practice. The practice should be supported by a National Network and be linked to an International Network.

Planning a Programme

Once the general practice as a whole has satisfied the basic criteria of a HPGP and, after consultations with its members, has commited itself, it will be necessary to develop a plan for future actions.

To achieve this, the Programme Manager of the HPGP should create a "working group" with the tasks of distributing roles among its members, and planning future activities.

The planning of the integration of health promotion and health education into the activities of a general practice should cover the following areas:

- carrying out a survey of the general practice, including its organisational structure, the decision making process, the inter-institutional relationships, and the relationships with external factors (authorities, other institutions and the community), as well as relationship with the patients;

- enabling each professional member of staff to select individual priorities, with special emphasis on the health issues;

- organising workshops or other forms of in-service training and transmission of information for members;

- allowing each professional member to develop his/her own plan of action, based on personal and professional priorities, and enabling him/her to decide on the requirements such as resources and necessary expertise;

- developing an institutional plan based on the plans of action developed by each professional;

- providing support for each carrier of a programme to develop indicators and criteria for the evaluation of the execution of the own plan of action;

- developing general indicators and criteria for evaluation of the activities of the whole institution;

- making provisions for carrying out the evaluation and audit of the activities within the individual programmes as well as within the institution;

- ensuring that there is feed-back and adjustment of the plan of action of the institution as a whole and each of the programmes.

The plan of action can be carried out only after it has been discussed and accepted by all the members of the institution. This can be achieved at a meeting where the plans are presented, discussed and accepted by all the members.

Once a plan of action has been accepted, the role definition of members will have to be carried out and put into action.

To achieve this, it may be desirable to organise workshops for members, where they will acquire the knowledge and skills related to their part in the overall plan and to the requirements for the evaluation of the activities.

The plan of action will have to cover both the health promotion and health education activities within the HPGP as well as a part of its relationship with other external factors. The plan of action will thus need to include the following parts:

- the HP/HE aspects of the activities within the HPGP (in general and for each programme);
- the HP/HE aspects of the relationship of the HPGP with the wider community (transport, commerce, communication, etc.);
- the HP/HE aspects of the relationship of the HPGP with the authorities (educational, health, legal, etc.);
- the HP/HE aspects of the relationship of the HPGP with other similar HPGPs;
- the HP/HE aspects of the relationship of the HPGP to other relevant institutions (health care providers, social support system, police, etc.).

Since the methods of carrying out a plan of activities can be "HPGP-specific" as well as "programme-specific", that is, different for each HPGP and for each programme within that HPGP, it may be desirable for the HPGP to precede the actual work by a small study of their requirements to be carried out by the relevant members of the HPGP, representing management and unit members. Such studies may include the following:

- the definition of the specific aims and objectives of the HPGP and each programme;
- the identification of those aspects of the aims which may benefit from integration of health promotion and health education into the objectives, designed for the achievement of the stated aims;
- agreement on the methods considered most appropriate for the achievement of such an integration;
- the acquisition of skills necessary for the execution of the plan of action;

- the development and management of mechanisms relevant for the collection, monitoring and assessment of information relevant to the evaluation of the plan of action.

The outcome of such studies should enable the HPGP to finalise its own plan of action, which should include:

- the timetable of activities;
- the role definition of members;
- the aims and objectives;
- the indicators and criteria;
- methods of monitoring and evaluation;
- feed-back mechanisms.

A Structural Analysis

It is a well known fact that people carry out their daily work without being aware of the structural and functional factors of which this work is composed. This is not a problem as long as one does not need to analyse such work and describe its various characteristics. The first step in transforming a general practice into a "Health Promotion General Practice" will be to carry out a structural and functional analysis of the practice. This will include a description of the following:

- location of the practice and the working conditions;
- composition of the practice;
- role definitions and power structure of the members of the practice;
- procedures in carrying out various services, with the relevant documentation;
- classification of the main services;
- the records of the practice in terms of type of patients, morbidity, mortality, referrals, etc.

This analysis should help the staff of the practice to see how the health promotion and health education can be incorporated into their work.

Division of labour

The role definition of each member of staff of a practice will require a detailed analysis of the tasks undertaken, concentrating on those which lend themselves to health promotion and health education interventions. This will include:

- task definitions;
- interrelationships between members of staff;
- interrelationship between staff members and the patients;
- the role definition of patients.

The importance of the establishment of role definitions of staff and patients lies in the fact that it provides a good framework for the analysis of individual health promotion and health education activities.

Evaluation, Quality Assessment and Audit

One of the main characteristics of most organisations is their accountability, which requires information about the services provided in terms of processes (how), contents (what) and outcomes (with what effect). There are three ways that accountability can be approached:

- **Evaluation**: Evaluation is programme based and involves the assessment of the achievement of the aims of a programme. It applies to the situation where health promotion and health education are integrated into certain aspects of the existing practice activities. It requires a clear statement of aims in measurable terms and the description of objectives which define the way these aims are planned to be achieved. It also requires the choice of indicators to be used for the assessment of achievement as well as the decision about the criteria which will be used in the definition of success or failure of a programme.

- **Quality Assessment:** Quality assessment of a production process is consumer based. The assessment takes place in the light of the recognised interests and needs of the consumers. The assessment of a health promoting setting uses existing methods, but modified for such a setting. The mechanisms of quality management should include in their specifications the health promotion and health education aims. A current approach is the Total Quality Management model. The main characteristics of this model are the examination of the whole process of production, i.e. looking at the "raw material", "the production process" and the "outcome", which in turn represents the "raw material" for the next stage. This implies that there is quality control of each stage of the process annd with necessary adjustments is as applicable to service industries as to manufacturing.

- **Audit:** Audit is the assessment of an activity against the existing social values, norms, laws, regulations and rules. It is carried out by professionally legitimised "auditors" who can be members of a profession (medical audit) or a government department (financial audit).

Intervention Studies

In addition to the study of the processes and outcomes of such an exercise, the staff of the general practice should plan and carry out a number of small studies related to their different activities, with the aim of finding out for themselves where health promotion and health education could best be applied and what the anticipated outcomes might be.

The expected outcome of the general study will have implications for health promotion and health education on different levels:

- it should provide experience in transforming a setting into a health promoting setting;

- it should produce a new curriculum relevant for teaching the application of an organisational model of health promotion and health education;

- it should indicate how best to introduce the concept of Total Quality Management into a general practice for the purpose of evaluation and quality management.

The activities of a general practice with a pilot status should be monitored, empirically tested and publicised for the benefit of others who wish to follow the same road.

The aims of the pilot intervention study for the purpose of creatinng a Health Promoting General Practice can be summarised along the followinng lines:

AIM 1: To develop a procedure for the transformation of a General Practice into a Health Promoting General Practice. To achieve this aim the intervention will have the following objectives:

Objective 1.1: To take the staff of the practice through the commitment procedure necessary for the acquisition of the recognised status of a Pilot Health Promoting General Practice;

Objective 1.2: To establish mechanisms necessary for carrying out the process activating the conditions for a health promoting general practice, i.e. creating a healthy environment, integrating health promotion and health education into daily activities, and to establish an outreach into the community in the form of networks and alliances.

AIM 2: To provide the necessary knowledge and skills to the staff of a General Practice for operationalisation of the preconditions relevant to a Health Promoting General Practice. To achieve this aim the intervention will have the following objectives:

Objective 2.1: Development of curricula for training programmes for the staff of the practice;

Objective 2.2: Organisation of workshops for training the Practice staff of the practice in the subject matter of health promotion and health education, including the planning, execution and evaluation of the activities;

AIM 3: To develop mechanisms for the evaluation of the activities of the Health Promoting General Practice, which, within an organisational model, should take the form of quality management and quality assessment; the main indicator is the

health gain of the patients; to achieve this aim, the intervention will have the following objectives:

Objective 3.1: Development of mechanisms for the constant monitoring and assessment of quality of the services provided, based on the Total Quality Management model;

Objective 3.2: Development of standards and specifications for the quality assessment of the services provided.

The Patient (Consumer) Level

It should never be forgotten that the purpose of the whole exercise is to enhance the health gain of the patient and at the same time to provide the staff with a feeling of competence and achievement. The processes of doctor-patient interaction relevant for the HP/HE interventions include:

Differential diagnosis

GP-patient interaction includes, as a vital component, the diagnosis of problems and the selection of appropriate interventions. Both the GP and the patient contribute to this interaction, each in a distinct but well defined way.

The GP

From a medical point of view a GP is trained to carry out a "differential diagnosis" of the patient. This means, in general terms, that the GP follows a line of inquiry, selecting the appropriate symptoms and eliminating the irrelevant ones, until a combination of presented symptoms matches a disease entity. Once a potential disease is assumed to be present, the GP introduces a number of specific examinations and tests to verify the presence of the assumed disease. If the findings fit the symptoms presented, the GP can express his/her opinion that a specific disease is present and prescribe a relevant course of treatment. During the treatment, the GP will monitor the outcomes and reverse the procedure if unexpected results are encountered. If the treatment works the patient will be considered cured.

From a psycho-social point of view, the GP-patient interaction can be considered as the means by which a GP legitimises the patient's various roles such as the sick role, the at-risk role and the chronically ill role, all with the relevant rights and duties that such statuses entail.

The interaction takes the form of an interview, during which the GP applies all the techniques of interpersonal communication (listening, interpreting verbal and non-verbal signs, prompting, and so on) to enable the patient to provide the information necessary for an accurate diagnosis.

The Patient

In most cases preliminary self-diagnosis will produce an indication of the nature of the problem. The patient presents this perception of the problem (right or wrong) to the GP. The level of medical sophistication of the patient's perception will influence the presentation of these symptoms. Where the patient is well informed about symptoms of the disease inferred during the process of self-diagnosis, he/she will be able to "press the right buttons" with the GP and may influence him/her to come to a similar initial diagnosis. This will, however, have to be confirmed by further observations and tests.

Once the patient comes to the practice and starts interacting with the GP, both actors manifest forms of behaviour implicitly defined by the norms (expectations) related to the patient's various roles, such as for example the "sick role". This role is characterised by the dominant position of the doctor and the dependent position of the patient. Both actors have a certain set of rights and duties towards each other. The doctor's actions are defined by the professional code of ethics whereas the patient's actions are defined by a whole set of social norms related to compliance and the wish to get better.

What really happens within the practice can be traced by using a Patient's Career Model (described earlier) which follows the patient through the whole process of acquiring a "sick role". Before confronting the GP, the patient will have (as we have seen) already undertaken a preliminary process of self-diagnosis, of exploring the opinions of the immediate environment, and of checking in the literature and observing the signs of the problem.

This will be followed by a decision-making process during which the patient will consider all the available options (to see if the symptoms will go away, to self medicate, or to see the GP). Once the decision to see a GP has been made, the patient explores the immediate social environment (spouse, colleagues, and family), to gain their approval and support for taking on a sick role. When the treatment is completed the patient can relinquish the sick role and acquire a well role.

The main characteristics of a "sick role" are:

- the sick person is exempt from certain social responsibilities;
- the person cannot be expected to take care of the health problem on his/her own;
- the person should strive to get better;
- the person should seek medical help, during which process the sick role will be legitimised;
- the person should cooperate with the doctor and comply with the prescribed treatment.

By analogy with the sick role, the patient can acquire an "at-risk" role, which has similar psycho-social characteristics to any social role It is linked with the patient's increased risk from a particular health threat or disease which may be due to specific environmental factors, family history (genetics), or behavioural patterns.

In some instances the sick role can be transformed into a "chronically ill" role, in case of the failure of the treatment returning the patient to a "well" role.

Within an organisational model of health promotion and health education the patient's career model has practical implications since it can serve as a guideline in defining the structure of the doctor-patient relationship and in examining the various stages or focal points in this process.

CASE STUDY: A PILOT GENERAL PRACTICE

Introduction

The study design described in this section relates to the experimental transformation of a general practice into a Pilot Health Promotion General Practice and is appropriate for the testing of the new concept in the new situation, for finding out the advantages and the possible barriers to such a transformation and for the development of general guidelines which could be applied to other general practices if it is deemed desirable and advantageous for the improved treatment of the patients.

In addition to a main study a number of small specific studies will be required. The main reason for the introduction of a number of small intervention studies in a HPGP lies in the fact that this is a way of solving the problem of shortage of empirically tested methods and outcomes that could be generally applied. Experimental testing of new approaches has been designed to cover following areas:

- the description of the practice in terms of the structure and the role definition of the practice staff, with special emphasis on the responsibilities and accountability of each member of staff towards other members as well as the patients;

- specific information about patients health promotion and health education needs is to be collected and recorded in addition to the existing medical records.

The general practice will have to go through the process on the "ground work" level as well as on the "organisational" level to gain recognition as a Health Promoting General Practice. The steps of that process have been already described in detail and will not be discussed hare. This part of the description is concerned with design of the process at the "patient" level of intervention.

Primary Care

When a patient becomes ill, this triggers can result in certain activities within primary health care or primary medical care.

Primary Health Care

Primary health care emerges at the first awareness of a health problem by a potential patient. It takes on a number of stages, such as:

- awareness of the symptoms or health threats;
- self-diagnosis and decision whether it applies to the patient;
- making a decision about the course of action:
    1. doing nothing and wait for it to pass;
    2. carrying out self-medication by choosing the traditional or most common remedies;
    3. seeking outside help;

- seeking outside help may include:
    1. help within the community (advice from friends and relatives, self-help groups etc.);
    2. approaching traditional healers and using traditional medication;
    3. seeking professional help.

Primary Medical Care

Primary medical care is defined as the first contact of the patient with the health care system. This is usually the general practitioner.

The GP can treat the patient or refer him/her to specialists or specialist institutions.

The Role of the GP

The role of GPs in health promotion and education can be seen in this case study designed for a GP practice (2 partners) in a town in Norther England and is concerned with the provision of preventive services (immunisation and screening). The purpose of the case study is to test some approaches specifically adjusted to the new role of GPs in the field of prevention.

The Needs and Aims

The services to be studied are the provision of immunisation (against diptheria, tetanus, whooping cough, tuberculosis, measles, rubella and polio) and of cervical smear tests.

The need of the client population is to benefit from desirable and to prevent undesirable effects of the immunization and vaccination of children and of thee cervical smear tests of women. The need of the GPs is to increase the utilisation of relevant preventive services by their patient population so that they can provide the required services.

The Aim of the intervention programme will be to increase the utilisation of the services provided. To achieve this aim, the programme will have the following objectives:

Objective 1: to organise the provision of services in a way which will be acceptable and convenient to the users.

Method: reorganisation of the provision of services to include:

a) the establishment or revision of adequate records of patients for the purpose of invitation for attendance and for monitoring their response;

Indicators : accurate records of the target population; distribution of appropriate invitations; effects of the invitation on attendance, which include the following criteria:

- criterion (1): accessible age/sex register and the age register of children;

- criterion (2): accurate records of immunised children and screened women;

- criterion (3): total coverage of the target population by invitations;

- criterion (4): readability test showing the appropriate composition of the invitation for the target population;

- criterion (5): interpretation and understanding of the message in the invitation;

- criterion (6): effects of the invitation on the utilisation of services;

b) *organisation of services to suit the needs and requirements of the patients;*

Indicators : organisation of services; needs of the target population;

- criterion (1): the needs of the target population in terms of place, time, transport, waiting time, supportive services (creches), reflected in the services provided;

- criterion (2): congruence between the patients' needs and the professional possibilities;

- criterion (3): recall system;

c) *provision of alternative services jointly with the Local Health Authority or other clinics;*

Indicators : provision of alternative services:

- criterion (1): expressed need for alternative services;
- criterion (2): accessibility of alternative services;
- criterion (3): utilisation of alternative services;
- criterion (4): exchange of records between all the available services;
- criterion (5): client satisfaction with the alternative services;
- criterion (6): recall system;

Objective 2: to create and/or reinforce the norms related to these preventive actions; the establishment and/or reinforcement of social norms concerning the preventive behaviour will include:

a) *the cooperation with the local Health Promotion Unit for the purpose of gaining their support in the establishment and/or reinforcement of social norms by means of mass media and other campaigns; ensuring an effective diffusion process and social support;*

Indicator : joint planning and execution of programmes; participation of mass media; support or changes in social norms; diffusion by the consumers; experience of social support by the consumers;

- criterion (1): existence of a joint plan;
- criterion (2): available resources for the plan;

- criterion (3): participation of the media;
- criterion (4): contents of the media messages appropriate for reinforcing or changing social norms;
- criterion (5): perception of social norms relevant to the required action by the target population and their social environment;
- criterion (6): diffusion of information about actions taken (positive, negative) within the consumers' peer group;
- criterion (7): positive or negative social support affecting decisions about actions;

b) *synchronisation of the campaign of the HP Unit with the activities within the GPs' surgery;*

Indicators : synchronisation of activities:

- criterion (1): timing of mass media campaigns preceding the GPs' activities;
- criterion (2): GPs' activities following closely the mass media campaign;
- criterion (3): GPs' reinforcement of mass campaign messages at appropriate times;

c) *monitoring and feed-back of the patients' response to the HP Unit and the media, thus maintaining the impetus of the campaign; achievement of goals;*

Indicators: consumers' reactions, comments, and actions; regular feedback and information exchange between main actors; impetus of the campaign; achievement of set goals;

- criterion (1): records of consumers' reactions;
- criterion (2): records of comments made by non-utilisers;
- criterion (3): records of comments made by providers of services;
- criterion (4): utilisation of services;
- criterion (5): comparative preferences between services offered;
- criterion (6): existence and utilisation of mechanisms for feedback and exchange of information and experiences;
- criterion (7): monitoring of utilisation through time;
- criterion (8): achievement of set goals;

Objective 3: to inform and motivate the patients to utilise the services offered by reinforcing their conformity to the social norms and by enabling them to make an informed decision within an atmosphere of social support; the information and motivation of patients will be the main aspect of the GP-patient interaction and will include:

a) examination of existing mass media concerning preventive actions; selection of the appropriate existing materials or producing new; materials; sending materials to the target group; inviting patients to attend; follow-up of nonattenders by house visit of the nurse;

Indicators: review of existing mass media about the problem area, content analysis and appropriateness; distribution to the target group; follow-up visits by the practice nurse;

- criterion (1): content analysis of accurate information about the problems and desired actions;
- criterion (2): content analysis of the approaches required for creation or changes of social norms;
- criterion (3): content analysis of the readibility and understanding factors;
- criterion (4): content analysis of the appeals used (positive or negative);
- criterion (5): total coverage of the target population by personal invitation and mass media;
- criterion (6): follow-up visits of nonattenders by the practice nurse at certain appointed times;
- criterion (7): establishment of reasons for non-attendance and feedback to the programme;
- criterion (8): follow-up visits of attenders of one activity (e.g.immunisation) and non-attenders of the other (smear test) or vice versa;

b) face-to-face interaction with patients, when the GP and/or the nurse will:

i) reinforce the message;
ii) legitimise the at-risk status;
iii) relieve any anxieties or uncertainties;
iv) enable patients to make an informed decision concerning the conformist behaviour to the norms;
v) confirm the rewards in terms of gaining protection from a health threat;

Indicators: face-to-face interaction of the GP or the nurse with the patients who come for some other reasons to the surgery;

- criterion (1): initiating the reinforcement of the message;
- criterion (2): legitimation of the at-risk role and the confirmation of the role-relevant norms;
- criterion (3): relieving anxieties and uncertainties;
- criterion (4): appropriateness of information for an educated decision about the services offered;
- criterion (5): conformity to the perceived norms;
- criterion (6): awareness of the positive gains following the utilisation of services;

c) *providing the service required; updating the records; informing the patient where appropriate; emphasizing the need for the patient to share their experiences with others; acknowledging the social support where appropriate;*

Indicators: provision of services; records; follow-up information of patients where appropriate; control and coping with side-effects; diffusion effects; recognition of social support;

- criterion (1): availability of services (GP and alternative);
- criterion (2): up-to-date records of attendance, of receipt of invitations, of exposure to and understanding of mass media messages; of role performance of professions involved;
- criterion (3): information about the outcome of each smear tests and recall services;

- criterion (4): monitoring for side-effects and coping with the existing ones;

- criterion (5): verbal recognition of the social support received by the patient;

- criterion (6): emphasis of the importance of sharing the experiences with others in the peer group and the diffusion effect.

Objective 4: to monitor and evaluate the process and the outcome of such an intervention.

The evaluation will be an integral part of planning and management of the intervention. It includes the establishment of indicators and criteria for each of the objectives selected for the achievement of the stated aim. Once the indicators are selected, the formative evaluation will be carried out through monitoring the whole period of the intervention. At the end, a summative evaluation will establish the extent of the achievement of the stated aim and any possible side effects.

The Role of the Patient

A doctor-patient interaction is characterised by the doctor's legitimation and the patient's acquisition of a number of socially recognised statuses and roles.

Sick role

After presentation of symptoms by the patient the doctor makes a diagnosis and defines the illness from which the patient suffers, thus legitimising the patient's sick role with all its implications.

Quasi-sick Role

Contact can occur between the doctor and the patient without the patient presenting some acute symptoms but asking for advice related to some other problems (obesity, smoking, etc.), or as a result of a health check-up. The doctor gives the patient personal advice and prescribes treatment, thus legitimising the patient's quasi-sick role with all its implications.

At-Risk Role

The patient may approach the doctor with some problems which are not directly related to any acute symptoms. Such contact can also result from the results of a screening programme such as a health check. The doctor may refer the patient to the nurse who is running different health promotion clinics, in which case the nurse will enable the patient to solve such a problem. In this case the doctor is legitimising the patient's at risk role with all its implications.

SPECIFICATIONS (INDICATORS) FOR QUALITY ASSESSMENT INDICATORS FOR THE PATIENT

	THE PATIENT
Location	place of residence type of accommodation access to the GP
Type of patient	social characteristics social position educational level occupation medical history
Family	composition conjugal roles family history
Social support	sick role decision making reinforcement
Decision making	self-diagnosis contacting GP
Symptoms	description of problems acquisition of sick role
Compliance	medication
Progress report	reappointment discharge acquisition of the well role

Access to General Practice

The location of the patient will influence the access to the general practice. The access can be influenced by:

- means of transport (on foot, private transport, or public transport);
- the cost of travel;
- provision for leaving home (babysitter etc.);
- access to a telephone.

Conjugal Roles

The relationship of the patient with the spouse will influence the decision making about contacting the GP. This relationship can be expressed in the following terms:

- merged (joint decisions);
- cooperative (supporting decisions);
- divergent (independent decisions).

Social Support

The readiness to see a GP will be enhanced by the willingness of the immediate and wider social environment to support the decision maker in terms of preconditions relevant to taking on a sick role, such as:

- approving the decision to see a GP;
- recognising the existence and seriousness of the symptoms;
- relieving the decision maker of social obligations;
- providing practical support in daily activities.

Competence in Self-diagnosis

When the awareness of the symptom is accompanied by appropriate perceptions the decision will be made to visit a GP. These perceptions include:

- recognition of the symptoms;
- assessment of severity;
- awareness of available solutions.

Presentation of Symptoms

The GP diagnosis will depend on the way the patient presents the symptoms, as well as on the combination of the symptoms presented. This is usually a part of doctor-patient interaction, where the communication is a result of questions and prompts by the doctor.

Understanding the GP Information

The doctor-patient interaction will depend on the patient's understanding of the questions raised and the information provided. This reflects:

- the language;
- the terminology;
- the procedures;
- the medication;
- the awareness of side-effects.

Compliance with Medication

The patient's compliance with the medication prescribed will depend on:

- affording the prescription;
- availability of medication;
- type of medication;
- continuity of medication;
- completion of the course.

Monitoring Progress

The success of treatment will depend on monitoring the patient's progress by looking at:

- possible side-effects;
- assessment of outcome.

INDICATORS FOR THE RECEPTIONIST

THE RECEPTIONIST	
Setting	**access to practice** **waiting room**
Contact	**friendliness** **initial interview** **appointment**
Records	**patient records**
Diary	**timing of appointment**

The Setting

The environment in which the receptionist works will influence the possibility of successful communication with the patient. This includes:

- access by telephone;
- seating arrangements;
- degree of privacy.

Contact

The receptionist - patient interaction will depend on:

- language;
- friendliness;
- reassurance;
- waiting time for making appointment and for seeing the GP.

Records

Following the identification of the patient the receptionist needs to locate the patient's records to be presented to the GP. This will depend on:

- access to records;
- identification of the patient.

Diary

The receptionist will need to have access to an accurate diary of the GP's appointments to be able to allocate the time to the new patient. This will depend on:

- up to date notes;
- checking with the GP.

Appointment

The receptionist will in agreement with the GP's timetable provide the patient with an appointment. This will include:

- exact day and time;
- waiting time;
- changes and cancellations.

THE GENERAL PRACTITIONER

Setting	**practice accommodation**
Records	**examination of records** **recorded history**
Contact	**establishing contact** **history** **examination** **tests**
Diagnosis	**sick role** **advice** **reassurance**
Medication	**prescriptions** **instructions**
Sick Note	**type and duration**
Referral	**community care team** **specialist** **hospital**
Monitoring	**reappointment** **progress report** **discharge** **well role**

Setting

The doctor-patient interaction will depend on the arrangement of the surgery accommodation. This will include:

- the size of the room;
- the seating arrangement;
- the available equipment;
- degree of privacy.

Records

The availability of records will depend on:

- servicing by the receptionist;
- computerised data;
- time to look at the records;
- accuracy of records.

Contact

The contact between the doctor and the patient includes taking of the patient's medical history, carrying out examinations and tests. This will depend on:

- welcoming effect;
- language;
- terminology;
- prompting;
- reassurance;
- listening;
- attention;
- professional efficiency;
- resources for tests and examinations.

Diagnosis

Based on the outcome of the contact, the GP will be able to make a diagnosis of the patient's state of health by:

- differential diagnosis;
- developing hypotheses;
- verifying hypotheses;
- defining the problem; through
  - examination,
  - on-site tests (height, weight, body mass; blood pressure, smoking, alcohol, family history. pregnancy, sight, visual activity, colour blindness, etc.)
  - outside tests (X ray, cholesterol, full blood count, thyroid, renal and liver function, estrogen level etc.)
- outcome of the health check according to "banding".

Medication

Based on the diagnosis arrived at the GP will prescribe medication which will include:

- informing the patient;
- reassuring the patient;
- checking the understanding of the patient;
- providing a prescription.

Sick Notes

Depending on the outcome of the diagnosis the GP can issue a sick note to the patient which will legitimise the patient's sick role and justify the absence from work. The sick note can invoke a reassessment of the patient by an outside professional who will carry out an examination of the patient and confirm or rescind the sick note.

Referrals

Part of the prescribed treatment may involve the need for support from other professionals or agencies, in such a case the GP may refer the patient to:

- a member of the community health team; such as:
  the District Nurse
  the Practice Nurse
  Physiotherapist, etc.;
- a specialist on an out-patient basis;
- a hospital for in-patient treatment.

Monitoring

The GP will monitor the progress of the patient's medication until recovery. This will include:

- patient's awareness of possible side-effects;
- arranging for a reappointment.

Discharging the Patient

After completion of the treatment the patient will get a reappointment before being discharged. This will include:

- interview;
- possible examination and tests;
- discharging the patient.

CASE : SICK ROLE I

Patient - presentation of symptoms

A middle-aged female patient went to see her GP complaining about abdominal pain.

GP - differential diagnosis at the first visit

The GP took the history of the patient by asking:

- How long the complaint had lasted?
- Whether she had eaten something that could have caused it?
- Whether she had had the pains before?

The GP carried out a physical examination of the patient. Following the examination, the GP made a diagnosis and prescribed appropriate medication, thus legitimising the patient's sick role.

The GP arranged a re-appointment for the patient in two weeks time with an indication that she should return earlier if the situation worsened.

The patient

The medication was successful in relieving the patient's symptoms. The doctor was able to legitimise the patient's return into the "well" or "healthy" role, with all its implications.

CASE : SICK ROLE II

Patient - presentation of symptoms

A middle-aged female patient went to see her GP complaining about abdominal pain and vomiting.

GP - differential diagnosis at the first visit

The GP took the history of the patient by asking:

- How long the complaint had lasted?
- Whether she had eaten something that could have caused it?
- Whether she had had the pains before?

The GP carried out a physical examination of the patient. Following the examination, the GP reached a conclusion that it could be one of the following problems:

- Gastritis
- Gastric ulcer.

The GP prescribed medication:

- to relieve pain
- to stop vomiting.

The GP arranged a re appointment for the patient in two weeks' time with an indication that she should return earlier if the situation worsened.

GP - differential diagnosis at the second visit

The GP took the history and found out:

- that the symptoms had persisted
- presence of additional symptoms - pain in the chest, onset of breathlessness

The GP carried out an examination and additional tests and confirmed the diagnosis that it could be a heart attack.

The GP referred the patient to a heart specialist for further examination and tests.

The Heart Specialist - differential diagnosis

The heart specialist carried out an examination and additional tests on the patient. The outcome was the confirmation of the new diagnosis of a possible heart attack.

The specialist prescribed medication for the patient and informed the GP.

The GP - monitoring the patient

The patient returned to the GP, who undertook to monitor the effects of the new treatment to see if it resulted in the improvement of the patient's condition.

The patient

The patient complied with new medication and reported an improvement in her condition to the GP.

The GP - legitimation of new role

Following the confirmed diagnosis and successful treatment the GP legitimised the at-risk role of the patient and noted it in the patients records.

CASE : SICK ROLE III

The patient

The patient presents symptoms to the doctor.

The doctor

The doctor takes the history and examines the patient. If necessary, the doctor carries out certain tests (either in the surgery or in a hospital).

The doctor makes a diagnoses and decides that the patient needs specialist treatment. The patient is referred to a specialist or a hospital.

The specialist

The patient undergoes a similar procedure of history, examination and tests carried out by the specialist. The specialist confirms the GP diagnosis and informs the GP.

The doctor

The GP informs the patient about the problem and prescribes medication. The patient is invited to re-visit the GP after a certain period of time.

The patient

The patient complies with the medication procedures and recovers.

The doctor

After confirming the patient's recovery the GP discharges the patient.

CASE: SICK ROLE IV

The patient

The patient (a middle-aged woman) requests a home visit of the doctor and presents him with symptoms (stomach pain, shortness of breath and pain the left arm).

The doctor

The GP takes the history, carries out an examination and decides to seek a second opinion of a specialist. The GP legitimises the patient's sick role.

The patient

The patient is referred to the hospital where again a history is taken, examination and tests carried out. The results of the tests do not confirm the GP's initial diagnosis (possible heart attack) and the patient is discharged from the hospital.

The doctor

The GP examines the patient for other possible causes and when none are found the GP informs the patient about the false alarm, discharges the patient and legitimises the patient's "well" role.

CASE: QUASI-SICK ROLE

The patient

The patient makes an appointment to see the GP and complains about certain behavioural patterns, such as obesity.

The doctor

The GP takes the patient's medical history, carries out an examination and a number of tests.

The GP diagnoses the presence of risk factors associated with heart disease. Based on the examination and family history the GP confirms the patient's specific risk of CHD and prescribes treatment in the form of behaviour modification (loss of weight).

The GP thus legitimises the patient's quasi-sick role with all its implications.

The patient

After receiving the necessary advice and possible medication, the patient is invited to pay regular visits to the GP as a part of the monitoring process.

CASE: AT-RISK ROLE

The patient

The patient makes an appointment to see the GP and presents him/her with certain behavioural problems such as over eating and obesity.

The doctor

The GP takes a history, carries out an examination and tests and makes a diagnoses of a general risk to the patient's welbeing due to being overweight.

The GP legitimises the patient's at risk role and refers the patient to the nurse who deals with such problems.

The nurse

The nurse is in charge of the anti-obesity clinic registers the patient for a sequence of sessions. She uses special methods for helping patients to reduce weight (information, diary, calorie counting, special diet, weight control, joining a group, etc.).

The patient

Complies with the weight loss procedures and loses weight.

The patient is referred by the nurse to the GP who confirms the patient's "well" role.

HEALTH PROMOTING HOSPITALS

INTRODUCTION

Provider units are those from which fund holders will purchase health care services - in the main, hospitals. Their primary contribution will be the provision of high quality services to patients, as required by DHA and GP Fund Holder contracts. In addition, the hospital sector can:

- ensure that health professionals are able to provide effective patient education and counselling as part of the diagnosis, treatment and care as well as ensuring appropriate ongoing care on discharge from hospital;
- maintain an environment which promotes and protects the health of all who come into contact with hospital services;
- ensure that all premises are smoke-free (purchasers will be able to address this in their negotiations with providers on the quality specifications in their contracts);
- provide more intensive counselling and advice linked with specific health programmes (prevention of childhood accidents, smoking cessation, particularly with advice to general medical and surgical patients) in liaison with the primary care services.

In the recent past, the World Health Organisation has applied their settings approach to hospitals, which is the result of the work carried out in a Vienna hospital by members of the Department of Medical Sociology of The Ludwig Bolzmann Institute at Vienna University. As a WHO Collaborative Centre, they are the organisers of an European Network of Pilot Health Promoting Hospitals. The idea has spread more rapidly than expected, mainly due to the attractiveness of this novel concept rather than tested and evaluated outcomes. At present there are 20 hospitals which have been accepted as "Pilot Health Promoting Hospitals" (see Appendix 8). Each of these hospitals has endeavoured to establish five innovative health promoting projects and expected the period of their 'Pilot Health Promoting Hospital' to run for at least five years (ending in 1996), in order to allow information dissemination, feedback of evaluation information and networking to occur. There are also hospitals, with individual projects, which have joined the WHO European Network of similar institutions, and have undertaken at least part of the commitment to intensify health promotion and health education activities in their institutions.

The WHO pilot network is based in Vienna and offers four levels of membership: full membership, associate membership, 'interested institutions' membership and 'interested individuals' membership.

The approach is based on the "Vienna Model". It requires the agreement of a hospital to undertake such a commitment, the establishment of an organising body within the hospital and the establishment of a health promotion/health education programme. This programme is based either on special hospital units or focuses on some specific health problems (e.g. The Department of Gynaecology or diabetes). The methods are conventional, and include transmission of knowledge and skills, as well as improvements in the hospital's physical environment. Initiatives may include, for example, special lectures for diabetics as well as improvements in the hospital catering.

This initial approach has been gradually modified in line with the requirements for the recognition of a hospital as a "Pilot Health Promoting Hospital". This includes, in addition to a general commitment of the whole hospital to health promotion and health education as integral parts of their services, the collection of base-line information, interventions using the new community participation methods, and the post-intervention phase which includes the evaluation, quality assessment and auditing of the processes and outcomes of such an intervention.

EUROPEAN DEVELOPMENTS IN HEALTH PROMOTING HOSPITALS

As mentioned in the last section the "health promoting hospital" movement in Europe originated in the work carried out in a Vienna hospital by members of the Ludwig Bolzmann Institute for Medicine and Medical Sociology at Vienna University, where, in collaboration with the WHO EURO, the newly created International Network of Pilot Health Promoting Hospitals is now located.

A brief historical review of the events initiating and influencing this development is set out below.

Date / Place	Event	Theme
1988 Copenhagen	*WHO-EURO Consultation*	Hospitals and Health Promotion
4/1989 London	*Joint Workshop WHO-EURO*	The Health Promoting Hospital Bloomsbury Health Authority
11/1989 Vienna	*Start of the Vienna WHO-Model Project*	"Health and Hospital"
9/1990 Vienna	*WHO-EURO Workshop*	Hospital and Health
6/1991 Budapest	*1st Business Meeting of the HPH*:	Next Steps on the Way to the Health Promoting Hospital
9/1991 Barcelona	*2nd Business Meeting of the HPH:*	Health Promoting Hospitals as a Means for Reorienting Health Services
3/1992 Milano	*3rd Business Meeting of the HPH*:	Specific Areas of Concern for HPH: Occupational Health and the Relationship to the Community

Date / Place	Event	Theme
9/1992 Dublin	*4th Business Meeting of the HPH*:	Improving the Implementation and Outcomes of HPH Project Management and Evaluation
4/1993 Warsaw	*1st Business Meeting of the European Pilot Hospital Project of HPH*	"Setting up the European Pilot HPH Project: Developing Common Goals, Strategies and Structures
4/1993 Warsaw	*1st International Conference on HPH*	"Establishing New Structures of the Network: The European Pilot Hospital Project and Tobacco-free Hospitals"
10/1993 Hamburg	*2nd Business Meeting*	"Next Steps in the Development of the Pilot Hospitals and the European Project: Consultation, Documentation and Evaluation."
4/1994 Padua	*3rd Business Meeting*	Exchange of Experiences: Visibility, Involvement of Staff, Evaluation, Partnership,etc.
4/1994 Padua	*2nd International Conference*:	Developing Health Promoting Organisations by Strengthening Intersectoral & Community Action.Healthy Nutrition Policies for Hospitals

This historical review shows the numerous activities that contributed to the further development of this idea, including the Budapest meeting in 1991, which produced the "Budapest Declaration" (see Appendix 6), defining the basic preconditions necessary for joining the movement. The "Budapest Declaration" was further refined at the Barcelona and Milan meetings in 1992, where an agreement was reached concerning the conditions and the categories of various hospitals who wish to join, according to the level of their development and commitment to health promotion. This is expected to take the form of a formal "statute" for the Pilot Health Promoting Hospitals European Network. It includes a set of activities such as:

- the formal recognition of the "Budapest Declaration";
- active participation in business meetings;
- conducting health promoting projects (minimum 5);
- being recognised by their Government as a pilot or a project hospital;
- including monitoring and evaluation;
- acting as a national coordinator.

THE UK DEVELOPMENTS

The initiative in the UK is based on the developments in Europe under the guidance of the WHO EURO, and has been elaborated in the Department of Health documents. One such document is the DoH Green Paper "The Health of the Nation", which lists the following potential roles of hospitals:

- ensuring that health professionals are able to provide effective patient education and counselling as part of diagnosis, treatment and care, as well as ensuring appropriate ongoing care on discharge from hospital;

- maintaining an environment that promotes and protects the health of all who come into contact with hospital services;

- ensuring that all premises are smoke free (which will be a part of the purchasing agreement);

- providing more intensive counselling and advice linked with specific health programmes in liaison with the primary care services.

These activities place a "health promoting hospital" within a "health promoting health care system" in a "health promoting community".

The other important Department of Health document is the White Paper "The Health of the Nation" (see Appendix 4) which is the result of consultations following the publication of the Green Paper. The White Paper confirms the "settings" approach and together with the Green Paper serves as a basis for the "health promoting hospital" movement.

The main protagonists of this idea in England were University of Salford, the Health Education Authority, London, and the Royal Preston Hospital, which ultimately became the first Pilot Health Promoting Hospital in England, recognised by the European Network and the Department of Health.

These developments achieved a formal recognition by the choice of Salford as the venue for the International Conference on Health Promoting Hospitals held in Preston in 1993, sponsored jointly by the WHO EURO, the European Network, the Department of Health, the Health Education Authority, and Preston Royal Hospital.

The English Charter

One of the outcomes of this Conference was the "The English Charter for Health Promoting Hospitals", based on the WHO Budapest Declaration on Health promoting Hospitals and sponsored by the Health Education Authority in London.

The Charter summarises the conditions and the processes of becoming a Health Promoting Hospital. To become a health promoting hospital in England it is necessary for the hospital management board to:

- acknowledge and support the concepts of health and health promoting hospitals;
- develop and implement the five-year programme of organisational development and change;
- develop and implement the process of project planning and management; the Charter also outlines the arrangements for future networking and support currently planned by the Department of Health and the Health Education Authority in England.

There is no "registration process" for becoming a health promoting hospital in England. Participation in and compliance with the Charter will depend on agreements made at local level between purchasers and providers through the contracting process.

In England, a number of initiatives are already under way. Royal Preston and Sharoe Green Acute hospitals have been nominated as model health promoting hospitals for England in the European network, and Sheffield and Trent Region have also been working to develop health promoting hospitals.

EVALUATION OF HEALTH PROMOTING HOSPITALS

Each setting will have a different set of HP/HE specifications according to its aims. Since such specifications do not exist ready-made they need to be developed. In some settings, such as a health promoting hospital, the idea of being health promoting includes the development of such specifications. This is expressed in the concept of Pilot Health Promoting Hospitals which are committed to carrying out at least five intervention studies with exactly the purpose of exploring their role in HP/HE, within the general role of a hospital. The outcome of such studies should be the development of specifications for the hospital in general and for each specialist service within such a hospital. Thus, the Pilot HPH will provide benchmarks for the specifications for other hospitals. A similar process is already in progress in Health Promoting Schools, and the intention is to extend it to other settings.

The intervention studies are, therefore, concerned with the development of specifications for the three main areas of activity, i.e. the working environment, integration and the community outreach. The general pattern of such studies is set out in the following sections.

Procedures

Once an agreement has been reached about the specifications for the three main areas, with a special emphasis on the role of HP/HE, there must be accepted procedures or practices to show the standards of the specifications have been met. In terms of the HP/HE planning process, these include the objectives of the intervention studies for the purpose of achieving the aims as described in the definition of specifications. In the case of a Health Promoting Hospital, the procedures used to ensure the meeting of the specification requirements in the three areas can be listed. They will include the following activities.

1. Creating a healthy working environment for staff and clients:

- create healthy and safe working conditions;
- ensure appropriate accommodation for staff and patients;
- provide a healthy balanced nutrition;
- ensure accident prevention at the work place;
- ensure appropriate care of the patients and good relationships between staff and staff with patients.

2. Integrating HP/HE into daily activities:

- meet the needs of the staff in terms of work and training;
- meet the HP/HE needs of the patients (case-specific);
- meet the needs of the immediate social environment (family, friends, relatives).

3. Outreach into the community:

- make provisions for a follow-up of patients after leaving the hospital and returning into the family and community;
- establish networking with other similar settings (hospitals);
- create healthy alliances with other settings in the community that are directly or indirectly relevant for the wellbeing of the patients.

The achievement of these HP/HE specifications will depend on the procedures or standard practices (objectives) applicable in the setting. It should be noted that different settings may have a different set of procedures appropriate for meeting the requirements of the above three specifications relevant to most of the health promoting settings.

Methods

Success in meeting the specification will, to a large extent, depend on the choice of the appropriate procedures (methods). HP/HE methods have been described elsewhere (Baric, 1993). These will have to be selectively chosen for each specification and procedure in each setting. The choice of methods requires a differential diagnosis of the problem which should indicate the appropriate methods. In case of a Health Promoting Hospital, one can examine this issue in greater detail by looking at specifications related to each of the three main commitments of a Health Promoting Hospital:

1. Creating a healthy working environment for staff and clients will include the following procedures:

- *creating healthy and safe working conditions; the related procedure should include the following practical steps:*

  i) a survey of the existing working environment and the establishment the areas where this working environment needs to be improved;

  ii) the provision of resources for the chosen improvements in the working environment by means of budgeting and/or attracting external resources;

  iii) planning the actual work in terms of allocating the internal supervisory roles and contracting external firms to carry out the improvements;

  iv) monitoring the ongoing activities and applying the required procedures for quality assessment of the work done.

- *ensuring appropriate accommodation for staff and patients; this can be achieved by carrying out the following work:*

  i) a survey of existing accommodation for staff and for patients in terms of comfort, privacy and appropriateness related to the expected outcomes for staff as a basis for their rest and recreation and for patients as a contribution to their healing process;

  ii) the provision of resources for the chosen improvements in the area of accommodation by means of budgeting and/or attracting external resources;

  iii) planning the actual work in terms of allocating the internal supervisory roles and contracting external firms to carry out the improvements;

iv) monitoring the ongoing activities and applying the required procedures for quality assessment of the work done.

- *providing a healthy balanced nutrition; this can be achieved by carrying out the following procedures:*

i) carrying out a survey of the existing catering system and checking on their meeting the dietary requirements of staff and patients;

ii) the provision of resources for the chosen improvements in the area of catering by means of budgeting and/or attracting external resources;

iii) planning the actual improvements in terms of allocating the internal supervisory roles and providing necessary training of staff involved;

iv) monitoring the ongoing activities and applying the required procedures for quality assessment of the work done.

- *ensure accident prevention at the work place; this can be achieved by carrying out the following procedures:*

i) carrying out a survey of the safety records related to the work place and the treatment procedures. Establishment of potential or existing "black spots" most prone to accidents;

ii) the provision of resources for the chosen improvements in the area of "black spots" by means of budgeting and/or attracting external resources;

iii) planning the actual improvements in terms of allocating the internal supervisory roles, providing necessary training of staff involved and if necessary contract out for the required improvements;

iv) monitoring the ongoing activities and applying the required procedures for quality assessment of the work done.

- *ensure appropriate care of the patients and good relationships between staff and staff with patients; this can be achieved by carrying out the following procedures:*

  i) redefine the term "appropriate care" to include the necessary HP/HE components. Explore by means of interviews the feelings and the needs of patients related to the HP/HE components of their treatment;

  ii) Make provision for staff training in carrying out these additional tasks by developing training programmes with appropriate curricula;

  iii) explore with the Personnel Department and by a staff survey the existence of any problems in the area of staff relationship (remuneration, time table, discrimination, harassment, etc.)

  iv) install procedures and mechanisms for dealing with the existing and potential staff problems;

  v) explore the quality of staff - patient relationship by surveying both parties. Make provisions for any necessary improvement by providing special training programmes for staff to enable them to deal with patients' needs and by special educational programmes for patients to adjust their wants to their needs.

2. Integrating HP/HE into daily activities. This can be achieved by addressing the following problems:

- *meeting the needs of the staff in terms of work and training; this will be achieved by carrying out the following procedures:*

  i) establish the existing levels of staff competence in HP/HE practices. This can be achieved by testing staff knowledge and skills and by observing their existing practices;

  ii) provide the necessary time and resources for staff training programmes based on appropriate curricula and including practical exercises;

iii) include specific HP/HE tasks into the job description of each member of staff by means of a role definition and specified outcomes;

iv) install necessary mechanisms for quality assessment of staff work in the area of HP/HE;

- *meet the HP/HE needs of the patients; this will be achieved by carrying out the following procedures:*

i) carry out a differential diagnosis of the needs for each case which are amenable to HP/HE interventions;

ii) allocate specific person(s) to carry out the required HP/HE intervention;

iii) monitor and evaluate the intervention in terms of immediate results, the quality of the intervention and the long term effects.

- *meet the needs of the immediate social environment (family, friends, relatives); this can be achieved by carrying out the following procedures:*

i) monitor and evaluate the needs and potentials for support of the patients by their family, friends, neighbours, etc. by observing the visiting patterns and recording the comments made by the patients;

ii) explore the needs of the immediate social environment (family, friends, etc.) concerning the existing situation while the patient is in the hospital and potential problems once the patient has been discharged;

iii) establish mechanisms for recording the observations and evaluating the interventions as well as ensuring the sharing of these observations and experiences with other staff (who are either directly involved or who may have expertise in that specific problem area);

3. Outreach into the community. This can be achieved by the following procedures:

- *make provisions for a follow-up of patients after leaving the hospital and returning into the family and community; this will require the following procedures:*

  i) ensure the existence of mechanisms for a "continuous care" approach, including the contact with the GP who referred the patient and the immediate and wider social environment (family, community) into which the patient will be discharged;

  ii) make provisions in the existing recording system for these information to be stored for use of other members of staff who may be concerned with the same patient;

  iii) establish contact with external settings (family, social services, general practice, etc.), exchange information about each patient's needs and make provision for sharing the responsibilities for each patient's follow-up care;

  iv) include the documentation and its utilisation into the quality assessment system and make provisions for feed-back into the process of "continuous care" of each specific patient;

- *establish networking with other similar settings (hospitals); this can be achieved by the following procedures:*

  i) publicise the health promoting aspects of the hospital and if appropriate announce the Pilot status of the hospital and what it implies;

  ii) organise meetings with other hospitals, serve as a source of information and expertise and raise these topics at regular meetings of hospitals in your area and region;

  iii) publicise the "progress reports" based on evaluation and quality assessment of the existing work;

iv) formalise the relationship with other hospitals by creating an organisational structure with allocated roles and tasks, regular meetings for the exchange of experiences, and mechanisms for further training and evaluating the progress in these settings;

- *create healthy alliances with other settings in the community which are directly or indirectly relevant for the wellbeing of the patients; this can be achieved by the following procedures:*

i) develop a "careers model" of your patients in their passage through the health care system, of which your hospital will be only one point on the continuum of patient care; establish the exact names and addresses of all the points in the system and locate the decision-makers (by name) for each point;

ii) establish contact with each decision-maker and organize discussions about the introduction of "organized" continuous care of your patients; provide them with information about the issues included in the continuous care of patients in general; acquire their commitments and agree on role allocations for each setting with the aim of meeting the needs of individual patients as they arise;

iii) formalise such "healthy alliances" by creating a formal structure, carrying out the role differentiation and by developing mechanisms for continuous exchange of information about each patient;

iv) create mechanisms for evaluation and quality assessment of the services provided on a community basis.

CASE STUDY : ROYAL PRESTON HOSPITAL

Introduction

For an example of a health promoting hospital we may take the Royal Preston Hospital and Sharoe Green Hospital, Preston England. These are managed as a single entity and offer a range of complementary services. They have been recognised as a Pilot Health Promoting Hospital by the European Network of Pilot Health Promoting Hospitals and by the Department of Health.

The Royal Preston Hospital has altogether 732 beds in the following departments: general medicine (200); paediatrics/SCBU (42); dermatology (8); neurology/YDU (36); geriatrics (60); general surgery (80); ENT (33); trauma and orthopaedics (104); ophthalmology (21); eurology (31); plastic surgery (38); oral surgery (9); neurosurgery (34); accidents and emergency (10); day beds (26).

The Sharoe Green Hospital represents the older part of the complex, having been constructed in the early part of the nineteenth century. It has undergone considerable redevelopment and has a total of 324 beds in the following departments: paediatrics/SCBU (20); eurology/YDU (25); geriatrics (88); trauma and orthopaedics (30); gynaecology (59); obstetrics (87); day beds (15).

Both hospitals have now been joined under a common name of Preston Acute Hospitals Trust, which has 3,023 staff, representing a whole-time equivalent of 2,325.51 staff.

Acquiring the Pilot Status

In summer 1991, the author as the Acting Consultant for WHO contacted the management of the Hospital and the Director of Health Promotion Services in Preston with the suggestions that it should become a Pilot HPH. The idea was accepted and all the preparations were made so that the Hospital could apply for Pilot status at the Dublin Business Meeting of the European Network of HPH (1992). This was subsequently approved at the Business Meeting in Warsaw (1993).

A Project Management Group was established, consisting of the representatives of the Hospital Management Team, the Health Promotion Unit and the consultant representing the local University. It identified the basic elements included in the planned changes which were:

- responding to the changing role of hospitals in society, i.e. shorter lengths of stay, development of services in localities, the increasing influence of general medical practitioners as to where care is provided, the need to promote health in a wider setting;

- maximising the benefits of the government's health service reforms, relating to greater autonomy, the marketing of services and the link between patient activity and income.

The Project Management Group defined its aims as follows:

- to plan, implement and evaluate the development of a Pilot Health Promoting Hospital in England over the five year period 1993-1997;

- to reorientate acute hospital-based services towards the values and organisational development necessary to achieve health gain outcomes through mediation, advocacy and alliance building with the community served;

- to develop and evaluate a wide range of hospital-based health promotion interventions aimed at achieving health targets identified in the government's White Paper "Health of the Nation";

- to provide a networking centre for the development of Health Promoting Hospitals throughout England and to represent England in the European Pilot Health Promoting Hospitals Network.

Intervention Sudies

Onc of thc prcconditions for acquisition of a "pilot" status is the commitment of the hospital to mount a minimum of five intervention studies dealing with health promotion aspects concerned with topics of their choice. The purpose of the intervention studies is to enable the hospital to develop mechanisms for the integration of health promotion and health education into its regular activities, by obtaining the commitment of heads of departments to introduce health promotion and health education into their daily work and to evaluate this introduction within the framework of an intervention study. The outcome of the intervention studies should be to provide knowledge and experience tested in practice and concerned with the new aspects of health promotion and health education in a specific setting. The Preston Acute Hospital Trust committed itself to the following five intervention studies:

Project 1 A Health Promoting Environment in a Health Promoting Hospital

The study is based on the DoH document "Health at Work in the NHS". It consists of a baseline study and an intervention study which includes the monitoring of outcomes within the general framework of health gains.

The aim of the baseline study is to establish information for Preston and another North West Regional Health Authority concerning the health of the NHS staff.

The aim of the intervention study is to examine whether:

1. a planned and evaluated programme of health promotion and health education (HP/HE) intervention can improve the health related knowledge, attitudes and practices of the NHS staff in the Pilot Hospital as compared to the health status of NHS staff in general;

2. a planned and evaluated programme of HP/HE intervention can increase the availability of HP/HE influences on the staff in the workplace and results in structural changes in work experiences, with special reference to mental health problems;

3. a planned intervention can increase the occasions on which NHS staff within the Hospital will undertake HP/HE interventions of

their own, targeted either at patients or the community as a whole;

4. a planned intervention of individualised and computerised health status assessment - counselling - reassessment can improve the measured health status of programme participants.

The monitoring and evaluation of the intervention study should indicate the possible improvements in the health status of NHS staff, which is directly or indirectly due to the HP/HE intervention. The indicators used will include (a) institutional changes, (b) changes due to the intervention, (c) effects on the community and (d) changes in observed health status of the participating NHS staff.

Project II The Management of Post Coronary Patients

The study is concerned with HP/HE effects on the management of post coronary patients and will be conducted within the existing Preston Cardiac Rehabilitation Programme. This programme has been initiated to complement the traditional medical interventions by introducing HP/HE methods of influencing patients, in the hope of reducing readmission rates, recurrence of symptoms, failure of convalescents to alter their lifestyles and inadequacy of rehabilitation.

The aims of the intervention study are:

1. the study of the changes in patient health gain due to the acquisition of the status of a Health Promoting Hospital;

2. the study of improvements in patient's coping capacity with post coronary problems;

3. the study of the outreach of the Hospital into the community related to prevention of coronary problems.

The HP/HE intervention will include the establishment of baseline information, the actual intervention and the evaluation of the outcomes. A series of HP/HE methods will be applied and tested to find out which of them are most effective and efficient, as well as most appropriate for implementation in a post coronary care hospital environment.

Project III Prevention of Accidents

This planned intervention study is concerned with the reduction of accidents by means of HP/HE and primarily directed at schools and colleges in the community. The study is a part of a wider programme already being carried out by the Accidents and Emergency Department of the Hospital dealing with the same problem. Through the HP/HE intervention the study will attempt to link the three types of environment (home - work - public places) that contribute mostly to the occurrence of accidents.

The study will be divided into collecting baseline information, an intervention and the evaluation of outcomes. The aims of the study include:

1. information about accidents in the area;

2. designing a comprehensive programme for the prevention of accidents based on the information collected on location and cause;

3. a HP/HE intervention to increase the competence of individuals and especially school children, related to preventing and coping with accidents at home, at work (school) and in public places;

4. to evaluate the HP/HE intervention.

The indicators used in the study include the existence of mechanisms for increasing competence, the actual changes in the level of competence and the effects on the reduction of accidents. In addition, a study of the environmental conditions as possible sources of accidents will be included.

Project IV The Health Promoting Hospital in the Community - Developing Healthy Networks and Alliances

This study is concerned with the possibilities of the outreach of the hospital into the community and the establishment of networks with other hospitals, as well as alliances with other institutions within the immediate and wider social environment. It will include a main study concerned with the methodological questions related to this new type of research and an intervention study concerned with actually establishing networks and alliances.

Based on the principles of community participation in promoting health the Health Promoting Hospital can be used as an entry point into a specific community, with the intention of spreading the "health promoting settings" movement to other institutions in the community and thus creating preconditions for recognition of that community as a "Health Promoting Community".

The main study has the following aims:

1. to establish the indicators for the collection of baseline information relevant to the planning and evaluation of an HP/HE intervention;

2. to collect baseline information based on a "community profile link";

3. to collect specific health information including health status and the available services;

4. to develop an HP/HE intervention approach appropriate for that community.

The aims of the intervention study are:

1. application of the HP/HE approach to the community;

2. definition of the role distribution of intervention agents within the hospital and the community;

3. preparation of the HP/HE methods and resources;

4. development of methods and instruments for monitoring and evaluation of the intervention.

A selection of HP/HE methods will be applied, tested, monitored and evaluated to establish a benchmark for future similar interventions in this area.

Project V The Health Promotion Aspects of Collecting and Disposing of Clinical Waste

This study is concerned with the HP/HE aspects of collecting and disposing of domestic and clinical waste within the hospital and as a service to the community. It is composed of a baseline study and a HP/HE intervention, which will also include the development and testing of new prototype equipment for waste disposal.

The main study will be concerned with identifying and assessing the existing procedures in the hospital concerning the collection and disposal of domestic and clinical waste, and to indicate the areas where this practice could be improved.

The intervention study will aim to develop and test new prototypes of equipment appropriate for collection and disposal of clinical and domestic waste. It will also aim to establish the potential role of HP/HE in improving the practice of collection and disposal of clinical and domestic waste.

The indicators used in the study will relate to the improvement in existing practices, reduction in directly or indirectly associated accidents and the increase in the level of satisfaction of the participants due to improved methods and approaches.

THE HEALTH PROMOTING GENERAL DENTAL PRACTICE

INTRODUCTION

The reform of the NHS in the UK, as described in the White Paper "The Health of the Nation" and reflected in the new contracts between the dentists and the NHS, made provision for the dentists' role in health promotion and the way they should be paid for such activities.

The Department of Health issued "An Operating Manual for Dentists" (DoH, 1990) which provides information about the changes involved in the new contract signed by the dentists and their Family Health Services Authority (FHSA) and the payment for the dentist's role in health promotion and health education as a part of these services to patients. The document states:

"The new General Dental Service Regulations have placed the practitioners' relationship with patients and the NHS on a continuing care basis.

This allows the GDS to embrace preventive care in addition to restorative treatment and has changed the legal obligations placed on GDPs.

There are new opportunities, new responsibilities for both dentists and staff, with new fee and administrative systems.

Dentists offer 'the care and treatment necessary to secure and maintain oral health'. This contrasts with the old contract whereby dentists aimed to secure 'dental fitness' at a specific point in time, with preventive care generally excluded......

...The new General Dental Service Regulations bring preventive care within the scope of the GDS for all patients. GDPs will, for the first time, receive a steady flow of income based on patient numbers which is independent of treatment provision....

There is ... a new standard of care applying to continuing care or capitation payments:

> *To provide, during the currency of the continuing care arrangements or capitation arrangements, dental advice and such care and treatment which the patient is willing to undergo, to such an extent, and at such intervals, as may be necessary to secure and maintain the oral health of the patient.*

Oral health is defined as:

> *such a standard of health of the teeth, their supporting structures and other tissues of the mouth, and of dental efficiency, as in the case of any patient is reasonable having regard to the need to safeguard his general health."*

The new contract also makes provision for "patient communication and information", which requires the GDPs to make sure that staff are trained to provide information to the patients about their rights, and the services on offer, as well as to be able to explain the difference between the treatment on NHS or by private arrangements. The GDPs are required to produce Patient Information Leaflets and to display the list of charges.

The new contract provides the dentists with an opportunity as well as a duty to engage in preventive work and be able to claim fees for such work on a "per capita" basis. The contract provides for the inclusion of health promotion and health education into the care of patients but does not make provisions for the new WHO approach concerned with the creation of "health promoting settings".

The reform of the dental services did not satisfy existing needs for better services, so the government initiated a number of reviews and consultations, with the aim of meeting all the objections and finding a solution to the existing problems. The outcome was the publication of the document "Improving NHS Dentistry" (DoH, 1994), which addresses all these issues. It was presented to Parliament in July, 1994. The document is based on the review of the dental services carried out by Sir Kenneth Bloomfeld and on the contributions to the debate that emerged from the procedings of the House of Commons Select Committee, which had published a comprehensive report on dental services on 10 June 1993.

The document "Improving NHS Dentistry" deals with two main issues: the state of oral health and the provision of dental services including the payment of dentists.

The state of oral health

In the 45 years since the NHS began there has been considerable improvement in dental health among the population. This has been illustrated by a number of surveys carried out between 1978 and 1991 which showed:

- the proportion of adults with no teeth fell from 28% to 17%;

- regional variations exist, with adults in the north of England being twice as likely to have no teeth compared to adults in the south; they are also three times as likely to have caries;

- the proportion of 15 year olds with active, untreated decay has fallen from 42% to 30%; more than five times as many are free from caries in 1993 (37%) than in 1983 (7%); the proportion with fillings is now 45% compared with 85% ten years ago; the number of extractions due to decay has also been reduced from 24% (1983) to 7% (1993).

In general one can conclude that there has been a considerable improvement in dental health among children as well as adults in the last decade.

The improvement has been due to a number of factors, such as improved nutrition, fluoridation, better oral hygiene and earlier and better services.

The dental services

Although the services have been extended and improved the way the dentists are being paid changed little since the introduction of the NHS.

A comparison of data between 1978/79 and 1993/94 shows:

- an increase of net expenditure "in real terms" by 37%;
- an increase in the gross expenditure "in real terms" by 57%;
- the number of children registered under capitation in UK has increased from 2.8 million in 1990 to 8 million in 1994;
- the number of NHS courses of treatment provided to adults by GDPs in UK has increased from 20 million in 1979 to 29 million in 1993-94;
- the number of adult patients registered under NHS is increasing steadily and in 1994 reached 25,379,251.

Dentists have traditionally been paid through fees for item of services provided. This is in principle still in operation with certain minor adjustments. The main change was introduced in 1990, with the new contract for primary dental care. This aimed at the improvement of oral health of the nation by encouraging patients to visit their dentists regularly, and dentists to practice preventive care. The reason for this was the changing needs of the patients, shifting from general restorative work to an overall need for a basic care and maintenance service.

This was followed by a new scale of fees, introduced in 1991, which manifested many weaknesses. It led to gross overpayments to dentists over and above planned expenditure. It was based on the intention to give to the average dentist a given level of income whilst meeting all NHS expenses and depended on accurate forecasts of the number and type of treatment to be done and the cost incurred providing them. The system failed badly, and the dentists grossed on average £12,500 each more than intended for that year at a total gross cost of some £200 million. This was due to a number of reasons, such as the non-existence of an "average" dentist, the over-bureaucratisation of the system and the lack of reliability of forecasts concerning the necessary expenditure.

The outcome was a number of reviews such as carried out by the Doctors' and Dentists' Remuneration Body (DDRB), the Bloomfield Review and the report of the House of Commons Health Select Committee. This was followed by extensive consultations with practitioners and a number of other concerned bodies and resulted in a number of Government proposals for reform covering the following areas:

- *A Local System* - more closely adjusted to local needs; the NHS managers could have money to purchase appropriate services based on a local strategy, agreed contracts, setting standards within the provision of a general health care as a part of a "purchaser - provider" relationship; the dental services would be closer to the mainstream of NHS; dentists should actively participate in decisions concerning the changes and their implementation; the Government, following the necessary legislation will introduce pilot schemes for the introduction of the purchasers and providers roles into dental services;

- *The Direction of Change* - the remuneration would be determined locally through negotiations; the pilot schemes for testing the "purchaser - provider" model will require some time and in the meantime the Government would introduce short-term reforms in addition to developing a new system for the future; the reforms will also address the problem of repayment of money owed by the profession to the Government; there is some evidence that incentives based on productivity can have adverse effects on quality and the existing mechanisms should ensure that this kind of misuse does not occur and that there are adequate incentives based on the quality of services provided;

- *Sessional Fees* - these are a way of managing changes during the intervening period until the new model will be decided upon; it puts emphasis on quality and focuses on patients; it is meant to divorce financial from clinical incentives and reward preventive work; sessional fees should reward the dentists for the time they spend with the patients; the fees will be set for full time NHS dentists a 35 hour week for 46 weeks in a year. Full time engagement is considered to be 10 sessions at 3.5 hours a week;

this would be the basis for payment within the upper limits set by the health department; the additional expenses and sessions will be dealt with individually; the treatments should be considered under three categories: diagnosis and prevention, maintenance and advanced treatment; this would address the problem of time spent on prevention, and non-acceptance of patients with a lot of treatment required;

- *Developing the Community Dental Services* - the aim of the Government is to ensure accessible services and the Community Dental Services are intended as a safety net for patients who are not registered with a GDP.

Patients' Rights

The best insight into the services available to patients and their expected contribution can be achieved by looking at the payment arrangements for these services.

Since 1990 the payments have been made through five categories of fees:

- adult continuing care payment;
- child capitation payments;
- child entry payments;
- child item of service fees;
- adult item of service fees.

The Health Select Committee's categories of treatment cover:

- diagnostic and preventive treatment (examinations, scaling, small X-rays);
- maintenance treatment (fillings, root fillings, extractions, exempt treatments, other);
- advanced treatment (other periodontal work, surgical, general anaesthetics, veneers, inlays and crowns, bridges, dentures, adult orthodontics).

Present exemptions and remissions from patient charges cover:

- children under 18;
- full time students under 19;
- pregnant women and mothers of children under 1 year;
- those receiving income support and family credit.

A health promoting setting

There appears to be a gap between the new developments recommended by WHO EURO and the Government's practical policies related to the reform of the NHS and developments of dental health care. The new proposals many of which will become law following consultations and agreement by the dental practitioners indicate the need for preventive work but do not set any standards, specifications or expectations concerning the process and outcome of such work.

There is at present an attempt being made to find out whether this preventive aspect of dental services could be carried out within a "health promoting setting" model.

The concept of a "health promoting dental practice" (HPDP), represents a new approach promoted by the WHO within an organisational model, and involves the total dental practice as in HP/HE activities, including staff, patients and members of the immediate and wider community. The procedure follows the general recommendations for the creation of a "health promoting setting" as presented in Part 2 of this book. The assessment of activities is based on quality management and uses the indicators related to the health gain of the patients. The formal recognition of a dental practice as a "health promoting dental practice" requires the dentist to undertake the commitment to fulfil the following conditions: a) creating a healthy working environment, b) integrating HP/HE into all the practice activities, and c) establishing links (alliances) with other relevant institutions in the community for the benefit of the staff as well as the patients.

HEALTH PROMOTING GENERAL DENTAL PRACTICE

The application of an "organisational model" to a GDP is characterised by a number of developmental phases:

- **ground work;** exploration; "testing the water"; consultations; choosing the appropriate candidates; selling the idea to management and staff; staff meeting;
- **implementation on the organisational level;** forming a work team; second staff meeting; programme planning and organisation; reaching agreement; link with external academic institution and consultant(s); commitment; structural analysis; role definition; division of labour; policy statement; training programme; development of mechanisms for implementation and evaluation including quality management; development of a plan of action including intervention studies;
- **implementation on the patient level;** execution of the plan of action; execution of intervention studies; choice of methods for intervention, monitoring and evaluation.

These phases cover the steps in becoming a "Health Promoting Setting" and in the case of a Health Promoting General Dental Practice, can be described in greater detail as follows:

Ground Work Level

The basic ground work includes the preliminary activities involved in selection of a GDP:

Exploration ("testing the water")

Whoever initiates the health promoting setting's idea among general dental practices in a specific area will have to become acquainted with the local situation and the availability of suitable candidates for such a transition.

Where the initiative originates within the GDP setting it will be necessary to explore the internal as well as external factors suitable for such a transition.

Consultation

Once the situation has been deemed favourable, it will be necessary to initiate a set of consultations or discussions with the various agents who are directly or indirectly involved in such a transition. These will include the representatives of the relevant Family Health Service Authority (FHSA), the British Dental Association, The Health Education Authority (and possibly WHO EURO), District Health Authority and their Health Promotion Service, Community Health Council, existing consumer associations or groups, the local academic institution (University or college) and any other institution deemed relevant for such a development.

Choice of a candidate

Familiarity with the situation should provide sufficient information for the choice of appropriate candidate practices.

Discussion with the chosen candidate(s) will limit the choice to one or more candidate GDP(s) who could participate in the project of creating HPGDPs.

The criteria for selecting the participant GDP(s) for the project will include the following indicators:

- the interest and willingness of the GDP to participate;
- the reason why the GDP wishes to participate, where priority should be given to the interests of the patients, although one should not disregard the interests of the GDP;
- the available resources within the GDP;
- the available support from the external institutions which will be involved in this process either as agents who should formally confirm this new status, or as organisers of national and/or international networks of HPGDPs to which the candidate GDP could be affiliated.

Selling the idea

Once the candidate has been selected (or self-selected) it will be necessary to initiate a set of meetings (management and staff), to clarify commitments and explore the various implications for the practice and individuals working in it.

This will include:

- the benefits and new duties relating to the practice;
- the benefits and new duties relating to the staff;
- the benefits and new duties relating to the patients.

Participants should not underestimate the depth and extent of changes involved in such a commitment and should be clear about the strength of their belief in the feasibility of such a project.

Staff meeting

Following this general preparation, the process of initiation should include the organisation of a staff meeting. This can be a special meeting or a part of an existing works meeting. A successful meeting includes the following stages:

- the notification of the meeting, including the title, the time, the place, the agenda and the speakers;

- the agenda should include the clarification of the concept, the outline of advantages and possible disadvantages and the role distribution of potential participants;

- the "questions and answers" period should be allowed sufficient time for clarification of any issues and constructive treatment of any objections;

- the outcome of the meeting should be the acceptance of the setting as a whole to undertake the commitment and enter into the exploratory process of finding out in reality what this commitment implies;

- the follow-up should sound out individuals according to the suggested role definition as part of the agenda, and organise a meeting with the members who agreed to actively participate in the attempts to improve the "life" of the setting, which could also include health issues.

Implementation on the organisational level

This concerns the management and staff of the practice and includes the support and help from external consultant(s) and academic institution(s).

Reaching agreement

The first step will be to reach an agreement between the managemnt and the staff based on full information about the nature of the commitments involved.

Forming a Working Team

The individuals concerned with the issue and willing actively to support the movement should be concerned with the following topics:

- forming a "working team" from among all the people interested;

- distributing the tasks among the members in relation to the organisational programme;

- taking on the task of studying and defining the problems in the setting.

Second Staff Meeting

Once the formation of the team has been completed, they should call a staff meeting to discuss the findings and inform all the staff of the GDP about the progress made towards organising the activities required. The outcome of this meeting should be a general agreement of the GDP about the priority of problems according to their seriousness and feasibility.

Programme Planning and Organisation

These preparations should produce a programme of future activities. (For details see the appropriate section in the programme for a workshop, i.e. the module 2).

External links

Once the GDP as a whole has decided to undertake the process of becoming a health promoting setting, it will be necessary to follow up the support promised by various external agents during the exploration phase.

This support needs to be formalised and specified in terms of the mutual expectations of such a collaboration. It will be important, for example to know what support can be expected from the FHSA, HEA and the DHA, in terms of advice, equipment, resources, etc. The same applies to consultants and academic insitutions, in terms of expertise for planning and the execution of different aspects of the plan of action, such as, for example, advice in management, quality assessment, HP/HE methods, research planning and data analysis, case study research methods, drawing inferences, publishing reports, etc.

In some cases, such as, for example, using the services of the external consultant it will be necessary to draw up a formal contract including the duties and remuneration fees.

The Commitment

As in the case of any other health promoting setting there are certain preconditions which the management of a setting needs to fulfil. In the case of a Health Promoting General Dental Practice, the manager or the dentist will have to become acquainted with these requirements, they will have to discuss them with the members of the practice and then take on a commitment to fulfil the necessary conditions which include:

- acceptance of the Ottawa Charter;
- development of a healthy working environment;
- integration of health promotion and health education into daily activities;
- outreach into community (networks and alliances);
- planning and execution of intervention studies in main areas of activity;
- evaluation in the form of quality assessment of the services provided;,
- in-service training programmes in health promotion and health education for the practice staff.

It is important to realise that the health promotion and health education activities should be "resource neutral" which means that they should be carried out within the existing resources of the practice and/or the existing contract with NHS.

If "pilot status" is recognised, a practice will have to make special efforts to monitor the activities and produce documentation which can serve other practices in carrying out a similar transformation. In this case, the pilot practice can apply for additional support in the form of resources and advice to enable them to carry out the monitoring activities.

Recognition of the status of a health promoting dental practice should enable the practice to join the National and European Networks of Health Promoting General Dental Practices. This will include a number of additional commitments such as participating in the Business Meetings of the Networks, organising workshops, publishing progress reports, etc.

The new role of dentists in health promotion and health education places new demands on the FHSAs as purchasers of these services. They will be expected to develop specifications for these services and provide training programmes for the staff working in General Dental Practices. To be able to do this, they will need to support and initiate research into tested methods before they can expect dentists successfully to provide the required services.

A Structural Analysis

As we have already mentioned, people carry out their daily work without being aware of the structural and functional factors of which this work is composed. This is not a problem so long as there is no need to analyse the work and describe its various characteristics. The first step in the effective transformation of a General Dental Practice into a Health Promotion General Dental Practice is to carry out a structural and functional analysis of the practice. This will include a description of the following:

- location of the practice and the working conditions;
- composition of the practice;
- role definition and power structure of the members of the practice;
- procedures in carrying out various services with the relevant documentation;
- classification of the main services;
- the records of the practice in terms of type of patients, morbidity, mortality, referrals, etc.

This analysis should help the staff of the practice to recognise the potential for including health promotion and health education into their work.

Division of Labour

The role definition of each member of staff of a practice will require a detailed analysis of the tasks allocated with special reference to those tasks which lend themselves to health promotion and health education interventions. This procedure includes:

- task definition;
- interrelationship between members of staff;
- interrelationship of staff members and the patients;
- the role definition of patients.

The importance of the establishment of role definition of staff and patients will provide a good framework for the analysis of their health promotion and health education activities.

Policy statement

The commitment should take the form of a policy statement of the HPGDP which is somewhatis similar to the policy statement required for meeting the standards for quality management. It includes:

- the organisation's image and reputation for quality;
- type of service to be provided (specifications);
- objectives for the achievement of service quality (procedures);
- approaches or methods used for the achievement of quality objectives;
- role of personnel responsible for implementing the quality policy.

The carrying out of policy will require a clear statement of the **aims** or goals of the service organisation to cover:

- effectiveness leading to customer satisfaction and consistent with professional standards and ethics;
- continuous monitoring and improvement of services;
- adjusting services to the needs of the society and the environment;
- efficiency in providing the services.

The achievement of these aims will depend on the selection of *objectives or specifications* including the following activities:

- clear definition of customer's needs which should include appropriate indicators and criteria related to quality assessment;
- application of appropriate procedures related to aims;
- preventive actions to avoid customer's dissatisfaction;
- optimising quality-related cost for the required performance and type of service;
- continuous review of service requirements and achievements to identify opportunities for service quality improvement;
- preventing adverse effects of the service activities on the society and the environment.

The achievement of the stated aims through the selected objectives will require the establishment of a *structure* for the effective evaluation and control of the service quality and resulting in possible improvements.

The purpose of such an analysis of structure is to provide a picture of the distribution of authority and role definitions (job descriptions) of the personnel in accordance with the requirements of the provision of services. This should pay special attention to the qualitative and quantitative aspects of the personnel-consumer relationship at all interfaces within and external to the organisation.

Top management should ensure the development and smooth operation of the requirements for a HP/HE system. The responsibility should be allocated to a *special person* or form a part of the general role of an individual. It is important, however, to understand the holistic character of the activities. They will not depend solely on a designated person or on the performance of an aspect of the role of a person; it is the outcome of a *total commitment and aggregated performance* of all the personnel, expressed in their commitment, motivation, involvement and networking. The main theme, however, is continuous improvement of services.

The Method

There is as yet no tested experience of the transformation of a General Dental Practice (GDP) into a Health Promoting General Dental Practice (HPGDP). This process needs help and support on different levels:

- the management team of the GDP needs advice from external consultants in different areas of activity such as the transformation process, the health promotion and health education methods and approaches, as well as in total quality management; this can be provided directly or in the form of workshops and other forms of in-service training;

- the staff of the GDP will need advice and help in establishing a set of intervention studies in different areas of activity for the purpose of finding out for themselves where and how their health promotion and health education activities could best benefit the patients and contribute to their health gain, using the differential diagnosis approach;

- the GDP as a whole will need to introduce appropriate systems for data collection and retrieval, related to the health promotion and health education activities concerned with identifying and satisfying patients' needs for the purpose of maximising their health gain and minimising any undesirable side-effects.

The Aims and Objectives

The translation of general aims of creating a Health Promoting General Dental Practice will be:

AIM 1: to develop a procedure for the transformation of a GDP into a HPGDP. To achieve this aim the intervention will have the following objectives:

Objective 1.1: to take the practice staff through the commitment procedure necessary for the acquisition of a recognised status of a Pilot HPGDP;

Objective 1.2: to establish the mechanisms necessary for carrying out the process activating the conditions for a HPGDP, i.e. creating a healthy environment, integrating health promotion and health education into daily activities, and establishing an outreach into the community in the form of networks and alliances.

AIM 2: to provide the necessary knowledge and skills to the staff of a GDP for operationalisation of the preconditions relevant to a HPGDP. To achieve this aim the intervention will have the following objectives:

Objective 2.1: development of curricula for training programmes for the practice staff;

Objective 2.2: organisation of workshops for training the practice staff in the subject matter of health promotion and health education, including the planning, execution and evaluation of the activities;

AIM 3: to develop mechanisms for the evaluation of the activities of the HPGDP, which, in line with the organisational model, should adopt quality management and quality assessment; the main indicator is the health gain of the patients. To achieve this aim, the intervention will have the following objectives:

Objective 3.1: development of mechanisms for constant monitoring and assessment of quality of the services provided, based on the Total Quality Management model;

Objective 3.2: development of standards and specifications for the quality assessment of the services provided.

The Outcome

The expected outcome of the study will have implications for health promotion and health education on different levels. It should:

- provide experience in transforming a setting into a health promoting setting;
- produce a new curriculum relevant for teaching the application of an organisational model of health promotion and health education;
- explore the introduction of the concept of total quality management into a GDP for the purpose of evaluation and quality management;

The activities of a GDP with a pilot status need to be monitored, empirically tested and publicised for the benefit of others who wish to follow the same road.

Training programme

The new tasks facing the staff of a GDP in the area of HP/HE will require additional training, including the acquisition of knowledge and skills. This can take the form of a Workshop which can be divided into following modules:

The **aims** of this module are to enable the participants in the GDP to become familiar with and competent in "selling" the idea of getting their setting recognised as a "Health Promoting Setting", to their patients and the people living in their community, by emphasising its advantages and presenting the realistic contributions expected from each community member and staff of the setting.

At the end of this "initiation period", the setting should have established a "working team", examined the existing problems and selected the priorities in preparation for the development of the "organisation programme." The part of the workshop covering this stage in the process should enable the participants to acquire skills in "directive interviewing", i.e. individual conversations with the aim of counselling ideas to colleagues with the idea and gathering opinions and possible objections.

The **content** should include information about raising issues, listening to opinions, providing arguments, answering questions, as well as about the ways to conduct an interview (introduction, questions and answers, conclusion).

The **method** of acquiring this knowledge as well as skills related to interviewing, should include simple explanation of the major points supported by numerous illustrations and followed by practice in the form of role play.

The **assessment** should include the views expressed by the participants, the opinions of their colleagues and the external observers, as well as the assessment of the supervisor.

The part of Module 1, covering the organisation of a staff meeting, should enable the participants to acquire skills in planning, advertising, organising, leading and participating in such meetings. The contents should include information about attracting the attention and using staff media; the considerations to be taken into account when planning a meeting (place, size of the auditorium, seating arrangements, acoustics, lighting, chairing and running a meeting, presentation of speeches, leading a discussion, answering questions, dealing with troublemakers, and getting a commitment or opinion by sounding out the participants). The method of acquiring knowledge and skills should include some general advice, a task and role play. The assessment should include the subjective feelings of the participants and subsequent evaluation of the meetings organised by the participants.

The part of Module 1 dealing with organising the second staff meeting should enable the participants to learn from the experiences gained during the organisation of the first staff meeting and avoid most of the mistakes made. The contents should include ways of critically analysing the outcomes and possible improvements. The method should include the simulation of tasks, where participants get information about an imaginary meeting and carry out the exercise of improving on it. The assessment should be based on the outcome of the exercises which should also include the level of confidence expressed by the participants during the exercise. A long term assessment should include the evaluation of the second staff meeting.

Module 2: Programme Planning and Organisation

The **aims** of this module are to enable the participants to become competent and confident in drafting a programme for action, testing it with the general staff of the setting and producing a final organisational and operational programme for action.

The first step in planning and organising a programme for action should be to make a diagnosis by examining the causes and prescribing relevant solutions. The "oral health" diagnosis should be available from thedental profession and it should include "causes and solutions" related to dental health. For a HP/HE intervention it should be necessary to carry out a differential diagnosis with the emphasis on "health promotional/educational solutions".

One should take into consideration the fact that the activities of a HPGDP should take into account the problems of the staff working in the practice, the problems of the patients using the practice and the community within which the practice is located. The solutions to the problems in each of these areas should be adjusted to the needs and possibilities of each one. The success of such a simultaneous set of activities in these interacting areas should require a mechanism for coordination, evaluation and feedback. The main steps can be envisaged as follows:

- *commitment:* the implementation of the chosen solution should require the agreement and commitment of the practice, the patients and the community concerning certain required actions. This commitment can include resources, working time, expertise, services etc. It should be defined by the nature and the character of the solutions prescribed.

- *tasks:* once the general commitment of the practice has been gained, the next step should be to specify the solutions in terms of activities. These activities should then be distributed in the form of task-distribution for practice and role definition for individual members of each practice.

- *action:* launching the whole programme requires actions on the part of the practice according to task distributions and role definitions. These actions will have to be synchronised to achieve maximum effectiveness.

- *coordination of activities:* synchronisation of activities requires a mechanism for coordination as well as close cooperation of all the actors involved.

The purpose of such a mechanism is the coordination of a programme and its success will depend on the management skills of the teams, dealt with in Module 3.

Module 3: Management of the Programme

The **aims** of this module are to enable the participants to acquire knowledge about issues involved in management of a programme as well as skills in carrying it out.

The main **objective** of management is to *coordinate* the various planned activities involving members of the setting and their patients. This coordination is vital for *simultaneous actions* to take place.

Some of the solutions will depend for their success on the *synchronicity* of actions, for example, changing the norms, values and opinions of the members of the practice and the patients.

The management of the programme should include synchronising the commitments of the setting as a whole and its different parts, their acceptance of specific tasks and roles, as well as the adjustments of their actions with the aim of supporting and reinforcing each other.

The degree of success needs to be evaluated and this is dealt with in Module 4.

Module 4: Evaluation and Feedback

The **aims** of this module are to provide participants with an understanding of the need for for evaluating a programme and the skills necessary to do it. It is also necessary to make use of the feedback mechanism for the adjustments and corrections of the programme. This module should clarify the distinction between the traditional evaluation process and the new forms of evaluation adjusted to the needs of a HPGDP, for which quality assessment procedures need to be employed.

Evaluation should be included in the planning stages of a programme. To achieve a successful evaluation, the following preconditions should be met:

1. The programme should have aims and objectives defined in a measurable way; the measurement requires a set of indicators defined by criteria for assessment and translated into instruments that can be used to carry out the measurements; in terms of quality assessment, the programme should have a set of specifications for the expected outcomes, agreed upon by the purchasers, providers and consumers.

2. The programme should be divided into steps or phases, and each requires a specific evaluation of the achievement of each sub-aim or sub-objective;

3. the programme should include a mechanism for utilising the feedback information and adjusting the programme accordingly.

In terms of a "community" type action in a practice, the phases involved are:

- *commitment*: it is necessary to make a critical assessment of the commitments undertaken within the practice as well as by the individual members; these should be synchronised and be supportive as well as specific; they should also be relevant to the aims of the programme; any problems noted at this stage should be fed back into the system and corrected before proceeding with the next phase;

- *tasks and roles*: it is important to distinguish between the general and specific aspects of commitments; the specific commitments will allow the task distribution and the role definition to take place; any problems due to the mismatch between the institutional tasks and individual role performance should be fed back into the system and adjustments should be made;

- *actions*: evaluation should link the commitments undertaken to the distribution of tasks and roles and the actions carried out; it should also link the actions monitored with the actual achievements in terms of programme aims; since a number of actions and activities will be carried out within the framework of the programme aims, each one should be assessed separately; the feedback mechanism should allow corrections and adjustments to be made since any action in the practice represents an ongoing programme and a continuous activity as a part of the changing life style of the practice.

Evaluation, Quality Assessment and Audit

One of the main characteristics of GDPs is their accountability which requires information about the services provided in terms of processes (how), contents (what) and outcomes (with what effect). This accountability can be achieved by following approaches:

- *evaluation:* it is "programme-based" and is the assessment of the achievement of the aims of a programme; it applies to the situation where health promotion and health education are being integrated in certain aspects of the settings' activities; it will require a clear statement of aims in measurable terms, the description of objectives or the way these aims are planned to be achieved; it also requires the choice of indicators which will be used for the assessment of the achievement as well as the decision on the criteria which will be used in the definition of a success or failure of a programme;

- *quality assessment:* quality assessment of a production process is "consumer-based" and will carry out the assessment against the recognised interests and needs of the consumers; the assessment of a health promoting setting will have to use the existing methods applied in such a setting i.e. the mechanism of quality management which should also include in its specifications the health promotion and health education aims; the present preferential approach is the Total Quality Management model; the main characteristics of this model are the examination of the whole process of production, i.e. looking at the "raw material", "the production process" and the "outcome", which represents the "raw material" for the next stage; it also means the quality control of each stage of the process with necessary adjustments;

- *audit*: audit is the assessment of an activity against the existing social values, norms, laws, regulations and rules; it is carried out by professionally legitimised "auditors" who can be members of a profession (dental audit) or a government department (financial audit).

Implementation on the patient level

The execution of the agreed upon plan of action will be based on the findings of the structural analysis of the GDP and the role distribution within the plan of action.

The GDP will be expected to apply the standard methods of HP/HE to their patients with the aim of improving their oral health.

Intervention studies

In addition to a structural study of the GDP, the processes and outcomes of such an exercise, the staff of the GDP with a pilot status will be required to plan and carry out a number of small studies related to their different activities with the aim of finding out for themselves where health promotion and health education could be best applied, which methods are effective and what are the anticipated outcomes. These could include the effects of the new contract on the need satisfaction of patients, the satisfaction of the dentists and their staff with new tasks, the reaction of patients in terms of satisfaction, compliance, health gain, etc.

Writing a protocol

The instructions for writing a protocol for a intervention study were fully described in Part 2 of this book. The following summary guide may help in drafting an initial protocol for an intervention study. This is, however, a very short summary of a process which will need to be tailored and expanded to meet the needs of differing kinds of research.

It is, therefore, recommended that appropriate academic or other research support is sought before proceeding too far with the project planning. The protocol should include the following descriptions:

- outline of a research proposal;
- the situation/problems;
- the study (aims, objectives, methods, resources,timing);
- monitoring and evaluation (practice, patient,community levels);
- management, accountability, reporting.

CASE STUDY: GENERAL DENTAL PRACTICE

The process of creating a Health Promoting General Dental Practice (HPGDP) described in this case study followed the phases defined in the description of creating a Health Promoting Setting in Part 2 of this book. This included the work on three different levels: ground work level, organisational and patient levels.

Ground Work Level

The external HP/HE consultant, who has been engaged in the creation of a number of different health promoting settings, took the initiative in trying to create a HPGDP in Manchester. The ground work in this attempt included:

Finding the appropriate GDP

After contacting a number of general dental practices, one was located which met most of the preconditions for such an experiment:

- interest of the dental practitioners;
- a history of health promotion and health education work;
- a mixed combination of NHS and private patients;
- strong academic links;
- interest of the practice staff.

Acceptance of the commitment

The initial discussions with the professional members of the practice (two dentists) included the following topics:

- clarification of the concepts of a health promoting setting;
- the range of HP/HE interventions;
- the need for introducing quality assessment methods;
- the need to plan intervention studies;
- reporting the outcomes.

The initial discussions were based on several papers prepared by the external consultant on the topics mentioned.

Following these discussions the partners in the GDP expressed their willingness to participate in the experiment. They were informed about the procedure leading to the commitment which includes:

1. a written policy statement of the HPGDP covering:

- acceptance of the Ottawa Charter;
- role distribution of staff;
- provision for quality assessment;
- publication of progress reports;

2. acceptance of the three main aims of the HPGDP which were:

- creation of a healthy working environment;
- integration of HP/HE into daily activities;
- outreach into the community;

3. initiation of the intervention studies by each of the partners, who chose the following topics:

- HP/HE and children as dental patients;
- HP/HE and the elderly patients.

Support by the local academic institution

The external consultant contacted the local University, Dental School and after explaining the idea, acquired their commitment for support and supervision of these activities.

Support by the health education services

The external consultant contacted the Health Education Authority and invited them to participate or approve of such a venture. The HEA could not at this stage get directly involved with the venture but assured the initiators of their approval and support.

The Organisational Level

The activities on the organisational level included:

The academic institution

The head of Oral Health in the Department of Oral Health and Development, at the local University expressed willingness to take the initiative in the following areas:

- support and expert advice for the research aspects of the HPGDP;
- provision of resources for research aspects of the venture;
- undertaking the initiative for the creation and running of a Network of HPGDP (on the English, UK and European level);
- selecting other GDPs who would be interested to participate in such a venture and join the Network;
- linking with the Royal College of General Dental Practitioners;
- linking with WHO EURO with the aim of initiating similar ventures in other European countries and gaining support for an European Network of HPGDPs;
- organising in 1995 an international workshop of HPGDP.

The General Dental Practice

The activities on the level of the practice included:

- data collection concerning the practice, the staff roles, the patients' problems;
- exploring the availability of support from external bodies such as Family Health Services Authority (FHSA), the local Health Promotion Units;
- organising training sessions for the staff;
- producing a plan for action for each member of staff;
- establishment of mechanisms for evaluation and quality assessment.

The Patient Level

The activities on the patient level included:

Plan of action:

- interventions based on information about the most prevalent problems among patients attending the surgery;

- interaction with registered patients who are at present "well";

- selection of methods according to the needs of patients and problems;

- collection and preparation of materials for a HP/HE intervention;

- establishment of methods for evaluation (base line data, intervention process, outcomes.

Intervention studies

One intervention study is concerned with health promotion and health education directed towards the children who are registered patients in the GDP.

Thhe other study is concerned with the health promotion and health education directed towards the elderly patients registered in the GDP.

Both intervention studies are based on a "Blueprint for a Pilot Study" which is presented in a matrix form. On one axis are the areas which a HPGDP needs to cover (creating a healthy working environment, integration of HP/HE into daily work of the GDP, and outreach of the GDP into the community). On the other axis are the levels of a HP/HE intervention within an organisational model (the ground work level, the organisational level and the consumer or patient level).

The matrix includes a number of aims, distributed within this two-dimensional model of a pilot intervention.

Blueprint For A Pilot Study

Based on the matrix the aims are distributed along the two dimensions i.e. the levels and areas of intervention:

AIM 1: To establish the working conditions for staff (premises, relationships, timetable, resources);

AIM 2: To establish the conditions available to patients (access, appointment system, waiting room, relationships);

AIM 3: To establish existing HP/HE activities in the practice (information system, resources, time, readability, contents);

AIM 4: To establish the needs of the patients (coping with the acute condition, aspects of lifestyle, access to practice staff);

AIM 5: To establish the needs of the staff (HP/HE knowledge and skills, relationship with patients, available resources);

AIM 6: To establish the influence of the family (social support, values and norms, lifestyle);

AIM 7: To establish the influence of the wider social environment (values and norms, lifestyle, relatives, friends, colleagues);

AIM 8: To plan the adjustment of the working environment for staff (premises, access, working conditions);

AIM 9: To plan the adjustment of the practice conditions for the needs of patients (records, waiting room, appointment facilities);

AIM 10: To plan the establishment of facilities for display and distribution of HP/HE materials;

AIM 11: To plan available time for providing information and coping with anxieties;

AIM 12: To plan the provision of resources for HP/HE (free samples, publications, videos etc.);

AIM 13: To plan the establishment of contacts with other services where necessary (referral, social support, transport);

AIM 14: To plan the establishment of contacts with external settings (family, school, work);

AIM 15: To adjust the setting to enhance patients' privacy;

AIM 16: To ensure the patients' wellbeing in the waiting room and in the surgery;

AIM 17: To provide patients with problem-specific and general information about lifestyles;

AIM 18: To provide patients with the necessary skills for prevention and coping with health problems;

AIM 19: To motivate the patient to comply with the necessary measures concerning prevention and coping with health problems;

AIM 20: To include other family members (where relevant) and mobilise their support;

AIM 21: To mobilise the support of other settings (leisure, school, work).

THE HEALTH PROMOTING SCHOOL

The role of health education in schools is very old. It was always considered to be convenient to carry out health education where a captive audience is available, and a school was an ideal situation for that purpose. As a result of the work of the Regional Office for Europe of the World Health Organisation, a review was carried out and new approaches within a "healthy school" model were introduced (Baric, 1991). The groundwork was laid as long ago as 1984, and was followed by a number of meetings, which refined the concept and finally produced the "health promoting school" approach, now being introduced in a number of European countries. In this activity, WHO worked in close collaboration with the Commission of European Communities, whose European Community Council of Education Ministers adopted in 1988 a resolution concerning health education in schools.

The "health promoting school" approach aims at promoting health within a school treated as a complex social system. It is not merely aimed at the pupils' health or school curriculum development, but focuses the whole school environment and all aspects of school life. The decisive factor for accepting a school into this programme is the school's commitment and intent to create a health promoting school.

The concept of "health promoting schools" is closely linked to the general WHO EURO policy towards HP/HE within a settings approach, which has resulted in creating a number of different "health promoting settings". There has, however, been little coordination in the implementation of this policy within WHO, which is reflected in the fact that different settings have taken different paths to creating a health promoting setting, used different methods of evaluation and are at different stages of development. An example is the different approach to evaluation between hospitals and schools. The health promoting hospitals are expected to use a quality assessment approach to evaluating their services to patients, whereas the health promoting schools have so far disregarded this approach although quality assessment is a part of the educational assessment of schools. The outcome of this is the lack of comparability between the successes and failures of different settings and the inability to draw a valid conclusion about the settings movement as a whole.

There are, however, some shared characteristics related to the process these settings are undergoing in their transformation into "health promoting settings". This is valid for schools as well as hospitals, as two of the most developed areas of the implementation of a health promoting settings approach.

These shared characteristics are reflected in the stages of the transformation process each setting is undergoing:

- ground work;
- implementation on the organisational level;
- implementation on the consumer level.

The "health promoting school" programme is being developed on the European, national and local level. Examination of progress made so far shows that it is limited to ground work and implementation on the organisational level. There has been a considerable amount of work done on these two levels, resulting in detailed understanding of the conditions of joining, elements of planning, development of structures, etc.

Effectiveness will depend on preparation as well as evaluation of results from the implementation on the consumer (pupil) level. This has been so far disregarded and the usual commonsense assumption is applied, that if structures and resources are provided then health promotion and health education will provide the methods. This naive assumption is probably the reason why most of the programmes have not progressed beyond the organisational level.

THE AIMS OF THE PROGRAMME

The key actions areas of the Ottawa Charter for Health Promotion indicate the wider aspects of the health promoting schools programme and they define the main aims and goals. In practical terms these are:

- a three year programme of health promoting activity in each school project;
- development of the school curriculum to include a significant level of education for health;
- formal policy support for the promotion of health in the school setting and the eventual legal establishment of education for health in the school curriculum.

There is a need to differentiate between the maximal, optimal (ideal) and minimal achievements within such a programme. To be able to carry out any assessment or evaluation of such a programme it will be necessary to list the optimal or "ideal" project aims agreed at the WHO Planning Meeting on the Health Promoting Schools (Copenhagen, 1991). These were defined by the following objectives:

- implement the areas of the Ottawa Charter for Health Promotion as already indicated;
- provide a healthy environment with regard to safety, meals, buildings, playgrounds, leisure facilities, etc;
- promote a sense of responsibility with respect to the individual's, the family's and the community's health;
- encourage a healthy way of life and present a realistic and attractive range of health choices;
- enable pupils to fulfil their physical, psychological and social potential and actively promote the self-esteem of the pupils;
- make clear for staff and pupils the social aims of the school and its potential for the promotion of health.;
- develop good staff/pupil and pupil/pupil relations in the daily life of the school and provide good school/home/community links;
- utilize the potential of specialist and other resources in the community for advice and support in education for health and action for health promotion;
- plan a coherent health education curriculum;
- provide a health knowledge base and skills in obtaining, interpreting and acting upon information related to health.

THE METHOD

The planners of the Health Promoting School Programme used a systems approach. The system was defined as the Health Promoting School. It started by defining a structure for the whole movement, which includes the school, represented by the School Programme Manager (SPM), the Project Support Centre (PSCs) and the International Support Centre (ISCs), with a National Advisory Council (NAC) which is concerned with the general programme and which could include a number of schools.

The movement initiated by WHO EURO, set up consultations (ground work) with a number of "core" schools from various countries (Czech and the Slovak Republics, Poland and Hungary, UK). This was followed by a workshop organised by the University of Salford (April, 1992) for the future co-ordinators of the movement in their own country who were participating in the European Network.

At present there is a fully operational European Network of Health Promoting Schools run by WHO EURO. It consists of 36 European countries, together with their National Networks, all at different stages of acceptance by the European Network.

THE EUROPEAN NETWORK OF HP SCHOOLS

This section reports on the document which has been published jointly by the World Health Organisation for Europe, the Council of Europe and the Commission of the European Community (WHO, 1993). The European Network of Health Promoting Schools is a tripartite project and the document provides the shared views of the three partners. The document includes the following statements:

"The concept of the health-promoting school

1. The health-promoting school aims at achieving healthy lifestyles for the total school population by developing supportive environments conducive to the promotion of health. It offers opportunities for, and requires commitments to, the provision of a safe and health-enhancing social and physical environment.

2. The setting up of a European network of health-promoting schools, as an effective way of exchanging experiences and information and disseminating examples of good practice, has been repeatedly proposed by health and education experts, government policy-makers, researchers and teachers in various meetings and international conferences organized by CEC, CE and WHO.

3. WHO, CEC and CE have agreed to support a European Network of Health-Promoting Schools which strives to:

- *provide a health-promoting environment for working and learning through its buildings, play areas, catering facilities, safety measures, etc.;*
- *promote individual, family and community responsibility for health;*
- *encourage healthy lifestyles and present a realistic and attractive range of health choices for schoolchildren and staff;*
- *enable all pupils to fulfil their physical, psychological and social potential and promote their self- esteem;*
- *set out clear aims for the promotion of health and safety for the whole school community (schoolchildren and adults);*
- *foster good staff - pupil and pupil - pupil relationships and good links between the school, the home and the community;*
- *exploit the availability of community resources to support action for the promotion of health;*
- *plan a coherent health education curriculum with educational methods that actively engage pupils;*
- *equip pupils with the knowledge and skills they need both to make sound decisions about their personal health and to preserve and improve a safe and healthy physical environment;*

- *take a wide view of school health services as an educational resource that can help pupils become effective health care consumers.*

The rationale for a joint effort

1. Joint planning of the European Network of Health-Promoting Schools was one of the recommendations of the CE - CEC - WHO Conference on the Promotion of Health Education (Strasbourg, 20-22 September 1990). It builds on the collaborative work done in the 1980s under the pilot project "Education for Health". This joint work is in line with WHO's current priorities for health promotion, and it is also in the spirit of EC Council Resolution of 23 November 1988 on the implementation of health education in schools and the European Conference on Health Education and Prevention in Schools organized by CEC and held in Dublin from 7 to 11 February 1990.

2. Collaboration between CEC, CE and WHO in setting up this European network is essential to avoid duplication and provide a coherent framework within which to foster and sustain innovation, disseminate models of good practice and make opportunities for health promotion in schools more equitably available throughout Europe.

The organisation of the Network

The network should be as decentralized as possible. Key requirements for effective management and coordination at local (school), national and European levels are:

- *the selection of schools (approximately 10 in each Member State);*

- *at school level, the appointment of a school project team and school project manager;*

- *at national level, the identification of a project support centre and the designation of a national coordinator;*

- *at international level, the establishment of an international planning committee.*

The framework should allow for adjustments according to local and national circumstances and priorities.

2. At school level, management and coordination will be achieved by appointing and training school project managers. The school project manager should be chosen on the basis of his/her commitment, management skills and capacity to provide motivation and leadership. The school project manager should be officially appointed and supported by the director of the school. He/she should be supported in bringing together a school project team to facilitate the implementation, review and further development of the project. A major responsibility of this team is to share responsibility and promote and maintain motivation among pupils, teachers, parents and other school education and health-related staff.

3. At Member State level, management and coordination should be carried out by a national project support centre under the responsibility of a national project coordinator. The project support centre should play an active role in the day-to-day development of the network at country level. Its functions could be performed by a health promotion or health education centre already working in the field at country or regional level. Its selection should meet the criteria established by the international planning committee, including easy access to all the schools involved in the network from a given country (as described in the next section).

Project support centres should:

- *provide guidelines for the schools in the national network and guarantee coordination at country level;*

- *support school project managers through the organisation of training programmes and other developmental activities;*

- *be responsible for national dissemination of supportive information through a country-based "clearing-house".*

The national project coordinator will provide the main link of communication with the international planning committee.

4. Strategic planning functions and support to the network will be provided by an international planning committee (IPC) comprising representatives of the three bodies concerned (CEC, CE and WHO). Its functions are to:

- *identify the criteria to be met by Member States, project support centres, national project coordinators and participating schools to ensure effective development of the network;*
- *liaise with and provide guidance to project support centres and national project coordinators;*
- *plan training (e.g. summer schools);*
- *facilitate twinning and other exchanges for the purpose of carrying out the project;*
- *support and review evaluation;*
- *organize meetings with all the partners in the network;*
- *plan field visits.*

The IPC should provide a focus and ensure links and opportunities for all the parties in the network.

Requirements for applying to join the Network

1. A Member State wishing to participate in the European Network of Health-Promoting Schools should guarantee commitment to the project and intersectoral cooperation between education and health authorities at the highest level.

2. In order to ensure proper selection of schools, Member States are invited to assess existing health education and promotion programmes in the schools under consideration and evaluate the schools in terms of physical environment, work organisation and human relations, training of staff and perceived needs for health promotion.

3. The schools participating in the European Network should meet a number of criteria. First and foremost is their commitment to the concept of the health-promoting school. School directors, staff and pupils would need to understand fully the implications of joining the network in terms of commitment to and time spent on carrying out the necessary activities such as project management, training, curriculum development and involvement of parents and the community.

4. A project of this nature will need detailed planning at school level, so objective evaluation and auditing must be key elements of the project as a whole. All school projects will be evaluated in the context of their chosen aims and objectives. National coordinators will play an important role in assisting the process of evaluation in their own countries and will have the opportunity to update their knowledge and skills through participation in specially designed workshops on planning and process evaluation.

5. A participating school would be expected to agree to work towards meeting a set of 12 criteria:

- *active promotion of the self-esteem of all pupils by demonstrating that everyone can make a contribution to the life of the school;*
- *the development of good relations between staff and pupils and between pupils in the daily life of the school;*
- *the clarification for staff and pupils of the social aims of the school;*
- *the provision of stimulating challenges for all pupils through a wide range of activities;*
- *using every opportunity to improve the physical environment of the school;*

- *the development of good links between the school, the home and the community;*

- *the development of good links between associated primary and secondary schools to plan a coherent health education curriculum;*

- *the active promotion of the health and wellbeing of school staff;*

- *the consideration of the role of staff exemplars in health-related issues;*

- *the consideration of the complementary role of school meals (if provided) to the health education curriculum;*

- *the realization of the potential of specialist services in the community for advice and support in health education;*

- *the development of the education potential of the school health services beyond routine screening towards active support for the curriculum.*

6. Countries and schools participating in the European Network should:

- *design a health-promoting school project plan for a minimum of three years;*

- *form a school project team and give the project definite high priority in school activities;*

- *implement projects to tackle issues which are important locally and at the same time have European relevance, so that such projects can subsequently be used as models of good practice;*

- *implement activities which demonstrably promote the health of young people, foster solidarity and support attitudes and behaviour favouring responsibility for personal and community health and greater safety awareness;*

- *make all necessary arrangements to ensure the visibility and credibility of activities related to the health-promoting school project and facilitate the evaluation and dissemination of results.*

Commitment to the Future

The future of the new Europe is its children. All children must be given the opportunity to achieve their maximum potential as healthy and educated adults who possess the energy, skills and sense of responsibility that are so essential in the modern world.

This initiative is dedicated to reaching that goal. Its accomplishment will depend on the full and sustained support of leaders at all levels in education, health, and socio economic development.

We must do this; we can do it: the European Network of Health-Promoting Schools will capitalize on the political will and technical expertise now evident in Europe."

THE UK DEVELOPMENTS

In 1992 the Health Education Authority (HEA, 1993) commissioned an investigation into health promotion in schools, which was carried out by the National Foundation for Educational Research (NFER). The conclusions from the survey were summarised as follows:

- "between a half and two thirds of schools now have a written health education policy and others are currently developing on, or up-dating their existing policies. In most cases these policies are emerging to ensure greater coordination and consistency of provision, and to respond effectively to growing public concern about the health, lifestyles and choices of many young people;

- just under two-thirds of the schools have appointed a member of staff as a health education coordinator but their impact tends to be severely constrained by the lack of non-contact time to facilitate coordination and support for colleagues;

- as a result the quality of health education in many schools is variable, depending on the commitment and teaching styles of individual members of staff;

- this potential problem is compounded by the lack of resources available for in-service training in this area of the curriculum. Although there appeared to be no shortage of good teaching materials, few schools had the necessary finance with which to purchase existing resources. Furthermore, there was reduced support from health education coordinators and LEA advisory teachers because of reduction in number of posts;

- there is a risk that health education may become increasingly marginalised in many schools, mainly because of the demands associated with the implementation of the National Curriculum, but also because of a shortage of suitably trained and supported staff. The risk of marginalisation is greatest in small primary schools but is also a matter of concern in many secondary schools and special schools;

- many schools have broadened their health education provision beyond the curriculum, recognising the value of a health promoting school and the need for widely understood procedures for pupils at risk from the use of drugs and solvents, sexual activity, smoking, consumption of alcohol, diet, or sexual abuse. However, few schools have as yet recognised the need to involve non-teaching staff, parents and other adults who help at the school in the process.

Nevertheless, in spite of the constraints and difficulties now facing many schools, the project team found a great deal of commitment not only from teachers and coordinators in schools, but also from hard-pressed school nurses, advisory teachers and the staff of Health Promotion Units, all determined to maintain or improve the standard of health education."

In the Preface to the document Lynda Finn gave a summary of the new developments:

"The White Paper, The Health of the Nation sets out a strategy for health in England which acknowledges the importance of health education for young people both in and out of school. The strategy includes a commitment to develop health promoting schools in England.

As part of our work in the education sector, the Health Education Authority believed that it was important to chart the development of health education in schools since our last survey in 1989 (Health Education in Schools, HEA/MORI, 1989). Since then there have been major developments. These include implementation of the National Curriculum; the publication of Curriculum Guidance 5, the National Curriculum Council's guidance to schools on health education; the government's decision that as from April 1993 the GEST (Grants for Education Support and Training) scheme for health education will end, causing a sharp reduction in the number of LEAs funding health education coordinator posts; implementation of Local Management of Schools which gives individual schools responsibility for determining whether or not health education is a priority; surveys of young people's health and lifestyles which show an alarming trend towards early sexual activity, no significant decrease in teenage smoking rates, and many other lifestyle trends which point to an even greater need to teach about health education in schools (Today's Young Adults, HEA, 1992).

In 1989, the findings of the MORI survey were generally positive: seven out of ten secondary schools had a written policy for health education or personal and social education (PSE) and most of the rest were planning to formulate one; 61 per cent of primary schools and 76 per cent of secondary schools had a sex education policy; just over half (55 per cent) of primary schools and 80 per cent of secondary schools had a designated health education coordinator.

By 1992 the picture was less positive. Although there was a great deal of commitment and good will towards health education in schools, the general pattern was one of increasing marginalisation. Unsurprisingly, schools were giving top priority to implementing the National Curriculum, to the detriment of health education. The two-thirds of schools who had appointed a health education coordinator were not able to give them sufficient non-contact time to carry out their work, and this severely limited their impact. This was combined with a lack of resources for in-service training or new teaching materials, and reduced support from health education coordinators (many of whose posts had already disappeared). The quality of health education was found to be variable, depending largely on the commitment and teaching styles of individual members of staff. However, some findings were encouraging: over two-thirds of schools in the survey had developed a written policy on sex education and a further 29 per cent were preparing one. A mere 4 per cent of schools had a policy against sex education. And between one-half and two-thirds of schools now have a written health education policy, with many others currently developing a policy or updating their existing one.

Although it is clear that some of the ground gained since the early 1980s is in danger of being lost, the targets set out in The Health of the Nation cannot be achieved without school-based health education. Schools have a major part to play in helping to meet many of the national objectives and targets. The cultivation of healthy alliances between health and education authorities, schools and youth organisations is of paramount importance if the full potential of young people is to be realised."

The UK Network

Following the European developments, the Health Education Authority accepted the change of emphasis from health education in schools to the creation of "health promoting schools" and undertook the development and the running of the UK Network of Health Promoting Schools, which became a recognised member of the European Network in 1994. The Network has been recognised by the Education and Health Departments in all the four countries (England, Scotland, Wales and Northern Ireland). Each country will have separate but complementary activities and will adopt appropriate strategies to meet their specific cultural and social needs, adjusted to their own organisational structures. The health promotion services in each country will manage the projects, utilising the HEA as the National Support Centre for the whole UK project.

It is envisaged that the whole project will include approximately 30 pilot schools with further 50 reference schools. The pilot schools will aim at exploring the various aspects of their constitutions and their organisational structures and their relevance for promoting health and influencing the pupils' lifestyles. Based on the findings, these schools will design and test various practices directed towards the improvements in pupils' knowledge, attitudes and lifestyles. Some of the selected schools are already involved in certain health promotion programmes, which will be supported by their new status. Some innovative programmes may include: the learning process, management, curriculum development, policy formation, school ethos, as well as outreach into the community in the form of alliances with health and other environmental institutions.

Northern Ireland

The Health Promotion Agency of Northern Ireland has been working with the Curriculum Council on the guidance for teachers involved in Health Promoting Schools. Health education is one of the six mandatory educational themes, and it aims at producing the objectives concerning the classroom practices in this area. It is also recognised as a WHO Collaborative Centre for health behaviour of school children and is planning to join the European Network.

Scotland

The Health Education Board for Scotland is a member of the European Network. It has allocated 5 schools to participate in the project and has produced a training manual "Promoting Health of Young People in Europe".

Wales

Health Promotion Wales will manage the Welsh project which will ultimately include 10 pilot schools as a part of the project. The project will build on the extensive work already being done in many Welsh schools.

England

In addition to being the coordinator for the UK Network, the Health Education Authority is also the coordinator for the English Network. The English project includes 16 pilot schools, each matched with 2 reference schools. The pilot schools include 6 primary, 7 secondary and 3 special schools. The project is now in the initial phase of carrying out a base line survey of the 48 schools. The pilot schools will be assisted by the staff of the HEA and a number of advisers and consultants.

EVALUATING HEALTH PROMOTING SCHOOLS

Introduction

In this section the description of a possible evaluation, quality management and auditing exercise is linked to the new "Health Promoting Schools" approach. The advantage of such an approach is the creation of an impressive organisational structure with a high profile, easily recognised by the media and the fund providers.

The disadvantage of such an approach is that is has a limited number of implicit objectives, or ways in which the programme planners expect the aims to be achieved. These can be described as the creation of an organisational structure and transmission of knowledge and skills as an officially recognised part of a school curriculum, promotion of staff/pupil relationship, involving the community and providing a better school environment. They can be summarised as operating on three levels: ground work, implementation on the organisational level and implementation on the pupil level. The explicit as well as implicit objectives may or may not produce the improvements in health of the staff and pupil population of a school.

The main problem with such a general description of wants or desires (as compared to objective needs) is that it does not allow for the evaluation of the activity owing to the lack of a link between aims and objectives and a lack of specifications expressed in the form of indicators and criteria.

One could, however, carry out an audit of such an intervention and measure the processes and outcomes against some general norms or social expectations of activities, such as:

- the recruitment policy and the interaction processes related to staff and pupils, using as an indicator the absence of any discrimination and observing the principle of equity;

- the provision of supportive mechanisms for staff and pupils for their fulfilment of the tasks intended by the educational programme, such as school environment, financial aspects, transport and communication, equipment, etc., using as indicators the criterion of minimal, optimal and maximal standards of need satisfaction;

- the success of the school in achieving its main aim which is to serve as the agent of formal socialisation of the pupils into their future roles, using as indicators the role performance of the staff and pupils and the expectations of the social environment (family, potential employers, institutions for further education, etc.);

- the reduction in prevalence and incidence of illness among staff and pupils, as well as positive changes in their behaviour related to certain health risks, using as indicators health records and observation of behaviour and actions related to health;

- the improvements in public health and other political decisions related to the school, using as indicators the staff /student ratio, the budget, the training of staff, etc.,

- the relationship between the school and the health care system, using indicators such as the access to health personnel and health services, the sharing of responsibility for pupil's health, the participation of parents in decisions relating to the health of pupils.

Evaluation, Quality Assessment and Auditing

The success of the project will depend on the detailed planning that makes possible an objective evaluation of the project. The evaluation in its wider sense represents the assessment of the activities as well as the measurement of the outcomes. It will include the assessment of the process in terms of its quality and production of desired outcomes, as well as auditing the programme in terms of the value system associated with the educational process involved.

Evaluation is defined as the assessment of the achievements of the aims of the programme; quality assessment is concerned with the process and outcome of the programme; auditing is the assessment of the programme against the general norms (social, cultural, professional) prevalent in that society.

Quality assessment is especially relevant to educational programmes since quite a number of schools will already have a quality management programme to which it will be necessary to add certain health promotional and health educational specifications.

The assessment procedure will require a clear definition of the **aims and objectives** of the project. These can be divided into aims and objectives concerning the following: the ground work including the establishment of base-line information, the execution of the intervention on the organisational level and the execution of the intervention on the pupil level, which will include also the post intervention activities.

The assessment of the project will require the choice of **indicators**, which will be used to measure the achievement of the set aims by means of the set objectives. These indicators will have to be translated into **instruments**, which will be used for the set measurements. The interpretation of the findings will depend on the agreed upon **criteria** for success or failure.

Set out below is an example of possible aims, objectives and indicators which could be used by someone planning a Health Promoting School Project. The development of instruments has been omitted since this requires technical detail, as does the setting of specifications and criteria, which will depend on the agreement of the people in charge of such a project as to expectations and what to consider a success and what a failure.

Aims, Objectives and Indicators

The aims and objectives of an intervention concerned with the creation and operations of a "Health Promoting School" could be envisaged within the framework of the Ottawa Charter and could cover the five main parts of the system which are the school environment, the school proper, the school staff, the pupils and the pupils' families.

Ground Work Level:

AIM 1: To establish the needs of the pupils in relation to the promotion of health and prevention and management of disease; to achieve this aim the intervention will have the following objectives:

Objective 1.1: to carry out a survey of pupils' health needs;

Indicators 1.1: pupils' opinion about their own health and their perception of the main health problems that they encounter, such as inequality, addictive behaviour, physical activity, nutrition, accidents, and some special problems;

Objective 1.2: to carry out the secondary data analysis of the health statistics related to the school population;

Indicators 1.2: morbidity statistics for the school and/or the community in which the school is located and which represents the catchment area for the pupils;

Objective 1.3: to carry out a survey of the family competence related to the prevention and management of disease, and the utilisation of health services;

Indicators 1.3: knowledge and skills of various family members concerning the most prevalent health threats and diseases affecting the school population;

Objective 1.4: to carry out a survey of the members of the school health service and the family health service related to the utilisation of such services;

Indicators 1.4: records and a survey of school children concerning the patterns of utilisation of school and family health services.

AIM 2: To describe the internal structure of the school as a means of satisfying pupils' needs; to achieve this aim the study will have the following objectives:

Objective 2.1: to define the organisational structure, power structure, role definition and role relationships, and the professional expertise of the school;

Indicators 2.1: the organisational structure and names of people occupying different positions within the school; name of the person(s) decisive for curriculum development and introduction of health topics into the teaching programme; name of the person(s) responsible for the physical environment; availability of health related expertise within the school and general standards of teaching;

Objective 2.2: to explore potential conflict areas and possible resolutions within the school staff, as well as between the staff and the pupils;

Indicators 2.2: existing health related behaviour of staff and pupils (smoking, obesity, etc.); any existing (reported or observed) conflict within the staff (on the basis of sex, age, religion, race, qualifications, etc.), or between the staff and the pupils and or parents;

Objective 2.3: to explore the available technology as well as school curriculum as a means of satisfying pupil's needs;

Indicators 2.3: assessment of school equipment, ranging from basic hygienic needs to modern information technology (visual presentation, computers, etc.)

Objective 2.4: to establish the existing links between the school and the parents, as well as to describe the existing mechanisms for parents' participation in school policy and practice decisions;

Indicators 2.4: existence of a parent-teacher association, its work and participants' opinions about its effectiveness; any other active involvement of parents in school activities; involvement of school staff and parents in some community activities; political engagement of parents and staff.

AIM 3: To describe the links of the school with other institutions, the community and the environment; to achieve this aim the study will have the following objectives:

Objective 3.1: to explore the means and the level of financing of the school and its activities;

Indicators 3.1: the school budget; the resources for the upkeep of the school; opinions of teachers and parents about the adequacy of the available resources;

Objective 3.2: to explore the relationship between the school, the educational and health authorities and other community and voluntary bodies;

Indicators 3.2: existing mechanisms for collaboration between the education and health systems; examples of such collaboration; existence of voluntary bodies engaged in health issues concerning the pupils (e.g. Junior Red Cross, etc.); any community groups concerned with health issues which are implicitly or explicitly related to pupils' health;

Objective 3.3: to explore the interaction between the school and the wider environment in terms of provision of extra mural services, source of employment, utilisation of transport and sources of waste disposal and other aspects of potential environmental contamination;

Indicators 3.3: records of employment of local staff; records of extra mural courses; communication and transport links between school and the settlement (town centre, other facilities, etc.); existing environmental health problems;

Objective 3.4: carry out a survey concerned with establishment of social norms related to the role of the school and the attitudes to most prevalent actions and behaviour of pupils in school and in the environment;

Indicators 3.4: legal norms related to the role and responsibility of the school staff; social norms related to the roles of pupils and parents; records of pupils' behaviour related to health; records of any actions carried out in schools or in the community which could affect the school population.

AIM 4: To describe, in addition to teaching, the preventive and "promotive" activities relevant to the promotion of pupils health; to achieve this aim the study will have the following objectives:

Objective 4.1: to explore the existing preventive measures and services on offer;

Indicators 4.1: listing of desired and existing preventive measures in the school and the community which could affect the school population;

Objective 4.2: to explore the existing health promotive activities;

Indicators 4.2: the place of health issues in the curriculum; records of health campaigns;

Objective 4.3: to explore the links between the school and other preventive and health promotive actions in the area;

Indicators 4.3: records of interaction between school and community in health promoting activities;

The Organisational Level

AIM 5: To explore with the school staff the possibility of undertaking a commitment to become a "Health Promoting School" within the WHO conceptualisation of the requirements for such a commitment; to achieve this aim the study will have the following objectives:

Objective 5.1: to explore the felt needs of the staff and possibility of meeting their requirements;

Indicators 5.1: answers to questions concerning the interest of the school staff and parents related to the Health Promoting School project; assessment of existing information about the project; awareness about the implications of the commitments by staff, parents and pupils;

Objective 5.2: to explore the necessary resources to meet the existing shortcomings within the provision of school services;

Indicators 5.2: designing a draft programme with an indication of the required resources; the assessment of the existing resources; the indication of additional sources for the necessary resources;

Objective 5.3: to organise a workshop for members of the school staff and other relevant institutions (educational, health) for the purpose of establishing a joint commitment for collaboration and support in this endeavour;

Indicators 5.3: records of the workshop including the curricula, the methods and the expected outcomes in terms of specifically listed commitments of named individuals.

AIM 6: The creation of a "Health Promoting School" movement in the school; to achieve this aim the study will have the following objectives:

Objective 6.1: the self-selection of members of staff who will undertake commitments and carry out role definition and task distribution among its members;

Indicators 6.1: the number of volunteers for different tasks; the willingness of individuals to take over tasks; fairness in task distribution; individual dominance in carrying out tasks;

Objective 6.2: the organisation of training ventures for staff concerning their commitments;

Indicators 6.2: records of such training ventures (curriculum, participants, assessment of outcomes);

Objective 6.3: provision of skills for monitoring and evaluating the progress of the intervention as well as the changes within the school;

Indicators 6.3: contents of the curriculum covering information about monitoring and evaluation; methods for acquiring the necessary skills to carry out such a task; names of people who undertook such a commitment.

AIM 7: The planning and provision of health promotion and health education ventures as a part of the normal activities of a "health promoting school"; to achieve this aim the study will have the following objectives:

Objective 7.1: integration of health promotion and health education topics into the school curriculum, as well as into the planning and everyday running of the school;

Indicators 7.1: record of health promotion and health education topics included in the curriculum; methods of transmitting knowledge and skills; mechanisms for application of acquired knowledge in everyday running of the school;

Objective 7.2: definition of indicators and criteria for the evaluation of each health promotion and health education venture;

Indicators 7.2: a list of planned health promotion and health education activities including specific aims and objectives, indicators and criteria;

Objective 7.3: carrying out the planned tasks;

Indicators 7.3: records of the tasks carried out including their evaluation;

The Pupil Level

AIM 8: Integration of school health promotion and health education activities into the overall activities of the "health promoting educational system"; to achieve this aim the study will have the following objectives:

Objective 8.1: collaboration with the existing activities of the Health Promotion Unit of the DHA;

Indicators 8.1: records of meetings with the local HP/E Unit with the minutes, including the undertaken tasks and the names of persons taking them on;

Objective 8.2: collaboration with the existing activities of the educational authorities;

Indicators 8.2: list of the existing health related and health directed activities; type of collaboration; role distribution with names of actors; differentiation between the existing and the desired activities by the educational authorities;

Objective 8.3: integration of all these activities into the health promotion and health education activities of the health care and educational systems in the district;

Indicators 8.3: records of meetings and activities concerned with such an integration; minutes of these meetings including the subject matter, the decisions and the role distribution (names) following the meetings.

AIM 9: To carry out the monitoring of the intervention study; to achieve this aim the study will have the following objectives:

Objective 9.1: developing computerised instruments for monitoring the ongoing activities within the intervention;

Indicators 9.1: recording the type of instruments used and the existing technology;

Objective 9.2: application of instruments for monitoring the activities;

Indicators 9.2: records of the existing availability of the data collected; records of the methods used for data collection and storage;

Objective 9.3: analysis of data collected by means of the monitoring process;

Indicators 9.3: relevance of the collected data for the assessment of the progress of the project with a built in feed-back for adjustments and corrections.

AIM 10: To carry out the evaluation of the intervention; to achieve this aim the study will have the following objectives:

Objective 10.1: survey for data collection related to the evaluation of the health promotion activities within the intervention study;

Indicators 10.1: records of the survey, the methods and the instruments used;

Objective 10.2: survey for data collection related to the evaluation of the health education activities within the intervention study;

Indicators 10.2: records of the survey, the methods and the instruments used;

Objective 10.3: evaluation of the outcomes of the intervention study in terms of staff, pupil and parent satisfaction and improvements in the school environment and school practices;

Indicators 10.3: utilisation of indicators defined at the planning stage of the project.

AIM 11: The auditing of the intervention in terms of staff and patient satisfaction of the expressed needs; to achieve this aim the study will have the following objectives:

Objective 11.1: measurement of changes in the existing professional and social norms related to the aims of the intervention;

Indicators 11.1: data analysis showing the changes if any; assessment of changes using the criteria defined during the planning stage of the project;

Objective 11.2: measurement of intervention outcomes in terms of the established professional and social norms;

Indicators 11.2: the set aims and objectives during the planning stage concerning the norms; causal relationship between the set aims and the measured outcomes;

Objective 11.3: definition of areas where the existing professional and social norms need reinforcement or change;

Indicators 11.3: choice of areas based on the needs of the staff and the pupils and their families;

Objective 11.4: measurement of changes in the attitudes of staff and pupils related to health issues;

Indicators 11.4: comparison of attitudes with the social norms related to health issues, desired actions and willingness to actively participate in their improvements and changes;

Objective 11.5: achievement of changes and improvements in the most effective and efficient way;

Indicators 11.5: the amount of effort and resources spent on the achievement of improvements and their lasting effects on the health of the school population;

Objective 11.6: to affect the general health culture in the community by the activities carried out in the school and by the interaction between the school and the community, including the health and educational services;

Indicators 11.6: recording of the new activities in the community and their links with the school project; effects of such activities on the health of the population and the provision of health and educational services.

AIM 12: The quality assessment of the health educational and health promotional aspects of the educational process; to achieve this aim the study will have the following objectives:

Objective 12.1: the adjustment of the existing mechanism for quality assessment within the school or the introduction of a new one;

Indicators 12.1: the adjustment of the policy document to include HP/HE aspects of the intervention;

Objective 12.2: the introduction of "health circles" based on the concept of "quality circles" for the execution of the intervention;

Indicators 12.2: the number of health circles and the number of members of each circle, as well as the contents and achievement of the circles' work;

Objective 12.3: development of standards and specifications for the quality assessment of the health promotion and health education services;

Indicators 12.3: they will depend on the role definition of each member in terms of their specific aims and objectives;

Objective 12.4: introduction of documentation and instruments for quality assessment;

Indicators 12.4: establishment of a data bank and mechanisms for collection and analysis of data;

Objective 12.5: development of the structure representing the production process associated with the services provided;

Indicators 12.5: role definition as represented for example in an "Ishikawa" diagram (several links in problems) to be used for the assessment of achievements of each part of the system;

Objective 12.6: production of reports concerning the evaluation of the process and outcome of the intervention;

Indicators 12.6: the number of progress reports on which the final report will be based with the statement of outcomes.

CASE STUDY : HP SCHOOLS IN POLAND

Introduction

The European "Health Promoting Schools" Programme commenced in 1991 with the participation of four European countries, Poland, Hungary, Czech Republic and Slovakia. They represented the core countries in the European Network, to be joined by other European countries.

In Poland, as one of the members of the core countries in the Network, there has been a considerable amount of development related to the Polish Network, which is presented here as a case study.

The National Coordinating Team is located in the National Research Institute of Mother and Child in Warsaw and is composed of representatives of Ministries of Health, Education and Environment Protection, Office of Physical Culture and Teachers' Union. It has an Advisory Council composed of the Project Coordinator and the Polish Team of Health Promoting Schools.

The movement has been popularised in the press and media and attracted the interest of 383 schools, out of which 15 pilot schools were selected (age 6-15 years). Each school appointed a Project Coordinator and a School Health Promotion Team. The schools have introduced a wide range of health promotion programmes according to the local interests and local needs. The health promotion activities in each case are school specific. They all, however, express the following ideas:

- understanding the differences between the traditional approach in health education and health promotion and the concept of Health Promoting Schools;

- enabling people to discover their own vision of the health promoting school and find their own interest in creating it with special reference to joint activities, participation, health gain and wider repercussions for the school life;

- a health promoting school is a concept, an expression of a value system and an "ideal" which can only be partly achieved by schools in a real life situation.

The development of an infrastructure for HPS has included:

- education of teachers on an in-service and postgraduate level;

- development of school health education curricula;

- additional activities (summer holidays), democratic elections of pupil representatives and partnership with teachers.

The HPS movement has helped schools to develop their own aims, define their objectives and choose indicators for assessing the programmes.

The Polish HPS Network produces a Journal "*Leader*", in which the process and the outcomes of various projects have been publicised.

The activities undertaken by the Pilot Schools can be summarised as follows:

- improvement of the school environment (flowers and plants, bicycle stands, benches, cleaning up of waste and creating waste disposal and collection facilities);

- installation of an in-house broadcasting system (improvement in communications between staff and pupils);

- improvement in the learning achievement and reduction of truancy (following the discussions raised at the pupil/staff meetings), introduction of modern learning methods;

- implementation of a preventive programme on drug abuse, addressing the question of nutrition and other health problems;

- establishment of a "mini parliament" in which pupils participate in the decision-making process and elect their representatives;

- an increase in the participation of parents in school life (especially in specific "days" devoted to different topics, such as "roasted potato", "autonomy", "mother earth", "green school" etc.), organisation of a canoe race following the "cleaning up" of the river;

- workshops for teachers, in-service courses and opportunities for further education;

- establishment of links with various other community institutions and mobilising their support;

- improvement of the working conditions of the staff and reduction of stress at work.

At present the evaluation of the achievements of HPS is mainly limited to descriptive impressions offered by members and visitors.

HEALTH PROMOTING COMMUNITY SERVICES

INTRODUCTION

The reform of the National Health Service (NHS) resulted in the changes of the functions of various parts of the NHS such as District Health Authorities (DHA), Family Health Service Authorities (FHSA), as well as the provider units such as hospitals and community services. One important aspect of this change has been the integration of health promotion and health education (HP/HE) into the aims and objectives of these different parts of the NHS.

The reform of the NHS provided an opportunity for the implementation of new developments sponsored by the World Health Organisation (WHO) in the practice of health promotion and health education. These are based on the Alma Ata Declaration and the Ottawa Charter and state that health is a basic human right, based on the primary care system, involving active community participation and a multi-sectoral approach. This can be achieved through the process of advocacy, enabling participants to achieve and mediating among the various agents involved in promoting health and preventing and treating disease.

The recent changes in the political situation in Europe have created a need to carry out the role of advocacy, and to enable and mediate in the newly liberated countries, in the attempt to allow them to catch up with the rest of Europe. HP/HE has been expected to provide concrete and effective methods for the achievement of such improvements. It has become obvious that the existing medical model has not been sufficiently effective. This model starts with the medical problems and then uses pidemiological studies to establish the distribution of each of these problems in a population with the aim of targeting the HP/HE interventions. Consequently, a shift from a problem-based to a settings-based approach has occurred. Instead of taking a problem and looking for the people who suffer from it, the new approach starts from people (in different settings) and looks at the health different problems they experience and the possible solution of these problems by means of HP/HE.

The application of this approach started with the development of the "Healthy City" movement which by now includes over 400 cities on three continents. This was followed with a "Health Promoting School", a "Health Promoting Hospital", and a "Health Promoting Enterprise" programmes.

The programme being described in this section uses the principles and concepts of creating Health Promoting Settings (see part 2 of this book), and applies them to a Health Promoting Community Service. At this stage, a pilot study is envisaged to test the various possibilities owing to the complex structure of community services and different needs of various service providers.

CASE STUDY : HEALTH PROMOTING COMMUNITY CARE

Following the NHS reform, the organisation of community services differs from District to District. The case study presented is based on an experimental pilot study developed for a Community Trust in the North West of England and representing one type of organisational model. It is appropriate because of the high motivation among the Trusts to achieve success, owing to the element of self-financing, and because they aim to deliver community services of the highest standard to the residents of that district.

The experimental Trust includes the following skills and services:

- Community Paediatrics
- Community Nursing including District Nursing, Health Visiting, School Nursing, MacMillan Nursing, and Continence Advisory Service
- Community Dentistry
- Speech Therapy and Chiropody
- Clinical Psychology
- Midwifery
- Community Support Teams including Community Mental Handicap Nurses
- Respite and Day Care Facilities for People with Learning Difficulties including Voluntary and Community Development Services
- Physiotherapy
- Occupational Therapy
- Community Family Planning and Cervical Cytology Services
- Welfare Foods
- All appropriate support services.

These services within the experimental Trust are currently provided by an equivalent of 530 whole time staff, with a revenue approaching £10 million.

The population to be served by these services includes three Primary Care Areas (PCAs).

Establishment of the Trust will benefit the patients because of a number of consequences including the merger of services, providing a larger pool of expertise and services, a better career pathway for the employees, better access to services, and a link with centres of excellence and training facilities.

The core purpose of the Trust is:

- to make a major contribution to the improvement of health status of all sections of the community served by the Trust;

- to improve the quality of services in terms of direct clinical care, continuity and integration, accessibility and local flexibility and responsiveness whilst always striving to provide value for money;

- to provide support and development for the Primary Health Care Team.

The organisational structure of the Trust includes the Trust Board, the Chief Executive and a Corporate Management Group.

Aims and Objectives of the Intervention

The main requirement for designating a Health Promoting Community Trust will be the integration of HP/HE into all the activities of the Trust. This will be reflected in the aims and objectives of the Pilot Intervention, such as:

Ground work level:

Aim 1: To develop a typology for the various services and institutions operating under the Trust according to their internal structure, their specialism, the type of services and the characteristics of the client population. To achieve this aim, the intervention will have following objectives and use the following indicators:

Objective 1.1: workshop-type consultations with representatives of each service and agreement on an acceptable classificatory system;

Indicators: type of organisation, type of management, type of services, type and expectations of clients;

Objective 1.2: a Delphi-type approach (exploration of shared views using professional judges) to link the professional specialism of the services with the characteristics of the client population;

Indicators: aspects of the professional specialism and the characteristics of the clients relevant for HP/HE.

Organisational level:

Aim 2: To define the HP/HE aspects of each service, based on their expertise and the needs of the client population; to achieve this aim the study will have the following objectives and use the following indicators:

Objective 2.1: establishment of HP/HE aspects of services using the existing and recruited expertise;

Indicators: the HP/HE requirements for the definition of problems and choice of solutions, methodological requirements and standards for evaluation;

Objective 2.2: description of the client population and their needs;

Indicators: HP/HE relevant characteristics of the client population and the recording of their HP/HE relevant needs.

Aim 3: To raise the competence of the members of various services within the Trust; to achieve this aim the study will have the following objectives and use the following indicators:

Objective 3.1: development of a training curriculum based on the needs of the various members of the services;

Indicators: existing expertise in HP/HE, specific requirements in terms of knowledge and skills, translation of these needs as well as other information into a curriculum;

Objective 3.2: organisation and execution of training programmes for members of the various services;

Indicators: motivation and interest of the members, their participation and the success rate recorded at the end of the training programme.

The patient level:

Aim 4: To raise the awareness of the clints as well as other members of the health care system about the existing services with special reference to their HP/HE aspects; to achieve this aim the study will have the following objectives and use the following indicators:

Objective 4.1: mass media approach to popularise the new character of services on offer;

Indicators: coverage of the new approach in the mass media, the explanation of the advantages of the new approach for the clients and the expectations from clients making use of these new services;

Objective 4.2: distribution of information through professional literature and direct publications for professionals in other services;

Indicators: advantages of the new approach, effective distribution of information, the level of utilisation of services by other professionals.
Aim 5: Development and execution of a pilot intervention, including the requirements for monitoring and evaluation of the process as well as the outcomes; to achieve this aim the study will have the following objectives and use the following indicators:

Objective 5.1: Planning and execution of the intervention including the requirements for evaluation;

Indicators: planning stages, role distribution for each type of agents, organisation of the intervention, levels of participation;

Objective 5.2: setting of standards for evaluation of the intervention, collection of data and the establishment of a feed-back mechanism for adjustments in existing plans for future implementation;

Indicators: choice of standards, indicators, criteria, and their translation into instruments for evaluation.

Aim 6: Monitoring and evaluation of the intervention and drawing of inferences; to achieve this aim the study will have following objectives and use following indicators:

Objective 6.1: carrying out regular monitoring of the process of implementation and the evaluation of findings;

Indicators: invested efforts, assessed efficiency; established effectiveness;

Objective 6.2: development of standards for each specific type of service and the integration of procedures for regular monitoring and evaluation;

Indicators: specific data relevant for each type of services in terms of HP/HE aims and objectives, methods and programmes.

Methods of the Intervention:

The intervention will use existing, tested methods relevant for the achievement of different aims:

- a survey method for data collection;
- a case study approach for collection of expert knowledge;
- the workshop method for training of personnel;
- personal, group and mass media methods for diffusion of information, influencing decision making and behaviour;
- publications in professional journals;
- standard methods of monitoring and evaluation;
- computer-assisted analysis of data and drawing of inferences.

The Outcome

The assessment of the outcomes of this study need to be linked to the study aims:

The fulfilment of Aim 1 should produce a typology of various services operating within the Trust according to their specific HP/HE characteristics. The characteristics, such as the type of service, the staff and the client's needs, should provide a basis for planning and execution of HP/HE activities specific for each type of service within the Trust.

The development of such a typology should enable the establishment of HP/HE aspects of each type of service (Aim 2). The specific aspects of the service expertise and the needs of their clients will help in setting up concrete programmes with well defined aims and objectives, methods and preconditions for a successful evaluation.

Once the HP/HE potential role for each type of service has been clarified, it should be possible to establish the educational needs of the staff (Aim 3). The new expectations may in many cases require additional in-service training in the form of workshops or short courses, aimed at providing the opportunity to gain knowledge and skills in various methods of enabling, mediating and advocating for their clients.

The "new" role of these services, now including HP/HE activities, need to be advertised among the potential clients as well as among the other members of the primary care team (Aim 4). The clients should know what to expect and the other members of the primary health team should know what is on offer so that they could consider using these services for their own patients if they themselves do not provide such service.

The acquisition of expertise and the setting of potential aims and objectives should result in each of the services in question developing and carrying out their own programme of HP/HE activities (Aim 5).

It should be possible to monitor and evaluate such programmes on the basis of set aims and built in mechanisms for collecting information about the achievements (Aim 6).

Overall, the most important result of such a pilot study will be the establishment of HP/HE standards, methods and evaluation procedures for each specialty within the existing Trust.

The advantage of such an achievement will be the improvement in the structural, managerial and executive side of the services in question.

The relevance of such an intervention will be achieved by basing it on the established needs of the client population and the available expertise of the service providers.

The novelty of such an approach should lead to national and international recognition as well as an increased use of the services by other members of the health care system.

HEALTH PROMOTING CHARITABLE ORGANISATIONS

INTRODUCTION

Recent developments in the delivery of health care, based on the WHO EURO conceptualisations and the strategy laid out in the White Paper "Health of the Nation" (see Appendix 4) have pushed health promotion into new, uncharted territory as far as approaches and methods are concerned.

WHO has contributed to this change by stating that health is one of the basic human rights, which can be promoted by means of active community participation and supported by healthy public policies and effective primary care. It has stressed the importance of health promotion and initiated the shift of emphasis in the approach from problems to the settings in which people live, work and spend their leisure time.

This shift of emphasis has been formalised by the development of standards and preconditions for various settings to achieve the status of a "health promoting institution". The first one was "the healthy city" status, followed by "health promoting hospital", "health promoting school", "health promoting enterprise" and most recently some other settings such as community care are contemplating a similar move. Now the first attempts are being made to enlarge this concept by including voluntary organisations, one of which will be the new "health promoting charitable organisation" status.

There are three main commitments such an institution should undertake to qualify as a health promoting institution:

- it should create a healthy working environment, which includes the physical as well as social aspects (e.g. prevention of accidents, control of air and water pollution, safe waste disposal, protection of environment, appropriate working relationships, protection of jobs and incomes, fight against any discrimination, etc.);

- it should integrate health promotion into the planning and execution of the main goals of the institution, which can be the output of products and/or type of cares. In the case of goods, production and distribution should include the responsibility for outcomes such as handling, use and storing of products. In the case of type of care, it should take into consideration the needs and rights of the consumers (e.g. production of toxic substances, drugs etc., or teaching of pupils, training of professionals, counselling clients, etc.);

- it should initiate and/or promote such approaches in the community in the form of networking with similar institutions and creating healthy alliances with other institutions, which could contribute to the improvement of community health (e.g. a health promoting hospital initiates the creation of a health promoting school in the district and links with other authorities to promote the spread of such an approach to all the other institutions in that community).

CASE STUDY : COMMUNITY INTEGRATED CARE

This is an experimental proposal using a case study to develop standards, methods and evaluated outcomes in an attempt to create a "health promoting charitable organisation" model as an addition to the other settings which have received or are going to receive this status. By increasing the variety of settings within the "health promoting institutions" movement, it will be possible gradually to reach the position of creating a "health promoting community" status, where all the institutions in that community will be "health promoting". It reflects the emphasis on meeting the patients' needs by providing comprehensive type of care of a health promoting character for the achievement of a health gain.

This example is concerned with a voluntary organisation, Community Integrated Care (CIC). It is based on the preliminary exploration of possibilities in a real-life situation and provides an opportunity for planning a case study. The outcomes should be useful for similar attempts by other charitable organisations.

The CIC in question is a "not for profit" organisation and is a registered charity. It is currently in partnership with a number of Health Authorities and provides supported living and residential care for over 700 people with special needs..

The aims and objectives of CIC are to provide for the care of residents who are suffering from disability or disease attributed to old age, mental illness, mental handicap, infectious diseases or terminal illness and to provide an environment in which these patients can live each day to the full and die in dignity without physical or emotional suffering.

To fulfil these aims the CIC establishes, maintains and conducts care within a residential and nursing home environment, together with day and home care, with other types of care provided as required.

CIC endeavour to ensure that for as long as possible the residents enjoy a level of care in an environment that provides a lifestyle as near as possible to a normal home life. This is governed by the extent of the resident's disability.

The management structure of CIC, is composed of a Chairman and a Council of Management. It has a Chief Executive Officer and is divided into sections according to the types of care provided in addition to an advisory board: operational care for people with learning disabilities and for the elderly mentally ill, elderly severely mentally infirm and people with mental illness. The selection of care is growing and the proportion of patients projected for 1992/3 (total of 783) includes 22% elderly infirm, 28% people with learning disabilities, 13% mentally ill and 37% elderly severely mentally ill patients.

The patients are recruited from a population of patients discharged from hospitals or directed by General Practitioners within the region. The financing of the type of care is by payments through the state benefit system, a grant support from the Health Authority or from patient's private means. The various types of care are distributed in various locations.

Aims and Objectives

The main requirement for designating a Health Promoting Institution will also apply to a Health Promoting Charitable Organisation and should be reflected in the aims and objectives of the Pilot Intervention, as follows:

Gound work level:

Aim 1: To develop a typology for the various types of care (service and institutions) operating within the charitable organisation according to their internal structure, their specialism, the type of care and the characteristics of the client population. To achieve this aim, the intervention will have following objectives and use the following indicators:

Objective 1.1: workshop-type consultations with representatives of each type of care and agreement on an acceptable classificatory system;

Indicators: type of organisation, type of management, type of care, type and expectations of clients;

Objective 1.2: a Delphi-type approach (exploration of shared views) using professional judges to link the professional specialism of the type of care with the characteristics of the client population;

Indicators: aspects of the professional specialism and the characteristics of the clients relevant for HP/HE.

Aim 2: To define the HP/HE aspects of each type of care, based on their expertise and the needs of the client population; to achieve this aim the intervention will have the following objectives and use the following indicators:

Objective 2.1: establishment of HP/HE aspects of type of care using the existing and recruited expertise;

Indicators: the HP/HE requirements for the definition of problems and choice of solutions, methodological requirements and standards for evaluation;

Objective 2.2: description of the client population and their needs;

Indicators: HP/HE relevant characteristics of the client population and the recording of their HP/HE relevant needs.

Organisational level:

Aim 3: Role definition and raising of competence of the members of various type of care within the CIC; to achieve this aim the intervention will have the following objectives and use the following indicators:

Objective 3.1: development of a training curriculum based on the role definition and the needs of the various members within the care services;

Indicators: existing expertise in HP/HE related to role definition, specific requirements in terms of knowledge and skills, translation of these needs as well as other information into a curriculum;

Objective 3.2: organisation and execution of training programmes for members of the various type of care;

Indicators: motivation and interest of the members, their participation and the success rate recorded at the end of the training programme.

Aim 4: To enable the Community Integrated Care, to initiate the creation of other health promoting institutions in the District; to achieve this aim the intervention will have the following objectives:

Objective 4.1: to publicise together with the local Health Promotion Unit the idea of health promoting institutions in the District;

Indicator 4.1.1: number of publications in the local media; number of distributed literature commenting on the White Paper and its consequences for various type of cares;

Objective 4.2: to contact other institutions in the District and help them to accept this idea (a school, an enterprise, the FHSA and general practices, etc.);

Indicator 4.2.1: number of meetings with other institutions; content analysis of the meetings; recording of outcomes in terms of commitments and actions.

Aim 5: To establish a network of health promoting institutions in the District along the lines of "healthy alliances" as proposed in the White Paper; to achieve this aim the intervention will have the following objectives:

Objective 5.1: to apply to the local institutions the recommendations of the White Paper related to the priority health problems and based on the specific needs of various population groups in the District;

Indicator 5.1.1: levels of integration of HP/HE into each aspect of care; analysis of the plans of these institutions in terms of worked out aims and objectives; level of consideration given to the needs of different population groups related to the priority problems;

Objective 5.2: to carry out a role distribution of various institutions within such a "healthy alliance" in terms of their health promoting activities;

Indicator 5.2.1: level of precision in role definition; aspects of coordination of activities; quality of cooperation in the achievement of set goals.

Aim 6: To enable the members of services providing various types of care to carry out the expected activities and evaluate the outcomes in terms of health gains of the client population; to achieve this aim the intervention will have the following objectives:

Objective 6.1: to organise meetings and workshops for participants in this health promotion activity, which will improve their competence in health promotion and health education knowledge and skills;

Indicator 6.1.1: number of workshops; number of attenders; contents of the curriculum for each learning situation; assessment of achievement of each participant;

Objective 6.2: to develop a system of monitoring and evaluating the processes and outcomes of this project.

Indicator 6.2.1: quality and scope of collected data for monitoring; data collection and analysis for evaluation; inferences on the basis of collected data.

The patient level:

Aim 7: To raise the awareness of the clients and their families as well as other members of the health care system about the existing types of care with special reference to their HP/HE aspects; to achieve this aim the intervention will have the following objectives and use the following indicators:

Objective 7.1: mass media approach to popularise the new character of each type of care on offer and the way they can be used;

Indicators: coverage of the new approach in the mass media, the explanation of the advantages of the new approach for the clients and the expectations from clients making use of these new types of care;

Objective 7.2: distribution of information through professional literature and direct publications for professionals in other caring services;

Indicators: clarity of the message about the advantages of the new approach, effective distribution of information, the level of utilisation of types of care by other professionals.

Aim 8: Development and execution of pilot interventions for each type of care, including the requirements for monitoring and evaluation of the process as well as the outcomes; to achieve this aim the intervention will have the following objectives and use the following indicators:

Objective 8.1: planning and execution of the interventions including the requirements for evaluation;

Indicators: planning stages, choice of methods, role distribution for each type of agents, organisation of the intervention, levels of participation;

Objective 8.2: setting of standards for evaluation of the interventions, collection of data and the establishment of a feed-back mechanism for adjustments in existing plans for future implementation;

Indicators: choice of standards, indicators, criteria, and their translation into instruments for evaluation.

Aim 9: Monitoring and evaluation of the interventions and drawing of inferences; to achieve this aim the intervention will have the following objectives and use the following indicators:

Objective 9.1: carrying out regular monitoring of the process of implementation and the evaluation of findings;

Indicators: invested efforts, assessed efficiency; established effectiveness;

Objective 9.2: development of standards for each specific type of care/patient group and the integration of procedures for regular monitoring and evaluation;

Indicators: specific data relevant for each type of care in terms of HP/HE aims and objectives, methods and programmes.

The Outcomes:

The assessment of the outcomes of the intervention will need to be linked to the intervention aims, which are related to the three main requirements a health promoting institution should meet.

The first requirement is the creation of a health promoting charitable organisation, which will require the assessment of the existing situation and the available potentials within this type of care.

The ground work should produce a typology of various types of care operating within the CIC according to their specific HP/HE requirements. Their characteristics, such as the type of care, the staff and the client's needs, should provide a basis for planning and execution of HP/HE activities specific for each type of care of the CIC.

The development of such a typology should enable the establishment of HP/HE aspects of each type of care. The specific aspects of the type of care expertise and the needs of their clients will help in setting up concrete programmes with well defined aims and objectives, methods and preconditions for a successful evaluation.

The second requirement is the integration of health promotion into the existing tasks and activities of a voluntary organisation such as CIC.

Once the HP/HE potential role for each type of care has been clarified, it should be possible to establish the educational needs of the staff. The new expectations may in many cases require additional in-service training in the form of workshops or short courses, aimed at providing

the opportunity to gain knowledge and skills in various methods of enabling, mediating and advocating for their clients.
The "new" role of these types of care, which will include HP/HE activities will need to be advertised among the potential clients and their families as well as among the other members of the primary care team. The clients should know what to expect and the other members of the primary health team should know what is on offer so that they could consider using these types of care for their own patients if they themselves do not provide such types of care.

The acquisition of expertise and the setting of potential aims and objectives should result in each of the types of care in question developing and carrying out their own programme of HP/HE activities.

It should be possible to monitor and evaluate such programmes on the basis of set aims and built in mechanisms for collecting information about the achievements.

The third requirement is the involvement health promoting voluntary organisation such as CIC in the creation of healthy alliances and developing a network of similarly oriented institutions in the District.

This will be achieved by initiating similar developments in the District by advertising the new trends and helping various institutions to discuss the advantages and disadvantages of such a commitment within their existing possibilities.

Once a number of health promoting institutions in the District exist it will be necessary to establish a network which will permit the exchange of information, expertise and methods of monitoring and evaluation.

The health promoting voluntary organisation, such as CIC will depend on the creation of healthy alliances with other institutions and authorities that have a role to play in the maintenance and improvement of community health.

A most important result of such a pilot intervention will be the establishment of HP/HE standards, methods and evaluation procedures for each specialty within the CIC, as an example of a health promoting voluntary organisation.

The advantage of such an achievement will lie the structural improvement, managerial and executive side of the type of care in question.

The relevance of such an intervention will, however, only be achieved by basing it on the established needs of the client population and the available expertise of the type of care providers.

The novelty of such an approach should bring about national and international recognition as well as an increased use of the different types of care by other members of the health care system.

Methods

The intervention will depend on the creation of a health promotion team in the District, as well as a number of intervention teams in the different types of care provided by CIC in order to carry out the intervention. These teams should actively participate in helping the CIC to meet the criteria for its recognition as a health promoting institution.

Each intervention team should develop and test the most effective approach for creating a health promoting type of care within a health promoting CIC and for initiating the extension of the idea to other institutions in the District.

This would include the establishment of needs and potentials for each institution and organising meetings with their decision makers.

The intervention team will organise workshops for the members of various institutions for their improvement of knowledge and skills in integrating health promotion into their activities and evaluating the processes and outcomes in terms of health gains and the establishment of "healthy alliances". This will include the development of criteria and instruments for the evaluation and assessment of outcomes.

As far as the specific methodology is concerned, the intervention will use existing, tested methods relevant for the achievement of different aims:

- a survey method for data collection;
- a case study approach for collection of expert opinions and patients needs;
- the workshop method for training of personnel;
- mass media methods for diffusion of information;
- publications in professional journals;
- standard methods of monitoring and evaluation;
- computer-assisted analysis of data and drawing of inferences.

Time

The intervention should be planned as a five year project. The first year is most important and should be spent on setting up the whole project and enabling those with different roles to acquire knowledge and skills in health promotion and health education. The following years should see the actions taking place and the intervention team should only be involved in monitoring and evaluation of processes and outcomes.

A HEALTHY ENTERPRISE IN A HEALTHY ENVIRONMENT

Introduction

On the occasion of the 30th session of the Regional Committee (WHO EURO 1980), the Member States of the European Region approved their common health policy, including the European Strategy for attaining Health for All by the Year 2000. At its 34th session in 1984, the Regional Committee endorsed 38 targets in support of the original strategy (see Appendix 7). Of these, seven mention education for health policy. One of the targets (No.25) deals directly with health and the working place and states: "By the year 1995, people of the region should be effectively protected against work-related health risks". The achievement of this target envisages improvements in occupational health services and implementation of technical and educational measures aimed at the reduction of risk at work.

The result of this commitment has been a number of meetings and publications produced by WHO, either alone ("Health aspects of wellbeing at the workplace", WHO EURO, 1980) or together with others (" Health promotion in the working world", WHO EURO and the Federal Centre for Health Education, Cologne, 1984). In Germany the initiative was taken by WHO EURO, together with the Bundesverband der Betriebskrankenkassen (BKK) in Essen, to establish in 1990 an Information and Documentation Centre for Health Promotion at the Workplace. This should be considered as a part of a Regional Institute of Public Health, which is now being considered. This could take the form of a loose confederation of a number of "centres of excellence", one of which may be the new Information Centre in Essen.

The WHO approach treats the workplace as one of a number of aspects of health promotion, the others including the family, school and community. The programme has been developed along the traditional lines of health promotion at the workplace and deals with the biological, chemical and physical hazards within the framework of occupational health. The UK approach is different insofar as it looks at health promotion/education and work as two distinct activities and examines the relationship between the two in terms of their effects on the health of a population. It treats work as a social institution with all its implications, some of which may affect the health of the people who engage in this activity. In other words, the UK approach is based on a holistic conceptual model and uses a systems approach in analysing the problems and choosing the solutions. In practical terms this implies that health can be affected by certain working conditions as well as by the lack of opportunity to work due to unemployment. This conceptualisation has required the adjustment of principles of health promotion and education to specific situations associated with work and the development of a new approach which is now being tested for general use. This article gives an outline of this new approach.

The Increased Demand

Theree has been a considerable increase in interest in health promotion/education related to work. There are a number of reasons for this new situation, some of which are:

- lack of necessary funds for a comprehensive health promotion/education intervention programme and the hope that industry and commerce will be sufficiently interested to provide the necessary funds;
- new marketing policies which increasingly exploit an "environment-friendly image" to gain a competitive edge over competitors in the selling of enterprises and their products. There is an increased realisation that health care is a product with good sales potential;
- the realisation that certain processes of production or consequences of expansion may be considered as threatening to the environment or community interests and cannot be imposed by some administrative act and have to be "sold" to the community. The health promotion/education methods of community participation seem to be effective in empowering communities to consider the advantages and disadvantages of any such development in their decision making processes;
- the political and economic changes in Europe, which have the consequence of bringing together two working cultures and will demand considerable readjustments, not only in terms of

production and marketing, but also in terms of human resources. Health promotion/education will have to meet the different needs and expectations and learn how to manage different mechanisms and processes within communities and enterprises;

- there is a strong belief that improving health in the community will affect the health of the workforce in local enterprises and that improving health in enterprises will increase productivity and raise the profitability of the enterprise;
- work and leisure are considered as two aspects of a lifestyle. Health promotion/education approaches with the emphasis on lifestyle instead of risk factors seem at last to promise some effective ways of achieving health improvements which have been so desirable but also so evasive in the past.

Conceptual Framework

It would be helpful to define the terms of reference and the concepts used such as:

Health

There are numerous definitions of health: in medical terms it is not only the absence of illness but includes physical, mental and social wellbeing; in sociological terms it is the ability to perform one's social roles; in economic terms health is considered to be a valuable resource; in legal terms it is considered to be a basic human right, and in terms of a health promotional/educational intervention it is the desired goal. The definition is of special relevance for health promotion/education and work, since work or lack of it affects all these different aspects of health.

Life-style

The concepts of health and work are two aspects of the life-style of individuals, families, groups and communities. In Western industrialised societies, work is the main source of a person's social identity and the means of acquiring resources for survival and leisure activities. Both work and leisure have a direct influence on health. The transition from work to leisure can be traumatic, as in the case of unemployment, retirement, etc. By treating both work and leisure as parts of a life-style, health promotion/education can provide a coherent framework to enable individuals to cope with stresses due to change, and to influence the system to provide acceptable transitions within a life-style.

Enterprise as a Community

The concept of "community" implies a comparatively large number of people living together and sharing certain values and interests as well as interacting for a certain purpose or a shared goal. This concept has been linked not only to settlements in which people live (usually villages), but also extended to networks such as a "community of scholars" or a "community of scientists". One of the new developments in health promotion/education has been concerned with community participation. This concept has been in most cases simply translated from the classical "community organisation" approach, which implied going into a community, finding the local leaders or "gate keepers" and selling the programme to the people living in that community through them.

One recent application of the community approach in general health promotion/education has been the development of the "Healthy City" concept. The idea is that the whole community should share the responsibilities for a healthy environment and a healthy lifestyle of the citizens. The characteristics that make a group into a community can be extended also to enterprises. Here we have a group of people working together, sharing certain values and interacting for the achievement of a shared goal. Some of these shared values will be associated with health matters and will be supported by norms. In this way the "Healthy City" concept can be extended to a "Healthy Enterprise" approach. The new "community participation" approach emphasises the self-reliance and self-determination of community members and uses HP/HE to raise their competence in dealing with their health problems. In terms of a "healthy enterprise" this implies that the management as well as the workers/employees should be trained to recognise and deal with their own problems concerning health at the workplace and in the community in which the enterprise operates.

Environment

Work is carried out within a physical, social, cultural, political and economic system, which is different in different industrial societies in Europe. This implies that the concept of environment needs to include the social as well as physical factors which can affect and be affected by work. HP/HE needs to take into account these factors in planning and executing interventions. It will also have to take into consideration the changes currently occurring in these systems in Europe and include this process of change into the models and approaches recommended.

Work

If work is the basis of individual's social identity, then the differences in the type of work should be taken into account (in enterprises or at home and in the community) when contemplating a HP/HE intervention. At present there are various sociological concepts in use such as social class, status, culture etc., which are partly characterised by work of the individuals. There is very little work done that relates such concepts to specific aspects of health promotion. Some of the newer concepts such as "culture of poverty" and "underclass culture", may confuse the issues related to work and health and will have to be dealt with when discussing different approaches to the promotion of health in relation to work and the effects of work on health. In contrast, the more traditional approach is mainly concerned with health at the workplace and the reduction of risks associated with different types of work.

Workers/Employees

The degree of participation of workers/employees in a decision-making process within the enterprise will have a direct influence on working conditions and health. Since in most industrial countries many workers are organised into trade unions, their participation in decision-making may be limited to the activities of their trade unions. It will, therefore, be very important in initiating any programmes, to bear in mind the different roles trade unions play in different countries, especially in the field of health promotion, and to be aware of changes that may result from the adoption of new work practices, for example, those arising from the Social Charter. At the same time one must recognise the role of social forces in affecting the opportunities for work in a community, the status given to different kinds of work, and the recognition of leisure as a legitimate part of a lifestyle and a social position It is necessary also to be aware that the concept of participation can have political implications and could be considered as a threat to the existing power structure within a community or an enterprise.

Work and Environment

Most of the work force lives within regular commuting distance of their work place. One can say that the work will not only affect the health of workers at the workplace but also the health and wellbeing of the families living in the community. It is for this purpose that environmental issues, as well as working conditions, should be a part of any health promotion activity.

Workers and Consumers

Most work, be it production or service, is meant to satisfy certain needs of consumers. The type of product or the nature of service produced in an enterprise should also be taken into consideration when planning health promotion, not only because workers and their families are also consumers, but because the enterprise should carry a certain responsibility for its products. This is particularly important in the light of the rapid growth in new technology and its impact on the life in the community.

Health Promotion and Health Education

Following the Alma Ata Declaration and the introduction of the term "health promotion" it has become necessary to differentiate between this new term and the well established term "health education". After a great number of expert committees, workshops and articles it is now generally agreed that health promotion deals with environmental factors, whereas health education is mostly concerned with personal factors affecting health. The demarcation is arbitrary and there are many overlapping areas. One could say that both health promotion and education are two aspects of the same activity which strives to improve the health of a population. This topic has been discussed in some detail in the first part of this book.

Health Service

Any health promotion at the work place should include the health care system in the planning of activities. A close link between occupational and community health services should be established in planning and execution of HP/HE activities. One should bear in mind that in addition to the health issues of general importance, enterprises, as well as their workers, will have specific problems, which HP/HE will be expected to solve if it is to obtain the necessary support from industry.

Health Promoting Enterprises

The differentiation between health education and health promotion has had far-reaching consequences for the improvement of health at work (Baric, 1990). The health education approach in the past has been mainly concerned with the prevention of accidents at work, depending on the type of enterprise, with some attempts at introducing preventive screening for women, reduction of absenteeism among workers and control of the working environment. With the introduction of the concept of health promotion, the scope of health problems has been extended to include the environment in which the factory is located, the output it produces, as well as the health problems of the workforce.

With the breaking down of barriers between East and West, it has become obvious that the Eastern European countries have major environmental problems in addition to health problems of their work force. These problems are closely linked with the economic situation and are practically unsolvable. There are situations where the only solution would be closing down of the enterprise, which may not be economically and politically acceptable.

The WHO has recognised the seriousness of the situation and as a collaborative venture has nominated the Centre for Documentation for Health Problems at Work, located in Essen (Germany), which has been established and financed by one of the major German health insurance organisations (BKK), to explore these problems. The author has served as a consultant in the establishment of this Centre and in setting up their programme of work.

The recent switch of emphasis from problems to settings has made it necessary to examine the existing programmes of HP/HE in enterprises and to develop the new concept of a Health Promoting Enterprise.

HP/HE in Enterprises

This activity has a long tradition and has scored a number of successes. WHO EURO, jointly with the Federal Centre for Health Education (FCHE, Cologne, Germany), has organised two international conferences on this topic and produced reports (WHO, 1993), which include a number of examples of good practice.

The first conference was organised by the FCHE in 1985. It dealt with HP/HE at the workplace and presented the first collection of examples of "good practice" from various enterprises. This was followed in 1990 by a conference on the topic "Investment in Health" organised by the FCHE in Bonn, Germany. The latest conference was held in Cologne, Germany and was organised jointly by the FCHE and the WHO EURO under the title "Health Promotion in the Work Setting".

In the key note papers the conference discussed the topics of health as a company task from the point of view of employers, trade unions and employees. The working groups were divided according to their special interests and dealt with such topics as "Development of an Enterprise Policy for HP", "Health Circles and other Participatory Procedures of Company HP", and "Example of Good Practice". All the papers as well as the group work were fully supported by examples from the industry and commerce.

The Report represents a very good overview of the HP/HE work taking place in various enterprises in Germany and demonstrates certain innovative approaches in addition to the more traditional methods of dissemination of knowledge and organisation of various health oriented groups.

This concept has only recently been introduced into company health programmes and needs to be tested and fully developed before one can expect it to become widespread and replace the existing ad hoc approach of HP/HE in various companies.

Like a number of other "health promoting settings" (hospitals, schools) the Health Promoting Enterprise will be required to meet certain preconditions before it is granted health promoting status (creation of a healthy working environment, integration of HP/HE into the daily activities, and the outreach into the community).

The "Total Health Management" Approach

This is based on the Total Quality Management concept, which has become increasingly popular in industry and commerce. Total Quality Management arose through realisation that the old "supply and demand" economic models are not adequate in a situation where supply outstrips demand, cheap labour has slashed the prices of many products and the fight is on to gain a "competitive edge" over competitors. This has been achieved by recognising that a crucial factor in consumer choice is the "quality" (including reliability) of the product.

The main assumption of this concept is relatively simple: the quality of a product is a function of the interaction between the management and the workforce of an industry. This implies that the old method of quality control (after the product has been completed) has become obsolete. The new approach includes quality control throughout the production process, both on the management and workforce levels. Quality has become the "leitmotif" of industrial production with the management responsible for creating an environment (including technology) conducive to high quality production and the workforce becoming committed and gaining work satisfaction from the high quality and consequently high reliability of their products.

The "consumerism" prevalent in the eighties, which depended on "quality" for a competitive edge, is, however, making a place in the nineties for environmental issues. If one considers the fact that an enterprise is closely related to its immediate and the wider environment (where it is located and from where it recruits its labour force), then the new concept of "total health management" should take into account not only the internal levels of health in an enterprise but also the effects that this enterprise has on the health of the environment in which it operates. In this way, the new concept is being extended to "Healthy Enterprise in a Healthy Environment" with all its implications. It represents a shift from "quality" to "image" for gaining a competitive edge. It extends the "user friendly" image to an "environment friendly" image of the enterprise with all the benefits that such an image could have for public relations and advertising. This sets standards against which other enterprises could be assessed and, consequently, makes the concern for health a "norm" for the "health at the workplace" movement.

The "Total Health Management" concept takes into account the fact that productivity depends to a large extent on the health (physical, mental, social) of the workforce, since illness and accidents are the most common reasons for absenteeism or reduced work capacity. The concept recognises the functional relationship of management-workforce interaction and postulates that health management needs the total involvement of management and the workforce on all levels and in every phase of production. It takes into account the wider implications of work in terms of providing social status in the community, the relationship between leisure and the role of stress, in addition to occupational health hazards, as the indicator of a healthy enterprise. It, thus, affects not only the productivity but also the "image" of the enterprise and its products.

The implementation of this new approach requires new methods, which should include the "total" commitment of the management and the workforce to improving, maintaining and recovering high levels of health in the enterprise as well as in the community. This can be achieved by making health a "norm" supported by positive sanctions and legitimised by the powerstructure in the enterprise. The methodology of this approach is now being developed in pilot studies and includes a strong emphasis on educating the management and the workforce in the ways and means of achieving this goal.

Pilot Studies

At present there is a difference of opinion between the occupational health and health promotion/education experts about how to improve health in the work place. Whereas the former are mainly interested in the prevention of accidents and reduction of absenteeism, the latter are interested in expanding the approach to include the health of the community as well as that of the enterprise, based on general healthcare and healthy lifestyles and mobilising the participation of all the various agents within the health care system

The lack of any generally accepted and agreed-upon models in this field prompts us to plan a series of pilot studies which should result in the development of a pretested approach applicable on a European scale.

In the first instance, a set of pilot studies is planned in the UK., with the possibility of other similar studies being carried out in various firms in Western as well as Eastern Europe. The introduction of a comprehensive health promotion and education programme as a part of HP/HE activities is envisaged as including the following phases:

- exploration of existing needs and opportunities for health promotion and education interventions in the complex organisational structure of the system within which the personnel works;
- a training programme for the main carriers of health promotion and education interventions within the framework of existing institutions;
- a pilot intervention with the aim of testing available opportunities for health promotion and health education and evaluating the process and the outcome of such an intervention;
- extension of the developed programme and methods of intervention to the whole organisation.

The UK programme of pilot studies is envisaged as including three types of firms:

- a large firm (approx. 10,000 employees and workers) with a well established health service in the work place;

- a middle sized firm (up to 1,000 workers) with a partial health service, possibly just a first aid station;
- a small firm (under 100 workers) without a health service in the work place and utilising the local health service.

The outcome of a pilot study would be to provide:

- a conceptual approach and intervention programme;
- a curriculum for in-service training of personnel;
- the approach and instruments for evaluation and auditing.

It is envisaged that the resources for the pilot study would be provided mainly by the firms participating in the study since their workers would benefit directly from the outcome. It is hoped that a secondary benefit would come from the development of the approach, which could be used in other firms in Europe.

The Training Programme

Aims and Objectives

The aim of the proposed training programme is to provideparticipants with an insight into the requirements for planning and implementing a health promotion and education intervention.

To achieve this aim, the course has the following objectives:

- to provide participants with an insight into the latest developments in behavioural sciences related to prevention and treatment of disease as well as the most recent models in use in health promotion and education;
- to provide participants with an opportunity to acquire knowledge relevant for their health promotion and education role and skills for planning and implementing an HP/HE intervention;
- to provide participants with an insight into certain research methods relevant for the evaluation and auditing of their activities in the area of HP/HE.

Method

The Modular Course will consist of three modules:

Module 1: New approaches and methods in HP/HE

The aim of Module 1 is to provide the participants with information about the most recent advances in HP/HE and provide them with a choice of available methods for a HP/HE intervention.

To achieve this aim, Module 1 will have the following objectives:

- provide the participants with an overview of approaches in HP/HE;
- Inform the participants about the available methods for intervention.

Module 2: Planning and execution of HP/HE interventions

The aim of Module 2 is to provide the participants with the necessary knowledge concerning the planning and execution of a HP/HE intervention.

To achieve this aim Module 2 will have the following objectives:

- to provide the participants with the principles and methods of planning an intervention;
- to enable the participants to practice the execution of an intervention.

Module 3: Methods of evaluation and auditing

The aim of Module 3 is to acquaint the participants with the requirements for integrating evaluation into the planning process and to be able to audit an intervention.

To achieve this aim, Module 3 will have the following objectives:

- provide information about the requirements for evaluation;
- provide information about auditing an intervention.

Assessment

At the end of the three course Modules, the participants will be assessed on the basis of a programme, which they will be expected to produce on a topic of their own choice. Successful participants will be issued with a Certificate of Attendance by the relevant University.

The Evaluation of Health Promoting Enterprises

In planning the evaluation of HP/HE in enterprises it will be necessary to distinguish between the evaluation of these activities when they are integrated into an enterprise and the evaluation of a "health promoting enterprise". In the first instance, evaluation will follow the procedures for the assessment of processes and outcomes as was described in Part 2 of this book. In the case of a "health promoting enterprise", however, evaluation will have to be included in the existing process of quality assessment which exists in most of the large and medium sized enterprises. In small enterprises, a combination of quality assessment and evaluation will have to be specially designed.

According to its aims each setting will have a different set of HP/HE specifications. Since such specifications do not already exist they will need to be developed. In some settings, such as that of the Health Promoting Enterprise, conceptualising the programme includes examining the possibilities of the development of such specifications. This is expressed in the idea of Pilot Health Promoting Enterprises, which are committed to carrying out a number of intervention studies with precisely the purpose of identifying their HP/HE role within the general role of an enterprise. The outcome of such studies should be the development of specifications for the enterprise in general according to their character. The Pilot HPE thus provides benchmarks for specifications for other enterprises. Similar processes are already in progress in Health Promoting Schools and Health Promoting Hospitals, so that they can be extended to other settings.

Intervention studies are, therefore, concerned with the development of specifications for the three main areas of activity which are included in the commitment of a health promoting setting, i.e. the working environment, integration and the community outreach.

Specifications

Once a commitment has been made concerning the three main areas to be defined in terms of specifications, with a special emphasis on the role of HP/HE, it is necessary to define the standard procedures or practices which will be employed to meet the requirements of the specifications. In terms of the HP/HE planning process, the objectives of the intervention studies are developed to achieve the aims, according to the defined specifications:

1. Creating a healthy working environment for employees and clients will include the following procedures:

- creating healthy and safe working conditions;
- providing a healthy balanced nutrition;
- ensuring that there is accident prevention at the work place;
- ensuring that good relationships exist between employees and clients.

2. Integrating HP/HE into daily activities will include the following procedures:

- meeting the needs of the employees in terms of work and training;
- meeting the HP/HE needs of the clients (case-specific);
- meeting the needs of the immediate social environment (family, friends, relatives).

3. Outreach into the community will include the following procedures:

- making provisions for a follow-up of products;
- cstablishing networking with other similar settings (enterprises);

- creating healthy alliances with other settings in the community which are directly or indirectly relevant for the productivity of the enterprise.

The achievement of these HP/HE specifications will depend on the procedures or standard practices (objectives) applied within the setting. It should, however, be noted that different settings may have a different set of procedures which will appropriate for meeting the requirements of the three specifications relevant to most of the Health Promoting Settings.

The specifications will need to be assessed according to the three levels of implementation of HP/HE in an enterprise, that is: ground work level, organisational level and the client level.

This will enable the planners of evaluation or quality assessment to envisage the requirements in the form of a matrix, in which the three areas of activity can be assessed according to the three levels of implementation.

Methods

Success in meeting the specification will, to a large extent, depend on the choice of the appropriate procedures (methods). Health promotion and health education methods (Baric, 1993) have been described in general. They need to be selectively chosen for each specification and procedure in each setting. The choice of methods will, therefore, require a differential diagnosis of the problems and the choice of appropriate methods.

Evaluation, Quality Assessment and Auditing

The success of the project will depend on the detailed planning that will make possible an objective evaluation of the project. The evaluation in its wider sense represents the assessment of the activities as well as the measurement of the outcomes. It should include the assessment of the process in terms of its quality and results affecting desired outcomes, as well as auditing the programme in terms of the value system associated with the production process involved.

Evaluation is defined as the assessment of the achievement of the aims of the programme; quality assessment is concerned with the process and outcome of the programme; auditing is the assessment of the programme against general norms (social, cultural, professional) prevalent in that society.

Quality assessment is especially relevant to the production process since many enterprises will already have a quality management programme (BS 5750) to which it will be necessary to add certain health promotional and health educational specifications.

The assessment procedure will require a clear definition of the standards and specifications of the outcomes of the process, i.e. the product.

The assessment of the project will require the choice of **indicators**, which will be used to measure the achievement of the agreed aims through the set objectives. These indicators will have to be translated into **instruments**, which will be used for the measurements. The interpretation of the findings will depend on the accepted **criteria** for success or failure.

Set out below is an example of possible aims which could be used by someone planning a Health Promoting Enterprise Project.

Aims

The aims and objectives of an intervention concerned with the creation and operation of a "Health Promoting Enterprise" can be drawn up within the framework of the Ottawa Charter. They should cover the four main parts of the system which are the environment, the enterprise proper, the employees and the employees' families.

Ground Work:

AIM 1: To establish the needs of the employees in relation to the promotion of health and the prevention and management of disease.

AIM 2: To describe the internal structure of the enterprise as a means of satisfying employees' needs.

AIM 3: To describe the links of the enterprise with other institutions, the community and the environment.

AIM 4: To describ the preventive and promotive activities relevant to promotion of employees health.

Organisational Level:

AIM 5: To explore, with the enterprise employees, the possibility of undertaking a commitment to become a "Health Promoting Enterprise" within the WHO conceptualisation of the requirements for such a commitment.

AIM 6: The creation of a "Health Promoting Enterprise" movement within the enterprise.

AIM 7: The planning and provision of health promotion and health education ventures as a part of the normal activities of a "health promoting enterprise".

Employee (Consumer) Level:

AIM 8: Integration of health promotion and health education specifications into the quality assessment based on the needs of the consumers.

AIM 9: To carry out the monitoring of the intervention study.

AIM 10: To carry out the evaluation of the intervention.

AIM 11: The auditing of the intervention in terms of employee and consumer satisfaction of the expressed needs.

AIM 12: The quality assessment of the health educational and health promotional aspects of the work process.

HEALTH PROMOTING COMMUNITIES

INTRODUCTION

The idea of "health promoting communities" has been carried out, in Europe and elsewhere, in two different types of settings: in villages and in towns. Although the general conception is similar, the implementation and the outcomes will be different. The case studies presented in this section cover both aspects and give examples of the similarities as well as differences.

THE HEALTH PROMOTING VILLAGE

This approach is specially adjusted to improvements in health in rural areas. It is based on the "new" community participation model which makes a clear distinction between the role of the agent of change and that of the community members. The activities of the agents of change are limited to sensitising the community to existing problems and available improvements, with the aim of enabling members of the community to take over the responsibility for improvements. The role of the change agent is then limited to providing support if and when it is required by the members of that community. This applies also to the assessment of the processes and outcomes which are done by the community with the help of the external agents. In this way, the changes become permanent and are within the limits of the existing community resources.

This approach was tested in a set of villages in Sudan as a part of a HP/HE intervention study carried out by a member of the University of Gezira (Abdelgadir, 1991). It should be noted that the study took place before the most recent political changes in Sudan. It is presented here in the form of a case study, which showed that encouraging community members to take responsibility for their own wellbeing and the acquisition of competence in dealing with the problems within their own limits, has had a positive influence and a lasting effect in community changes.

Case Study : A Health Promoting Village in Sudan

This is a report on an intervention study carried out in two experimental villages in Sudan, using a community participation approach within the framework of the "healthy community with healthy children" concept.

Self-reliance and self-care approaches, within the primary health care system, using health promotional and educational programmes, were shown to be very effective in promoting health, in a country like the Sudan, with one million square miles, 22 million population, with 90% living in remote rural areas, with poor means of communication, high infant and maternal mortality rates, low literacy level, poor environmental sanitation, predominance of communicable diseases and poor health services.

Raising family competence, at the experimental villages was the theme of this study. This came about because health care should begin at home; individuals should become more knowledgeable about health issues, and develop skills to deal with them. Thus lay self-care, and mutual self-reliance have an essential role to play in improving people's health in developing countries. There were, however, a number of other factors such as, cultural, political, economic and religious, which were taken into consideration during this study, since the promotion of health depends to a large extent on improving people's socio-economic conditions.

For effective community participation, the study used a health promotion approach, as part of the process of enabling the village population to increase control over and to improve their health. A health education approach was also used as a process of development and change through which individuals, families and community become competent in the promotion, maintenance and management of their own health.

The practice of community participation was already a part of community life in the experimental villages. Therefore, during this study, it was necessary to work in collaboration with the already established network of community groups and sectors at the village level (e.g. Sheikhs, Faki, religious leaders, youth groups, women's groups and others), which ensured that the felt *needs* of the population were given top priority.

The existing approach to community development in the Sudan depended on the interaction between, external factors and the community pressures. The external factors included the services available, the initiation of a new programme or any similar activity coming from outside the community. It was not clear how far the communities were dependent on the external agents. The choice of community problems by the external agents might not actually be a community need. The long term benefits were usually limited, and once the outside support dried up, the community reverted to its previous state.

Taking into account the disadvantages of the existing approach to community development and the need for a better alternative approach, there was a rationale and justification, for testing a new approach to community participation (Baric, 1990) at the Sudanese village level.

The new approach to community participation, is based on the concepts of self-reliance and self-determination of the communities in taking care of their own health. It emphasises a shift in responsibility from the health care system to the communities. Following this new approach health activities should be integrated into the everyday life of the community, and should be shaped by the available community resources. External support should be mainly concered with raising the community's competence in dealing with its own health problems. The new approach to community participation should be a part of primary health care, within the framework of health education as a part of a wider concept of health promotion.

The intervention study was conducted in *Alamelhuda and Keriba* villages at the central part of Gezira Region of the Sudan, where the support of the health care system was not easily available and the health and future wellbeing of a child depended on the competence of family members and their immediate social environment to cope with the problems as they arose.

The study had the following four aims:

1. To raise the level of self-reliance and self-competence of communities in looking after their own health, including the health of their children.
2. To introduce and test the potential of Baric's community participation approach method in the experimental villages.
3. To make the experimental villages an outlet for community-based training programmes for the students at Gezira University.
4. Gradually to introduce the tested new community participation approach to the rest of the Gezira villages.

The population for the study consisted of families with at least one child. The main respondent was the mother, who was either interviewed alone or in the presence of the father and/or other members of the households. A representative random sample of 100 families from "Keriba", a big village, and 50 families from "Alamelhuda", a small village, were studied.

The methods and instruments used in this study included the following:

- establishment of external conditions;
- establishment of personal characteristics;
- development of a detailed intervention programme;
- application and evaluation of the intervention programme.

The establishment of the external conditions at the villages were carried out through a survey during a visit to the villages, observing the situation, talking with various members in authority, with health services and villagers and examining the existing records. The systemisation of information was achieved by the use of an "aide mémoire", as a guidance for the description of the external conditions.

A *baseline survey* consisting of two structured questionnaires, was carried out in both villages. Questionnaire 1 included coverage of villagers' social characteristics, health status and their utilisation of health services, while questionnaire 2 included questions about villagers' competence in dealing with preventative and curative aspects of illnesses within a family framework. The questionnaires were linked to the aims and objectives of the study and were administered by previously trained interviewers.

After the baseline survey, an intervention programme was planned, including community leaders' workshops in both villages.

The participants in the workshops were leaders and representatives of communities with different backgrounds ranging from highly educated leaders to illiterate community members. The teaching programme of the workshop was divided into four modules: Initiating a movement, and organising, managing and evaluating community programmes.

The analysis of the frequency distribution of the baseline survey, provided a basis for the development of the workshop curriculum, reflected in the contents, which included topics related to the lack of adequate knowledge and skills within the competence of the participants.

The curriculum contents were divided into four units:

Unit I: Included basic information about concepts of community participation, initiation, organisation, implementation and evaluation of community health programmes.

Unit II: Included a description of health problems related to pregnant women, including delivery.

Unit III: Included child health problems, common endemic diseases, environmental sanitation, and home accidents with relevant first aid topics.

Unit IV: Was mainly devoted to the process of planning and evaluation of village health programmes.

At the end of the community leaders' workshop, the participants decided to carry out the commitment by declaring their villages to be as "health villages with healthy children". They divided themselves into different village health committees. Each village health committee took the responsibility for dealing with a specific health problem area in their village.

The community leaders started their activities by conduting similar training workshops for villagers, who had not attended the main community leaders workshop. Alongside this activity, they carried out different health promotional and educational programmes at their villages.

The health activities and programmes that were carried out by the village health committees at the experimental villages mainly concentrated on the following areas:

- promotion of villagers' knowledge and skills related to pregnancy and delivery;
- promotion of child health care;
- control and prevention of endemic diseases at the villages level;
- improvement of villages' environmental sanitation;
- prevention of home accidents and transmitting knowledge and skills related to first aid.

After finishing one programme, the villages' health committee would turn to another. In this way, the activities and the health programmes in both villages were still continuing six months after the main intervention.

During the six months' period of ongoing village health promotional programmes and activities, the health education team used frequently to visit the villages, offering advice and support for the village health committees. At the same time, the team was monitoring and observing the changes that occurred after the intervention, checking health records for patterns of decline in morbidity and mortality as well as getting feedback from the villagers. Six months after the intervention programmes, a second evaluation survey was conducted. This survey used the same questionnaire as the one used in the baseline survey which had been conducted six months earlier before the intervention. In both villages, the information collected after the intervention was compared with the data collected before the intervention.

Statistical tests were performed on the comparison (T-test). Variables from the research questionnaire were then cross-tabulated with variables from the first questionnaire, and a bivariate analysis was performed, to determine the associations. Chi-square tests were computed for association between health predictors and socio-economic factors.

Outcomes:

- almost all criteria, regarding the health of the respondents, the health of the children and the health of other members in the family, at both villages, showed highly significant differences in health knowledge after the intervention;

- the University of Gezira decided to use the experimental villages as an outlet for the training of students in community-based programmes;

- the villages, represented by their community leaders, permitted the students of Gezira University to be trained in their villages, and promised support and co-operation with them in the future;

- the villagers' health committees renewed their commitment for the continuation of health programmes aimed at raising villagers competencies in matters related to their health;

- the HP/HE team promised to offer the continuous help and support for further promotion of the experimental villages;

- the Regional Ministry of Health undertook the commitment of introducing this tested, innovative approach to community participation in the villages in the rest of Gezira Region as well as offering help and support for the health promotion in the villages;

- the community leaders coming into the training project have developed a much more positive self-image, and their understanding of health and health care issues has increased enormously, so that they became a useful health resource for their local community;

- this study has demonstrated that, lay community members with opportunity for training could be an effective way of stimulating community involvement and organisation in health education and promotional health care issues;

- it was demonstrated that through health education, health promotion and the new approach to community participation, the desirable health practices could become a part of daily village life;

- based on the statistical tests and observations during different phases of this two year study, showed the new approach to community participation to be very effective in raising the awareness, increasing the health knowledge and competence of the population in the experimental villages.

HEALTH PROMOTING CITIES

Introduction

The Healthy City movement has already had some impact and has been described elsewhere (Baric, 1993). One of the consequences of this movement has been the "EnviroNet Project" sponsored by WHO EURO and including five European cities. This is a progress report on the project and the outcomes, which are a part of an ongoing process in these cities.

The CEC Projects

The Commission of the European Communities was charged by Article 10 of the ERDF regulations (1988) with the exploration of innovative means of achieving regional policy objectives. This resulted in the funding under this article of 36 inter-regional cooperative network projects as a selection from a great number of received proposals concerning the promotion of inter-regional co-operation.

The general objectives of the inter-regional cooperation projects has been identified as follows:

- to encourage the rapid transfer of know-how particularly from more advanced to less advanced regions;
- to create economics of scale through the implementation of common programmes and in response to shared problems and challenges;
- to promote the efficiency of administrations, particularly concerning the regional development process in less favoured regions;
- to help the development of Community policies particularly where they have an impact on regional development;

These objectives represent the main criteria for the assessment of the selected projects.

The EnviroNet Project

EnviroNet is a pilot project supported by the Commission of the European Communities for a duration of 5 years, of which the first two years are treated as the pilot stage. It started in 1992 with and agreement between the 5 cities involved in the project.

EnviroNet refers to the Environment-oriented Network of Cities on the periphery of the EEC. Its purpose is to share knowledge and skills in the areas of public administration, urban planning and environmental protection. This knowledge is to be transferred from two advanced cities (Wurzburg, Horsens) to the three less favoured cities (Patras, Greifswald and Suhl).

The aims of EnviroNet include:

- establishment of five local EnviroCentres to act as catalysts for key projects and publicity, as mediators for interaction between citizens, the public sector and other EEC cities, and as generators for enhanced social welfare, economic performance and efficiency of administration;

- initiating three key projects, coordinated by EnviroCentres and carried out by citizens related to the following topics: *Environmental Master Plan* (waste treatment, sewage system, water supply, traffic control, green areas, monitoring/information system and saving energy); *Public Administration Retraining* (ecological city planning, management/administration of health and environmental services, intersectoral approach, strategic information and management training); *Health Plan* (self-help groups, adequate care for elderly, neighbourhood networking and open future labs, and reduction in medicine consumption);

- the financial breakdown of expenditure which is financed during the two-year pilot phase by a budget of 5.2 million ECU of which 3 million ECU will be co-financed by an EU programme for regions and cities in Europe, the EC RECITE (the less favoured cities obtain 60% of the EC RECITE co-financing, the advanced cities 37% and consultants and non-specific experts only 3%).

The general idea behind this approach is based on the assumption that the citizens will be more satisfied due to the mechanism of participatory democracy. Mechanism for mediating between the interested groups should ensure the success of new initiatives. Health and environmental regulations should ensure good working conditions for industry and a healthy and motivated labour force. This should attract new industries into the region and serve as an indicator for future industrial investments.

The expected outcomes of the EnviroNet project are:

- improvement in quality of life;
- improvement of social and cultural values;
- protection and improvement of health conditions;
- protection and maintenance of the environment by using natural resources carefully and sensibly;
- increase in economic growth, business integration and social welfare;
- a long term regional plan for health and environment.

These outcomes are intended to be achieved through the following management structure:

- the overall coordinator is the City of Horsens represented by Health and Environment Group Horsens AS;
- board of Mayors and Presidents;
- key political personalities;
- EnviroCentre coordinators;
- operational key persons and citizens.

In their work the EnviroNet avoids:

- convincing politicians by budgets and promises of savings;
- trying to tell the inhabitants how they should live;
- smart technological solutions.

On the other hand, it attempts to:

- convince politicians by real life examples which are hard to disregard;

- mobilise the under-utilised resources of citizens to solve their own local problems;
- visualise the benefits from investment in sustainable health and environmental processes.

This is to be achieved by:

- establishing EnviroCentres as small shops in the city centres manned by 2-4 volunteers able to mediate between citizens and politicians and industry;

- initiating and generating health and environmental pilot projects such as those for specific diseases, social welfare, efficiency of public administration, strategic planning and information.

Case Study : City of Greifswald

The city of Greifswald in Germany (former GDR) is one of the more developed partners of the five-city partnership under the EnviroNet project. It has 68,000 inhabitants and is participating in the EnviroNet project with the support of the local "Ernst-Moritz-Arndt" University.

The aims defined by Greifswald include:

The City Health Promotion Action Plan , consisting of:

- Self-help Information and Nutrition Centre;
- youth and child health promotion;
- video lab for youngsters;
- an "Alcohol-free Cafe";
- a senior citizens committee;
- school health.

City Environmental Action Plan, consisting of:

- environmental education in schools;
- exhibitions and competitions;
- neighbourhood planning;
- environment library;

- support for a noise reduction programme.

Public Administration Training, consisting of:

- experience exchange with other cities;
- language courses;
- project management course;
- self-help support.

The focal point for the development of the EnviroNet project in Greifswald is the Centre for Health and Environment. The Centre produced an interim report about the achievements in the first two years of operation. A number of things have been achieved:

- establishment of a locally and internationally effective Centre for Health and Environment in Greifswald;

- support of existing and creation of new infrastructures for the promotion of health and the environment in Greifswald, such as the Office for Self-help and Nutritional Information, the Video Lab for Youngsters, the "Alcohol-free Cafe", the Environment Library and the Noise Reduction Plan;

- creation of a network for health promotion and environment protection with many partners on the local and regional level (e.g. the University; the City Offices for Health, Environment, Town Planning, Youth and Schools; the sickness funds and social welfare associations; private and government organisations for health promotion and environmental protection);

- partnership on the national and international level (e.g. the Federal Centre for Health Education; the German Nutrition Society; the Federal Environmental Office; the German Healthy Cities Network; and the Baltic Cities WHO Working Group);

- cooperative links with the EnviroNet Project Cities Wurzburg, Suhl, Horsens and Patras;

- a number of new jobs created by the EnviroNet Project.

These achievements open a whole range of new perspectives for future developments on a local, urban, national and international level within the Centre for Health and the Environment, based on the local and international experience gained through the successful implementation of the EnviroNet Project in Greifswald.

SUMMARY

In the third part of the book a sample of case studies has been presented in the hope that they would illustrate a number of points related to the introduction of the new organisational model of health promotion and health education applied to settings, as well as the problems encountered within these settings. The main issues are:

- the spread of the movement to encompass a whole range of settings;

- the different levels of development of various settings;

- the different types of management within each setting and their specific agendas;

- the important role of the WHO EURO in initiating and encouraging developments in different countries;

- the exceptional opportunity that exists in the UK as a result of the reform of the NHS and the policy documents published by the Department of Health;

- the long road ahead to achieve improvements on the population level.

The experience of the author acting as consultant to people working in these settings has indicated a number of problems which need to be addressed and, it is to be hoped, solved if health promotion and health education are to meet the expectations facing them. These can be summarised as follows:

- there is an urgent need to carry the organisational model further by means of research and intervention studies, especially with respect to its application on the client level;

- it would be useful now to shift the focus from the macro level (various types of settings) to the micro level (various characteristics of the same type of a setting) and explore the consequences at this level of applying the organisational model of health promotion and health education;

- there is a need to develop further the concept of accountability in the field of health promotion and health education by making new assessment approaches, such as total quality management, applicable to the needs of health promotion and health education interventions;

- the first task facing health promotion and health education will be the rethinking of the training programmes in this area, with a special emphasis on curricula design, to include the needs of the various professions and the various statuses of people expected to play a role in their operationalisation;

- the redistribution of resources should reflect the new developments and be integrated into budgets on a national and local level.

The new challenges facing health promotion and health education as a means of contributing to the improvement of people's health promise an exciting time for those directly or indirectly involved in this field. Success, however, will depend on an effective shift in priorities and influence within organisations in favour of health promotion and health education professionals who are directly involved in ensuring the health gain of the clients.

APPENDICES

THE OTTAWA CHARTER

THE ADELAIDE RECOMMENDATIONS

THE SUNDSWALL STATEMENT

THE HEALTH OF THE NATION

THE PATIENT'S CHARTER

THE BUDAPEST DECLARATION

WHO TARGETS FOR HP

EUROPEAN PILOT HOSPITAL PROGRAMME

THE ENGLISH CHARTER FOR HPH

HEALTH AND SAFETY

APPENDIX 1
THE OTTAWA CHARTER

The first international Conference on Health Promotion meeting in Ottawa was held on 21st of November 1986, and produced a Charter for action to achieve Health for All by the year 2000 and beyond. The text of the Charter is as follows:

"This conference was primarily a response to growing expectations for a new public health movement around the world. Discussions focused on the needs in industrialised countries, but took into account similar concerns in all other regions. It built on the progress made through the Declaration on Primary Health Care at Alma Ata, the World Health Organization's Targets for Health for All document, and the recent debate at the World Health Assembly on intersectoral action for health.

Health Promotion

Health promotion is the process of enabling people to increase control over, and to improve, their health. To reach a state of complete physical, mental and social well-being, an individual or group must be able to identify and to realise aspirations, to satisfy needs, and to change or cope with the environment. Health is, therefore, seen as a resource for everyday life, not the objective of living. Health is a positive concept emphasising social and personal resources, as well as physical capacities. Therefore, health promotion is not just the responsibility of the health sector, but goes beyond healthy life-styles to well-being.

Prerequisites for Health

The fundamental conditions and resources for health are peace, shelter, education, food, income, a stable eco-system, sustainable resources, social justice and equity. Improvement in health requires a secure foundation in these basic prerequisites.

Advocate

Good health is a major resource for social, economic and personal development and an important dimension of quality of life. Political, economic, social, cultural, environmental, behavioural and biological factors can all favour health or be harmful to it. Health promotion action aims at making these conditions favourable through advocacy for health.

Enable

Health promotion focuses on achieving equity in health. Health promotion action aims at reducing differences in current health status and ensuring equal opportunities and resources to enable all people to achieve their fullest health potential. This includes a secure foundation in a supportive environment, access to information, life skills and opportunities for making healthy choices. People cannot achieve their fullest health potential unless they are able to take control of those things which determine their health. This must apply equally to women and men.

Mediate

The prerequisites and prospects for health cannot be ensured by the health sector alone. More importantly, health promotion demands coordinated action by all concerned: by governments, by health and other social and economic sectors, by non-governmental and voluntary organisations, by local authorities, by industry and by the media. People in all walks of life are involved as individuals, families and communities. Professional and social groups and health personnel have a major responsibility to mediate between differing interests in society for the pursuit of health.

Health promotion strategies and programmes should be adapted to the local needs and possibilities of individual countries and regions to take into account differing social, cultural and economic systems.

Health Promotion Action

Build Healthy Public Policy

Health promotion goes beyond health care. It puts health on the agenda of policy makers in all sectors and at all levels, directing them to be aware of the health consequences of their decisions and to accept their responsibilities for health.
Health promotion policy combines diverse but complementary approaches including legislation, fiscal measures, taxation and organisational change. It is coordinated action that leads to health, income and social policies that foster greater equity. Joint action contributes to ensuring safer and healthier goods and services, healthier public services, and cleaner, more enjoyable environments.
Health promotion policy requires the identification of obstacles to the adoption of healthy public policies in non-health sectors, and ways of removing them. The aim must be to make the healthier choice the easier choice for policy makers as well.

Create Supportive Environments

Our socicties are complex and interrelated. Health cannot be separated from other goals. The inextricable links between people and their environment constitutes the basis for a socio-ecological approach to health. The overall guiding principle for the world, nations, regions and communities alike, is the need to encourage reciprocal maintenance - to takc care of each other, our communities and our natural environment. The conservation of natural resources throughout the world should be emphasised as a global responsibility.

Changing patterns of life, work and leisure have a significant impact on health. Work and leisure should be a source of health for people. The way society organises work should help create a healthy society. Health promotion generates living and working conditions that are safe, stimulating, satisfying and enjoyable.

Systematic assessment of the health impact of a rapidly changing environment - particulary in areas of technology, work, energy production and urbanization - is essential and must be followed by action to ensure positive benefit to the health of the public. The protection of the natural and built environments and the conservation of natural resources must be addressed in any health promotion strategy.

Strengthen Community Action

Health promotion works through concrete and effective community action in setting priorities, making decisions, planning strategies and implementing them to achieve better health. At the heart of this process is the empowerment of communities, their ownership and control of their own endeavours and destinies.

Community development draws on existing human and material resources in the community to enhance self-help and social support, and to develop flexible systems for strengthening public participation and direction of health matters. This requires full and continuous access to information, learning opportunities for health, as well as funding support.

Develop Personal Skills

Health promotion supports personal and social development through providing information, education for health and enhancing life skills. By so doing, it increases the options available to people to exercise more control over their own health and over their environments, and to make choices conducive to health.

Enabling people to learn throughout life, to prepare themselves for all of its stages and to cope with chronic illness and injuries is essential. This has to be facilitated in school, home, work and community settings. Action is required through educational, professional, commercial and voluntary bodies, and within the institutions themselves.

Reorient Health Services

The responsibility for health promotion in health services is shared among individuals, community groups, health professionals, health service institutions and governments. They must work together towards a health care system which contributes to the pursuit of health.

The role of the health sector must move increasingly in a health promotion direction, beyond its responsibility for providing clinical and curative services. Health services need to embrace an expanded mandate which is sensitive and respects cultural needs. This mandate should support the needs of individuals and communities for a healthier life, and open channels between the health sector and broader social, political, economic and physical environmental components.

Reorienting health services also requires stronger attention to health research as well as changes in professional education and training. This must lead to a change of attitude and organisation of health services, which refocuses on the total needs of the individual as a whole person.

Moving into the Future

Health is created and lived by people within the settings of their everyday life; where they learn, work, play and love. Health is created by caring for oneself and others, by being able to take decisions and have control over one's life circumstances, and by ensuring that the society one lives in creates conditions that allow the attainment of health by all its members.

Caring, holism and ecology are essential issues in developing strategies for health promotion. Therefore, those involved should take as a guiding principle that, in each phase of planning, implementation and evaluation of health promotion activities, women and men should become equal partners.

Commitment to Health Promotion

The participants in this conference pledge:

- to move into the arena of healthy public policy, and to advocate a clear political commitment to health and equity in all sectors;

- to counteract the pressures towards harmful products, resource depletion, unhealthy living conditions and environments, and bad nutrition; and to focus attention on public health issues such as pollution, occupational hazards, housing and settlements;
- to respond to the health gap, within and between societies, and to tackle the inequities in health produced by the rules and practices of these societies;
- to acknowledge people as the main health resource; to support and enable them to keep themselves, their families and friends healthy through financial and other means, and to accept the community as the essential voice in matters of its health, living conditions and well-being;
- to reorient health services and their resources towards the promotion of health; and to share power with other sectors, other disciplines and most importantly with people themselves;
- to recognise health and its maintenance as a major social investment and challenge; and to address the overall ecological issue of our ways of living.

The conference urges all concerned to join them in their commitment to a strong public health alliance.

Call for International Action

The conference calls on the World Health Organization and other international organisations to advocate the promotion of health in all appropriate forums and to support countries in setting up strategies and programmes for health promotion.

The conference is firmly convinced that if people in all walks of life, nongovernmental and voluntary organisations, governments, the World Health Organization and all other bodies concerned join forces in introducing strategies for health promotion, in line with the moral and social values that form the basis of this Charter, Health For All by the year 2000 will become a reality."

APPENDIX 2
THE ADELAIDE RECOMMENDATIONS

The adoption of the Declaration of Alma Ata a decade ago was a major milestone in the Health for All movement which the World Healthy Assembly launched in 1977. Building on the recognition of health as a fundamental social goal, the Declaration set a new direction for health policy by emphasising people's involvement, co-operation between sectors of society, and primary health care as its foundation.

The Spirit of Alma Ata

The spirit of Alma Ata was carried forward in the Charter for Health Promotion which was adopted in Ottawa in 1986. The Charter set the challenge for a move towards the new public health by reaffirming social justice and equity as prerequisities for health, and advocacy and mediation as the processes for their achievement.

The Charter identified five health promotion action areas: build Healthy Public Policy, create supportive environments, develop personal skills, strengthen community action, and reorient health services.

These actions are interdependent, but Healthy Public Policy establishes the environment that makes the other four possible.

The Adelaide Conference on Healthy Public Policy continued in the direction set at Alma Ata and Ottawa, and built on their momentum. Two hundred and twenty participants from forty-two countries shared experiences in formulating and implementing Healthy Public Policy. The following recommended strategies for Healthy Public Policy action reflect the consensus achieved at the Conference.

Healthy Public Policy

Healthy Public Policy is characterised by an explicit concern for health and equity in all areas of policy and by an accountability for health impact. The main aim of Healthy Public Policy is to create a supportive environment to enable people to lead healthy lives. Such a policy makes healthy choices possible or easier for citizens. It makes social and physical environments health-enhancing. In the pursuit of Healthy Public Policy, government sectors concerned with agriculture, trade, education, industry, and communications need to take account of health as an essential factor when formulating policy. These sectors should be accountable for the health consequences of their policy decisions. They should pay as much attention to health as to economic considerations.

The Value of Health

Health is both a fundamental human right and a sound social investment. Governments need to invest resources in Healthy Public Policy and health promotion in order to raise the health status of all their citizens. A basic principle of social justice is to ensure that people have access to the essentials for a healthy and satisfying life. This, at the same time, raises overall societal productivity in both social and economic terms. Healthy Public Policy in the short term will lead to long-term economic benefits as shown by the case studies presented at this Conference. New efforts must be made to link economic, social, and health policies into integrated action.

Equity, Access, and Development

Inequalities in health are rooted in inequities in society. Closing the health gap between socially and educationally disadvantaged people and more advantaged people requires a policy that will improve access to health-enhancing goods and services, and create supportive environments. Such a policy would assign high priority to underprivileged and vulnerable groups. Furthermore, a Healthy Public Policy recognises the unique culture of indigenous peoples, ethnic minorities, and immigrants. Equal access to health services, particularly community health care, is a vital aspect of equity in health.

New inequalities in health may follow rapid structural change caused by emerging technologies. The first target of the European Region of the World Health Organization, in moving towards Health for All, is that:

"By the year 2000, the actual differences in health status between countries and between groups within countries should be reduced by at least 25% by improving the level of health of disadvantaged nations and groups."

In view of the large health gaps between countries, which this Conference has examined, the developed countries have an obligation to ensure that their own policies have a positive health impact on developing nations. The Conference recommends that all countries develop Healthy Public Policies that explicitly address this issue.

Accountability for Health

The recommendations of this Conference will be realised only if governments at national, regional, and local levels take action. The development of Healthy Public Policy is as important at the local levels of government as it is nationally. Governments should set explicit health goals that emphasise health promotion.

Public accountability for health is an essential nutrient for the growth of Healthy Public Policy. Governments and all other controllers of resources are ultimately accountable to their people for the health consequences of their policies, or lack of policies. A commitment to Healthy Public Policy means that governments must measure and report the health impact of their policies in language that all groups in society readily understand. Community action is central to the fostering of Healthy Public Policy. Taking education and literacy into account, special efforts must be made to communicate with those groups most affected by the policy conerned.

The Conference emphasises the need to evaluate the impact of policy. Health information systems that support this process need to be developed. This will encourage informed decision-making over the future allocation of resources for the implementation of Healthy Public Policy.

Moving Beyond Health Care

Healthy Public Policy responds to the challenges in health set by an increasingly dynamic and technologically changing world, with its complex ecological interactions and growing international interdependencies. Many of the health consequences of these challenges cannot be remedied by present and foreseeable health care. Health promotion efforts are essential and these require an integrated approach to social and economic development which will re-establish the links between health and social reform, which the World Health Organisation policies of the past decade have addressed as a basic principle.

Partners in the Policy Process

Government plays an important role in health, but health is also influenced greatly by corporate and business interests, non-governmental bodies, and community organisations. Their potential for preserving and promoting people's health should be encouraged. Trade unions, commerce and industry, academic associations, and religious leaders have many opportunities to act in the health interests of the whole community. New alliances must be forged to provide the impetus for health action.

Action Areas

The Conference identified four key areas as priorities for Healthy Public Policy for immediate action:

Supporting the Health of Women

Women are the primary health promoters all over the world, and most of their work is performed without pay or for a minimal wage. Women's networks and organisations are models for the process of health promotion organisation, planning, and implementation. Women's networks should receive more recognition and support from policy-makers and established institutions. Otherwise, this investment of women's labour increases inequity.

For their effective participation in health promotion women require access to information, networks, and funds. All women especially those from ethnic, indigenous, and minority groups, have the right to self-determination of their health, and should be full partners in the formulation of Healthy Public Policy to ensure its cultural relevance.

This Conference proposes that countries start developing a national women's Healthy Public Policy in which women's own health agendas are central and which includes proposals for:

- equal sharing of caring work performed in society;
- birthing practices based on women's preferences and needs;
- supportive mechanisms for caring work, such as support for mothers with children, parental leave, and dependent health-care leave.

Food and Nutrition

The elimination of hunger and malnutrition is a fundamental objective of Healthy Public Policy. Such policy should guarantee universal access to adequate amounts of healthy food in culturally acceptable ways. Food and nutrition policies need to integrate methods of food production and distribution, both private and public, to achieve equitable access to food at affordable prices.

A food and nutrition policy that integrates agricultural, economic, and environmental factors to ensure a positive national and international health impact should be a priority for all governments. The first stage of such a policy would be the establishment of goals for nutrition and diet. Taxation and subsidies should discriminate in favour of easy access for all to healthy food and an improved diet.

The Conference recommends that governments take immediate and direct action at all levels to use their purchasing power in the food market to ensure that the food-supply under their specific control (such as catering in hospitals, schools, day-care centres, welfare services, and workplaces) gives consumers ready access to nutritious food.

Tobacco and Alcohol

The use of tobacco and the abuse of alcohol are two major health hazards that deserve immediate action through the development of Healthy Public Policies. Not only is tobacco directly injurious to the health of the smoker but the health consequences of passive smoking, especially to infants, are now more clearly recognised than in the past. Alcohol contributes to social discord, and physical and mental trauman. Additonally, the serious ecological consequences of the use of tobacco as a cash crop in impoverished economies have contributed to the current world crisis in food production and distribution.

The production and marketing of tobacco and alcohol are highly profitable activities, especially to governments through taxation. Governments often consider that the economic consequences of reducing the production and consumption of tobacco and alcohol by altering policy would be too heavy a price to pay for the health gains involved.

This Conference calls on all governments to consider the price they are paying in lost human potential by abetting the loss of life and illness that tobacco smoking and alcohol abuse cause. Governments should commit themselves to the development of Healthy Public Policy by setting nationally determined targets to reduce tobacco growing and alcohol production, marketing, and consumption significantly by the year 2000.

Creating Supportive Environments

Many people live and work in conditions that are hazardous to their health and are exposed to potentially hazardous products. Such problems often transcend national frontiers. Environmental management must protect human health from the direct and indirect adverse effects of biological, chemical, and physical factors, and should recognise that women and men are part of a complex ecosystem. The extremely diverse but limited natural resources that enrich life are essential to the continuing survival, health, and well-being of the human race. Policies promoting health can be achieved only in an environment that conserves resources through global, regional, and local ecological strategies.

A commitment by all levels of government is required. Co-ordinated intersectoral efforts are needed to ensure that health considerations are regarded as integral prerequisites for industrial and agricultural development. At an international level, the World Health Organisation should play a major role in achieving acceptance of such principles and should support the concept of sustainable development.

This Conference advocates that, as a priority, the public health and ecological movements join together to develop strategies in pursuit of socio-economic development and the conservation of our planet's limited resources.

Developing New Health Alliances

The commitment to Healthy Public Policy demands an approach that emphasises consultation and negotiation. Healthy Public Policy requires strong advocates who put health high on the agenda of policy-makers. This means fostering the work of advocacy groups and helping the media to interpret complex policy issues.

Educational institutions must respond to the emerging needs of the new public health by reorienting existing curricula to include enabling, mediating, and advocating skills. There must be a power shift from control to technical support in policy development. In addition, forums for the exchange of experiences at local, national, and international levels are needed.

The Conference recommends that local, national, and international bodies:

- establish clearing-houses to promote good practice in developing Healthy Public Policy;
- develop networks of research workers, training personnel, and programme managers to help analyse and implement Healthy Public Policy.

Prerequisites for health and social development are peace and social justice; nutritious food and clean water; education and decent housing; a useful role in society and an adequate income; conservation of resources and the protection of the ecosystem. The vision of Healthy Public Policy is the achievement of these fundamental conditions for healthy living. The achievement of global health rests on recognising and accepting interdependence both within and between countries. Commitment to global public health will depend on finding strong means of international co-operation to act on the issues that cross national boundaries.

Future Challenges

1. Ensuring an equitable distribution of resources even in adverse economic circumstances is a challenge for all nations.

2. Health for All will be achieved only if the creation and preservation of healthy living and working conditions become a central concern in all public policy decisions. Work in all its dimensions - caring work, opportunities for employment, quality of working life - dramatically affects people's health and happiness. The impact of work on health and equity needs to be explored.

3. The most fundamental challenge for individual nations and international agencies in achieving Healthy Public Policy is to encourage collaboration (or developing partnerships) in peace, human rights and social justice, ecology, and sustainable development around the globe.

4. In most countries, health is the responsibility of bodies at different political levels. In the pursuit of better health it is desirable to find new ways for collaboration within and between these levels.

5. Healthy Public Policy must ensure that advances in health-care technology help rather than hinder the process of achieving improvements in equity.

The Conference strongly recommends that the World Health Organisation continue the dynamic development of health promotion through the five strategies described in the Ottawa Charter. It urges the World Health Organisation to expand this initiative throughout all its regions as an integrated part of its work. Support for developing countries is at the heart of this process.

Key Issues: Equity And Accountability

The Concern with equity and accountability illustrates the new environmental emphasis in health promotion policy. The past two decades of public health have focused on individual behaviour modification, achieved through information, education, and the development of personal skills. The gains achieved by this approach should be seen in the context of supportive environments. The Conference repeatedly highlighted the hazard of blaming the victim if programmes and policies assume that people will make healthy choices, which in fact are not available to them. Governments should be held accountable to their people for creating supportive environments before they ask their people to be accountable to them for behaviour that puts their health at risk. The future of public health must be characterised by stronger emphasis on the creation of structural, institutional, and legislative supports that make healthy living accessible to the whole population.

Equity

The Conference saw equity as the fundamental and overriding issue in promoting health. Representatives from all regions of the World Health Organisation emphasised that health inequality and social inequity are endemic. Inequities in health have been reduced in some countries over the past decade but it was made clear to the Conference that this has not occurred with sufficient speed or impact on a global level. This was underlined in the major speeches to the Conference.

Equity in health is created or destroyed by public policy in all sectors at the national, regional, and local levels. Policies on taxation and subsidies influence the supply of goods and services that most affect the poor. Transport policy affects people's access to the community.

Agricultural policy has a major impact on the supply of foods to the people. Education policy, especially for women, is reflected in literacy levels that determine people's capacity for self-care and participation in community life.

The case studies illustrated the many forms that inequities take and the people most affected: women, homosexuals, drug users, old people, the disabled.

Workshop: "Equity and Access"

The results of a workshop on "Equity and Access" highlighted the Healthy Public Policy approach to health inequities:

Healthy Public Policy is concerned with treatment of causes rather than symptoms, and emphasis should not, therefore, be on disease and unhealthy habits, but rather on issues of structure, equity, and access to overcome maldistribution of power and resources.

The contextual definition of Healthy Public Policy must make distinctions between indigenous dispossessed peoples, minority immigrant ethnic groups, movements of oppressed people, citizens' movements (e.g. for environmental issues, peace), and consumer movements.

The Workshop Outlined Priorities for Action:

- training in participative skills for disadvantaged people;
- language access;
- change of image - health images of beautiful people need to be changed to include people with handicaps (mental, physical, age, gender) of a variety of racial and ethnic origins;
- re-allocation of resources from national to regional levels and away from institutions dominated by professional groups. Caution was expressed, however, that this should not be interpreted as a move to "community care" which most often means more work for women, particularly women of disadvantaged groups. True community care needs adequate resourcing and properly paid workers;
- linking of local movements with national and global networks.

The Workshop Set Future Challenges:

- World Health Organization to include minority groups and representatives of all disadvantaged people including indigenous minority peoples in all future conferences. The achievement securing full participation (rather than token representation) will involve provision of adequate interpreting facilities and training in participating skills;
- World Health Organization to set up independent monitoring systems to demonstrate the effects of public policy and be responsive to changing needs;
- World Health Organisation should develop its role as advocate in the legitimising of policies of Health for All -especially at times when many governments are legitimising inequalities;
- World Health Organization should spread information regarding both good and bad policies in an accessible way (not turgid tables but readily comprehensible statements which can be utilised at national and local levels);
- ways should be sought of bringing together the functions of management and control to encourage both accountability and ownership.

Panel Debate : "Equity and Development"

Equity was also highlighted in a panel debate which emphasised the following points:

- new types of development aid are badly needed, to give more funds for human and social investment and move away from models with little value for developing countries;
- modernisation and development have too often become synonymous. This has been at great economic and ecological cost and in many cases has led to massive national debt;
- because of international monetary sanctions, public expenditure in many developing countries has to be reduced; this leads to massive cuts in social programmes, education, and health, thereby widening the already existing gap;
- there are still stark inequalities in the developed countries; in many cases the health gap is static, if not widening.

Global Interdependence and Responsibility

The main result of the debate on equity during the Conference was the recognition of global interdependence and responsibility.

The Conference saw Healthy Public Policy as being as relevant and necessary to the developing nations as to the industrial world. Participants recognised the need for varying content and application, however, as an acknowledgement of the myriad political, social, and economic conditions in the different regions. Healthy Public Policy may focus on reducing excess in one region, at the same time as it deals with increasing access in another. For example, clean water and better food supplies are central issues in many countries, whereas changing diets and reducing alcohol use are priorities in others.

Healthy Public Policy in the developing world implies initial support for the basic prerequisites for health and for the development of essential infrastructures. The most fundamental challenge is to overcome the increased risk of international dependence and negative influences on lifestyle.

Accountability

Accountability emerged as the second central issue during the course of the Conference. By definition, accountability implies clear direction in policy development and assumes an ability to assess progress.

If societies truly place a high value on health and see it as the right of each citizen, then each government policy needs to be assessed also in terms of its positive or negative health impact.

The Conference recommended that all countries should establish national goals for health. These should be broken down into a timetable of targets for implementation at national, regional, and local levels. The exercise of setting goals and targets gives the opportunity for health to take priority within the context of other policy issues.

For example, Health for All Australians took two factors as its starting point: the need to put more emphasis on health promotion and disease prevention; and the existence of stark inequalities in health status. In the spirit of Federal cooperation, all Australian States have agreed, as the first step, to establish national health goals. However, goals for Healthy Public Policy will have meaning only if there is a mechanism for measuring the health impact of all government policies, or lack of them, at all levels. This will enable progress to be assessed and gaps to be identified, and will contribute significantly to informed decision-making by those who control the nation's resources. A comprehensive information system must be established to measure health and equity outcomes, and the process of policy implementation.

Community participation is at the heart of accountability. People's access to accurate, timely, and understandable information affects their ability to hold the policy-makers accountable for their decisions. Access to information is one of the essential steps along the path to equity.

The Conference concluded that each country should publish regular reports on the state of the nation's health. These should be communicated to all sectors of society in ways that are both understandable and culturally acceptable. Participants overwhelmingly endorsed the view that the mass media could play an essential role in health communication to the public and in providing a vehicle for response from community organisations.

APPENDIX 3
THE SUNDSVALL STATEMENT

The Third International Conference on Health Promotion: Supportive Environments for Health (WHO, 1991) was held in Sundsvall, Sweden. The Conference issued a Statement which calls upon people in all parts of the world to engage actively in making environments more supportive to health. Examining today's health and environmental issues together, the Conference pointed out that millions of people are living in extreme poverty and deprivation in an increasingly degraded environment that threatens their health, making the goal of Health for All by the Year 2000 extremely hard to achieve. The way forward lies in making the environment - the physical environment, the social and economic environment, and the political environment - supportive to health rather than damaging to it.

The Sundsvall Conference identified many examples and approaches for creating supportive environments that can be used by policy-makers, decision-makers and community activists in the health and environment sectors. The Conference recognised that everyone has a role in creating supportive environments for health.

A Call for Action

"This call for action is directed towards policy-makers and decision-makers in all relevant sectors and at all levels. Advocates and activists for health, environment and social justice are urged to form a broad alliance towards the common goal for Health For All. We Conference participants have pledged to take this message back to our communities, countries and governments to initiate action. We also call upon the organizations of the United Nations system to strengthen their cooperation and to challenge each other to be truly committed to sustainable development and equity.

A supportive environment is of paramount importance for health. The two are interdependent and inseparable. We urge that the achievement of both be made central objectives in the setting of priorities for development, and be given precedence in resolving competing interests in the everyday management of government policies.

Inequities are reflected in a widening gap in health both within our nations and between rich and poor countries. This is unacceptable. Action to achieve social justice in health is urgently needed. Millions of people are living in extreme poverty and deprivation in an increasingly degraded environment in both urban and rural areas. An unforeseen and alarming number of people suffer from the tragic consequences of armed conflicts for health and welfare. Rapid population growth is a major threat to sustainable development. People must survive without clean water or adequate food, shelter and sanitation.

Poverty frustrates people's ambitions and their dreams of building a better future, while limited access to political structures undermines the basis for self-determination. For many, education is unavailable or insufficient, or, in its present forms, fails to enable and empower. Millions of children lack access to basic education and have little hope of a better future. Women, the majority of the world's population, are still oppressed. They are sexually exploited and suffer from discrimination in the labour market and many other areas which prevents them from playing a full role in creating supportive environments.

More than a billion people worldwide have inadequate access to essential health care. Health care systems undoubtedly need to be strengthened. The solution to these massive problems lies in social action for health and the resources and creativity of individuals and their communities. Releasing this potential requires a fundamental change in the way we view our health and our environment and a clear, strong political commitment to sustainable health and environmental policies. The solutions lie beyond the traditional health system.

Initiatives have to come from all sectors that can contribute to the creation of supportive environments for health, and must be acted on by people in local communities, nationally by government and nongovernmental organizations, and globally through international organizations. Action will involve predominantly such sectors as education, transport, housing and urban development, industrial production and agriculture.

Dimensions of Action on Supportive Environments for Health

In a health context the term **supportive environments** refers to both the physical and the social aspects of our surroundings. It encompasses where people live, their local community, their home, where they work and play. It also embraces the framework which determines access to resources for living, and opportunities for empowerment. Thus action to create supportive environments has many dimensions: physical, social, spiritual, economic and political. Each of these dimensions is inextricably linked to the others in a dynamic interaction. Action must be coordinated at local, regional, national and global levels to achieve solutions that are truly sustainable.

The conference highlighted four aspects of supportive environments:

1. The **social** dimension, which includes the ways in which norms, customs and social processes affect health. In many societies traditional social relationships are changing in ways that threaten health, for example, by increasing social isolation, by depriving life of a meaningful coherence and purpose, or by challenging traditional values and cultural heritage.

2. The **political** dimension, which requires governments to guarantee democratic participation in decision-making and the decentralisation of responsibilities and resources. It also requires a commitment to human rights, peace, and a shifting of resources from the arms race.

3. The **economic** dimension, which requires a re-channelling of resources for the achievement of Health For All and

sustainable development, including the transfer of safe and reliable technology.

4. The need to recognise and use **women's skills and knowledge** in all sectors, including policy-making, and the economy, in order to develop a more positive infrastructure for supportive environments. The burden of the workload of women should be recognised and shared between men and women. Women's community-based organizations must have a stronger voice in the development of health promotion policies and structures.

Proposals for Action

The Sundsvall Conference believes that proposals to implement the Health for All strategies must reflect two basic principles:

1. **Equity** must be a basic priority in creating supportive environments for health, releasing energy and creative power by including all human beings in this unique endeavour. All policies that aim at sustainable development must be subjected to new types of accountability procedures in order to achieve an equitable distribution of responsibilities and resources. All action and resource allocation must be based on a clear priority and commitment to the very poorest, alleviating the extra hardship borne by the marginalised, minority groups, and people with disabilities. The industrialised world needs to pay the environmental and human debt that has accumulated through exploitation of the developing world.

2. Public action for supportive environments for health must recognize the **interdependence** of all living beings, and must manage all natural resources taking into account the needs of coming generations. Indigenous peoples have a unique spiritual and cultural relationship with the physical environment that can provide valuable lessons for the rest of the world. It is essential, therefore, that indigenous peoples be involved in sustainable development activities and negotiations be conducted about their rights to land and cultural heritage.

It Can Be Done: Strengthening Social Action

A call for the creation of supportive environments is a practical proposal for public health action at the local level, with a focus on settings for health that allow for broad community involvement and control. Examples from all parts of the world were presented at the Conference in relation to education, food, housing, social support and care, work and transport. They clearly showed that supportive environments enable people to expand their capabilities and develop self-reliance. Further details of these practical proposals are available in the Conference report and handbook.

Using the examples presented, the Conference identified four key public health action strategies to promote the creation of supportive environments at community level.

1. **Strengthening advocacy** through community action, particularly through groups organized by women.

2. **Enabling** communities and individuals to take control over their health and environment through education and empowerment.

3. **Building alliances** for health and supportive environments in order to strengthen the cooperation between health and environmental campaigns and strategies.

4. **Mediating** between conflicting interests in society in order to ensure equitable access to supportive environments for health.

In summary, empowerment of people and community participation were seen as essential factors in a democratic health promotion approach and the driving force for self-reliance and development.

Participants in the Conference recognised in particular that education is a basic human right and a key element to bring about the political, economic and social changes needed to make health a possibility for all. Education should be accessible throughout life and be built on the principle of equity, particularly with respect to culture, social class and gender.

The Global Perspective

Humankind forms an integral part of the earth's ecosystem. People's health is fundamentally interlinked with the total environment. All available information indicates that it will not be possible to sustain the quality of life, for human beings and all living species, without drastic changes in attitudes and behaviour at all levels with regard to the management and preservation of the environment.

Concerted action to achieve a sustainable, supportive environment for health is **the** challenge of our times.

At the international level, large differences in per capita income lead to inequalities not only in access to health but also in the capacity of societies to improve their situation and sustain a decent quality of life for future generations. Migration from rural to urban areas drastically increases the number of people living in slums, with accompanying problems including a lack of clean water and sanitation.

Political decision-making and industrial development are too often based on short-term planning and economic gains, which do not take into account the true costs to our health and the environment. International debt is seriously draining the scarce resources of the poor countries. Military expenditure is increasing, and war, in addition to causing deaths and disability, is now introducing new forms of ecological vandalism.

Exploitation of the labour force, the exportation and dumping of hazardous waste and substances, particularly in the weaker and poorer nations, and the wasteful consumption of world resources all demonstrate that the present approach to development is in crisis. There is an urgent need to advance towards new ethics and global agreement based on peaceful coexistence to allow for a more equitable distribution and utilization of the earth's limited resources.

Achieving Global Accountability

The Sundsvall Conference calls upon the international community to establish new mechanisms of health and ecological accountability that build on the principles of sustainable health development. In practice this requires health and environmental impact statements for major policy and programme initiatives. WHO and UNEP are urged to strengthen their efforts to develop codes of conduct on the trade and marketing of substances and products harmful to health and the environment.

WHO and UNEP are urged to develop guidelines based on the principle of sustainable development for use by Member States. All multilateral and bilateral donor and funding agencies such as the World Bank and International Monetary Fund are urged to use such guidelines in planning, developing and assessing development projects. Urgent action needs to be taken to support developing countries in developing their own solutions. Close collaboration with nongovernmental organizations should be ensured through the process.

The Sundsvall Conference has again demonstrated that the issues of health, environment and human development cannot be separated. Development must imply improvement in the quality of life and health while preserving the sustainability of the environment.

The Conference participants, therefore, urge the United Nations Conference on Environment and Development (UNCED), to be held in Rio Janeiro in 1992, to take the Sundsvall Statement into account in its deliberations on the Earth Charter and Agenda 21, which is to bee an action plan leading into the 21st century. Health goals must figure prominently in both. Only worldwide action based on global partnership will ensure the future of our planet.

APPENDIX 4

"THE HEALTH OF THE NATION"

The White Paper published by the Department of Health represents a cornerstone in the role of health promotion. It was published in July 1992 and is based on the preceding Green Paper under the same heading and published in 1991.

The aim of the consultative document "The Health of the Nation" was to stimulate a period of widespread public and professional debate on health and how it might be improved. The White Paper sets out a strategy for health for England which takes account of the response to consultation. The strategy:

- selects five Key Areas for action
- sets national objectives and targets in the Key Areas
- indicates the action needed to achieve the targets
- outlines initiatives to help implement the strategy
- sets the framework for monitoring, development and review.

The Strategic Approach

The strategy is set against the background of a continuing overall improvement in England's general state of health. It emphasises disease prevention and health promotion as ways in which even greater improvements in health can be secured, while acknowledging that further improvement of treatment, care and rehabilitation remains essential.

Key Areas for Action and National Targets

Five Key Areas, in which substantial improvements in health can be achieved are selected. Each Key Area has national targets, and is supported by action needed to secure progress. In the main, the targets relate to the year 2000, but some look further to the future. Within Key Areas, emphasis is placed on risk factors, such as smoking or dietary imbalances.

The Key Areas are:

- Coronary heart disease and stroke
- Cancers
- Mental illness
- HIV/AIDS and sexual health
- Accidents

Working to Take the Strategy Forward

Everyone has a part to play if the strategy is to be successful. At national level the Government has set up a Ministerial Cabinet Committee to coordinate Government action and oversee implementation of the health strategy. Others with major roles include the NHS and health professions, statutory and other authorities, the Health Education Authority, voluntary bodies, employers and employees, and the media.

The importance of active partnerships between the many organisations and individuals who can come together to help improve health ("healthy alliances") are also highlighted. action on a wide variety of fronts will include work in "settings" such as healthy cities, healthy schools or healthy hospitals, specific action on general health promotion in the workplace and of the environment at large.

The Particular Role of the NHS

The NHS has a particularly important role in improving health in addition to its responsibilities for health care. Not only will it work towards achieving progress in the national Key Areas, but it will add to them identified local priorities. the success of the strategy will depend to a great extent on the commitment and skills of the health professionals within the NHS.

Monitoring, Developing and Reviewing the Strategy

The strategy must be monitored and the tools to do so developed. A range of action to meet information and research needs, including major new health survey work, is put in hand. Monitoring and reviewing progress will be overseen by the Ministerial Committee on Health Strategy, assisted by the three Working Groups set up at the start of the initiative. Periodic progress reports will be published.

Summary and Discussion

A great step forward

The present reform of the NHS, as outlined in the Green Paper, has brought about some radical changes reflected in a shift of emphasis from the provision of services to the promotion of health. The changes in the provision of services have put the accent on meeting the needs of people by purchasing the best available services provided by the health care system. This is being achieved by contracting these services from those providers that meet the standards expected to match the needs of the people. The changes in promotion of health are reflected in the shift from a 'problem' approach to a more general 'settings' approach.

These changes have been reinforced in the White Paper and have been taken a step further. The White Paper spells out the need to take into account the settings in which people live, work and play, as well as five priority problem areas. The emphasis is on a health promoting environment, in which all the various institutions are "health promoting" (cities, schools, hospitals, enterprises, health authorities, etc.). As far as the five priority problem areas are concerned, the White Paper sets a strategy for the achievement of improvements and defines the targets which should be used to evaluate these achievements within a specific period of time. Although the five problem areas (coronary heart disease, cancers, mental illness, HIV/AIDS and STD, and accidents) should receive priority attention, the White Paper does not exclude any other health problems from its strategy. Within this combined problem/settings approach, the White Paper mentions specific population groups which need special attention (infants and children, women, elderly, ethnic minority groups, specific socio-economic groups, people with physical, sensory or learning disabilities and other groups such as unemployed).

The main criticism of the opposition party and some other individuals, which has been voiced in Parliament and in the media, concerns the allegedly disregard in the White Paper of the "major" causes of ill health in the population such as unemployment, poverty, inadequate housing, etc. If one accepts the intention of the White Paper to be an extension of the previously published Green Paper, then such criticism does not seem to be fully justified. The White Paper emphasizes the need for the responsibilities for health of the nation to be shared between various Government Departments and not only by the Secretary of State for Health. The Green Paper outlines in great detail the role of these Departments (e.g.Environment, Transport, Education and Science, Social Security, Trade and Industry, Energy, Employment, etc.). The commitments in both these documents allow for enough scope to tackle the most important threats to health by the Government as a whole and not just one Department.

Research and Evaluation

A more serious criticism concerns the basic assumption in both the Green and the White Paper, which is, that Research and Development activities should continue to concentrate on the study of the problems (and now also the settings), since the solutions are self-evident and common-sensical. This one-sided approach to research has been evident throughout the period during which health promotion has become "respectable" and even desirable. There has been a noticeable absence of any serious research into the solutions which health promotion and health education use to solve the existing health problems.

Examples for this can be found in most of the areas covered by the new strategy. The new contract between the NHS and the General Practitioners provides for health promotion clinics and sets targets for some preventive activities. Both will depend on the efficient and effective methods used, although these have not been defined nor is there any scientifically tested evidence that those used so far could be effective. This tendency has been perpetuated by the White Paper, which sets well defined targets in terms of levels and timing of the expected achievements. It does not, however, recognise the fact that some of the presently used methods do not always work, some do not work because of the way they are being used, and some that could work may not be acceptable to the professionals and/or the population. In a number of cases the solutions applied are limited to the use of resources (human and financial) for the establishment of complex organisational structures (committees, task forces, etc.) with limited effects on the ground level.

The reason for this is a lack of systematic evaluation and of any objective auditing of the organisations and programmes related to different problems. This usually results in blaming the consumers for any failure and not the agents or the methods. Recently there have been statements (media, newspapers, publications) which were critical of the way the solutions to the problems of health in general have been applied ("More staff than patients in booming Aids industry" The Sunday Times, 19.7.92; "Action 'failed to reverse inner-city decline'" Independent, 14.7.92; "Jobs 'cost £32,965 each' to create", Independent, 15.7.92; etc.) The Institute of Health Education, in its Journal, has taken the lead in this area for a number of years, by publishing articles which draw the reader's attention to such needs, and also introduced for the first time the concept of auditing health promotion and health education activities ("Evaluation -A Tool for Planning, Management and Auditing Health Promotion/Education Interventions" Vol.27, No.2, 1989).

One could summarise that the White Paper, together with the earlier published Green Paper, represents an important step in the improvement of the health of the nation. The emphasis on health promotion reflects the recent developments in the world, and the combination of the problem-, settings- and special population groups-approach provides a realistic opportunity for the achievement of better health in this country. The proposed strategy is clear and sets realistic targets within the foreseeable future.

The main question facing health promotion is whether in its present state of development it will be able to meet these expectations. It seems that the only hope lies in a radical change being introduced in the allocation of priorities and resources for research and evaluation, which would result in the study of the solutions in addition to the present emphasis on the study of problems.

APPENDIX 5
THE PATIENT'S CHARTER

The Patient's Charter sets out clearly for the first time your rights to care in the National Health Service and the National and Local Charter Standards which the Government intends to see achieved.

In addition to seven well-established rights, the Government is introducing three important new rights for you from 1st April 1992.

The Government is also introducing National Charter Standards in nine key areas. These are not legal rights but major and specific standards which the Government looks to the NHS to achieve, as circumstances and resources allow. They are set out on pages twelve to fifteen.

The Government will be ensuring the collection and publication of information on the achievement of these Standards at national and local level. Where performance is unsatisfactory, the Secretary of State will require the Chief Executive of the NHS to take action to put things right.

National Charter Standards are essential in the nine key areas. The Government believes that other Standards are better set at local level where they can more accurately reflect differing local circumstances. The Government will require health authorities to develop and publish their own Local Charter Standards from 1st April 1992.

The Patient's Charter Rights

Seven existing rights: every citizen has the following established National Health Service rights:

1. to receive health care on the basis of clinical need, regardless of ability to pay;
2. to be registered with a GP;
3. to receive emergency medical care at any time, through your GP or the emergency ambulance service and hospital accident and emergency departments;

4. to be referred to a consultant, acceptable to you, when your GP thinks it necessary, and to be referred for a second opinion if you and your GP agree this is desirable;
5. to be given a clear explanation of any treatment proposed, including any risks and any alternatives, before you decide whether you will agree to the treatment;
6. to have access to your health records, and to know that those working for the NHS are under a legal duty to keep their contents confidential;
7. to choose whether or not you wish to take part in medical research or medical student training.

Three new rights from 1st April 1992:

1. *To be given detailed information on local health services, including quality standards and maximum waiting time.* Your district health authority and, in some cases, GP, are now arranging services from hospitals and community services. They must make information about these services and National and Local Charter Standards available to you. You will be able to get this information from your health authority, your GP or your local Community Health Council. Your health authority will make sure that all local NHS hospitals publicise current maximum admission times for each speciality;

2. *To be guaranteed admission for treatment by a specific date no later than two years from the day when your consultant places you on a waiting list.* The great majority of patients will be admitted well before their guaranteed date. Currently, of patients admitted from waiting lists, half come in within five weeks and 90% are admitted within a year. Exceptionally for some treatments it may be necessary to set a date more than two years away. Your health authority (or GP) will be responsible for ensuring that the guaranteed times are met, if necessary by offering you treatment in an alternative hospital;

3. *To have any complaint about NHS services - whoever provides them - investigated and to receive a full and prompt written reply from the chief executive or general manager.* From 1st April 1992, health authorities and NHS hospitals will have to publish details regularly of both the number of complaints received and how long it has taken to deal with them. If you are still unhappy with the way

your complaint about the administration of an NHS service has been handled, you have the right to take the matter up with the Health Service Commissioner.

National Charter Standards

1. *Respect for privacy, dignity and religious and cultural beliefs.* The Charter Standard is that all health services should make provision so that proper personal consideration is shown to you, for example by ensuring that your privacy, dignity and religious and cultural beliefs are respected. Practical arrangements should include meals to suit all dietary requirements, and private rooms for confidential discussions with relatives.

2. *Arrangements to ensure everyone, including people with special needs, can use services.* The Charter Standard is that all health authorities should ensure that the services they arrange can be used by everyone, including children and people with special needs such as those with physical and mental disabilities, for example, by ensuring that buildings can be used by people in wheelchairs.

3. *Information to relatives and friends.* The Charter Standard is that health authorities should ensure that there are arrangements to inform your relatives and friends about the progress of your treatment subject, of course, to your wishes.

4. *Waiting time for an ambulance service.* The Charter Standard is that when you call an emergency ambulance it should arrive within fourteen minutes if you live in an urban area, or nineteen minutes if you live in a rural area.

5. *Waiting time for initial assessment in accident and emergency departments.* The Charter Standard is that you will bee seen immediately and your need for treatment assessed.

6. *Waiting time in outpatient clinics.* The Charter Standard is that you will be given a specific appointment time and be seen within thirty minutes of that time.

7. *Cancellation of operations.* The Charter Standard is that your operation should not be cancelled on the day you are due to arrive in hospital. However, this could happen because of emergencies or staff sickness. If, exceptionally, your operation has to be postponed twice you will be admitted to hospital within one month of the date of the second cancelled operation.

8. *A named qualified nurse, midwife or health visitor responsible for each patient.* The Charter Standard is that you should have a name, qualified nurse, midwife or health visitor who will be responsible for your nursing or midwifery care.

9. *Discharge of patients from hospital.* the Charter Standard is that before you are discharged from hospital a decision should be made about any continuing health or social care needs you may have. Your hospital will agree arrangements for meeting these needs with agencies such as community nursing services and local authority social services departments before you are discharged. You and, with your agreement, your carers will be consulted and informed at all stages.

Local Charter Standards

In addition to the National Charter Standards, there are many other aspects of service which are important to you and which your health authority, therefore, needs to consider.

From 1st April 1992, authorities will increasingly set and publicise clear Local Charter Standards on these matters, including:

- waiting time for first outpatient appointments;
- waiting times in accident and emergency departments, after your need for treatment has been assessed;
- waiting times for taking you home after you have been treated, where your doctor says you have medical need for NHS transport;
- enabling you and your visitors to find your way around hospitals, through enquiry points and better sign posting;
- ensuring that the staff you meet face to face wear name badges.

Your health authority will also publicise the name of the person you should contact if you want more information about the Local Charter Standards they have set.

Performances and Progress

Charter Rights.

These are guaranteed. If you think that you are being or are likely to be denied one of the National Charter rights you should write Duncan Nichol, Chief Executive of the NHS Department of Health, Richmond House, 79, Whitehall, London SW1A 2NS. Mr Nichol will investigate the matter and if you have been denied a right he will take action to ensure that this is corrected.

National Charter Standards.

Your health authority will publish information about performance against the Standards annually, with the name of the person to whom you should write with any comments. Every year the Secretary of State will discuss performance with the Chief Executive, who will take action where this has been unsatisfactory. The Department of Health will publish details of this action.

Local Charter Standards.

Your district health authority will publish an annual report of achievement against its local standards, and the name of the person to whom you should write with any comments. In the following year's report, the authority will say what action has been taken where necessary to improve its performance.

Better Information About Services

The Government wants you to know what services are available. From 1st April 1992, the Government will require regional and district health authorities to publish information about the services they provide and their performance in relation to Local and National Charter Standards, to help you to make informed choices about care and treatment.

Your health authority must provide information about the specific services it has arranged. In addition, your health authority will set up more general information services to help people to find their way around the NHS and to understand what is available. From 1st April 1992, you will be able to get information about:

- Local Charter Standards;
- the services your health authority has arranged;
- waiting times for outpatient, day case and inpatient treatment by hospital, speciality and individual consultant, set out in a standard way;
- common diseases, conditions and treatments;
- how to complain about NHS services;
- how to maintain and improve your own health.

From 1st April 1993, you will be able to find how successful your health authority has been in relation to the National and Local Charter Standards.

The new rights and standards in this Charter are designed to meet the commitments in the Citizen's Charter. The NHS will play a full part in the Chartermark scheme when it is launched.

APPENDIX 6

BUDAPEST DECLARATION

Following extensive discussion, the Budapest meeting agreed a set of three documents which have become known as The Budapest Declaration on Health Promoting Hospitals. These set out the Content and Aims of the health promoting hospital, the Criteria for participation including the types of working structures and procedures to be adopted and finally, the possible degrees of Commitment which parties interested in becoming involved in the initiative, can consider. The main thrust of these three documents are presented here.

Content and Aims for Model Hospitals participating in the International WHO-Network of Health Promoting Hospitals : Beyond the assurance FO good quality medical services and health care, participants agreed that the health promoting hospital would encourage and support health promoting perspectives, activities etc. amongst staff, patients, relatives, visitors and the wider community.

It was felt that it was desirable to develop within the hospital an organisational culture which adopted health promotion as a core value. This would involve, inter alia, support for a more active, participatory role for patients and relatives and the encouragement of self-help and community involvement.

The fostering of good working and living conditions within the hospital was seen as an essential aspect of health promotion in hospitals. It was felt that the physical environment of hospital buildings should support all users, particularly long stay patients. Food policy was seen as an important area for action by the health promoting hospital.

There was general agreement that the health promoting hospital should improve information and communication throughout the hospital and provide opportunities for education and training for staff, patients and relatives. It was felt that the needs and values of different population and cultural groups should be acknowledged.

Participants felt that communication and collaboration with existing social and health services in the community should be fostered and that services in general should be better coordinated. In addition, it was recommended that ht health promoting hospital develop an epidemiological data base specifically related to the prevention of illness and injury. It was agreed that this information would be communicated to public policy makers and other relevant institutions in the community.

Criteria for Participation : Basic recommendations for participation in the WHO-Network as a health promoting hospital involves acceptance of the Ottawa Charter and the Content and Aims document from the Budapest Declaration, described above. Eleven specific recommendations were agreed. These provide guidance regarding the organisation, management and implementation of a health promoting hospital initiative and outline the information dissemination responsibilities involved.

It is possible for any type or size of hospital to participate. Approval to become a Health Promoting Hospital must be sought from the owner, management and personnel of the hospital. A written submission to WHO - Healthy Cities Programme and LBI (-joint Network coordinators) is required. Cooperation with an independent institution in relation to planning, consultation, documentation, monitoring and evaluation is recommended. Members of this institution and the hospital are recommended to form a Joint Project Committee which would agree working procedures, personnel and financial resources. In addition, the hospital is recommended to nominate a project manager to oversee the initiative.

It was agreed that participating hospitals would endeavour to establish at least five innovative health promoting projects. Examples of such projects are presented below. It is recommended that the Health Promoting Hospital projects are linked with congruent local health promotion programmes, especially those within the Healthy Cities Network.

Finally, recommendations were agreed in relation to information dissemination, feedback of evaluation information, networking etc. within the hospital, its environment and more broadly to a national and international audience. It is envisioned that the running period for a Model Hospital initiative would b e at least 5 years.

Degrees of Commitment Possible : Four levels of commitment to the WHO-Network of Health Promoting Hospitals were agreed. It was felt that these different levels of commitment would accommodate the needs and interests of all those who wished to become involved.

The strongest level of commitment involved participation as an accepted Model Hospital in the WHO-Network of Health Promoting Hospitals. Hospitals which would like to participate at this level but may not be quite ready to do so, can become affiliated as a Potential Model Hospital with the option of participation in the Network of accepted Health Promoting Hospitals, at a later stage. It is also possible for hospitals which are considering the possibility of becoming a Model Hospital to commence their involvement as nominated observers within the Network.

The third level of commitment agreed, involves temporary affiliation of Individual Projects of relevance to the Health Promoting Hospital concept. Finally, those Interested Institutions or Persons who wish to be kept informed of developments in the area, can receive the planned Newsletter of the Network on submission of contact information to LBI.

Joining the Network

Hospitals could apply for the following categories of the European Pilot Network membership: full, associate, affiliate and observer membership. Each category has a different set of commitments which a hospital must undertake.

The approval of membership depends on the joint decision of the WHO EURO and the European Network of Pilot Health Promoting Hospitals . At present there are 20 hospitals that have been accepted as "Pilot Health Promoting Hospitals", whereas there is also a more general European Network of Health Promoting Hospitals run directly by WHO EURO which caters for the needs of any hospital which is interested in these developments and wishes to establish international means of communication with the help of WHO. The main difference is in the commitments of the various categories. Whereas the Pilot hospitals are required to serve as a developmental experiment and produce tested models of the application of this idea, and have a time limitation of 5 years concerning their special Pilot status, other hospitals within the European network are expected to benefit from the experiences of Pilot hospitals and provide a continuous process of integrated health promotion and health education as a part of their institutional goals.

Each of the Pilot hospitals, however, to fulfil their Pilot role, has endeavoured to establish five innovative health promoting projects with a running period of at least five years in order to allow information dissemination, feedback of evaluation information, networking etc. to occur.

This approach is based on the "Vienna Model" and requires the agreement of a hospital to undertake such a commitment, the establishment of an organising body within the hospital and the establishment of a health promotion/health education programme. This programme is based either on special hospital units or some specific health problems (e.g. the Department of Gynaecology; diabetes). The methods are conventional and include transmission of knowledge and skills as well as improvements in the hospital's physical environment. Initiatives may include, for example, special lectures for diabetics or improvements in the hospital catering.

Contents and Aims

A model hospital participating in the international WHO Network of Health Promoting Hospitals will have the following aims and contents which go beyond the assurance of good quality medical services and health care and are associated with their health promoting role:

1. Provide opportunities throughout the hospital to develop health-orientated perspective, objectives and structures;

2. Develop a common corporate identify within the hospital which embraces the aims of the Health Promoting Hospital;

3. Raise awareness of the impact of the environment of the hospital on the health of patients, staff and community. The physical environment of hospital buildings should support, maintain and improve the healing process;

4. Encourage an active and participatory role for patients according their specific health potentials;

5. Encourage participatory, health gain orientated procedures throughout the hospital;

6. Create healthy working conditions for all hospital staff;

7. Strive to make the Health Promoting Hospital a model for healthy services and workplaces;

8. Maintain and promote collaboration between community based health promotion initiatives and local governments;

9. Improve communication and collaboration with existing social and health services in the community;

10. Improve the range of support given to patients and their relatives by the hospital through community based social and health services and/or volunteer groups and organisations;

11. Identify and acknowledge specific target groups (e.g. age, duration of illness etc.) within the hospital and their specific health needs;

12. Acknowledge differences in value sets, needs and cultural conditions for individuals and different population groups;

13. Create supportive, humane and stimulating living environments within the hospital especially for long-term and chronic patients;

14. Improve the health promoting quality and the variety of food services in hospitals for patients and personnel;

15. Enhance the provision and quality of information, communication and educational programmes and skill training for patients and relatives;

16. Enhance the provision and quality of educational programmes and skill training for staff;

17. Develop in the hospital an epidemiological data base specially related to the prevention of illness and injury and communicate this information to public policy makers and to other institutions in the community.

Criteria

The model hospitals participating in the international WHO Network of Health Promoting Hospitals are supposed to meet the following preconditions:

Basic Recommendations

1. Acceptance of the principles declared in the "Ottawa Charter for Health Promotion";

2. Acceptance of the document "CONTENT AND AIMS for Model Hospitals participating in The International WHO Network of Health Promoting Hospitals".

Specific Recommendations

1. Approval to become a Health Promoting Hospital to be sought from the owner, management and personnel of the hospital (including representatives of unions, working council). A written submission will be required;

2. Willingness to cooperate and ensure the funding of programmes with an independent institution in relation to planning, consultation, documentation, monitoring and evaluation.

Evaluation to be undertaken annually in order to guide future action;

3. Willingness to develop an appropriate organisation structure and process, supported by project management to realise the aims of the Health Promoting Hospital;

4. Establishment of a Joint Project Committee (with representatives form the Model Hospital and institutions of research and/or consultation). Nomination of a project manager by the hospital, who is accountable to the Joint Project Committee;

5. Provision of necessary personnel and financial resources as agreed by the Joint Project Committee;

6. Readiness to develop at least five innovative health promoting projects related to the hospital, the people who work within it, and the population served, with goals, objectives and targets for each project. Projects should be complementary to health promotion initiatives in primary health care;

7. Public discussion of health promotion issues and possible health promoting activities within the hospital by
   - Internal Newsletter
   - Public presentations within the hospital;

8. Provision of evaluation information at least annually to
   - the Joint Project Committee
   - Management
   - Workers
   - the public and to those who provide funding
   - other organisations, both local, national and international including WHO and the Coordinating Institution for the Network;

9. Exchange experience by networking with
   - other hospitals
   - the international WHO Network of Health Promoting Hospital (participation in business meetings etc.)

National Network (group of nominated observers from different institutions with an interest in health);

10. Link the Health Promoting Hospital projects with congruent local health promotion programmes, especially those within the Healthy Cities Network;

11. Prospective running period of the model : 5 years.

Creation of Task Forces

The original problems with which the European Network of Health Promoting Hospitals had to deal was the assessment of applications of various hospitals in the European region applying for a Pilot status. This task has now been successfully completed with the nomination of 20 Pilot Health Promoting Hospitals.

The new problem facing the European Network is to ensure the fulfilment of the commitment by Pilot Hospitals. These include:

1. Restructuring of the hospital to meet the HP/HE needs;

2. Implementing the five research projects;

3. Evaluating the projects and producing annual, as well as the final report.

For this purpose the European Network has at its second Business Meeting in Hamburg (October 1993) decided to establish a number of "Task Forces". At present there are in operation the following Task Forces:

- Financing and Funding
- Consultancy and Links with External Institutions
- Evaluation and Assessment.

APPENDIX 7

WHO EURO TARGETS FOR HEALTH PROMOTION

Following the WHO EURO Regional Committee in 1985 a set of targets have been agreed upon in support of the European strategy for the achievement of Health for All by the Year 2000. The document includes 38 targets which are summarised as follows:

Equity

a) Equity in health

Target 1: reducing the difference in health status between countries and between groups within countries by at least 25%;

b) Adding life to years

Target 2: by the year 2000 people should have the basic opportunity to develop and use thcir health potential to live socially and economically fulfilling lives.

Target 3: by the year 2000 disabled persons should have the physical, social and economic opportunities that allow at least for a socially and economically fulfilling and mentally creative life.

c) Adding health to life

Target 4: by the year 2000 the average number of years that people live free from major disease and disability should be increased by at least 10%.

Target 5: by the year 2000 there should be no indigenous measles, poliomyelitis, neonatal tetanus, congenital rubella, diphtheria, congenital syphilis or indigenous malaria in the region.

d) Adding years to life

Target 6: by the year 2000 life expectancy at birth in the region should be at least 75 years.

Target 7: by the year 2000 infant mortality in the region should be less than 20 per 1000 live births.

Target 8: by the year 2000 maternal mortality in the region should be less than 15 per 100,000 live births.

Target 9: by the year 2000 mortality in the region from diseases of the circulatory system in people under 65 should be reduced by at least 15%.

Target 10: by the year 2000 mortality in the region from cancer in people under 65 should be reduced by at least 15%.

Target 11: by the year 2000 deaths from accidents in the region should be reduced by at least 25% through an intensified effort to reduce traffic, home and occupational accidents.

Target 12: by the year 2000 the current rising trends in suicides and attempted suicides in the region should be reversed.

Lifestyles Conducive To Health

e) Better opportunities and improved capacities

Target 13: by 1990 national policies in all Member States should ensure that legislative, administrative and economic mechanisms provide broad intersectoral support and resources for the promotion of healthy lifestyles and ensure effective participation of the people at all levels of such policy-making.

Target 14: by 1990 all Member States should have specific programmes which enhance the major roles of the family and other social groups in developing and supporting healthy lifestyles.

Target 15: by 1990 educational programmes in all Member States should enhance the knowledge, motivation and skills of people to acquire and maintain health.

f) Promoting healthy behaviour

Target 16: by 1995 in all Member States, there should be significant increases in positive health behaviour, such as balanced nutrition, non-smoking, appropriate physical activity and good stress management.

Target 17: by 1995 in all Member States, there should be significant decreases in health-damaging behaviour, such as over use of alcohol and pharmaceutical products; use of illicit drugs and dangerous chemical substances; and dangerous driving and violent social behaviour.

Healthy Environment

g) Environmental health policies

Target 18: by 1990 Member States should have multisectoral policies that effectively protect the environment from health hazards, ensure community awareness and involvement, and support international efforts to curb such hazards affecting more than one country.

h) Monitoring, assessment and control

Target 19: by 1990, all Member States should have adequate machinery for the monitoring, assessment and control of environmental hazards which pose a threat to human health, including potentially toxic chemicals, radiation, harmful consumer goods and biological agents.

Target 20: by 1990 all people of the region should have adequate supplies of safe drinking-water, and by the year 1995 pollution of rivers, lakes and seas should no longer pose a threat to human health.

Target 21: by 1995 all people of the region should be effectively protected against recognised health risks from air pollution.

Target 22: by 1990 all Member States should have significantly reduced health risks from food contamination and implemented measures to protect consumers from harmful additives.

Target 23: by 1995 all Member States should have eliminated major known health risks associated with the disposal of hazardous wastes.

i) Improving environmental conditions

Target 24: by the year 2000 all people of the region should have a better opportunity of living in houses and settlements which provide a healthy and safe environment.

Target 25: by 1995 people of the region should be effectively protected against work-related health risks.

Appropriate Care

j) Priorities of a health care system

Target 26: by 1990 all Member States through effective community representation, should have developed health care systems that are based on primary health care and supported by secondary and tertiary care as outlined at the Alma Ata conference.

Target 27: by 1990 in all Member States the infrastructures of the delivery systems should be organised so that resources are distributed according to need, and that services ensure physical and economic accessibility and cultural acceptability to the population.

Target 28: by 1990 the primary health care system of all Member States should provide a wide range of health - promotive, curative, rehabilitative and supportive services to meet the basic health needs of the population and give special attention to high-risk, vulnerable and underserved individuals and groups.

Target 29: by 1990 in all Member States, primary health care systems should be based on cooperation and team work between health care personnel, individuals, families and community groups.

Target 30: by 1990 all Member States should have mechanisms by which the services provided by all sectors relating to health are coordinated at the community level in a primary health care system.

k) Quality of services

Target 31: by 1990 all Member States should have built effective mechanisms for ensuring quality of patient care within their health care systems.

Research for HFA

Target 32: before 1990 all Member States should have formulated research strategies to stimulate investigations which improve the application and expansion of knowledge needed to support their health for all developments.

Health Development Support

l) Healthy policy formulation

Target 33: before 1990 all Member States should ensure that their health policies and strategies are in line with health for all principles and that their legislation and regulations make their implementation effective in all sectors of society.

m) Managerial process

Target 34: before 1990 Member States should have managerial processes for health development geared to the attainment of health for all, actively involving communities and all sectors relevant to health and, accordingly, ensuring preferential allocation of resources to health development priorities.

Target 35: before 1990 Member States should have health information systems capable of supporting their national strategies for health for all.

n) Human resource development

Target 36: before 1990 in all Member States the planning, training and use of health personnel should be in accordance with health for all policies, with emphasis on the primary health care approach.

Target 37: before 1990 in all Member States education should provide personnel in sectors related to health with adequate information on the country's health for all policies and programmes and their practical application to their own sectors.

Target 38: before 1990 all Member States should have established a formal mechanism use of health technologies and of their effectiveness, efficiency, safety and acceptability, as well as reflecting national health policies and economic restraints.

APPENDIX 8
EUROPEAN PILOT HOSPITAL PROJECT - LIST OF SUBPROJECTS

Alten Eichen Hospital, Hamburg, D.

1. Employee Questionnaire towards Health and Well-being 07/92
2. Improvement of Organization of Wards towards a more Holistic and Patient-centered care 07/92
3. Health and Environment Check up/Hospital Catering-Health and Social Aspects 07/92
4. Health and Safety at Work and Improving Psychosocial Working Conditions 04/1994
5. Health Promotion for the Patient 09/1994

Altnagelvin Area Hospital, Londonderry, UK

1. Cardiopulmonary Resuscitation Training Programme 01/92
2. Nutrition and Health 11/92
3. Children's Education Programme 07/92
4. Accidents at Work 10/92
5. Breast feeding Promotion Programme 12/91
6. Implementation of the Workplace Alcohol Policy 01/93
7. Implementation of the New Smoking and Health Policy 01/93

Areteion Hospital, Athens, GR

1. Hygiene and Safety in the Hospital 01/93
2. Control of Hospital Acquired Infections 01/93
3. Health Education Program for the Training of Young Mothers on Issues of Perinatal Care 01/93
4. Study of Patient Satisfaction at the Areteion Hospital 01/93
5. The Development of a Quality Control Program in the Surgical Department of the Areteion Hospital 01/93
6. The Link of Areteion to a National Database of Antibiotics 10/93

Vittore Buzzi Hospital, Milano, 1.

1. Survey on Relationships in the Hospital 08/92
2. Early Discharge from Hospital of Puerpera and Newborn 08/92
3. Psychological Impact of Hospitalization on Children and their Families 08/92
4. Socialization of Children affected by invalidating Diseases 08/92
5. Adolescent Suicide Attempters: Diagnosis and Psychotherapy 08/92
6. Family Risk of Premature Atherosclerosis 08/92
7. Physical Rehabilitation of Children submitted to Heart Surgery 08/92
8. Postmenopausal Osteoporosis 08/92
9. Indoor Pollution in Hospital Environment 08/92
10. Surveillance of Operating Theatre Staff 08/92
11. Smoke Free Hospital 04/94
12. Air Quality Control in the Wards 04/94
13. An Information and "Welcome" Booklet 04/94
14. Monitoring of Hospital Infections 04/94
15. Criteria for the Purchasing of Furniture, Equipment, Material for Hospital Wards and Services 04/94

Hospital of the City of Chemnitz, Chemnitz, D.

1. Introduction of an Effective Patient Information and Counselling System Designed for the Lessening of Hospital Anxieties and for Helping Patients to Cope with their Diseases 04/93
2. Problems, Reserves and Development Trend in the Implementation of Comprehensive Care 04/93
3. Conceptional Framework for Establishing a Complex Quality Management Concept in the Chemnitz Municipal Hospital 04/93
4. Public Relation Work for Health Education 04/93
5. Efforts Directed at Ensuring that Chemnitz Municipal Hospital Will Enjoy an Ever Greater Acceptance Among the Children and Youth of the Catchment Area and Translating this Acceptance in to an Adequate Health Consciousness of the Young 04/93

Child's Health Centre, Warsaw, PL.

1. Nutrition and Health 01/93
2. The CHC: A Nonsmoking Environment 01/93
3. Prevention of Type B Hepatitis in Children and Hospital Staff 01/93
4. Involvement of the Child Health Centre's Paediatric Stomatology Department in the Hospital's Health Promotion Program 01/93
5. Promotion of Psycho-Social well-being of Hospitalized Children 01/93
6. The Hospital: One of the Sources of Health Education 01/93
7. Exercise Trail 01/93
8. Implementation of Health Education 01/93

James Conolly Memorial Hospital, Dublin, IR.

1. Cardio-Pulmonary Resuscitation Training Scheme 10/92
2. Stress Management Project 10/92
3. Smoke Awareness Project 10/92
4. Back-Care Project 10/92
5. Waste Disposal Project 10/92
6. Community Nutrition Health Project 10/92
7. Promotion of Healthy Lifestyles 10/93

Emergency Care Hospital, Prague, C.

1. Education of Family Members of High Risk Patients in Efficient Prophylactic Measures in First Aid and in Priorities for their Future Life 1/93
2. Information and Assistance of the Family in an Early Psychosomatic Rehabilitation of Patients in Life Crises 1/93
3. Psychological Assistance to Young Nurses Confronted with the Stress Situations of Emergency and Critical Care Medicine 1/93
4. Education of Paramedical Personnel in the Mountain Rescue Service 1/93
5. Multilingual Dictionary and Modes of Non-Verbal Communication with Compromised People, Refugees and People in a Life - Crisis 1/93

Koranyi Institute, Budapest, H.

1. Club Movement for Diabetic, Alcoholic and Asthmatic Patients 01/93
2. Healthy Catering Service 01/93
3. Postgraduate Training 01/93
4. Preventive Measures Against Hospital Infections Among Staff 01/93
5. Avoidance of Harmful Environmental Factors 01/93

Linköping University Hospital, Linköping, S.

1. Management Towards a Decentralised Responsibility 11/92
2. Tobacco: The Smoke Free Hospital 11/92
   The Unit for Tobacco Absence Support 11/92
   Midwives and Health Advice to Pregnant Women, Developing the Professional Dialogue 10/93
3. Nutrition: Healthy Food for the Family 11/92
   Shopping for a Better Life 11/92
4. Caring for Patients with Alcohol Problems Identified in the Emergency Ward 11/92
5. Hospital Accident Analysis in the Prevention of Accidents 11/92
6. Psychological and Social Support to Patients, Relatives and Staff Suffering from Crisis 11/92
7. Swedish Health Care and the Meeting with Refugees 11/92
8. Östergötland Osteoporosis Prevention Project 11/92
9. Environment Protection and Pollution Control 11/92
10. Rehabilitation of Personnel with Sick Leave 11/92
11. Total Quality Care - Project 11/92

Padova University Hospital, Padova, I.

1. A Smoke Free Hospital 4/92
2. Quality Improvement of Birth 4/92
3. Nutrition and Health 4/92
4. Occupational risk for Health Workers 4/92
   (Project to prevent vertebral column pathology in health operators)
5. Changing Demand of an Ageing Population 4/92

Philipps Hospital, Riedstadt, D.

1. Health in the Workplace 12/92
2. Psycho educational Program 12/92
3. Improving the Integration of the Hospital into the Region 12/92
4. Counselling Centre for Foreign Fellow Citizens 12/92
5. Implementation of an Intensive Rehabilitation Unit 12/92
6. Horse Riding Therapy as a New Therapeutic Agent for Patients with Psychosis 10/93
7. Inpatient Therapy on Neurotic and Borderline Patients as a New Therapeutic Inpatient Service 10/93
8. Theatre group 10/93
9. Cultur-Cafe 10/93
10. An Aviary within the Hospital Area to Encourage Communication 10/93
11. Networking of a Hospital Ward with the Outpatient Services 10/93
12. Medical Emergency Service Cooperating with the Hospital 10/93
13. Making the Health care Activities Open to the Community 10/93
14. Public Relations within the Region 10/93

Prince Philip Hospital NHS Trust, Llanelli, Wales

1. Health Promotion Manual 10/92
2. Llanelli Lifting Programme 10/92
3. Diabetic Education Programme 10/92
4. Healthy Choice Eating in Young Physically Disabled 10/92
5. Staff Health and Physical Exercise Studio/SHAPES 10/92

Repty, Silesian Rehabilitation Centre, Ustron, PL

1. The Fight Against Tobacco Addiction 1/93
2. Separation and Collection of Waste from the S.R.C. Repty in Ustron 1/93
3. Correction of the Epidemiological Environment in the Hospital and a Project for Preventive Treatment against HIV HBs 1/93
4. The Principles of Healthy Diet in the Preventive Treatment of Illnesses brought on by Lifestyle 1/93
5. The Health School 1/93

6. The Fight against Stress 1/93
7. An Ergonomical and Aesthetically Pleasing Workplace 1/93
8. Activities for the Staff and the Local Residents - (CANCELLED)
9. The Health Promoting Hospital as a Place for the Encouragement of Cultural Events 1/93
10. Healthy Eating 10/93
11. The Effect of Climatic Conditions on the Rehabilitation Process 10/93

Preston Acute Hospitals NHS Trust, Preston, UK

1. Health at Work in the NHS 8/92
2. The Health Promotion Aspects of Collecting and Disposing of Clinical Waste 8/92
3. The Health Promoting Hospital in the Community 8/92
4. The Management of Post-Coronary Patients 8/92
5. Prevention of Accidents Through Self Care 8/92

Rudolfsstiftung Hospital, Vienna, A.

1. Health at the Workplace 6/90
2. Organization of Hospital Hygiene 11/90
3. Reorganization of a Ward 6/90
4. The Outpatient Department as Interface between In- and Outpatient Care 6/90
5. Healthy Food in the Hospital 6/90
6. Training of Diabetics 6/90
7. Nursing 1/91
8. Support for Patients by Volunteer Services 2/92
9. Interprofessional Co-operation (CANCELLED)
10. Organizational Development 9/93

St. Bernward Hospital, Hildesheim, D.

1. Management of Health Support in the Operation-Department 12/92
2. Health Consulting-Promoting Healthy by Information, Consultation, and Environmental Changes 12/92
3. Development of an Integrated EDP Infra-Structure 12/92

4. Outpatient Department: Admission Unit - Reception of Patients in the Hospital 12/92
5. Interdisciplinary Cooperation within and among Wards and Departments 12/92
6. The Bernward Hospital as a "Learning organization": Construction of a Wide Span Further Education Method 12/92

St. Irmingard Hospital, Prien/Chiemsee, D

1. Health Promoting Enhancement of Hospital Environment 4/92
2. Healthy Food for Staff Members 9/91
3. Hospital Waste 4/92
4. Doctor Patient Seminar 9/91
5. Resuscitation Training 4/92
6. Diabetic Seminar 4/92
7. Total Quality Management (TQM) 4/94
8. Quality Circles Interne with Co-workers and Externe with Other Hospitals 4/94
9. Effective Doctor-Patient Communication PLANNED

Stobhill NHS Trust, Glasgow, UK

1. Health Promotion and Quality Management 10/92
2. Health Promotioon Coordinator 10/92
3. Hospital Nutrition Project 10/92
4. Minimal Intervention Alcohol Project 10/92
5. Clinical Care and Smoking Cessation 10/92
6. Cardiac Rehabilitation 10/93

Vaugirard Hospital, Paris, F.

1. The Gerontology Network of the Vaugirard Hospital and the XVth District of Paris 9/93
2. Inform the Professionals of the District 9/93
3. A New Conception of the Life of Elderly People in Hospital through Special Training for the Hospital Employees 9/93
4. The Social Plan 9/93
5. The Development of a Work with Voluntary Associations 9/93

APPENDIX 9
THE ENGLISH CHARTER FOR HEALTH PROMOTING HOSPITALS

The English Charter on Health Promoting Hospitals has evolved from the experience of English hospitals who have already begun work on these issues.

Organisational development and change

In order to develop a health promoting hospital it is necessary to establish an agenda for long-term organisational development and change that will provide the infrastructure and support for effective prevention work.

This section of the charter outlines key aims, objectives and tasks that will need to be undertaken incrementally over an initial five-year period.

Central to the concept of a health promoting hospital is the precondition that all initiatives arise from a redirection of existing resources. The organisational development outlined below will, therefore, need to be guided by senior managers and integrated carefully into the long-term mission, contracts and business plans of the hospital as a whole.

Aims

1. To reorientate hospital-based services towards the values and organisational development necessary to achieve health gain outcomes through mediation, advocacy and alliance building with the community served by the hospital.

2. To develop the hospital's role within the community as an advocate of good public health policy and practice, particularly in its function as a model employer, workplace and service provider.

3. To develop the ability of the hospital as an institution, and the skills of staff as facilitators, to strengthen and support community action for positive good health.

Objectives

To achieve Aim 1, the following objectives and tasks should be undertaken;

Objective 1.1: Develop or acquire by collaboration an epidemiological database of hospital admissions, treatments and outcomes of all activity. This database should be developed to identify the scope of preventive action available to avoid the identified illness or injury being treated. This data should be publicly available and actively communicated to public policy makers and other institutions in the community.

Much of this work is probably best handled within sub-units of the hospital such as clinical directorates or departments and should feature in clinical audits of work within the hospital. Key findings should offer insights into service developments and reorientation of resources for new interventions that provide health gain outcomes that will secure more efficient and effective use of existing resources for improving community health. Evaluated outcomes of existing resource use should feature in contracting negotiations with service purchasers, and may also be used to inform local public opinion about the nature of the services they may want.

Objective 1:2: Develop a common corporate identity within the hospital that focuses on the hospital as a health promoting institution dedicated to improving community health as well as providing high quality treatment and care for ill people.

Hospital management and staff should redefine their mission, service agreements and contracts to reflect their goals in terms of health improvements (not just illness treatment).

Objective 1:3: Develop mechanisms for identifying and acknowledging specific target groups of clients with special needs within the hospital. These mechanisms should involve the development of strategies to meet these needs and the monitoring of identified outcome measures. This process should involve identification in particular of clients with different values, cultures and religious needs.

Providing sensitive and appropriate prevention, treatment and care for a diversity of local needs should be an issue identified in the quality and standards specification of the hospital. Mechanisms for translating this commitment into reality will require explicit policy development, staff training and management review. Alliances with agencies and community representatives outside the hospital can be of great assistance in these tasks.

Objective 1:4: The hospital should develop health promoting policies for staff and patients and pursue an active programme of training, implementation and monitoring to ensure compliance.

Policies should include: smoking prevention, problem drinking (alcohol), exercise. heart disease prevention, equal opportunities. health and safety at work, good nutrition, fire safety, the control of substances hazardous to health, Aids/HIV and employment, maternity and paternity leave, breast-feeding, public and patient participation and confidentiality.

Objective 1:5: Create supportive, humane and stimulating living environments within the hospital especially for long-term and chronic patients.

Hospital managers and staff should seek to establish programmes to "open up" their hospitals, particularly long-stay hospitals, to a wide variety of social, cultural and caring agencies within the community. Hospital arts projects, the involvement of voluntary groups and activities outside the hospital environment should be particularly encouraged. The hospital should be a vibrant part of the local community, not a place apart.

Objective 1:6: Develop mechanisms for networking and sharing examples of successful innovation and good practice in the processes of reorienting the hospital towards prevention.

All hospitals within England will to a greater or lesser degree be attempting similar processes of organisational development and change. Twinning with another similar hospital, networking conferences or publications, and other similar strategies may help to avoid the unnecessary duplication of work within the hospital. The nomination of a senior officer within the hospital responsible for this process may help with internal and external communications and data processing.

To achieve Aim 2, the following objectives and tasks should be undertaken:

Objective 2:1: Develop the hospital's advocacy role as "champion of the community's health",

A programme should be established of communicating with the local media about the preventable causes of hospital admissions. This should be followed up by suggestions of action the hospital is supporting to help take action on the issues identified.

Objective 2:2: Develop "healthy alliances" with local agencies and groups in the hospital's catchment area, to plan action on the identified causes of ill health within the district.

Alliances with social services, primary health care teams, local government and voluntary community groups and local commerce and industry are particularly important. The hospital should seek to nominate key relevant staff to collaborate in healthy alliances, particularly in the Health of the Nation target areas.

Objective 2:3: Review the impact of the hospital and its environment on the health of patients, staff and the surrounding community.

The physical environment of the hospital buildings should make a positive contribution to the healing process of patients. It should also promote staff well-being and not damage the natural environment. Managers and staff should conduct an environmental audit of the hospital to identify areas where improvements could be made.

Objective 2:4: Create healthy working conditions for all hospital staff.

Hospital managers and staff should regularly review all aspects of working and living conditions within the hospital. A programme to promote "Health at Work in the NHS" should be established.

Objective 2:5: The hospital should develop and promote itself as a model healthy workplace.

All hospital-based health promotion developments. particularly those which exemplify good environmental, employment or industrial practice should be shared with local employers. This could involve marketing the hospital staff's skills, e.g. good food hygiene, or offering advice and consultancy to local employers on health policies - smoking prevention, alcohol etc

To achieve Aim 3, the following objectives and tasks should be undertaken:

Objective 3:1: Develop active mechanisms for public, patient and staff participation in the planning and operation of hospital services.

Hospitals should have written strategies or protocols on public, patient and staff participation. In some cases these will already be informally operated, and may simply require codification and dissemination throughout the hospital. The NHSME document *Local Voices* (1992) gives guidance on these issues.

Objective 3:2: Improve and develop the support given to patients and their relatives within the hospital through community-based social and health services and volunteer groups and organisations.

Hospitals should have clearly identified discharge procedures and protocols. They should also have a well developed patient information service which gives information to all patients who require it, about the nature of their illness, its prevention and treatment and a listing of local and national voluntary or self-help groups who can support the patient in their own home. Hospitals should regularly review any programmes (or lack of them) for joint care with primary health care teams. Hospitals should also review whether they can give support such as a room or telephone access to local self-help groups who may need support themselves to provide services to patients and their families. The Patient's Charter (DoH, 1992) provides guidance on some of these issues for patients and NHS staff.

Objective 3:3: Develop staff knowledge, skills and good practice in health promotion by enhancing the provision and quality of basic and post-basic education and training within the hospital.

Much basic training of NHS staff now includes a greatly expanded syllabus of health promotion. However, staff already trained in particular should be given the opportunity to develop specific skills and academic qualifications in this area. Apart from locally run training by health promotion officers, consideration should be given to seconding staff to study part-time promotion and research qualifications. Courses can be established in local partnerships with academic institutions. The Health Education Certificate or the Postgraduate Diploma in Health Education (open learning) may be particularly appropriate for NHS staff running health promotion programmes.

Objective 3:4: Hospital staff of all grades should be encouraged to develop and manage their own health promotion intervention studies, based on their knowledge of their own clients' needs or service provision.

All NHS staff should have the management support and practical facilities they need to develop their own health promotion project in their own workplace. This can be aimed at improving staff, patient or community health. Hospital managers will need to develop supportive mechanisms, e.g. a nominated adviser such as a health promotion officer to guide and support staff in developing an intervention protocol, implementing the programme and evaluating the outcomes. Staff undertaking such projects should be encouraged to register for an academic research qualification. Resources for this work should be made available within routine service and training budgets.

APPENDIX 10
HEALTH AND SAFETY

The Health and Safety Executive (HMSO 1993) produced a booklet on the procedure for managing health and safety at work.

Five Steps to Health

Step 1: Set your policy

Identifying hazards and assessing risks, deciding what precautions are needed, putting them in place and checking they are used, protects people, improves quality and safeguards plant and production. The Health and Safety Policy should influence all the activities, including the selection of people, equipment and materials, the way work is done and how one designs and provides goods and services. This should be produced in a written statement defining the policy and the organisation for implementing measures to reduce hazards and risks.

Step 2: Organize your staff

To make health and safety policy effective it will be necessary to get staff involved and committed. This is often referred to as "Health and Safety Culture".

To achieve this it will be necessary to implement the four "C's".

- Competence : recruitment, training and advisory support.
- Control : allocating responsibilities and securing commitment.
- Cooperation : between individuals and groups.
- Communication : verbal, written and visible.

Step 3 : Plan and set standards

Planning is the key to ensuring that health and safety efforts really work. Planning involves.

- Setting objectives.
- Identifying hazards.
- Assessing risks.
- Implementing standards of performance.
- Developing a positive culture.

Setting standards helps to built a positive culture and control risks. They should identify who does what, when and with what result. This should apply to:

- Premises, place of work and environmental control.
- Plant and substances, purchase, supply, transport, storage and use.
- Procedures, design of jobs and the way work is done.
- People, training and supervision.
- Products and services, design, delivery, transport and storage.

The three key points about standards are: they must be measurable, achievable and realistic.

Step 4 : Measure your performance

Just like finance, production or sales it will be necessary to measure the health and safety performance to find out whether it is successful. This includes:

- Where you are.
- Where you want to be.
- What is the difference and why.

There are two key components of the monitoring system.

- Active monitoring (before things go wrong). This means implementing the standards and finding out whether they are effective.

- Reactive monitoring (after things go wrong). This includes investigating injuries, cases of illness, property damage and near misses. It means identifying in each case why the performance was substandard.

The information from monitoring should be fed-back into the system and initiate activities to improve the situation. This should be done by defining priorities and seriousness of the things that need to be improved.

Step 5 : Learn from experience : Audit and review

Monitoring provides the information which will enable the review of activities and influence decisions for the improvement of performance. Audit by staff or outsiders complement monitoring activities to see whether the policy organisation and system are actually achieving the right results.

In monitoring and auditing health and safety at work one should look at the following indicators:

- The degree of compliance with health and safety performance standards (including legislation).
- Areas where standards are absent or inadequate.
- Achievement of stated objectives within given time scales.
- Injury, illness and incident data: analysis of immediate and underlying causes, trends and common features.

In conclusion one can state: you get the level of health and safety that you demonstrate you want. Health and safety is no accident : it has to be managed.

Five Steps to Risk Assessment

The Health and Safety Executive (HSE, P.O. Box 1999, Sudbury, Suffolk, CO10 6FS) produced a leaflet on this topic which reminds the management of the necessary steps to risk assessment.

Step 1 : Look for the hazards

This can be done within the enterprise or one can contract external assessors. Employees should also participate in this work.

Step 2 : Decide who might be harmed and how

In addition to the workforce one should also take into consideration those who are not present all the time, such as cleaners, visitors, contractors, maintenance personnel, etc.

Step 3 : Evaluate the risk arising from the hazards and decide whether existing precautions are adequate or more should be done

Even after all precautions have been taken some risk remains. For each significant hazard it will be important to decide whether the remaining risk is high, medium or low. After this one should decide which level of risk is legally expected and acceptable by the employeeds.

Step 4 : Record your findings

Small firms (under five employees) need not write down anything related to risk assessment. Any larger firm, however, must record the significant findings of such an assessment, which includes writing down the more significant hazards and recording the most significant conclusions. The assessment needs to be suitable and sufficient, not perfect. The real points are: are the precautions reasonable, and is there something to show that a proper check was made.

Step 5 : Review your assessment from time to time and revise it if necessary

This is specially important if one introduces new equipment, substances or procedures which could lead to new hazards. This should be done mainly for new significant hazards which should be dealt with.

The assessment of risk is a legal requirement and one should seek advice from the local Health and Safety Inspector.

REFERENCES

Abdelgadir, M. (1991) *"Community Development in Two Villages in Sudan"* (PhD Thesis, University of Salford), University Library, Salford.

Alderfer, C.P. (1972) **Existence, Relatedness and Growth**, Collier Macmillan, London.

Argyris, C. (1972) **The Applicability of Organizational Sociology**, Cambridge University Press, London.

Atkinson, J.W. (1957) "Motivational Determinants of Risk-taking Behaviour" in *Psychol. Rev.* 64. (pp.359-372).

Bandura, A. (1977) Social Learning Theory, Prentice-Hall, Englewood Cliffs, N.J. 1977.

Baric, L. (1969) "Recognition of the 'at-risk' role: a means to influence health behaviour" in *Behaviour Change Through Health Education*, Report of the Int.Seminar on Health Education, Hamburg, 1969, Federal Centre for Health, Cologne.

Baric, L. (Ed.) (1972) **Behavioural Sciences in Health and Disease** published by International Journal of Health Education, Vol. XV No.1, 1972, Geneva, Switzerland.

Baric, L. (1975) "Conformity and Deviance in Health and Illness" in *Int. Journal of Health Education*, Supplement to Vol. XVIII, No.1, Jan-Mar 1975, Geneva.

Baric, L., & Fisher, C. (1978) "Primary Socialisation and Smoking" in *Research Monographs*, No.1., 1978, the Health Education Council, London.

Baric, L. (1979) "The Way Forward" in **Proceedings of a Health Education Conference, Dundee 1978**, The Health Education Unit, Edinburgh 1979.

Baric, L. (1979) "Non-smokers, Smokers, Ex-smokers" in *International Journal of Health Education*, Vol.22, No.1 (Supplement) (pp.3-20).

Baric, L. (1980) "Evaluation - Obstacles and Potentials", *International Journal for Health Education*, Vol. XXIII, No.3 (pp.142-149).

Baric, L. (1985) "The Meaning of Words : Health Promotion" in *Journal of the Institute of Health Education*, Vol. 23, No.1, 1985, (pp.10-15).

Baric, L. (1989) "Inequalities in Health (Education)" *Journal of the Institute of Health Education* Vol. 27, No.1, (pp30-33).

Baric, L. (1989) "Evaluation - A Tool for Planning, Management and Auditing Health Promotion/Education Interventions" in *Journal of the Institute of Health Education,* Vol.27, No.2, 1989 (pp.53-63).

Baric, L. (1990a) **Health Promotion and Health Education : Problems and Solutions,** Barns Publications, 1990.

Baric, L. (1990b) "Health Promotion and Health Education in a Situation of Radical Change" *Journal of Institute of Health Education,* Vol.28, No.4 (pp.105-108).

Baric, L. (1990c) "New Approaches to Community Participation" *Journal of the Institute for Health Education,* Vol.28 No 2.

Baric, L. (1991) "Health Promoting Schools : Evaluation and Auditing", *Journal of the Institute of Health Education,* Vol. 29 No.4.

Baric, L. (1992a) "Promoting Health New Approaches and Developments", *Journal Institute of Health Education,* Vol. 30, No.1. (pp.6-16).

Baric, L. (1992b) "Health Promoting Hospitals" *Journal of Institute of Health Education,* Vol.30, No.4 (pp.144-148).

Baric, L. (1993) "The Settings Approach - Implications for Policy and Strategy" *Journal of the Institute of Health Education,* Vo.31 No.1, 1993 (pp.17-24).

Barnard, C.I. (1938) **The Functions of the Executive,** Harvard University Press, Cambridge.

Beck, J.D. (1972) "Role Inconsistency and Health Status", *Social Science and Medicine,* 6. (pp.737-751), Pergamon Press, London.

Becker, M.H. (Ed.) (1974) "The Health Belief Model and Personal Health Behaviour" in *Health Education Monographs,* Volume 2, No.4.

Bennetto, J. (1994) "Hair holds personal diary of drug-taking" *The Independent,* 1994.

Bennis, W.G. (1966) "The Coming Death of Bureaucracy", *Think,* November-December, 1966, pp.30-35.

Berelson, B. and Steiner, G.A. (1964) **Human Behaviour: An Inventory of Scientific Findings,** Brace and World Inc. New York.

Berelson, B., (1965) "KAP Studies on Fertility" in Berelson, B., et.al. (Ed.) **Family Planning and Population Programmes,** University of Chicago Press, Chicago.

Berger, P.L.,Luckmann, T., (1967) **The Social Construction of Reality,** The Penguin Press, London.

Bettman, J.R. (1979) **An Information Processing Theory of Consumer Choice,** Addison-Wesley, Reading, Mass. 1979.

Blake, R.B., and Mouton, J.S. (1985) **The Managerial Grid III**, Gulf Publishing Co.

Blau, P.M. (1970) "A Formal Theory of Differentiation in Organizations" in *American Sociological Review*, April 1970, pp.201-218.

Blau, P.M. & Schoenherr, R.A. (1971) **The Structure of Organizations**, Basic Books, New York.

Brown, T.A. (1989) **Genetics - A Molecular Approach**, Van Nostrand Reinhold, London.

Brown, W. (1974) **Organization**, Penguin, London.

Cameron, K.S. (1984) "The Effectiveness of Ineffectiveness", in B.M. Staw and L.L. Cummings, eds., **Research in Organizational Behaviour**, Vol.6, JAI Press, Greenwich, Conn. p.276.

Carter, C.O. (1976) "The Global Incidence of Genetic Disease" in Carter & Peel (Ed.) **Equalities and Inequalities in Health**, Academic Press, London.

Clark, J.V., & Krone, C.G. (1972) "Towards an Overall View of Organizational Development in the Early Seventies", in J.M. Thomas and W.G. Bennis (eds), **Management of Change and Conflict**, Penguin, Harmondsworth.

Cloward, R.A., Elman, R.M. (1974) "Advocacy in the Ghetto" in Cox et.al **Strategies of Community Organization**, F.E. Peacock Publishers, Inc. Itasca, Illinois. (pp.207-214).

Connor, S. (1993a) "Homosexuality linked to genes", *The Independent*, 16.7.1993.

Connor, S. (1993b) "Scientists link defective gene to aggression", *The Independent*, 26.6.1993.

Connor, S. (1994) "Geneticists to fight against blood tests for homosexuality, *The Independent*, 23.2.1994.

Connor, S. (1994b) "The Gene Dilemma", *The Independent*, 6.1.1994.

Cook, T.D., & Gruder, C.L. (1978) "Metaevaluation Research" in *Evaluation Quarterly*, 2:5-15.

Cox et.al (Ed) (1974) **Strategies of Community Organization**, F.E. Peacock Publishers, Inc. Itasca, Illinois.

Crosby, P.B., (1984) **Quality Without Tears**, McGraw Hill, New York.

Davis, R.C., (1951) **The Fundamentals of Top Management**, Harper & Row, New York.

Dawkins, R., (1989) **The Selfish Gene**, Oxford University Press, Oxford.

Dawson, S. (1992) **Analysing Organisations,** 2nd edn. Billing & Sons, Worcester.

Deming, W.E. (1986) **Out of the Crisis**, Massachusetts Institute of Technology Center for Advanced Engineering Study, Cambridge, Mass.

Department of Education (1994) **The Parent's Charter**, HMSO, 1994, London.

Department of Environment (1994) **Inner City Research Programme: Assessing the Impact of Urban Policy,** HMSO, 1994, London.

Department of Health (1988) **Public Health in England**, The Report of the Committee of Inquiry into the future Development of the Public Health Function, Acheson Chairman, HMSO, 1988.

Department of Health (1989) **Promoting Better Health**, HMSO, London.

Department of Health (1989) **General Practice in the NHS**, HMSO, London.

Department of Health (1990) **Working for Patients**, HMSO, London.

Department of Health (1990) **The New Contract - An Operating Manual for Dentists**, Wyvern Corporate Communications, London.

Department of Health (1991) **The Patient's Charter**, HMSO 1991, London.

Department of Health (1992) **Health of the Nation**, The White Paper, HMSO 1992, London.

Department of Health (1993) **Five Steps to Health and Safety,** Health & Safety Executive, HMSO, London.

Department of Health (1994) **Improving NHS Dentistry**, HMSO, 1994, London.

Derrida, J. (1976) **Speech and Phenomenon**, Northwestern University Press, Evanston, IL.

Dobson, R. (1994) "X plus Y equals sexual confusion", *The Independent*, 24.5.1994.

Drucker, P.F. (1968) **The Practice of Management**, Pan Books,London.

Etzioni, A. (1964) **Modern Organizations**, Prentice-Hall, Englewood Cliffs, N.J.

Fayol, H. (1916) **Administration Industrielle et Generale**, Dunod, Paris.

Fayol, H. (1949) **General and Industrial Management**, Pitman, London.

Fishbein, M. & Ajzen, I. (1975) **Belief, Attitude, Intention and Behaviour: An Introduction to Theory and Research,** Addison Wesley.

Foucault, M. (1977) **Discipline and Punish,** Pantheon, New York.

Frank, A.W. (1991) " From Sick Role to Health Role - Deconstructing Parsons" in Robertson et al.(Ed) (1991) **Talcott Parsons - Theorist of Modernity,** Sage Publications, London (pp205-216).

Galbraith, J. (1973) **Designing Complex Organizations,** Addison-Wesley, Reading, Mass.

Giddens, A. (1990) **The Consequences of Modernity,** Polity Press, Cambridge.

Glanz, K., Lewis, F.M., & Rimer, B.K. (Eds) (1990) **Health Behaviour and Health Education : Theory Research and Practice,** Jossey Bass, Oxford.

Gleick, J. (1987) **Chaos - Making a New Science**, Sphere Books Ltd.,London.

Golzen, G. (1994) "Real Task for Virtual Companies", *The European,* 24-30. 6. 1994.

Gombrich, E.H. (1968) **Art and Illusion,** (3rd edition),Phaidon Press Ltd, Oxford.

Graham-Smith, Sir F. (ed) (1994) **Population - The Complex Reality, Report of the Population Summit, New Delhi 1993,** The Royal Society, London.

Green, L.W. (1970) "Status Identity and Preventive Health Behaviour", University of California, Berkeley, *Pacific Health Education Report* No.1. 1970.

Green, L.W. (1990) **Community Health,** Times Mirror/Mosby College Publishing, Boston.

Grossmann, R. & Scala, K. (1993) **Health Promotion and Organisational Development,** WHO EURO and IFF, Vienna.

Guskin, S.L., & Ross (1974) "Advocacy and Democracy : The Long View" in Cox et.al **Strategies of Community Organization,** F.E. Peacock Publishers, Inc. Itasca, Illinois. (pp.340-351).

Habermas, J. (1971) **Toward a Rational Society,** Heinemann, London.

Hall, C. (1993) "Baby to get first gene transplant", *The Independent,* 18.3.1993.

Hammer, M., & Champy, J. (1993) **Reenginneering The Corporation -A Manifesto for Business Revolution,** Nicholas Brealey Publishing, London.

Harsanyi, Z. & Hutton, R. (1983) **Genetic Prophecy - Beyond the Double Helix,** Paladin Book, Granada, London.

Health Education Authority (1993) **A Survey of Health Education Policies in Schools,** HEA, London.

Hertzberg, F. (1974) **Work and the Nature of Man,** Granada Publishing Ltd, London.

Hochbaum, G.F. (1958) **Public Participation in Medical Screening Programmes**, Dept. of HEW, USPHS Publ. No. 572 (mimeo), 1958.

Hudson, J. & McRoberts, H.A. (1984) "Auditing Evaluation Activities" in Rutman (1984) **Evaluation Research Methods**, Sage Publications, London (pp.219-236).

Hunt, J. (1979) **Managing People at Work**, Pan Books, London.

Hunt, L. (1992) "Intelligence in babies linked to parenting skills" *The Independent*, 10.4.1992.

Hymas,C. and Cohen, J. (1994) "The trouble with boys", *The Sunday Times*, 19.6.19945.

Illey C. (1994) "Decline and fall of the nuclear family", *The Sunday Times*, 19.6.1994.

Illich, I. (1975) **Medical Nemesis**, Calder & Bogars, London.

Ishikawa, K. (1976) **A Guide to Quality Control**, Asian Productivity Organization, Tokyo.

Jones, S. (1993) **The Language of the Genes**, Flamingo, Harper Collins, London.

Juran, J.M. (1988) **Quality Control Handbook**, McGraw Hill, New York.

Katz, D. and Kahn, R.L. (1966) **The Social Psychology of Organizations**, John Wiley, New York.

Kast, F.E., and Rosenzweig, J.E., (1985), **Organization and Management : A Systems and Contingency Approach**, 4th edn. McGraw-Hill International, Singapore.

Keeney, R.L. (1982) "Decision Analysis : State of the Field" in *Operations Research*, 30 (pp.803-838).

Kegeles, S.S. (1963) "Some Motives for Seeking Preventive Dental Care", *Journal American Dental Association*, Jnl.Dent.Assoc. 67:90.

Kickbusch, I. (1986) "Introduction to the Journal" *Health Promotion*, Vol. 1 No.1, 1986.

Kickbusch, I. (1990a) **A Strategy for Health Promotion**, WHO EURO, 1990.

Kickbusch, I. (1990b) **Action on Health Promotion : Approaches to Advocacy and Implementation**, WHO EURO, 1990.

Kosko, B. (1993) **Fuzzy Thinking - The New Science of Fuzzy Logic**, Harper Collins, London.

Kuhn T.,(1970) **The Structure of Scientific Revolutions**, 2nd Ed. University Press, Chicago.

Langford, V. (1979) "Managerial Effectiveness : A Review of the Literature" in Brodie, M. and Bennet, R. (Eds) **Perspectives of Managerial Effectiveness**, Thames Valley Regional Management Centre.

Lewin, K. (1935) **A Dynamic Theory of Personality: Selected Papers**. Translated by Adams D.K. and Zener K.E., McGraw Hill Book Co. Inc. New York.

Leventhal, H., Rosenstock, I.M., Hochbaum, G., & Carriger, G., (1960) "Epidemic Impact on the General Population in Two Cities", in **The Impact of Asian Influenza on Community Life**, USPHS Publication No. 766, U.S. Gov. Printing Office, Washington, D.C.

Lightfoot, L. (1994) " 'Flawed' gene tests put rape verdicts in doubt", *Independent*, 8/5/94.

Likert, R. (1961) **New Patterns of Management**, McGraw Hill, London.

Lussato, B. (1976) **A Critical Introduction to Organization Theory**, Macmillan, London.

Mahler, H. (1986) "Towards a New Public Health" *Health Promotion*, Vol. 1 No.1, 1986.

March, J.G., and Simon, H. (1958) **Organizations**, John Wiley, New York.

Marcuse, H. (1964) **One-Dimensional Man**, Beacon Press, Boston, USA.

Marsden, G. & Peterfreund, N. (1984) "Marketing Public Health Servics" in *International Quarterly of Community Health Education*, 5, (pp.53-71).

Maslow, A.H. (1943) "A Theory of Human Motivation" in *Psychological Review* 50,pp.370-396.

Mattison, K., McAllister, F., & Roberts, K. (1994) **One plus One** The Marriage and Partnership Research Charity, London.

Mayo, E. (1933) **The Human Problems of Industrial Civilization**, Macmillan, New York.

Mayo, E. (1945) **The Social Problems of an Industrial Civilization**, Graduate School of Business Administration, Harvard University, Boston.

McClelland, D.C. (1962) "Business Drive and National Achievement", *Harvard Business Review* 40, pp.99-112, New York.

McGregor, D. (1960) **The Human Side of Enterprise**, McGraw-Hill, New York.

McGregor, D. (1987) **The Human Side of Enterprise**, Penguin, London.

McKinlay, J.B. (1971) "The Concept 'Patient Career' as a Heuristic Device for Making Medical Sociology Relevant to Medical Students" , *Soc. Sci. & Med.*, 5, (pp.441-460) Pergamon Press, London.

M'Gonigle, G.C.M., Kirby, J., (1936) **Poverty and Public Health**, London, Victgor Gollancz.

Miles, R. (1994) **The Children We Deserve: Love and Hate in the Making of the Family**, Harper-Collins, London.

Milio, N. (1981) **Promoting Health Through Public Policy**, Philadelphia, F.A. Davis, 1981.

Ministry of Health (1966) **The Challenge to Public Health from Urbanization**, Twentieth World Health Assembly, Technical Discussions Paper from United Kingdom (mimeo).

Mintzberg, H. (1979) **The Structure of Organizations**, Prentice-Hall, Englewood Cliffs, N.J.

Mitchell, T.R. (1982) "Motivation: New Directions for Theory, Research and Practice", *Academy of Management Review* Vol.7 No.1, pp.80-88.

Mitchell, T.R. and Larson, J.R., (1987) **People in Organizations**, McGraw-Hill, New York.

Moi, T. (1985) **Sexual/texual Politics: Feminist Literary Theory**, Methuen, New York.

Moreno, J.L. (1953) **Who Shall Survive?**, Beacon House, New York.

Morgan, G. (1993) **Imaginization - The Art of Creative Management,** Sage Publications, London.

Mullins, L.J. (1992) **Management and Organizational Behaviour**, Pitman, London.

Newwell J., (1990) "The new way to put on genes", *The Independent*, 21.5.1990.

O'Donnell, M. (1992) **A New Introduction to Sociology**, Thomas Nelson & Sons Ltd, Walton-on-Thames, Surrey. (3rd edn).

Ouchi, W.G. (1984) **Theory Z : How American Business Can Meet the Japanese Challenge,** Addison Wesley.

Pallot, P. (1994) "GPs £200m Health Drive 'is a Flop' ", *Daily Telegraph* 19.7.93.

Parkinson, C.N. (1957) **Parkinson's Law**, Houghton Mifflin, Boston, p.33.

Parsons, T. (1951) **The Social System**, Glencoe Illinois Free Press, USA.

Parsons T. (1978) **Action Theory and the Human Condition**, Free Press, New York.

Pascale R.T. (1990) **Managing on the Edge: The Learning Organization**, Simon and Schuster, New York.

Pelikan, J.M., Demmer, H., Hurrlemann, K., (1993) **Gesundheits-förderung durch Organisationsentwicklung**, Juventa Verlag Weinheim und München.

Perrow, C. (1967) "A Framework for the Comparative Analysis of Organizations" *American Sociological Review*, April 1967, pp.194-208.

Peter L.J and Hall R., (1969) **The Peter Principle: Why Things go Wrong**. Morrow, New York.

Pfeffer, J. (1978) **Organizational Design**, AHM Publishing, Arlington Heights, Ill. USA.

Pfeffer, J. (1981) **Power in Organizations**, Pitman Publishing,Marshfield, Mass. USA.

Pflanz, M. & Rohde, J.J. (1970) "Illness Deviant Behaviour and Conformity", *Soc. Science & Medicine*, 4. (pp.647), Pergamon Press, London.

Popper, K. (1945) **The Open Society and its Enemies** (p.13), Routledge & Kegan Paul, London.

Price J.L. and C.W.Mueller (1985) **Handbook of Organization Measurement**, Pitman Publishing, Marshfield, Mass.,1985.

Pugh, D.S., Hickson, D.J., Hinnings, C.R., and Turner, C., (1969) "The Context of Organization Structures", *Administrative Science Quarterly*, March 1969, pp.91-114.

Pugh, D.S. Ed (1971) **Organization Theory : Selected Readings**, Penguin Book, Harmondsworth.

Pugh, D.S. (1991) "Foreword" in Huczynski, A., & Buchanan, D., **Organizational Behaviour,** Prentice Hall, Hemel Hempstead, Herts.

Reddin, W.J. (1970) **Managerial Effectiveness**, McGraw Hill, London.

Rennie, J. (1993) "DNA's new twists", *Scientific American*, March, 1993.

Robbins, S.P. (1990) **Organization Theory : Structure, Design, and Applications**, 3rd edn. Prentice Hall International, Inc. London.

Robertson R., and Turner B.S. (Ed.) (1991) **Talcott Parsons - Theorist of Modernity**, Sage Publications, London.

Roethlisberger, F.J., and Dickson, W.J. (1939) **Management and the Worker**, Harvard University Press, Cambridge.

Rogers, R.W. (1975) "A Protection Motivation Theory of Fear Appeals and Attitude Change" in *Journal of Psychology* 91, (pp.93-114).

Rosenstock, I.M., Hochbaum, G.M. et.al (1960) **The Impact of Asian Influenza on Community Life,** U.S.P.H.S. Publications 766.

Rosenstock, I.M. (1966) "Why People Use Health Services", *Milbank Memorial Fund Quarterly,* 44:94.

Rotter, J.B. (1966) "Generalised Expectancies for Internal Versus External Control of Reinforcement" in *Psychological Monographs,* 80.

Royal College of Physicians (1989) **Medical Audit,** Report of the Royal College of Physicians, London.

Rutman,L. (1984) **Evaluation Research Methods,** Sage Publications, London (2nd Ed.).

Ryan, S. (1994) "Surfing, genes and the meaning of life", *The Sunday Times,* 15.5.1994.

Ryan, S. & Reeve, S. (1994) "Revealed: the nation's most polluted cities", *The Sunday Times,* 10.7.1994.

Schien E.H.(1985): "Organizational Culture" in *Organizational Dynamics,* Vol.12,pp.13-28.

Schutz, A. (1964) "The Stranger" reprinted from Collected Papers Vol.2, Martinus Nijhoff (pp91-105) in Berger B.(Ed) **Readings in Sociology,** Basic Books Inc, 1974.

Scott, W.R., (1978), "Theoretical Perspectives", in Marshall W. Meyer, ed., **Environments and Organizations,** Jossey-Bass, San Francisco, (pp.21-28).

Scott, W.R., (1992) **Organizations : Rational, Natural, and Open Systems,** 3rd edn. Prentice-Hall International Inc. London.

Selznick, P. (1949) **TVA and the Grass Roots,** University of California Press, Berkeley.

Shingo, S. (1986) **Zero Quality Control : Source Inspection and the Poka-yoke System,** Productivity Press, Cambridge, Mass. USA.

Sigerist, H.E. (1929) "The Special Position of the Sick", first written in 1929, republished in M.I. Roemer, **Sigerist on the Sociology of Medicine,** New York, M.D. Publications 1960.

Simon, H.A. (1947) **Administrative Behaviour: A Study of Decision-Making Processes in Administrative Organizations,** Macmillan, New York.

Simon, H.A. (1976) **Administrative Behaviour,** 3rd edn., Macmillan, New York.
Simopoulos, A.P., Herbert, V., Jacobson, B., (1993), **Genetic Nutrition,** Macmillan Publishing Co. New York.

Sobel, H.J. (Ed) (1981) **Behavioural Therapy in Terminnal Care**, Bellington, Cambridge.

Solomon, D.S. (1981) "A Social Marketing Perspective on Campaigns" in **Public Communication Campaigns**, (Eds, Rice, R.E. & Paisley, W.J.), Sage, Beverly Hills.

Stouffer, S.A. et al (1949) **The American Soldier : Adjustment During Army Life**, Princeton University Press, Princeton.

Suchman, E.A. (1963) **Sociology and the Field of Public Health**, Russell Sage Foundation, New York.

Suchman, E.A. (1965) "Stages of Illness and Medical Care" in *Journal of Health and Human Behaviour*, 6/3/1965.

Suchman, E.A. (1966) "Health Orientation and Medical Care" in *Am. Jnl. Publ.Health*, Vol.56, No.1, 1966 (pp.97-105).

Suchman, E.A. (1969) "Social Factors in Illness Behaviour" in *Milbank Memorial Fund Quarterley*, 47, Jan.1969.

Suchman, E.A. (1970) Health Attitudes and Behaviour, *Arch. Environ.Health* 20, (pp.105-110) Jan. 1970.

Taguchi, G. (1981) **On-line Quality Control During Production**, Japanese Standards Association, Tokyo.

Taylor, F.W. (1911) **The Principles of Scientific Management**, Harper & Row, New York.

Thompson, J.D. (1967) **Organizations in Action**, McGraw-Hill, New York.

Tones, K., Tilford, S., Robinson, Y. (1990) **Health Education Effectiveness and Efficiency**, Chapman and Hall, London.

Townsend, P., & Davidson, N., (1982) **Inequalities in Health : the Black Report**, Penguin Books Ltd, Harmondsworth, Middlesex.

Trofimov,Y. & Kalpana Vora (1993) "Gene tests could create European underclass" *The European*, 1993.

Tse, K.K. (1985) **Marks and Spencer**, Pergamon Press, London.

Turney, J. (1994) "Kudos and chaos in a cancer breakthrough" *The Independent*, 6.6.1994.

Twaddle, A.D. (1973) "The Concept of Health Status", *Soc. Science & Medicine* 8: (pp.29-38), Pergamon Press, London.

Walton, M. (1989) **The Deming Management Method**, Mercury Books, Gold Arrow Publications Ltd, London.

Watson, J.D., (1968) **The Double Helix,** Weidenfeld & Nicholson, London.

Watts, S. (1994) "Ethics of DNA ownership under scrutiny", *Independent*, 8.1.94.

Weber, M., (1947) **The Theory of Social and Economic Organizations,** ed., Talcott Parsons, trans. A.M. Henderson and Talcott Parsons, Free Press, New York.

Weber, M., (1968) **Economy and Society : an Interpretive Sociology,** 3 vols., eds. Guenther Roth and Claus Wittich, Bedminster Press, New York.

Weick, K.E. (1969) **The Social Psychology of Organizing**, Addison-Wesley, Reading, Mass. USA.

Wilkie, T. (1992) "Gene transplants offer hope for sufferes of inherited disorders", *The Independent*, 16.1.1992.

Wilkie, T. (1992b) "Scientists investigate the genetic anatomy of human intelligence" *The Independent*, 11.4.1992.

WHO (1978) **The Alma Ata Declaration** in Alma Ata 1978 Primary Health Care, Geneva, WHO 1978 "Health for All" series No.1.

WHO (1980) Regional Strategy for Attaining Health for All by the Year 2000, WHO EURO, (EUR/RC30/8).

WHO (1981) **Analysis of the Content of Eight Essential Elements of PHC,** Final Report to the HPC by the HPC Working Group on PHC, 10/8/1981, HPC/PHC/REP/81.1, Geneva.

WHO (1982) "Lifestyles and Their Impact on Health", WHO/ EURO/ RC33/ Tech.Disc. 30/5/82.

WHO (1983) "New Approaches to Health Education in Primary Health Care", WHO Tech. Reports Series, 690, 1983, Geneva.

WHO (1984) **Targets for Health for All**, WHO, Geneva.

WHO (1986) **The Ottawa Charter for Health Promotion** in Health Promotion No.1, 1986, iii-v.

WHO (1988) **The Adelaide Recommendations: Healthy Public Policy** in Health Promotion 3 (2) 183-186, 1988.

WHO (1989) **Ethics in Health Promotion**, WHO EURO, Copenhagen, 1989 (EUR/ICP/HSR/ 634,5119v).

WHO (1991) **Work for Health?** Briefing Book to the Sundsvall Conference on Supportive Environments. Sundsvall, Karolinska Institute and National Board of Health and Welfare, 1991.

WHO, CE , CEC (1993) The European Network of Health Promoting Schools, WHO EURO, Copenhagen, 1993, (EUR/HPS3).

WHO (1993) **Health Promotion in the Work Setting**, jointly with the Federal Centre for Health Education, Cologne, Germany, Verlag fur Gesundheitsforderung, G. Conrad, Gamburg, 1993.

Woodward, J. (1965) **Industrial Organization : Theory and Practice**, Oxford University Press, London.